BRITISH MANUSCRIPT DIARIES

JOHN STUART BATTS

BRITISH MANUSCRIPT DIARIES OF THE 19th CENTURY: AN ANNOTATED LISTING

CENTAUR PRESS LTD.
1976

First published 1976 by Centaur Press Limited
Fontwell, Sussex, and 11–14 Stanhope Mews West,
London, S.W.7

ISBN 0–90000084 8

Printed in Great Britain by
Bristol Typesetting Co. Ltd.,
Barton Manor, St. Philips,
Bristol

INTRODUCTION

A generation ago William Matthews in the introduction to his annotated bibliography of *British Diaries: 1442–1942* (Los Angeles, 1950) promised to publish a supplement to the work if readers sent him enough further material. We may presume that public response was not sufficiently encouraging because when I approached Professor Matthews a few years ago he was not proposing to produce such a supplement. It was at that stage that I began systematically to collect information on a number of unpublished diaries of the Victorian period, the majority of which had come to light since 1950. My collection then broadened to include diaries which were started after 1800.

The restricted focus upon one segment of the centuries covered by *British Diaries* is explicable in terms of three main considerations: first, the increased attention currently being given to the nineteenth century not only by the general reader but also by many branches of scholarship; second, there has been an increase in the availability of the nineteenth century's manuscript materials; and third, the sheer volume of diaries written in that century seemed to demand attention.

The past two decades have seen a quite remarkable growth in Victorian studies. Much of this scholarship has been of an interdisciplinary nature, and recent calls for an assessment of the literary culture and its relationship with literary art suggest that the value of diaries has yet to be realized.

More obviously, nineteenth-century manuscripts in Great Britain have become more readily available to public perusal since the end of the Second World War. There are several reasons for this. Owners of manuscripts and papers in private hands have been able to place their possessions in the care of an expanded network of archives and record offices. Further, with the coming of the welfare state and the break-up of many estates and large houses, family records, collections and papers have emerged into the public domain. Again, sufficient time has now elapsed to allow references to material which formerly might have been restricted out of deference to the susceptibilities of persons still living. Finally, mention may be made of a growth of civic interest among those cities, boroughs, and towns of England and Wales which are in effect the offspring of the nineteenth century—especially the industrial cities of the Midlands and the North of England—and who have actively aided the emergence and preservation of Victorian manuscripts. This new awareness has been evident in the past twenty years, sharpened perhaps by the recognition among local authorities of the increasingly rapid disappearance of the recent past, of the changing face of their urban environments, and of the very pattern of living.

The annotated list presented here focuses upon the unpublished diaries of the nineteenth century; to have included published diaries would have been

[v]

to make the list excessively bulky and to duplicate diaries covered in
Matthews' collection ; and whereas certain diaries have been published since
British Diaries, it was felt that these would be already known to those who
might wish to use them. Furthermore, partial publication of a manuscript
diary has been judged to constitute a published diary, for in such cases the
editors usually give some indication as to the volume of omitted material,
its nature, and its location.

Many of the unpublished items which appear in *British Diaries* also appear
here, sometimes with additional information incorporated. For example,
some of the manuscripts are now deposited in different locations; in some
instances additional volumes or facts about the diarist have been brought to
light ; some attributions of anonymous manuscripts have been since con-
firmed ; occasionally dates have been corrected ; and finally I have found
out from a few private owners of manuscripts that no diaries as such exist
among the papers in their possession even though cited in *British Diaries* ;
(these must be the "ghosts" to which Matthews alludes in his introduction).

The format of *British Diaries* has been followed, though not without some
misgivings. The list is arranged year by year with the earliest diary of a
writer determining the year of its inclusion ; while such a system is less
helpful with the diarist of longevity, it should be recalled that the majority
of diaries are of short span. Within each year's entry, the order is alphabetical. The arrangement of each entry explains itself. I have tried to impose
a basic pattern on diverse material which has meant that short diaries are
often given the same space as the longer. Where diarists with titles are
involved, usually the highest rank has been given ; it is more convenient to
find out more about a General, for example, even though he was only a
subaltern when he kept his diary. Each entry notes the number of volumes
(whenever possible), if only because the lines of comment on the contents
have often been severely restricted.

The compilation was achieved through a deal of letter writing and
pleasant visits to a variety of libraries in the United Kingdom. The latter
were most useful not only on account of the cooperation received but also
for the encouragement given by many librarians and archivists. The visits
frequently led to a more thorough search of possible repositories. Individual
appeals were mailed to several hundred libraries, including county archives
and record offices, the libraries of major cities and towns, libraries of
universities and colleges, and private libraries.

Manuscript diaries in private hands were elusive. I tried to confirm the
locations of those diaries listed in *British Diaries*, mostly in vain. However,
the National Register of Archives furnished me with some new ones, as did
a number of archivists who either had privately-owned diaries on loan or
had knowledge of journals owned by people in their locality. The total
number of privately-owned diaries in the list is disappointingly small, but in
view of developments alluded to above it may well be that the percentage of

such diaries omitted in this survey is less than in Matthews' work. While collecting material I encountered several instances when owners discreetly asked that my list should not include mention of manuscript diaries in their possession. I have respected such wishes; no diarist or diary which was subject to such a request has been consciously included.

While the methods of approach are reasonably wide, I can only claim to have an adequate representation of the century's British diaries. Among the diaries excluded was a number which begin in the late eighteenth century and overlap into the nineteenth, sometimes by many years; at the other end of the century, a number of diaries which begin in the last years yet belong to undeniably twentieth-century figures (such as Beatrice Webb whose journals are at the London School of Economics), are also omitted.

I am not sure that any citation, however extended, would suffice to include all the people to whom I am indebted for their help in the compilation of this annotated listing. I should like to thank the many patient and generous archivists and librarians without whose aid this project would never have been possible. The following were kind enough to spare me much labour, (and I list them alphabetically): C. G. Allen, L.S.E.; M. E. Allen, Ipswich & East Suffolk R.O.; J. N. Allen, Brighton P.L.; H. Appleyard, Litchfield P.L.; M. Y. Ashcroft, North Riding of Yorkshire R.O.; W. H. S. Ashmore, Haringey Borough Libraries; W. H. Baker, Monmouth C.R.O.; F. U. Batchelor, Halifax A.O.; Jane Bebbington, India Office Library; John Bebbington, Sheffield City Libraries; Geraldine Beck, Guildford Muniment Room; Patricia Bell, Bedford C.R.O.; A. Betteridge, Halifax P.L.; H. Bilton, Bradford P.L.; R. Bingle, India Office Library; S. J. Butcher, Barnet P.L.; J. Campbell, Northumberland C.R.O.; G. A. Capel, Harrogate P.L.; N. Carrick, Liverpool R.O.; G. A. Carter, Warrington Borough Libraries; Margaret Cash, Hants. C.R.O.; D. T-D. Clarke, Colchester & Essex Museum; G. E. Clarke, Margate Borough Library; H. S. Cobb, House of Lords R.O.; I. P. Collis, Somerset C.R.O.; E. H. Cornelius, Royal College of Surgeons Library; A. B. Craven, Leeds City Library; A. N. Cross, Ipswich & East Suffolk C.R.O.; E. J. Davis, Bucks. C.R.O.; S. C. Dean, Darlington Borough Library; S. T. Dibnah, Huddersfield P.L.; R. Drummond-Hay, Queen's College, Oxford; E. G. Earl, Isle of Wight R.O.; C. A. Elliot, Islington Borough Libraries; Jon Elliot, Rawtenstall P.L.; Madeleine Elsas, Glamorgan C.R.O.; J. S. English, Gainsborough P.L.; D. W. Evans, Birmingham University Library; M. W. Farr, Warwick C.R.O.; J. M. Farrar, Cambridge C.R.O.; J. M. Fewster, Durham University Library; H. G. Fletcher, Cheltenham P. L.; Eric Follows, Friends' Meeting House, Worcester; A. M. Fowler, Cheshire R.O.; Levi Fox, The Shakespeare Centre, Stratford-upon-Avon; Norah Garney, Borthwick Institute, University of York; D. E. Gerard, Nottingham P.L.; Joan Gibbs, University of London Library; Phyllis Giles, The FitzWilliam Museum; J. L. Gilham, Sheffield University Library; Patricia Gill, West Sussex

C.R.O.; Marguerite Gollancz, Surrey C.R.O.; T. W. Graham, Glasgow University Library; Miss Green, Berkshire R.O.; G. Hampson, Southampton University Library; W. Best Harris, Plymouth P.L.; K. C. Harrison, Westminster City Library; L. Helliwell, Southend P.L.; A. J. M. Henstock, Notts. C.R.O.; N. Higson, East Riding of Yorkshire R.O.; Mary Hill, Salop C.R.O.; R. A. Hill, Huntly House Museum, Edinburgh; Jennifer Hofmann, Dorset C.R.O.; A. E. J. Hollaender, Guildhall Library, London; S. H. Horrocks, Reading P.L.; Felix Hull, Kent C. Archives; P. L. Hull, Cornwall C.R.O.; Meryl Jancey, Herefordshire R.O.; A. G. Jones, U.C. of North Wales Library; B. C. Jones, Cumberland and City of Carlisle R.O.; F. Jones, Carmarthen C.R.O.; T. Kaye, Trinity College Library, Cambridge; Rosemary Keen, C.M.S., London; P. A. Kennedy, Devon C.R.O.; M. Knight, Wigan A.O.; G. Langley, Bristol P.L.; S. Lawrence, Maidenhead P.L.; Hilda Lofthouse, Chetham's Library, Manchester; E. H. Lowe, Lancaster P.L.; H. K. MacKay, Baillie's Library, Glasgow; Maj-Gen. A. MacLennan, R.A.M.C. Museum; Sheila MacPherson, Westmorland C.R.O.; J. C. Marl, South Shields P.L.; Glenise Matheson, Rylands' Library; Douglas Matthews, The London Library; M. F. Messenger, Shrewsbury P.L.; B. Mollo, National Army Museum; C. S. Minto, Edinburgh City Libraries; Miss Morcom, William Salt Library and Staffs. C.R.O.; Catherine Murdoch, Glasgow City Archives; K. C. Newton, Essex C.R.O.; S. C. Newton, East Sussex C.R.O.; A. E. B. Owen, Cambridge University Library; B. G. Owens, National Library of Wales; Peter Pagan, Bath Municipal Library; L. A. Parker, Leicestershire R.O.; A. J. I. Parrott, Gloucester City Libraries; B. R. Parry, Caernarvon C.R.O.; L. M. Payne, Royal College of Physicians; Mrs. Percival, University College, London; M. R. Perkin, Liverpool University Library; Jean F. Preston, Huntington Library, San Marino, California; N. S. E. Pugsley, Exeter City Library; Elizabeth Ralph, Bristol A.O.; R. D. Rates, Lewisham Borough Libraries; M. G. Rathbone, Wilts. C.R.O.; Dora Rayson, Manchester P.L.; L. M. Rees, Swansea City Libraries; Susan Rice, National Maritime Museum; W. A. L. Seaman, Durham C.R.O.; Joan Sinar, Derbyshire R.O.; B. C. Smith, Glos. C.R.O.; F. Smith, Dewsbury P.L.; W. J. Smith, G.L.R.O. (Middlesex); W. H. Southern, Hull Maritime Museum and Hull P.L.; M. P. Statham, Bury St. Edmunds & West Suffolk C.R.O.; Anabel Stewart, The Plunkett Foundation; Marion Stewart, Scottish Record Office; R. Suddaby, Imperial War Museum; W. A. Taylor, Birmingham P.L.; O. S. Tomlinson, York C.L.; K. Twinn, Dr. Williams's Library; P. Walne, Herts. C.R.O.; T. Walsh, Manchester Local History Library; Mrs. Welch, Nottingham University Library; G. H. Williams, Merioneth C.R.O.; Miss Williams, The Minet Library, Lambeth; and M. J. W. Willis-Fear, Portsmouth City R.O. I would like to acknowledge also the help and hospitality of the staffs of the Bodleian Library; The British Museum; Edinburgh University Library; The Mitchell Library, Glasgow; The London School of Economics

Library; The National Army Museum; The National Library of Wales; The National Register of Archives; and Wigan Central Public Library. I am grateful to a number of my colleagues for their suggestions, especially Richard N. Pollard and Irene Spry, and to the British Council for a bursary which allowed the search to begin in earnest. Finally, I express my appreciation to my wife and children who have been long-suffering in this cause.

A*

CONTENTS

1800

ANON.
Diaries, 1800–01.
Contents: *Journal of our proceedings in Wig* and *Journals upon the coalworks since their Commencement.*
Scottish Record Office: GD 221/52.

ANON.
Diary, 1800–01. 1 vol.
Contents: looseleaf journal of expedition to Egypt.
Scottish Record Office: GD 45/4/16.

ANON.
Diary, no date but believed to be written in 1800. 1 vol.
Kent Archives Office: Faunce Delaune MS., F 18. (Presented in 1946).

BROWNE, William George (1768–1813), writer.
Diaries, Oct., 1800–March, 1804. 11 vols.
Contents: notes of travel in Europe and Middle East.
Shrewsbury School Library: MS. 4. ix. 31–41.

CLARK, Isaac Stockton, of Whitby, Yorkshire.
Diary, Dec., 1800–March, 1813.
Contents: notes of family events; extracts from poems; cash accounts; little value.
University of Leeds, Brotherton Library: MS. No. 76.

CLIFFORD, Arthur.
Diary, entitled *Journal of my Studies,* 1800–25, 1 vol.
East Riding of Yorkshire County Record Office. MS. DDCC/150/276.

CLINTON, Sir William Henry.
Diaries, 1800–45.
Manchester, John Rylands Library: Clinton Papers (not yet numbered).

CUST, Honourable C.
Diary, *Journal of a Tour,* 1800. 1 vol.
Lincolnshire Archives Office: Brownlow Muniments.

DUNCAN, (? Jonathan), Imperial civil servant.
Diary, 27-30 May, and 13-14 June, 1800. 1 vol.
Contents: notes on proceedings at Bombay by a Governor.
India Office Library: Home Misc. 473/3.

FENTON, Richard (1746–1821), Welsh topographer and poet.
Diaries of travel, c. 1800, 1804–10.
Contents: notes kept of various travels in Wales.
Cardiff Public Library: MSS. coll.

GELL, Sir William (1777–1836), archaeologist.
Diaries of travel, Oct., 1800 and 1801. 2 vols. (see also p. 13).

Contents: travel in southern Europe; illustrations.

Bristol University Library: MS. No. 8 & 7.

GIBBINS, William (1778–1839), constable of Cookham Dean.

Diary, May, 1800–Jan., 1840.

Contents: mainly local births and deaths (many violent), scandals, accidents, and crimes; local events, Thames valley; interesting spellings.

Maidenhead Public Library: MSS. coll.

GOULD, George.

Diary, 1800–01. 1 vol.

Contents: journal kept aboard H.M.S. *Mercury*.

National Maritime Museum: JOD 47, MS55/036.

GRAY, Jonathan (1779–1837), of York, a solicitor.

Diaries, 1800, 1802, 1815. 3 vols.

Contents: tour journals in North Wales, the West Country and South Wales, and Belgium.

York Public Library: Archives Dept., Gray's Court Papers MSS. Acc. 5 & 6 T / 3 a, b; 4, 5, 6. (Presented 1959).

Mrs. Edwin Gray, *Papers and Diaries of a York Family: 1764–1839*, (Sheldon Press, 1927).

GREENOUGH, George Bellas (1778–1855), M.P., of Regent's Park, London.

Diaries, Dec., 1800–1854 (with gaps). 28 vols.

Contents: early diaries are of tours in France, Italy, and Scotland; there is nothing between 1806 and 1821, and later diaries have very sparse entries. Writer was latterly President of the Geological Society: comments are on geography, architecture, social conditions etc.

London, University College Library: Greenough Papers 5–7.

HILL, C. Fitzmaurice, a Captain in the Indian Army.

Diary, Oct., 1800–Aug., 1802. 1 vol.

Contents: relates to the expedition from India to Egypt, and covers general orders, military details, and writer's own views; journey from Bombay to Mocha; to Cairo; ruins of Temple of Isis; Alexandria, etc.

India Office Library: MSS. Eur. D. 108. (Acquired 1919).

HOBBES, Robert, of Stratford-upon-Avon, solicitor.

Diaries, Jan., 1800–March, 1803. 2 vols.

Contents: personal and business affairs at Stratford.

Stratford-upon-Avon, Shakespeare's Birthplace Library.

HUGHES, John (1776–1843), a Welsh Methodist preacher.

Diaries, 1800–08. 2 vols.

Contents: diarist was one of the first two missionaries appointed by the Methodist Conference to introduce Wesleyan Methodism into North Wales.

Present MSS. location unknown.

LEYDEN, Dr. John (1775–1811), Scottish physician and poet.

Diaries of travel: June, 1800, and July–Oct., 1800, and Sept., 1823.

Contents: June, 1800, in the Border country; Gilsland and Lake District;

July–Oct., in the Highlands and Western isles; visits to literary celebrities. 1823, in the eastern Border country.

Journal of a Tour in the Highlands . . ., ed. James Sinton (Edinburgh, 1903). Also, *Trans. Hawick Archaeol. Soc.*, 1906

METCALFE, Charles Theophilus, Baron (1785–1846), Governor-General of India, and of Canada.

Diary, c. 1800.

Contents: schoolboy at Eton; classical studies.

Quotations in *Notes and Queries*, 182 (1942), 262.

MONSON, Honourable Charlotte. (Cousin of 6th. Lord Monson).

Diaries, 1800–1823. 7 vols.

Lincolnshire Archives Office: Monson coll. MS. 14 F.

NELSON, Horatio, Viscount (1758–1805), admiral.

Diaries, Feb.–March, 1800; May–Aug., 1805; Sept., 1805– until his death at Trafalgar, Oct. 21, 1805.

Contents: details of naval service.

London, British Museum: Add. MSS. 34902; 35191; 34966; 34968; 34922 (copy).

National Maritime Museum: JOD 14, MS9642 (1805 only).

SLOANE, WILLIAM, son of Hans Sloane, of Paultons House, Hants.

Diary, 1800. 1 vol.

Hampshire Record Office: MS. 10M55/102.

STACKHOUSE, Rachel (Mrs. William Rashleigh), of either Trehane near Truro or Pendarves, near Camborne.

Diary, 1800. 1 vol.

Contents: journal of a journey to Bath and Salisbury etc.

Cornwall County Record Office: MS. DD.R.(S)1/174.

STEADE, B.B., of Beauchief, Derbyshire.

Diary, 1800–50. 5 vols.

Contents: commonplace jottings.

Nottinghamshire Record Office: MS. DDCW 8c./2, 3, 4; 8d/4, 5.

WELLS, Rev. George, Prebendary of Chichester Cathedral, 1822–39.

Diaries, 1800–09, 1818, 1820, and 1828. 13 vols.

Contents: mainly accounts.

West Sussex County Record Office: Add. MSS. 1937–1949.

WHITE, Sampson, of Maidford, Northamptonshire.

Diary, 1800–23 (with gaps). 4 vols.

Diarist is the eldest son of Henry White of Selbourne, Hampshire, and the nephew of Gilbert White the naturalist.

Oxford, Bodleian Library: MSS. Eng. misc. b 33–37, c 154–157, c 198, d 230, d 241, f 65.

WILSON, Sir Robert Thomas (1779–1849), engineer and general.

Diaries, 1800–23 (with gaps).

Contents: military matters; service abroad, public events, military escapades; prison in Paris; volunteer in the Spanish revolution; diplomacy of the day.

Private Diary of Sir Robert Wilson, ed. H. Randolph, 2 vols. (London, 1861), deals with military diary, April, 1812–June 1814 only. *Life of Sir Robert Wilson*, ed. H. Randolph, 2 vols. (London, 1862).

London, British Museum: Add. MSS. 30095, 30096, 30099, 30102, 30103.

1801

ANON.

Diary, 1801–12.

Contents: journal of a tour through Wales.

Private: Sir Robert Throckmorton, Coughton Court, Alcester, Warwickshire.

ANON.

Diaries, Feb., 1801–May, 1803. 2 vols.

Contents: diary kept by a young man of twenty-one years; descriptions of social life in Dublin; comments on affairs at home and abroad; topographical descriptions; of interest to students of the evolution of social history at the turn of the century.

Dublin, Royal Irish Academy: SR. 24K. 14–15 Vols. 5 & 6 only.

ANON.

Diary, 1801–12.

Private: Lt.-Col. J. T. B. Bretherton Hawkshead-Talbot, Pool Farm, Willersley, Near Broadway, Worcestershire.

ANON.

Diary, 1801.

Contents: travel journal of a tour from Kinrosshire to Mull; scenery and sights.

National Library of Scotland: MS. No. 3038.

ANON.

Diary, 1801–02. 1 vol.

Contents: journal of campaign in Egypt.

Scottish Record Office: GD 45/4/22.

ANON.

Diaries, 1801–02 and 1804–06. 2 vols.

Scottish Record Office: GD 253/215–216.

ADDISON, Thomas (d. 1869) of Llanelli, Wales.

Diaries, 1801–29 (extracts).

Contents: service on East India Company's ships; extracts for conditions of service and relation to Royal Navy.

Naval Misc. I (Naval Records Soc., XX, 1901), 335–374.

BOSANQUET, [?]
Diaries, 1801–04, 1811–21, and 1821–31.
London, Public Record Office: MSS.30/3 Nos. 16–18, Bosanquet Papers.

CARLYLE, Joseph Dacre (1759–1804), Professor of Arabic at Cambridge.
Diary, March–April, 1801.
Contents: journal of a scholar kept while at Mount Athos, cataloguing monastic libraries.
London, British Museum: Add. MS. 27604.

COOPER, Samuel.
Diary, 1801–02.
Contents: entries made on board H.M.S. *Dreadnought* in the Mediterranean.
Sheffield University Library: MSS. coll.

DALRYMPLE, Capt. Robert, soldier.
Diaries, 1801–06.
Contents: mostly concerned with military matters; writer served with 3rd. Guards, and was killed at Talavera.
Scottish Record Office: GD 135/152/1–3.

DURHAM, General James, of Largs, soldier.
Diary, 1801–17 (microfilm).
Scottish Record Office: RH 4/15/1.

ECCLESTONE, Thomas.
Diaries, 1801, 1803, and 1804.
Lancashire County Record Office: Scarisbrick MSS., DDSc.

FOX, George Townshend, of Westoe, South Shields, and later of Durham, a rope-maker.
Diaries, 1801, 1818–28, 1825, 1834, 1835–40, and 1837. 6 vols.
Contents: a domestic journal, 1835–40; a journal pertaining to business, 1818–28; travel journals: to London and the West of England, Lake District, and Boulogne.
South Shields Public Libraries: Fox coll.

FREDERICK, General E., C.B., soldier.
Diaries, March–Sept., 1801, Nov., 1802, and Jan.–Sept., 1810.
Contents: first kept while campaigning in Egypt; second, on a trip to the Persian Gulf; third kept in Persia: places visited, people met, local legends, historical accounts, etc.
India Office Library: MSS. Eur. D. 109–111. (Acquired 1907).

GODSCHALL, William Man, F.R.S. (d. 1802), of Weston Manor, Albury, Surrey, a landowner. (Formerly he was William Man, but took the name Godschall in 1752 upon marrying a Godschall heiress.)
Diary, July, 1801–June, 1802. I vol.
Contents: notes on estate farming and building work; books read; social visits paid and received; weather; diarist's health; some national events mentioned.

Guildford Muniment Room: MS. 52/1/2.

GOWER, Capt. R.H. (1768–1833), mariner.
Diary, 1801. 1 vol.
Contents: journal kept on the ship *Transit*, an experimental vessel; some sketches and loose notes about the ship and the diarist's other inventions including patent log; voyage to Lisbon and back.
National Maritime Museum: JOD 74, MS59/0.

KNATCHBULL, Sir E.
Diaries, 1801–46 and 1834–48 (with gaps). 2 vols.
Contents: the first is a series of private entries on family matters; the second is a detailed account of his political activities as member of Sir Robert Peel's Cabinet, as Paymaster General, 1834–35, 1841–45 when he resigned, with additional notes added 1846 and 1848.
Kent Archives Office: MSS. U951 Knatchbull, F 20/21.

LLOYD, Louisa (née Harvey), wife of William Lloyd of Aston.
Diaries, 1801–60 (with gaps).
Travel Diaries, 1812–47 (with gaps.)
Contents: tours in the Continent: Portugal, France, Switzerland, Belgium, Italy; a stay with the Duke of Wellington at Cambray, 1816.
National Library of Wales: Aston Hall MSS. 4407–4480, 4710, 4711, 4715, 4720, 5196–5204, 7047–49, 7051–52, 7060.

LLOYD, William (d. 1843), of Aston.
Diaries, 1801–42. 30 vols.
Hunting diaries, 1810–30 (with gaps).
Contents: record of runs, lists of hounds, game killed.
National Library of Wales: Aston Hall MSS. 4704, 4680, 4697–98, 4716, 4768–98, 8354.

MacKINTOSH, Catherine, wife of Sir James MacKintosh.
Diary, 18 June–28 July, 1801. 1 vol.
London, British Museum: Add. MS. 52450. (Presented in 1964 by Dowager Lady Farrar).

M———— ?
Diary, August, 1801.
Contents: an account by Mr. M————, illustrated by a few water-colour sketches, of a journey from London to South Wales.
National Library of Wales: MS. 13400.

PIERREPONT, Hon. Henry Manvers (1780–1851).
Diaries, July, 1801–Feb., 1802, 1814, 1817, 1823–25. 3 vols.
Contents: first, a journal of a diplomatic mission to Scandinavia, Russia, and Germany; then journals of tours of pleasure to France and Italy, 1814 onwards.
Private: The Duke of Wellington, Stratfield Saye House, Reading Berkshire.

RACKETT, Dorothea, of Spetisbury, Dorset.
Diary, Jan.–Dec., 1801. 1 vol.
Contents: very brief notes of daily activities of a young girl at home.
Dorset County Record Office: MS. NU140.

RIDLEY, Matthew White, 3rd. Bart. (1778–1836), of Blagdon.
Diaries, 1801, 1806, 1811, 1813–15, 1817–18, 1822–26, and 1828–30. 25 vols.
Contents: some are merely engagement books, others are journals of tours to the Continent.
Northumberland County Record Office: Ridley of Blagdon MSS. (NRO 138), ZRI 31/1.

RODD, Col. Francis (1732–1812), of Northill, landowner.
Diaries, 1801, 1802, 1807, and 1810. 4 vols.
Contents: personal and family matters, local events.
Cornwall County Record Office: MSS. AD.360/15–18.
Bryan Latham, *Trebartha, The House By The Stream* (1971).

RUMFORD, Sir Benjamin Thompson, count.
Diary, Sept.–Dec., 1801. 1 vol.
Contents: journal of a journey from London to Munich and Paris; (copied by Lady Palmerston, wife of 2nd. Lord Palmerston).
Birmingham University Library: MS. 6/iv/29.

SEYMOUR, Lady Anne Horatia.
Diary, 1801. 1 vol.
Contents: mostly engagements.
Warwickshire Record Office: MS. CR114A/363.

SMITH, Ebenezer (b.1785), of Nether Chapel, Sheffield.
Diary, Oct., 1801–Jan., 1804.
Contents: record of religious experiences only; the family were Congregationalists.
Sheffield City Libraries: misc. documents, 1874.

STUART, Lord Stuart of Rothesay.
Diary, 1801. 1 vol.
Contents: journal of the journey to Austria.
Oxford, Bodleian Library: Eng. misc. c 256.

WOOLLEY, Joseph, of Clifton, a framework knitter.
Diaries, 1801–15. 6 vols.
Contents: matters of trade interest; personal and local items.
Nottinghamshire Record Office: MS. DD 311/1–6.

YOUNG, William Weston, of Glamorgan, South Wales.
Diaries, 1801–43. 30 vols.
Contents: accounts and household matters.
Glamorgan County Record Office: D/DXch.

1802

ANON.

Diary, Sept.–Oct., 1802. 1 vol.

Contents: journal of a tour to Paris; description of various small towns and Paris; sketch of the character of Buonaparte; description of various works in the Louvre.

Birmingham University Library: MS. 6/iii/2.

ANON.

Diary, 1802.

Contents: journal of a tour made through parts of England and Wales.

National Library of Wales: MS. 789b.

ANON.

Diary, July–Sept., 1802. 1 vol.

Contents: journal of a tour in France and Savoy; Paris mainly; tourist's notes on sights, hotels.

Cambridge University Library: Add. MSS. 6302.

ANON.

Diary, 1802. 1 vol.

Contents: journal kept on the voyage from Gibraltar to Cape Finisterre.

Scottish Record Office: GD 45/4/57.

ALLEN, Dr. John.

Diaries, 1802–41.

Contents: political journals, and journals kept abroad.

London: British Museum: Add. MSS. 52198–52503, 52204–5. (Holland House Papers).

DAVIES, Walter

Diaries, 1802–45 (with gaps). 7 vols.

Contents: journals of tours throughout Wales, some undertaken on behalf of the Board of Agriculture; interested in the geology of the counties, their agriculture and other industries. Some of the entries are made in Welsh.

National Library of Wales: MS. 1659b, 1730b, 1755–56a, 1757, 1762b, 1844. (Crosswood MSS.).

ELPHINSTONE, – – (Not in *D.N.B.*).

Diaries, 1802–3, 1805–6, 1807–8. 1 vol.

Contents: journals of his voyages to Bombay and China; gives boat's position each day, otherwise only a few comments.

Stafford, The William Salt Library: MS. M. 162.

FOX, C. J.

Diary, 1802.

London, British Museum: Add. MS. 51475, (Vol. 158 of Holland House papers), (acquired 1963).

GURNEY, Hannah.
Diary, 1802. 1 vol.
Contents: journal of a coach tour in England, including Castle Howard.
Durham Cathedral: Chapter House, DD/2.
McD————(?), A. and A. C.
Diary, 1802.
Contents: journal of a stay in the Highlands.
Edinburgh University Library: MS. La.II.378.
MAUDE, Rev. John Barnabas (1781?–1851), sometime Fellow of Queen's
College, Oxford.
Diary, June, 1802–May, 1814. 2 vols.
Contents: experiences and reflections during his detention at Verdun
as a prisoner of War during the Napoleonic wars.
Oxford, Queen's College: MSS.403–404.
MIFFLIN, Ann.
Diary, 1802–03.
Contents: accounts of visits to the Indians.
Warrington County Borough Municipal Library: MSS. coll.
RANSOM, Mercy (1728–1811), of Hitchen, Hertfordshire.
Diary, April, 1802–Nov., 1810. 71 pp.
Contents: religious musings of a Quaker, sufferings, and ill health; God's
providences.
Hitchen Public Library: MSS coll.
RUSSELL, Mary and T. P.
Diaries, 1802–04 and 1835–42.
Contents: journals of tour in Wales and elsewhere.
Gloucestershire Record Office: MSS. D. 388: F 1–10.
RUSSELL and Pakington families.
Diaries and engagement books, 1802–31.
Private: Curtler and Hallmark (present location unknown).
SCOTT, James (1768–1827), of Cradley, Staffordshire, a Unitarian minister.
Diary, April, 1802–Aug., 1827. 1 vol.
Contents: journal kept in shorthand of tours made in Britain.
London, Dr. William's Library: MS. 28. 111.
STEWART, Mrs., of Bonskeid, Scotland.
Diary, Feb.–Dec., 1802. 40 fols.
Contents: domestic and social life; sharp-tongued comment and gossip;
her reading; amusing and lively picture of good Scottish life.
National Library of Scotland: MS. No. 982.
SYKES, Tatton, of Malton, Yorkshire.
Diaries, 1802–32 (with gaps). 19 vols.
Contents: estate matters, brief details of wine, horses, accounts, estate
memoranda.
East Riding of Yorkshire Record Office: MSS. DDSY/102–35–36, 38–55.

TWISDEN, Capt. John.
Diaries, 1802–51. 6 vols.
Contents: notebooks containing numerous entries of a diary nature with some miscellaneous accounts.
Kent County Archives Office: Twisden MS. U49 Twisden F6/1–6.
WELLS, J.
Diary, 1802. 1 vol.
Contents: account of a voyage to Guinea and Grenada.
Cambridge University Library: MS. Add. 3871.

1803

ANON., an Army officer.
Diary, Aug.–Sept., 1803. MS Copy.
Contents: journal kept in India while serving with General Wade's detachment; expedition in Mahratta territory; brushes with the enemy, storming of forts at Allighur and Delhi; siege of Agra.
India Office Library: MSS. Eur. D. 117. (Acquired 1899).
ANON.
Diary, 1803.
Contents: man's diary and account book.
Surrey County Record Office: Goulburn MSS. (Acquired 1954).
BOURNE, Rev. Hugh (1772–1854), of Bemersley, Staffordshire.
Diary, Feb., 1803–Jan., 1852 (extracts).
Contents: his work as a Methodist preacher; evangelism; his founding of English camp meetings; travel and work therein; founding and editing of Primitive Methodist magazines; the busy life of a Methodist dignitary; the origin, expansion, and organization of Primitive Methodism to 1850.
John Walford, *Memoirs of the Life and Labours of Ven. Hugh Bourne*, 2 vols. (London, 1856).
Manchester, Hartley-Victoria Methodist College Library.
FITZPATRICK, General R.
Dairy, 1803.
London, British Museum: Add. MS. 51455 (Vol. 88 of Holland House Papers) (Acquired 1963).
GIDDY, Rev. Edward (1734–1839), of Tredea in St. Erth, Cornwall.
Diaries, 1803–06 and 1807–10. 2 vols.
Contents: memoranda, appointments, and accounts.
Cornwall County Record Office: MSS. DD.DG1/5–6.
A. C. Todd, *Beyond the Blaze: A Biography of Davies Gilbert* (Truro, 1967).

GILBERT, Mary Ann (1776–1845), wife of Davies Gilbert (formerly Giddy).
Diary, Nov., 1803–Sept., 1804. 1 vol.
Contents: journal kept mainly while in Sussex, London, and Kent.
Cornwall County Record Office: MSS. DD.EN.1917.

HILL, John (1787–1855). Principal of St. Edmund Hall, Oxford.
Diaries, 1803–55. 23 vols.
Oxford, Bodleian Library: MSS. St. Edmund Hall 66/1–3, 67/1–20.
J. S. Reynolds, *The Evangelicals at Oxford: 1735–1871* (Oxford, 1953).

[?]HODGKINSON, Richard. Agent for the Atherton Estate, Lancs.
Diaries, 1803–40 (with gaps).
Contents: travel journals.
Lancashire Record Office: MSS.DDX/211.

HOLWORTHY, Captain Matthew (1783–1836), sometime Captain 63rd.
Foot, and Rector of Elsworth, Cambridgeshire, 1827–36.
Diary, March, 1803–Oct., 1804. 1 vol. (transcript only).
Contents: family and social life at Elsworth, and recruiting for his
regiment in Suffolk and Cambridgeshire.
Cambridgeshire Record Office: MS. 327/F1.

MOSELEY, Jeremiah, of Somersham Park.
Diaries, 1803–76. 18 vols.
Huntingdonshire Record Office: MSS. coll.

UPCOTT, William (1779–1845), librarian, of Old Jewry, London.
Diaries, 1803–07, 1809, and July–Aug., 1823.
Contents: early diaries concerned with his bookselling business, with
London life, people met, entertainments attended; personal affairs, his
reading, books bought, expenses; last volume is of travel from London to
the Peak District of Derbyshire.
London, British Museum: Add. MS. 32558.
London, University College Library: Ogden MS. 93.

WALKER, Josias (1761–1831), of Glasgow.
Diaries, Jan., 1803–Aug., 1831. 3 vols.
Contents: kept by the professor of Humanity at Glasgow University;
written in Greek characters.
University of Glasgow: MSS. Gen. 1103(30).

WESLEY, Charles (1757–1834), musician.
Diaries, 1803, 1804, 1818, and 1824. 4 vols.
Contents: brief entries concerning music; family affairs; weather; visits;
etc.
Dorset Record Office: MS. D40G/F1–4.
Diaries, 1805, 1810, 1820.
Contents: brief notes of religious life and his work.
London, Methodist Book Room: MSS.

Diary, 1819.
Contents: similar to the preceding.
Private: Mrs. Ethel Lawson, formerly of Plymouth.

1804

ANON.
Diary, 1804. 1 vol.
Contents: journal kept on a voyage from Bushire to Calcutta in the ship *Rahumshar*.
India Office Library: MSS. Eur. A 37.
ANON.
Diary, 1804–07. 1 vol.
Contents: journal containing observations on weather and national events, etc.
Berkshire Record Office: MS. D/ECr Z1.
ANON.
Diary, 1804.
Contents: journey from Kilstay, Wigtownshire, to Edinburgh; notes on stages and places.
National Library of Scotland: MS. No. 735.
ANON.
Diary, 1804.
Contents: journal of tours in Somerset and Kent.
Private: Moncrieffe of Moncrieffe MSS. (Enquiries N.R.A., Scotland).
ARUNDEL, Katherine (m. Sir Edward Doughty, 1827).
Diaries, 1804–70.
Contents: few entries in the earlier volumes, but the 1814–20 vols. describe meetings with French emigres, tours and pilgrimages to Rome and other Continental cities.
Private: Sir Everard Radcliffe, Bart., Rudding Park, Harrogate, Yorkshire; Radcliffe (Rudding) MS. 567.
BANT, Eliza and Millicent.
Diaries, 1804–16. 6 vols.
Contents: journals describing tours in England, Scotland, and Wales.
Essex Record Office: Mayron Wilson MSS. (on loan).
BISS, James (1776–1807), Baptist missionary.
Diary, March–April, 1804.
Contents: journal-letter describing his voyage to India; journey from Madras to Serampore.
London, Baptist Missionary Society: MS. IN/2.
BLACKWELL, Thomas, soldier in the 36th. Regiment.
Diary, Sept., 1804–Dec., 1810.

Contents: fragmentary journal kept by a Lieutenant in the Napoleonic Wars; service in River Plate Expedition in the Peninsular at Corunna.
National Army Museum: MS. 6907/336.

CLARKSON, Rev. Townley (d. 1833), clergyman: vicar of Hinxton, 1802–25; Rector of Acton Scott, Salop, 1825–33; and of Beyton, Suffolk, 1830–33.
Diary, June, 1804–Oct., 1811. 1 vol.
Contents: description of tours through England, Scotland and Wales.
Cambridgeshire Record Office: MS. R57/11/1.

DAVIS, Timothy (1779–1860), of Coventry and Evesham.
Diary, 1804–58. 10 vols.
Contents: journals in English and Welsh; letters received or written by him; household accounts etc; work of Unitarian pastor.
National Library of Wales: MSS. 5487–96. (Acquired 1924).

DUNDAS, Chief Baron.
Diary, 1804–19. (Microfilm).
Contents: journal, including cruise on H.M.S. *Illustrious*.
Scottish Record Office: RH 4/15/1.

DUNN, James, of Patrington, Yorkshire.
Diary, 1804–06.
Contents: matters of local interest in a Yorkshire village.
Hull, University College Library: typed copy only.

EVERETT, Rev. James (1784–1872), of Alnwick, Northumberland.
Diary, 1804–66. 20 vols.
Contents: Methodist work, travel, introspection, largely in Yorkshire; diarist was a leader in the reform movement which split the Weslyan Methodist Convention c. 1849–50; matters of more general interest, topographical, industrial, literary, theological; copious illustrations with letters, etc.
Manchester, Hartley-Victoria Methodist College: MSS.
Richard Chew, *James Everett* (London, 1875).

GELL, Sir William.
Diaries, 1804–05 and Jan–March, 1806. 2 vols. (see also p. 1).
Contents: notes on a journey to Greece, and travels; the later one contains notes with sketches made during travels with Edward Dodwell in the Peloponnese.
Oxford, Bodleian Library: MSS. Eng. misc. e 154 and f 53.
(Purchased 1927–28).

HOGHTON, Major-General Daniel.
Diaries, 1804, 1807, 1810–11.
Contents: journals concerned with India, Copenhagen, and the Peninsular War respectively.
Lancashire Record Office: De Hoghton of Hoghton MSS., DD Ho.

KING, Thomas, of Thelnetham, Suffolk.
  Diary, 1804–38.
  Contents: much about building work.
  West Suffolk Record Office: typed copy.

KNATCHBULL, Fanny, second wife of 9th. Bart.
  Diaries, 1804–72 (with gaps). 69 vols.
  Contents: detailed entries ; domestic, etc.
  Kent Archives Office: MSS. U951 Knatchbull, F24/1–69.

LARKEN, Edmund, (father-in-law of 6th. Lord Monson).
  Diary, 1804–08.
  Lincolnshire Archives Office: Monson coll. (Acquired 1951).

MacKINTOSH, Sir James, P.C., M.P. (1765–1832), philosopher and
  historian.
  Diaries, Aug., 1804–Dec., 1826. 12 vols.
  Contents: partly in form of letters to his wife, Katherine.
  London, British Museum: Add. MSS. 52436–48. (Presented in 1964 by
  Dowager Lady Farrar).
  R. J. MacKintosh, *Memoirs of the Life of Sir James MacKintosh*, 2 vols.
  (London, 1835).

MONCK, Sir Charles Miles Lambert (1779–1867), of Belsay, Northumber-
  land.
  Diaries, 1804–06, 1830–31, and 1831. 7 vols.
  Contents: the earliest journals are of a tour of Germany, Venice, and
  Greece ; then a journal of a tour of France and Italy, 1830–31, and a
  separate one kept in Sicily.
  Northumberland Record Office: Middleton of Belsay MSS. (NRO 79)
  ZMI B52/1/1–3, ZMI B52/3/1–3, and ZMI B52/4.
  R. Welford, *Men of Mark 'Twixt Tyne and Tweed*, Vol 2 (1895).

PARKER, Edward, and Thomas GOULBURNE.
  Diaries, 1804, 1814, 1818, 1823–24, 1827, 1844, 1846–57, 1859–62, 1864.
  Lancashire Record Office: Parker of Browsholme MSS., DDB.

PLUMPTRE, Rev. James.
  (i) Diaries and memoranda, 1804–29. 25 vols.
  Contents: brief notes of personal and parish affairs.
  (ii) Travel diaries of tour in Scotland and the Lake District, etc. 1790–1800.
  Cambridge University Library: (i) Add. 5835–60 ; (ii) Add. 5794, 5802,
  5804, 5808–19.

POOLE, Henry.
  Diary, Oct., 1804–11. 1 vol.
  Contents: deals mostly with his wife's illness, written in narrative style
  and "designed for the perusal and satisfaction of my children when I am
  no more".
  East Sussex County Record Office: Add. MS. 4530.

REID, Rebecca Ann (b. 1783), sister of Thomas Whitehead Reid.
Diaries, 1804 and 1809. 2 vols.
Contents: first is brief journal of a sail on the Bristol Channel and visit to
Southerndown ; later journal records a visit to Liverpool.
London, University College Library: Sharpe Papers 158-9.

RUSSELL, Anne, daughter of Sir Henry Russell (2nd. Bt.)
Diary, April–Aug., 1804. 1 vol.
Oxford, Bodleian Library: MS. Eng. misc. e 391 (Russell of Swallowfield
Papers).

SPURRELL, Richard, of Carmarthen, Wales.
Diary, 1804–05. (Copy).
Carmarthenshire Record Office: Museum 302.

STACKHOUSE, Edward William (1775–1853), (surname changed from
Wynne in 1815), landowner, reformer, and M.P., of Pendarves, near
Camborne.
Diaries, 1804–07. 4 vols.
Contents: mainly scattered notes on engagements and cash accounts ; a
note on his marriage, 5 July 1804, to Tryphena Trist.
Cornwall County Record Office: MSS. DD.PD.329–332.

TOMLINSON, Matthew, of Doghouse Farm, Lupset, Wakefield, Yorkshire.
Diary, Feb., 1804–June, 1839 (vols. 4, 5, 9, 11 only).
Contents: farming diary of farm life and work ; local people ; deaths.
Wakefield Public Library: MSS.

VEALE, William (1783–1867), squire and vicar, of Gulval and Zennor,
Cornwall.
Diaries, 1804–66 (with gaps). 46 vols.
Contents: sparse though often interesting entries ; early items deal with
education at New College, Oxford ; later he was vicar of Gulval (1813–17),
then of Zennor (1824–37) ; also squire of Trevaylor ; many entries with
personal cash accounts.
Cornwall County Record Office: MSS. DD.ML. (uncatalogued).

WHITE, Rev. Francis Henry, of Maidford, Northamptonshire.
Diary, Jan–Dec., 1804.
Contents: country matters ; weather, personal and natural history at
Fyfield, Hampshire.
Oxford, Bodleian Library: Eng. misc. d 241.

WHITE, John, soldier.
Diary, 1804–08. (Copy).
Contents: journal of his service in the 36th. Regiment in India.
Private: Lady Napier.
India Office Library: MSS. Eur. F 108.

WOOD, Searles and SPENCER, Edward.
Diaries, 1804–12. 2 vols.
Contents: entries made in co-partnership and covering voyages to St.

Helena, Madeira, Calcutta, Madras, Bombay, and other Indian ports, Cape Town and London.
East Suffolk Record Office: MSS. 50/20/3.1, 3.2.

1805

ANON. (Formerly attributed to Samuel Rogers, poet).
Diary, (?) 1805. 1 vol.
Contents: tour of the Lake District made sometime between 1805 and 1821.
London, University College Library: Sharpe Papers 165.

ATKINSON, Thomas. Ship's Master.
Diary, Jan–June, 1805. 1 vol.
Contents: journal of H.M.S. *Victory*.
Oxford, Pembroke College Library: MS. 22.

BLACKETT, Henry.
Diary, 1805.
Private: present location unknown.

BLUNDELLS, William.
Diaries, 1805, 1818, and 1821.
Contents: journals of tours in the British Isles, France, Germany and the Netherlands, and the Netherlands respectively.
Lancashire Record Office: Blundells of Crosby MSS.

COOKE, Thomas William (d. 1825), of Theberton and Polstead, Suffolk.
Diaries, 1805–18. 18 vols.
Contents: personal and farming diaries; sport; journeys abroad; supplemented by vouchers and accounts.
Ipswich Public Library: MS. S1/1/81.1–81.18.

FIELD, James, of Dublin.
Diary, Dec., 1805–Sept., 1849.
Contents: service as a soldier with Moore during the Peninsular War; personal adventures in Portugal, Spain and France; military life; return to England; work as a Methodist preacher; travels; life and religion in Cork and Dublin.
A Devout Soldier (Dublin, 1869).

GIBBON family, of Benenden, Kent.
Diary, Aug–Sept., 1805. 1 vol.
Contents: journal of a visit to Hastings and Winchelsea.
Kent Archives Office: MS. U1272 F2.

GREEN, Lieut. William Pringle, mariner.
Diary, 1805–08.
Contents: journal kept aboard H.M.S. *Conqueror* while chasing the French Fleet; some notes on training a ship's crew to the use of arms.
National Maritime Museum: JOD 48, MS. 55/030.

HOTHAM, Rear-Admiral Sir George.
Diaries, April, 1805–March, 1824 (with gaps).
(i) Sea diaries: on board various vessels: *Medusa, Minden, Seringapatam, Eurylus, Prince Regent.*
(ii) a tour through the Netherlands, Rhineland and France, Aug.–Oct., 1821 ; and a tour through France, Switzerland, and Italy, July, 1823–March, 1824.
East Riding of Yorkshire Record Office: MSS. DDHO/9/6–7.

MOORE, Thomas, continental trader.
Diary, March, 1805–Oct., 1806. 1 vol.
Contents: travels of a merchant ; his business during the Napoleonic Wars ; Riga, St. Petersburgh, Stockholm, Danzig, Copenhagen, Gothenburg, etc.
Wigan Central Public Library: Edward Hall coll.

MUSHET, George, of The Hermitage, near Alfreton Iron Works.
Diary, Nov., 1805–Aug., 1815. 1 vol.
Birmingham University Library: MS. 7/iii/21.

PALMER, John (1769–1840), Professor of Arabic at Cambridge.
Diaries of travels, 1805–30 (with gaps).
Contents: in the East, 1805–17 ; in France and Switzerland, 1821 ; France and Italy, 1823–24 ; Spain and Portugal, 1826–27 ; Holland, 1830 ; scholary interests.
Cambridge, St. John's College Library: MSS. coll.

PARKER, Robert, F. S. A.
Diaries, 1805 and 1823.
Contents: journal of a tour from Bath to Anglesea, 1805 ; one of a tour from Bath to Newcastle, 1823 ; and an undated tour in Wales.
Hampshire Record Office: MSS. coll.

PECHELL, Lady (Katherine Annabelle Bishopp) (1791–1891).
Diaries, 1805–55 (with gaps).
Contents: notes of her social life ; domestic details ; country house pleasures ; impressions and sketches of people ; court life in London and Brighton ; sport, dancing, reading.
Private: Mrs. Somerset, Worthing, Sussex.
Arthur Ponsonby, *More English Diaries* (London, 1927), pp. 170–178.

PRICE, Mrs.
Diary, 1805. 1 vol.
Contents: record of a tour in Devonshire.
Berkshire Record Office: MS. D/EEg Z1.

RAIKES, Henry.
Diary, 1805–06.
Contents: journal of a Grecian tour.
Liverpool University Library: Special coll.

RASTRICK, John Urpeth (1780–1856), civil engineer.
Diaries, Sept., 1805–53 (with gaps). 15 vols.

Contents: daily entries of varying lengths; his pioneer work in developing the steam engine; railway work in the West Midlands and concerning the London and Brighton Railway.

University of London Library: MSS. 242/I/2–4, 242/II/1–4, 242/III/2–7, (G. L.) I. 828. (Joan Gibbs, Palaeographer). T. D. Rogers, *The Rastrick Papers: a Handlist* (London, 1968). N. Mutton, "An Engineer at Work in the West Midlands: the Diary of J. U. Rastrick for 1820", *Journal of West Midlands Regional Studies* (Spec. Pub. No. 1, 1969).

ROSS, John, soldier.
Diary, 1805–16.
Contents: service in Spain, Portugal, France during the Peninsular War; notes kept while deputy commissioner of ordnance department.
Oxford, Bodleian Library: MS. Eng. hist. e 31.

SOCKETT, Rev. Thomas, a tutor to the sons of 3rd. Earl Egremont.
Diary, 1805–07. 1 vol.
Contents: journal includes visits to Stanstead Ho., Portsmouth and the Isle of Wight coinciding with Nelson's sailing from Portsmouth.
West Sussex County Record Office: Petworth House Archives, 1679.

STANLEY, Rev. Edward (1779–1849), Rector of Alderley, Cheshire, and later a Bishop of Norwich.
Diaries, 1805–1827. 10 vols.
Contents: contains observations and notes, etc. concerning parish work while rector of Alderley (1805–37).
Alderley Church, Cheshire: Parish Records.

THORP, W., a seaman.
Diary, 1805. 1 vol.
Contents: journal kept in the form of minutes during the battle of Trafalgar by a seaman on H.M.S. *Minotaur*.
National Maritime Museum: JOD 41, MS. 9735.

WILLIAMS, Maria Jane.
Diaries, 1805, 1840, 1849–50, 1852–53, 1855–57, 1860–61.
Contents: entries made in printed pocket books and almanacs.
National Library of Wales: Aberpergwm MSS. 1308–17 (Deposited 1940).

1806

ANON.
Diary, 1806–32.
Contents: a listing of day-to-day events; diary found in Nevis, British West Indies.
Oxford, Rhodes House Library: MSS. W. Ind. S.24.

ANON.
Diary, 1806–52 (with gaps).
Contents: journals of tours in Wales.
Private: Porter MSS. (Present location unknown).
ANON.
Diary, 1806–08.
Contents: ship's log, H.M.S. *Pompée*.
Cambridge University Library: Add. MSS. 4638–40.
ALLWYN, John, merchant.
Diary, 1806.
Contents: sea journal from Falmouth to Gibraltar; attack by Spanish pirates; religion, business gossip, graphic details of dangers at sea; interesting spellings.
Eclectic Magazine, CIX (1887), 87–93.
ASHBURTON, Alexander Baring, 1st. Baron (1776–1848), statesman.
Diary and Memorandum book, 1806–1827.
Contents: farming and estate development; Rosehall estate, Sutherland; full account.
Harpenden, Hertfordshire: Rothamsted Experimental Station.
BOSWELL, James (son of the biographer), student at Oxford.
Diary, Jan–Feb., 1806.
Contents: very brief journals of two tours by an undergraduate at B.N.C. in London.
Oxford, Brasenose College Library: MS. 43.
CAMPBELL, Archibald.
Diary, May, 1806–Feb., 1812. 1 vol.
Contents: journal of a voyage around the world from 1806 to 1812, in which Japan, Kamschatka, the Al(e)utian Islands, and the Sandwich Islands were visited.
University of Glasgow: MS. Euing 24.
CECIL, Rev. R.
Diary, 1806–07.
Contents: journal of prayers and reflections by an Anglican clergyman.
Private: Cecil MS. (Present location unknown).
FITZHERBERT, Sir Henry (1783–1858).
Diaries, 1806–58, 1808–49, 1852, and 1857.
Contents: the first diary, 1806–95, was continued by his son after 1858 and contains notes on farming, crops, cows and weather; the second group are annual copies of Goldsmith's Almanack and contain entries of varying lengths on family, social, and County matters; finally, diaries covering parts of the years 1852 and 1857 contain fuller notes, mostly family and personal.
Derbyshire Record Office: MSS. D.239/1,4,5,.

FOX, Mrs. Charles James, wife of famous Whig statesman.
Diaries, 1806–40. 31 vóls.
London: British Museum: Add. MSS. 51476–51507 (Holland House MSS.
Vols. 159–190) (Acquired 1963).

GULSTON, A. S., landowner, of Carmarthenshire, South Wales.
Diaries, 1806, 1826, 1833.
Carmarthenshire Record Office: MSS. Derwydd H 27.

HALL, Dr. Benjamin (d. 1825), Chancellor of diocese of Llandaff.
Diary, July–Nov., 1806.
Contents: includes a Greek vocabulary by him with Latin and English
equivalents.
National Library of Wales: MS. 2871A.

INGILBY, William Bates.
Diaries, 1806–56 and 1855.
Contents: brief journal of the career of diarist, 1806–56; and a notebook
containing a journal of a journey from Grahamstown to Capetown, 1855.
Leeds Public Libraries (Sheepscar): Archives Dept., MS. No. 3599.

KENNAWAY, Richard, of Exeter.
Diary, 1806.
Contents: journal of journey to India.
Exeter City Record Office: MS. Ref. 58–9, Box 30.

MARDON, Richard (1776–1812), Baptist missionary.
Diary, 1806–07.
Contents: itinerant work in Goamalti area; a visit to Burma with fellow
missionary.
London, Baptist Missionary Society: MS. IN/25.

NIMMO, Alexander.
Diary, 1806.
Contents: travel journal along the east coast of Inverness-shire; scenery
and beauties.
National Library of Scotland: MS. 34.4.20.

REEVE, General John.
Diary, 1806–13.
Contents: journals of Sicilian Expedition, 1806–08, and of the Spanish
Expedition, 1808–13.
Private: MSS. at Leadenham House, Lincolnshire.

ROBERTSON, Anne (later Mrs. Traill).
Diary, 1806. 1 vol. (see also p. 112).
Contents: journal of a tour from Liverpool to Edinburgh.
Liverpool Record Office: Arch. 920 PAR III.

SHERBROOKE family, of Oxton, Southwell, Notts.
Diary, Jan., 1806–Dec., 1829. 1 vol.
Contents: sporadic jottings, including principally gardening notes, lists of

flowers, thermometer readings; little personal comment.

Oxford, Bodleian Library: MS. Eng. misc. d. 640. (Acquired 1968.)

SMITH, Sir Harry G. W., Governor of the Cape Colony.

Diary, 1806–08.

Contents: entries concern the Montevideo Expedition.

London, Public Record Office: Harry Smith Papers (W. O. 135). (Presented 1941).

THOMLINSON, Matthew.

Diaries, 1806–12, 1832–36, 1836–39. 3 vols.

Contents: recording family life and domestic incidents; state of his health; the weather; the parish offices which he held; notes on farming; melancholy philosophical reflections, usually occasioned by the deaths of relatives and acquaintances.

Wakefield Public Library: MS. 82.

WRIGHT, Miss Lucy, of London.

Diary, Aug–Sept., 1806. 1 vol.

Contents: leisurely account of a tour to the Welsh Marches, Tintern, Chepstow, Bath, Southampton, and Cowes, by curricle.

Wigan Central Public Library: Edward Hall coll.

1807

ANON.

Diary, 1807.

Contents: journal of journey into South Wales.

Private: Bledisloe MSS. Present location unknown.

BARNARD, William, of Harlow, Essex, a farmer.

Diary, 1807–23. 1 vol.

Contents: a weekly journal; farming matters.

Essex Record Office: MS. D/DU 676.

BISHOP, Harriet Anne (13th Baroness Zouche).

Diaries, 1807–64.

Private: formerly by the late Hon. Clive Pearson of Parham, Sussex. (Present location unknown).

BLOOMFIELD, Robert (1766–1823), poet.

Diary, Aug., 1807. 1 vol.

Contents: journal of a tour of Wye Valley, Malvern, etc., lengthy sketches and pictures; literary romantic descriptions of scenes.

London, British Museum: Add. MS. 28267.

BULLEN family, of Suffolk.

Diaries, 1807–69.

West Suffolk Record Office: MSS. Acc. 2151.

B

BUSH, Miss R. M. (later Mrs. Smith).
  Diaries, 1807 and 1812. 2 vols.
  Contents: brief entries in printed *Ladies Useful Repository* and *The London and Fashionable and Polite Repository*.
  National Library of Wales: Aberpergwm MSS. 1318/1319.

COLLINGWOOD, Cuthbert (1750–1810), 1st. Baron of Newcastle, admiral.
  Diary, Dec., 1807–Jan., 1810.
  Contents: naval diary; service in the Mediterranean.
  Newcastle-upon-Tyne Reference Library: L 920 (typewritten copy.) Also; Northumberland Record Office: MS. ZAN M13 F21 (Typescript).

CUYLER, A. M.
  Diary, 1807.
  Contents: an account of a visit to Llanbedr, Brecknock, with remarks on an excursion down the River Wye.
  National Library of Wales: MS. 784A.

DAVIES, Henry, of Llanycrwys, Carmarthen.
  Diary, 1807. (Transcript).
  Contents: journal kept aboard H.M.S. *Repulse*, by a Royal Marine.
  Carmarthen County Record Office: MSS. Acc. 4361.

DUNDONALD, Sir Thomas Cochrane (1775–1860), 10th. Earl of, admiral.
  Diary, Nov., 1807–July, 1849. 27 vols.
  Contents: naval journal in West Indies; naval life and work; social life and travels.
  National Library of Scotland: MSS. 2577–2604. (S.R.O.: GD 233/65/11).

ELKINGTON, (——), Army Officer.
  Diaries, 1807–14 and 1826.
  Contents: journal kept during the Peninsular War, and one later with few entries.
  Royal Army Medical Corps, Historical Museum: MSS. 336/484.

GROSVENOR, Field-Marshal Thomas.
  Diary, 1807. 1 vol.
  Contents: journal relating to the English expedition to Copenhagen, when the diarist was a Major-General.
  London, British Museum: Add. MS. 49059 (Jellicoe Papers).

HOLLAND, Col. Lancelot, soldier.
  Diary, 1807–08. (Typescript extracts).
  Contents: deals mainly with his service as DQMG of the expedition to the River Plate on the staff of General Crawford.
  National Army Museum: MS. 6807/236.

HOWARD, Luke (1772–1864), of Plaistow, Essex and of Ackworth, near Pontefract, Yorkshire. He was the founder of Howards & Sons, chemical manufacturers (now Laporte Industries Ltd.).
  Diary, July–Aug., 1807. 1 vol.
  Contents: journal of a journey to Westmorland and visits to places en

route, with attendances at meetings of the Society of Friends; a meeting with Robert Southey at Keswick.

Greater London Record Office (Middlesex Records): MS. Acc. 1017/1397.

JOHNS, William, Baptist missionary.

Diary, (?) 1807 (extracts).

Contents: portion from his journal 28 Jan–March, 6; Lord Minto ordered him to be deported in 1813, since he had not obtained permission to land from the court of Directors.

London, Baptist Missionary Society: MS. IN/5.

LYON, Rev. James Radcliffe (1786–1869), rector of Pulford, Cheshire.

Diaries, Oct., 1807–Jan., 1811. 9 vols.

Contents: description of personal affairs and social life at Eaton Hall, Cheshire, while tutor to the sons of Robert, 2nd. earl Grosvenor.

Cheshire Record Office: MSS. DDX 197.

MARTIN, Lieut. William (1789–1882), soldier.

Diary, 1807–38 (with gaps). 1 vol.

Contents: journal begun on his joining the 10th. Bengal Native Infantry, and includes his subsequent service, especially long marches and expeditions.

National Army Museum: MS. 7207/10.

MOLYNEUX, Henry More.

Diary, log book and Papers, 1807–15.

Private: Loseley MSS. (Present location unknown).

PARISH, John (1743–1829), of Bath, merchant, philanthropist, and eccentric.

Diaries, (i) Aug., 1807; (ii) Aug–Sept., 1807.

Contents: (i) details of what occurred at Table Bay during the last weeks of his residence before Copenhagen; (ii) expedition in H.M.S. *Cruizer*, appointed to take the Trade to Southward under convoy, and Parish's passage to the Nore.

Bath Municipal Library: MSS. 29:971.

PROTHEROE, Mrs. Emma (nee Jones), of Carmarthen.

Diaries, Sept., 1807–Sept., 1809 and Jan–Dec., 1818. 2 vols.

Contents: diaries kept while living at Gellydowyll and Dolwilym respectively.

Carmarthen County Record Office: MSS. Protheroe Beynon 214–5.

RATHBONE, Elizabeth (1790–1882)

Diaries, 1807 and 1811–69.

Contents: typewritten copy of extracts from her journal as a young girl, 1807; the remainder are pocket diaries.

Liverpool University Library: Rathbone Papers.

SMITH, Major William (d. 1810), of 45th Regiment.

Diary, Aug., 1807–March, 1809.

Contents: service in South America; Montevideo; later reconnoitering

and military service in Spain during the Peninsular War.
Sherwood Foresters' Regimental Annual (London, 1929), pp. 169–186.

STANHOPE, John Spencer (1787–1873), of Cannon Hall, Cawthorne, Yorks., author.

Diaries, 1807–69. 35 vols.

Contents: with intermittent entries, 1810–13 ; covers the travels in Spain, Greece and Italy, and the author's imprisonment in Spain ; sparse entries, 1825–69.

Sheffield City Library: Spencer Stanhope Papers, 60642–60644. (John Bebbington, City Librarian).

Memoirs of Anna Marie Wilhelmina Pickering, ed. Spencer Pickering, (Privately printed, 1904), pp. 347–553.

STEER, George, of Comforts Place Farm, Godstone, near Redhill, Surrey, tenant farmer.

Diary, Sept., 1807–July, 1814. 1 vol.

Contents: diary-cum-ledger containing accounts and memoranda ; family items ; includes some later insertions: family births, newspaper cuttings, etc.

Surrey Record Office: MS. Acc. 511.

STUART, Charles, a soldier.

Diaries, Oct., 1807–March, 1812 (with gaps). 4 vols.

Contents: describes expedition under Maj-General Dickens which reduced forts at Komona & Ganauri of a refractory chieftain ; a journey from Keitah to Benares ; expedition into Bundelkhand ; a journey to Calcutta to command Cadet College at Baraset.

National Army Museum: MSS. 6404/74/5.

VAWDREY, Mrs. Sarah Darell (1789–1837), of Kinderton by Middlewich, Cheshire.

Diaries, 1807, 1811, and 1829. 3 vols.

Contents: memoranda, observations, appointments, personal accounts, household matters, provisions etc. Irregular entries.

Cheshire Record Office: MSS. DMD/L/8.

1808

ANON.

Diary, June, 1808. 1 vol.

Contents: journal of a trip from the Isle of Wight to Oxford.

National Library of Wales: Pitchford MS.

ANON.

Diary, 1808. 1 vol.

Contents: north Cardiganshire attorney's diary for the year.

National Library of Wales: MS. 5916A.

ANON.
  Diary, 1808.
  Private: Col. R. G. Parker, Bronsholme Hall, Clitheroe, Lancs.
ANON. [? William Blundell]
  Diary, Aug., 1808–34.
  Contents: "the idea of this journal is to assist me by thus retaining such things as might otherwise escape my memory".
  Lancashire Record Office: Blundell Coll. (Deposited 1947).
BARCROFT family.
  Diary, 1808.
  Contents: matters relating to the Barcroft family; Lancashire interest.
  Private: Col. R. G. Parker, Bronsholme Hall, Clitheroe, Lancs. Deposited on loan at Lancashire Record Office, Preston.
CALL, George Cotsford.
  Diaries, 1808, 1810.
  Contents: journey to Spain, 1808; journey to the Continent in company with his sister, Mrs. Philleda Bathurst, in search of her missing husband, Benjamin Bathurst, British Envoy to Austria.
  London, British Museum: Add. MS. 52284. (Presented 1963).
COLTHURST, Lieut. James, a soldier of the 32nd. Foot.
  Diary, 1808–09. 1 vol.
  Contents: journal kept on service with the 1st. Bn. 32nd. Foot during the Spanish campaigns.
  National Army Museum: MSS. 6807/166.
DOBREE, Lieut. Augustus Frederick, a soldier of the 14th. Foot.
  Diary, 1808–09. 1 vol.
  Contents: brief (6pp.) journal kept in the Peninsular campaign by an Ensign of the 14th. Foot.
  National Army Museum: MSS. 6807/148.
ELEY, James.
  Diary, 1808. 1 vol.
  Contents: journal of a tour from Thornbury, Glos., to Leominster and Pembridge in Herefordshire; interesting information about Non-Conformism in Leominster.
  Private: K. G. Marling, Esq., Malvern, Worcs.
  Herefordshire Record Office: MS. J 18/1 (typescript).
FORTESCUE, Hugh, 2nd. Earl (1783–1861), of Castle Hill, Filleigh, Devon.
  Diaries, 1808–15, 1842–43, 1849–50 (travel, 9 vols); 1811–61, (daily, 10 vols).
  Contents: the travel journals have detailed daily entries in narrative style; Wales, Spain, Portugal, Tangier, Sardinia, Sicily, Malta, Elba, Italy, and Switzerland 1808–15; Belgium, Germany, Prussia, Italy and Greece, 1842–43; France and Italy, 1849–50. The daily diaries contain brief

entries of personal, social, and political activities while in Devon, London, Ireland, and on the Continent.

Devon Record Office: MSS. 1262 M/FD 3–8, 19–20; 22, 9–17, 21.

HODGE, Capt. Edward, a soldier of the 7th. Hussars.

Diary, Oct., 1808–March, 1809.

Contents: journal of service with the 7th. Hussars during the Corunna campaign of the Peninsular War.

Warwick, Queen's Own Hussars Museum: MSS. coll.

JONES, Rev. David (1735–1810), rector of Llangan, Glamorgan.

Diaries, 1808 and Jan–Aug., 1810.

Contents: notes of preaching engagements, home pursuits, etc.

National Museum of Wales: Folk coll. 28.608/1–2.

(Loaned)

LEITH-HAY Andrew, politician and soldier.

Diaries, 1808, 1812–13, 1833, 1844–46, 1854 and 1855. 5 vols.

Contents: early diaries kept in Spain and Portugal with sketches of towns and battle of Corunna ; parliamentary diaries for 1833 and 1855 are brief notes of business; journal of a shooting expedition in Lower Canada while stationed at Montreal; finally one kept while serving in the Crimea.

Scottish Record Office: GD 225/ Boxes 39–40.

LEY, John.

Diary, 1808–09.

Exeter City Library: Brooke MS.

MacKENZIE, John Randoll (d. 1809), of Suddie, major-general.

Diary, Oct., 1808–May, 1809.

Contents: service during the Peninsular War, in Portugal and Spain ; military movements; notes on Spanish towns, etc.; Spanish social life; strategy and military operations.

London, British Museum: Add. MS. 32901.

OTWAY, L. W., a soldier of the 18th. Hussars.

Diary, 1808–09. 1 vol.

Contents: journal kept during the Peninsular campaign; service at Corunna.

National Army Museum: MSS. 6810/35.

PALMERSTON, Henry John Temple, 3rd. Viscount (1784–1865), statesman.

Diary, Feb., 1808–Sept., 1844 (extracts).

Contents: his legal career and trials ; public events at home and abroad ; current political issues and parliamentary affairs while he was secretary of war ; Napoleonic wars ; quarrel of Whigs with George III ; visits to Paris and Germany.

Hampshire Record Office: (?) unlisted collections.

Evelyn Ashley, *Life and Correspondence of Lord Palmerston*, 2 vols. (London, 1879). Also, Sir H. Lytton Bulwer, *Life of Lord Palmerston*, 3 vols. (London, 1870–74).

RICHARDSON, George (1773–1862), of North Shields.
Diary, June, 1808–April, 1842.
Contents: various Quaker missionary and visiting journeys mostly through the north of England; visits to Friends' meetings; work in ministry; prayers, etc.
A Journal of the Gospel Labours of George Richardson (London, 1864).

ROWNTREE, Elizabeth, of Scarbrough, Yorkshire.
Diary, May, 1808–Oct., 1835 (with gaps).
Contents: brief notes; Quaker meetings, religious introspection and observances; travel in many parts of Great Britain; social life of Friends; family life and children.
London, Friends' Society Library: Box T.

WELLESLEY-POLE, Hon. William (1763–1845), later Baron Maryborough.
Diary, Aug., 1808–22.
Contents: military matters; Spain; first landing in the Peninsular War, etc.
Private: Duke of Wellington, Reading, Berkshire.

1809

ANON.
Diary, 1809. 1 vol.
Contents: diary covering the Walcheren expedition.
Scottish Record Office: GD 45/4/60.

ANON.
Diaries, 1809–10, 1820, 1823–30. 9 vols.
Contents: a farmer's journal, mainly relating to sales, carriage and purchase of crops and livestock with tasks given to labourers.
Leeds Central Library: MSS. BW/Di/1. (Battie Wrightson MSS.)

ANON.
Diary, Sept., 1809. 1 vol.
Contents: journal of a brief visit to Portsmouth and the Isle of Wight.
East Sussex County Record Office: De la Warr MS. 556.

ANON.
Diary, 1809. 1 vol.
Contents: journal of a tour in Ireland.
Cambridge University Library: MS. 4342.

BEDINGFELD, Lady Charlotte (d. 1854), of Oxburgh, Norfolk.
Diary, July, 1809–Sept., 1833 (extracts, and large gaps).
Contents: domestic life and social affairs in high society; the illness of her father; religion; her later life in a convent at Hammersmith.
Private: Sir Edmund Paston-Bedingfeld, Oxburgh Hall, King's Lynn, Norfolk.
The Jerningham Letters, ed. E. Castle (London, 1869).

BROUGHTON, John Cam Hobhouse (1786–1869), 1st Baron, statesman. Diaries, June, 1809–April, 1852 (with gaps).

Contents: autobiographical introduction; career of a radical Whig statesman; politics and public affairs; travels abroad, with Byron in Italy; social life and entertainment; life of a country gentleman; notes on famous literary and stage figures of the day.

London, British Museum: Add. MSS. 43744–43765, 47231–47235.

Recollections of a Long Life, 6 vols. (London, 1909–11).

BUXTON, Sir John Jacob, bart. (d. 1842).

Diary, 1809. 1 vol.

Contents: brief pocket diary.

Oxford, Christ Church College Library: MS. coll.

CALDWELL, J. S., of Lindley Wood, Talke, Staffordshire.

Diary, Jan., 1809–Sept., 1811.

Contents: include many references to local families and lists of debtors with whereabouts; brief entries only.

Stafford, William Salt Library: MS. 167.

CAREY William (the younger) (1787–1853), son of the founder of the Baptist Mission Society.

Diary, Sept., 1809–Jan., 1810.

Contents: journal describing journey from Serampore to Katwa; missionary work; his coffee plantation.

London, Baptist Mission Society: MS. IN/26.

DILLWYN, Lewis Weston.

Diary, July–Aug., 1809.

Contents: journal of a tour from Swansea to Killarney; notes on Irish scenery and towns.

Dublin, Trinity College Library: MS. Cat. No. 967.

DUNDAS, Sir Robert L., of Loftus, Cleveland, Yorkshire.

Diary, 1809–10.

Contents: three campaign diaries by the youngest son of 1st Lord Dundas, and brother of 1st. Earl Zetland; diarist held the rank of Lieutenant-General.

North Riding of Yorkshire County Record Office. MS. ZNK X/4.

ERSKINE, William (1773–1852), of Edinburgh, orientalist.

Diary, Dec., 1809–Oct., 1850 (many gaps).

Contents: mostly notes on his reading and his critical opinions.

London: British Museum: Add. MS. 39945.

FOLEY, Rev. Edward Walwyn (1809–1899), of Holt, Worcestershire.

Diaries, 1809–92 (very brief), and 1831.

Contents: (i) brief diary of events in the life of the diarist; (ii) journal of a tour, July–Aug., 1831, through North and Mid-Wales made on foot with E. Cockey and T. G. Simcox; food & accommodation; meets future wife; reception by the locals.

Wigan Central Public Library: Edward Hall coll. M970 EHC178 (Presented 1951)

GORDON, Hon. Robert, diplomatist.
Diary, 1809–13.
Contents: reflections of an attaché to the British Embassy in Persia.
London, British Museum: Add. MSS. 43217 and 49273.

GRAY, William (Snr.) (b. 1751), of York.
Diaries, 1809–11 and 1836–41. 2 vols.
Contents: mostly journals of tours; in Derbyshire; York to Bath. (Also a tour of Scotland, ?1796).
York Public Library: Gray's Court Papers, T/5, T/1, D/2.
(Presented 1959). Mrs. Edwin Gray, *Papers of a York Family* (Sheldon Press, 1927).

GRIFFIN, Jane (later Lady Franklin) (1791–1875).
Diary, 1809–71. Nearly 150 vols.
Contents: public events and celebrities; details of her extensive travels; record of life-long attempts made to trace her husband's missing Arctic expedition.
Cambridge. Scott Polar Research Institute: MSS.

HAWKSHEAD-TALBOT family, of Chorley, Lancashire.
Diaries, 1809–20, 1824–27.
Lancashire Record Office: Hawkeshead-Talbot MSS., DDHk.

LIVERPOOL. Hon. Charles C. Cope Jenkinson, 3rd. Earl of (1784–1851).
Diary, March–July, 1809.
Contents: his personal activities; much information on the House of Commons; Canning, Liverpool, Huskisson; inspecting militia and defences; details about London society and governmental activities.
National Library of Wales: Pitchford MS.

LOVEDAY, Ann.
Diaries, 1809–39. 3 vols.
Warwickshire Record Office: MSS. coll. (Acquired 1960).

MEYNELL, Anna Maria (b. 1770), younger daughter of Edward Meynell of Kilvington and Yarm.
Diary, c. 1809–48.
North Riding of Yorkshire County Record Office: MS.

NEVILLE, Henry, a brother of the 3rd. Lord Braybrooke.
Diary, 1809. 1 vol.
Contents: kept during the Peninsular Campaign while the diarist was serving as a Captain in the Dragoons.
Essex Record Office: MS. D/DBy F16.

POWYS, Philip, of Fawley, Buckinghamshire.
Diary, 1809.
Oxfordshire Record Office: MS. PL. Acc. No. 8.

B*

RIDLEY, Capt. John, soldier.
Diary, 1809–13. 1 vol.
Contents: kept by a Royal Marines officer while prisoner of war in Verdun.
Northumberland Record Office: Ridley of Blagdon MS., NRO 138, MS. ZR1 32/4.

ROCHE, Captain Joseph, R.N.
Diary, Oct.,[?]1809.
Contents: journey by carriage from Liverpool to Worcester with a detachment of cavalry; notes on places, route.
N&Q, 12th. ser., III (1917).

SACKVILLE, [?———].
Diary, 1809.
Contents: journal of journey to Palermo.
Kent Archives Office: Sackville of Knole MSS., U269.

SHIELD, Admiral William (c. 1762–1842), of London and Exeter.
Diaries, 1809–12, and 1815–41. 26 vols.
Contents: brief daily entries of happenings at work and at home, including information on the weather and the state of his health; 1809–12 kept at Cape Town as Commissioner of the Navy, 1815 in London, then while at Plymouth, and from 1829 onwards kept at Exeter.
Devon Record Office: MSS. 74 B/MFS 4–29.

SILLS, John, of Ashford, Kent, a grocer.
Diary, 1809–21. 2 vols.
Contents: he included many references to national events as well as personal affairs; whimsical in places.
Kent Archives Office: MSS. Z6–1,2 (U442 Gordon Ward coll.)

SIMMONS, Major George (b.1786), of the Rifle Brigade.
Diary, May, 1809–June, 1815.
Contents: accounts of six campaigns in Spain and Portugal during the Peninsular War, and of the Waterloo campaign; military movements, battles; civilians; French atrocities.
Private: Sir Edward Le Breton, Loder's Court, Nr. Bridport, Dorset.
A British Rifle Man (London, 1899).

SOUTHEBY, Rose.
Diary, c. 1809
Contents: journal of a tour through parts of Monmouthshire and Glamorgan during the early part of the nineteenth century; illustrated by over 30 watercolours and unfinished pencil sketches by the diarist.
National Library of Wales: MS. 6497C.

STAIR, North Dalrymple, 9th. Earl of.
Diaries, 1809–10 and 1812–13. 2 vols.

Contents: first is diary kept in India; both kept before Dalrymple succeeded to the earldom.

Scottish Record Office: GD 135/155 and Box 43.

THOMAS, Rev. D. (1757–1837), of Penmain.

Diaries, 1809–20 (with gaps).

Contents: notes of sermons, church work and services.

National Library of Wales: Add. MS. 389–A.

TIMEWELL, Pte. John (b. 1782), of Milverton, Somerset.

Diary and narrative, June, 1809–June, 1815.

Contents: service with 43rd. Light Infantry during the Peninsular War in Spain and Portugal; American War; New Orleans; accounts of campaign; interesting spellings.

MacMillan's Mag., LXXVII (1877–78).

TRENCH, Gen. Sir Frederick (1775–1859), a soldier.

Diary 1809–13. 1 vol.

Contents: includes an account of the Walcheren expedition in Holland of 1809 and the Peninsular campaigns, 1811–13, of the Napoleonic Wars.

National Army Museum: MSS. 6807/261.

VERULAM, Charlotte Grimston, Countess of (d. 1863), of Gorhambury, St. Albans, Hertfordshire.

Diary, Nov., 1809–May, 1814. 1 vol.

Contents: brief entries mostly family and social.

Hertford County Record Office: MS. Ref. AR 942.

WELLINGTON, Catherine Dorothea Sara (1772–1831), later Duchess of, wife of the 1st. Duke of Wellington.

Diary, 1809–12. 1 vol.

Contents: kept during her husband's absence in Spain and Portugal during the Peninsular Campaign.

Private: the Duke of Wellington, Reading, Berkshire.

1810

ANON.

Diary, 1810–20.

Contents: journal relating to the cultivation of peppermint on two acres of land at Wisbech, Cambridgeshire.

Sheffield City Library: Jackson coll.

ANON.

Diary, 1810.

Contents: few entries in *Young Ladies Useful Pocket Book*; cash accounts.

Kent Archives Office: U120 Filmer, MS. F27/1.

ANON.

Diary, 1810–45.

Contents: personal interests of the diarist, a resident of Nuneaton.

Nuneaton Borough Library: MSS. (Deposited 1938).

ANON., of Frinton Hall Farm, Essex.

Diary, 1810–34. 3 vols.

Contents: interesting local and personal details.

Private: Mrs. Stone, The Garage, Priory Street, Colchester, Essex. (MSS. could not be traced in March, 1969).

ABBOT, Charles (later 2nd. Lord Colchester).

Diaries, 1810, 1811, and 1818, 1820–21 ; journals, 1819–26, and 1829–35.

Contents: accounts of various voyages in ships, *Liffey, Racehorse, Columbine,* and *Rose* ; a sojourn at Naples, and account of the Austrian campaign there ; deaths and funerals of his father and brother.

London, Public Record Office: Colchester Papers, 30/9.

ADDINGTON, Henry Unwin (1790–1870), permanent Under-Secretary for Foreign Affairs, 1842–45.

Diaries, in form of reminiscences, 1810–40. 10 vols.

Contents: narrative style giving details of places visited and of his work ; in Sicily at the Court of Naples ; on a commission in Cadiz, 1812, and in Berlin, 1813–14 ; with a legation to the Court of Denmark, 1821–22, and to the U.S., 1824–28 ; some journeys in France, Italy, and Germany, 1839–40.

Devon Record Office: MSS. 152 M/Box38/F1–10.

Bradford Perkins, ed., *Youthful America: Selections from Henry Unwin Addington's Residence in the United States of America:* 1822–25 (Los Angeles: University of California Publications in History, No. 65, 1960).

ARNOLL-DAVIS, Capt. Thomas (1794–1887), mariner.

Diaries, Jan., 1810–August, 1828. 9 vols.

Contents: personal copies of the official logs kept during nine voyages to India and China in the maritime service of the East India Company.

India Office Library: MSS. Eur. E. 286.

CARRINGTON, John (junior) (1763–1833), innkeeper, of Tewin, Hertford-shire.

Diaries, May, 1810–Dec., 1812. 7 vols.

Contents: personal, family, reflective, etc. Less lively continuation of his father's diary.

Hertford County Record Office: MSS. Ref. D/EX3.17–23.

CROFT, John.

Diary, March 1810–Dec., 1832. 3 vols.

Contents: records limited details of the transactions of a merchant.

Liverpool Record Office: MSS. 380MD 39–41.

DAVIS, Miss, of Ambleside, Westmorland.

Diary, Jan.–Dec., 1810.

Contents: irregular notes of a lady of leisure and consequence in the Ambleside group; holiday at Lytham; some personalia.

Wigan Central Public Library: Edward Hall coll. (Typed copy also available).

DYER, Mrs. Elizabeth (b. 1735).

Diary, 1810–13. 3 vols.

Contents: daily round of life at Belmont, Faversham, Kent; enormous amount of visiting; the weather; diarist's health.

Kent Archives Office: MSS. F1/1–3 (Harris coll. U 624).

Deposited 1957.

FEA, Peter, of Hull, Yorkshire, a Royal Naval seaman.

Diary, 1810–14. 1 vol.

Contents: daily entries recording the diarist's own movements and the comings and goings of other prisoners and French soldiers, following the capture of his ship by French privateers and his imprisonment at St. Malo, at Auxonne, and other places; lodgings and treatment described; list of prisoners who died; his freedom in 1814 and journey via Calais to Hull.

Devon Record Office: MS. 1317 M.

FORD, Henry (c. 1777–1840), estate agent to the Wilton estate of the Earls of Pembroke.

Diaries, 1810–40. 31 vols.

Contents: simple account of daily life.

Wiltshire Record Office: MSS. 867/1–31.

HIBBERT, Mary Anne.

Diaries, 1810–18, and 1823–68. 24 vols.

Contents: family affairs; description of tours taken, mostly in England.

Gloucestershire Record Office: D1799 F 317–340, Dyrham Park MSS.

HOBLYN, C. (apparently a woman).

Diaries, 1810. 2 vols.

Contents: journals kept of a visit to Bath, Wiltshire.

Cornwall County Record Office: MSS. DD.X.53/15.

HOTHAM, Admiral Sir Henry, G.G.M.G.

Diaries, 1810–11, 1814–15, 1830, 1832–33. 10 vols.

East Riding of Yorkshire County Record Office: DDHO/17/52–62.

MORRIS, Rev. Thomas.

Diaries and notebooks, 1810–19 (extracts), 1820, 1825–26, and c. 1836.

Contents: twentieth-century extracts from the early part of the journal; journal of a voyage from Calcutta to Benares, 1820; accounts of India; 1836, voyage to India and experiences in the subcontinent in the 1820's.

Bristol Archives Office: MS. Acc. 15400.

NAPIER, Lieut-General Sir Charles James, G.O.B. (1782–1853).

Diary, 1810–47.

Contents: full and detailed record of his army life and career; interspersed with letters; much about his personal and social life.

London, British Museum: (Napier Papers) Add. MSS. 49131–49134.
(Presented 1956).
Sir W. Napier, *The Life and Opinions of General Napier* (London, 1857).
POWELL, Commander George Eyre, R.N. (1790–1855).
Diaries, Dec., 1810–Aug., 1843, and Jan., 1847–Nov., 1855.
Contents: miscellaneous memoranda; some of his own poems.
National Library of Wales: MSS. 13271–13285.
ROSS, John Clunies, a seaman.
Diary, Nov., 1810. (extract).
Contents: journal kept on a South Seas whaler while serving as a
harpooner; joins brig *Olivia.*
India Office Library: MSS. Eur. C. 36.
STEWART, William, a soldier of the 30th. Foot.
Diary, Sept., 1810–May, 1811.
Contents: journal kept during the Peninsular campaign during the
Napoleonic Wars.
National Army Museum: MSS. 6112/33.
VAUGHAN, Sir Charles Richard (1774–1849), diplomatist.
Diary, 1810–14.
Contents: entries made while acting minister at Cadiz during the
Peninsular War.
Oxford, All Souls College Library: MSS.
VENN, Henry.
Diaries, 1810, 1824, and 1826.
Contents: journals of tours in Yorkshire and in Wales.
London, Church Missionary Society: MSS. (Acquired 1958).
WEST, Jane.
Diary, 1810.
Contents: journal of a tour of Ireland.
Cambridge, University Library: Add. MS. 738.

1811

ANON.
Diary, 1811–54. 2 vols.
Contents: journal of a farmer; stock and stores bought and sold, yields,
etc.
Private: Lt-Col. T. Fetherstonhaugh, Kirkoswald, Penrith, Cumberland.
ANON.
Diary, 1811. 1 vol.
Contents: journal of a lady's driving tour in North Wales in the summer;
scenery and beauties.
Cardiff Public Library: MSS.

ANON. [? Smith family of Horbling, Lincolnshire].
Diaries, 1811–54.
Contents: family interests, etc.
Lincolnshire Archives Office: Smith of Horbling MSS. (Some are still at Horbling).

ANON., a Quaker, of Hitchen, Hertfordshire.
Diaries, Sept–Oct., 1811 and Oct., 1814. 2 vols.
Contents: pleasure journeys: one to the Isle of Wight, the other to Dorset and Somerset; descriptive details.
Hertford County Record Office: MSS. Ref. 61174–5.

ANON. (a Flintshire lady)
Diary, Aug–Oct., 1811.
Contents: journal recording repeated visits to Gwenhaylod and Brynypys, and a journey to Tanyrallt, near Tremadoc, and elsewhere.
National Library of Wales: MS. 3565B (Puleston MSS).

ANON.
Diary, 1811–13.
Contents: daily work of a farmer, near Liverpool.
Harpenden, Hertfordshire, Rothamsted Experimental Station.

ANON.
Diary, 1811.
Contents: journal of the Honeymoon tour through England of J. F. Burnett and his wife, written by the chief bridesmaid, who accompanied them.
Private: Robert Burnett Esq., formerly of Devizes, Wiltshire.

ANON.
Diary, 1811–12. 1 vol.
Contents: journal of a voyage to and from the West Indies in the store ship, *Dromedary*.
National Maritime Museum: JOD 34, MS. 51/048.

BUNCE, Lieut-Col. Richard, of the Royal Marines.
Diary, 1811. 1 vol.
Contents: journal of a campaign in Java with the Royal Marines and H.M.S. *Scorpion*; memoranda, testimonials of service.
National Maritime Museum: JOD 8, MS. 56/010.

CALL, Capt, George Isacc, a soldier of the Light Dragoons.
Diary, Sept., 1811–Feb., 1812. 1 vol.
Contents: relating to his service in the Peninsular War with the 27th. (late 24th.) Light Dragoons.
National Army Museum: MSS. 6807/150.
Journal of the Society for Army Historical Research (XXIX, 55).

CLIFT, William (1775–1849), F.R.S., Conservator of Hunterian Museum, R.C.S., a naturalist.
Diaries, 1811–42. 33 vols.

Contents: memoranda concerning the museum, the buildings of the Royal College of Surgeons, and persons connected therewith.
London, Royal College of Surgeons Library: MSS. 276.g.1–33.

CLOWES, Col. P. L., a soldier.
Diary, 1811–12.
Contents: journal kept in Portugal and Spain during the Peninsular campaign of the Napoleonic Wars.
National Army Museum: MSS. 5807/10.

CROSSE, Dr. John Green (1790–1850), of Norwich, physician.
Diaries, 1811–14, 1814–15; d. with letters, 1815–35.
Contents: early diaries are ones kept in Paris.
Norwich Public Library: MSS.

CULLUM, Sir Thomas Gery.
Diary, 1811.
Contents: journal of a tour made through South Wales.
National Library of Wales: MS. 5446B (transcript only).
Y Cymmrodor 38, 45.

CURRY, John (1774–1850), of Walcot, Bath, overseer.
Diary, June, 1811–Jan., 1831.
Contents: journal of tours undertaken for the parish; notes mileage each year; comments on the operations of the Poor Law and relief practice.
Bath Municipal Libraries: MS. 1243.

GAIRDNER, James Penman, a soldier of the 95th. Rgt.
Diaries, Nov., 1811–June, 1816. 4 vols.
Contents: journals kept by a Lieutenant of the Rifle Brigade in the Peninsular campaign, and at Waterloo.
National Army Museum: MSS 6902/51.

HOW, Jonathan.
Diaries, 1811–12. 2 vols.
Contents: notes on the lead-mining business.
Derbyshire Record Office: MSS. 504B/L255–256.

HOWLAND, Harriet.
Diary, 1811.
Contents: journal of an American's tour in England; notes on towns, scenery, antiquities, customs.
Washington, Library of Congress.

LETHBRIDGE, Henrietta, daughter of Rev. Charles Lethbridge (1763–1840), possibly of Egloskerry, Cornwall.
Diary, 1811. 1 vol.
Contents: entries for certain days only; family affairs.
Cornwall County Record Office: MS. DD.X.76/5.

[MacKENZIE, Hon. Francis ?]
Diary, March–May, 1811 and Nov., 1813. 1 vol.

Contents: family, society, social life at Sidmouth; coach journey to London.

National Library of Scotland: MS. 2540.

MOGG, William, sailor.

Diary, Dec., 1811–68. 6 vols.

Contents: account of his voyages and travels in the navy from the time of his joining; in the Arctic with Capt. Parry; later his life as a citizen.

Southampton University Library: MSS. G469–o/s, 6169–6175.

MONCK, Lady Louisa Lucy (1778–1824), of Wheatley.

Diary, 1811–16. 1 vol.

Contents: entries concerning social events, etc., made by the daughter of Sir George Cooke, Bart.

Northumberland Record Office: MS. ZMI B52/2 (Middleton of Belsay MSS., NRO 79).

NAPLES, Joshua (b. ca. 1774), resurrectionist.

Diary, 1811–12. 1 vol.

Contents: an account of the work of a resurrection gang.

London, Royal College of Surgeons Library: MS. 67.a.5.

James Blake Bailey, *The Diary of a Resurrectionist, to which are added an account of the Resurrection Men in London and a Short History of the Passing of the Anatomy Act* (London: Swan Sonnenschein, 1896).

OAKLEY, Capt. R. C. (d. 1835), soldier of the 20th. Regiment.

Diaries, 1811–Jan., 1824. 2 vols.

Contents: includes some reflections on events from 1808 onwards; fairly detailed account of service in the Peninsular War; journeys to and from Bombay, etc.

Dorset County Record Office: MSS. D320.

PICKMORE, R. R. (d. 1851), of Warrington, gentleman.

Diary, Aug., 1811–May, 1821.

Contents: mainly notes on the comings and goings of himself and family, with a few observations of local interest.

Warrington Municipal Library: MS. 1164.

PLAYFAIR, William Henry (1789–1857), architect.

Diary, May, 1811. 1 vol.

Contents: notes of a journey from Edinburgh to Saltcoats, Ayrshire, with remarks on canals, locks, bridges, etc.

Cambridge, University Library: Add. MS. 6305.

R------- [?], C., of Peover, Cheshire.

Diary, Aug–Sept., 1811. 1 vol.

Contents: the Mainwarings on tour in Lake District; the picturesque (Salvator Rosa style); notes on local worthies and yokels.

Manchester, John Rylands Library: Mainwaring coll. 50.

RICH, Claudius James (1787–1821), East India Company resident in Bagdad.

Diaries, March, 1811–May, 1821 (with gaps). 9 vols.

Contents: mostly expeditions and journeys undertaken, to Bussora, Khales, Stamboul, Nineveh, Ctesiphon, Suleimania, etc.; observations and inspections.

India Office Library: MSS. Eur. A.12–15, B.44–46, D. 232.

Narrative of Residence in Koordistan etc. ed. Mrs. Rich, 2 vols. (London, 1836).

Constance M. Alexander, *Bagdad in Bygone Days* (London, 1928).

SMIRKE, Sir Edward (1795–1875).

Diary, 1811. (Typescript only).

Contents: journal kept while at school; of interest for those who wish to establish the family background of two extremely gifted nineteenth-century architects.

Royal Institute of British Architects: Smirke family MSS.

SMITH, Henry Nelson, a Lieutenant in the Royal Engineers.

Diaries, 1811 and 1815. 2 vols.

Contents: journals of tours in Italy.

Bedfordshire Record Office: MSS. X 143/12–13.

SMITH, Capt. William, a soldier of the Light Dragoons.

Diary, May, 1811–Oct., 1812. 1 vol.

Contents: journal relating to the Peninsular War by an officer of the 11th. Light Dragoons.

National Army Museum: MSS. 6807/52.

ST. JOHN, Lady Emma.

Diary, 1811.

Contents: account of tour in the West of England.

Private: Samuel Whitebread, Southill Park, Beds., MS. 1123.

STANLEY, Catherine (1792–1862), of Alderley, Cheshire, and latterly of Norwich.

Diary, June, 1811–Jan., 1820. 1 vol.

Contents: personal journal; gives an account of the physical and mental development of her four children, including Arthur Penrhyn; informative on child development.

Cheshire Record Office: MSS. DSA 75.

A. P. Stanley, *Memoirs of Edward and Catherine Stanley*, 3rd. edit., (London, 1880).

STEPHENSON, William, a soldier of the 3rd. Dragoons.

Diary, 1811–14. 1 vol.

Contents: includes details of his service in the Peninsular campaign; writer was a sergeant.

National Army Museum: MSS. 6807/215.

STEVENS, Rev. Henry, a Justice of the Peace, of Reading.

Diary, 1811.

Contents: includes mention of a visit to the County Gaol.

Berkshire Record Office: MS. D/ESv(M) F91.

STOCK, Rt. Rev. Joseph (1740–1813), Fellow of Trinity Coll.,
Dublin ; Bishop of Killala, and of Waterford.
Diary, May, 1811.
Contents: remarks on incumbents ; state of repairs of various churches,
rectories, and schools during the first visitation of his second diocese.
Dublin, Trinity College Library: MS.

SWAIN, Rev. Joseph (1754–1831), of Leeds.
Diary, April–Dec., 1811 and Aug–Dec., 1814.
Contents: his morals ; clerical social life and friendships ; local drunken-
ness and misdemeanors ; visits to Lightcliffe ; local people.
Leeds, Thoresby Society Library: Box 5.

VAWDREY, Thomas (1786–1839), of Newton by Middlewich, Cheshire.
Diaries, August, 1811–39. 4 vols.
Contents: initially a commonplace book, noting the principal events of
his life ; later diaries are personal: events, observations on the weather
(with weather-table), memoranda, etc.
Cheshire Record Office: MSS. DMD/M/1.

WESTCOTT, John, bandmaster of 26th. Regiment.
Diary, June, 1811–12 (really a narrative).
Contents: account of campaign in Portugal ; activities of the band ; notes
on foreign soldiers ; Portuguese life and customs.
London, British Museum: Add. MS. 32468.

WILLIAMS WYNN, Sir Henry Watkin (1783–1856), diplomat.
Diary, 1811–12. 1 vol.
Contents: journal of a tour on the Continent: Zante, Greek Islands,
Turkey, Cyprus, Egypt, Spain ; things seen, events, people met, buildings,
weather, his health.
Oxford, Bodleian Library: MS. Eng. misc. c.488. (Acquired 1969).

1812

ANON., of Sudbury, Suffolk.
Diary, April–June, 1812. 1 vol.
Contents: journal of tour from Suffolk to Wales and Lake District and
back through Derby ; tourist's observations and descriptions ; the pictur-
esque and romantic.
Manchester, John Rylands Library: Eng. MS. 421.

ANON.
Diary, 1812–13.
Contents: the Log of the brig, *Adventurer*, under Capt. Mossip ; left
Liverpool Sept., 1812 for Newfoundland ; notes of goods discharged there.
To Gibraltar by Dec., thence to Tobago and back to London.
Liverpool Record Office: Arch. 387 MD 5 Acc. 20 (Old Ref. MD 71).

ATKINSON, Richard, of Bassenthwaite Halls, a surveyor.
Diaries, 1812–48.
Contents: a set of business diaries, referring to enclosure and tithe commutation surveys as well as to ordinary surveying work.
Cumberland & Westmorland Record Office: MSS. D/Lec/ATK.

BEAVER, George (1809–1895), surveyor.
Autobiography and diary, Dec., 1812–April, 1895.
Contents: development of the Hitchen area, local affairs, national events, surveying.
Hitchin Public Library.

DEANS, Rear Admiral Robert.
Diary, 1812. 1 vol.
Contents: journal kept when he was a Lieutenant in H.M.S. *Venerable* off the coast of Spain during the Peninsular War.
National Maritime Museum: JOD 43, 37. MS. 1735.

DICKENSON, [?——], of Manchester.
Diaries, 1812 and 1819.
Contents: journals of tours in England.
Lancashire Record Office: MSS. DDX/274.

ELLIS, Rev. Robert (1812–1875).
Diaries and papers of a Baptist minister.
National Library of Wales: MSS.

FARQUHAR, Arthur, Captain R.N.
Diary, May–Dec., 1812.
Contents: log book of H.M.S. *Desiree*, while cruising off the Dutch coast.
Private: Messrs. Davidson and Garden, Aberdeen, Scotland.
[Enquiries to The Secretary, National Register of Archives (Scotland).]

FOX, Miss Isabella, of South Shields and Durham.
Diary, 1812–35. 3 vols.
Contents: journeys and accounts of Westoe village, her home, and the district.
South Shields Public Library: Fox coll.

FRANKS, Mrs. Elizabeth (nee Firth) (1797–1837), wife of Rev. James Charles Franks, of Thornton, Yorkshire.
Diaries, 1812–25 and 1829. 16 vols.
Contents: a simple record of day-to-day happenings, social and church occasions; writer was a friend of the Bronte family and godmother to two of the sisters.
Sheffield University Library: MS. Q 091 (F).

GRIMSTON, Hon. Charlotte Mary (1778–1830), of Berkhamsted, Hertfordshire, England.
Diaries, 1812–23. 13 vols.

Contents: family, social, literary, moral, etc. Most entries brief but some extended.

Hertford County Record Office: MSS. Ref. AR 942.

HAMILTON, [? Sir Alexander].

Diary, 1812.

Contents: farming details.

Exeter City Record Office: MS.

HEATHCOTE, Gilbert John.

Diaries, 1812–13. 3 vols.

Lincolnshire Archives Office: Ancaster Deposit XV.

HEYWOOD, George (b. 1788?), of Manchester, grocer.

Diary and autobiography, July, 1812–June, 1840. 1 vol.

Contents: notes on his courtship, marriage, and family; domestic life in Manchester; business life; social life, amusements; a record of middle-class life.

Manchester, John Rylands Library: Eng. MS. 703.

HODGKINSON, Mary, of Atherton, Lancashire.

Diary, July–August, 1812. 1 vol.

Contents: account of a journey to Lilford, Northamptonshire: Buxton; French prisoners; goose farming.

Manchester Central Library: MS. L15/2/11.

HOOD, Lady Mary Frederica Elizabeth.

Diaries, 1812 and n.d. 2 vols.

Contents: journey to Seringpatam and Mysoor, and cruise from Trincomalee to Bombay with inland journeys in Ceylon and India; one undated journal of travels in France.

Scottish Record Office: GD 46/17/vol 39–40; GD 46/15/124.

LISTER, Samuel (1793–1813), soldier of Shibden Hall, Southowram, near Halifax, Yorkshire.

Diary, 1812–13. 1 vol.

Contents: personal and social matters.

Halifax Central Public Library: MS. SH:3:AB:22.

MANGIN, Edward.

Diaries, 1812 and 1819.

Contents: journals kept in Paris.

Oxford, Bodleian Library: MS. Eng. misc. e 608.

McGREGOR, Lieut. Alexander.

Diary, 1812. 1 vol.

Scottish Record Office: GD 50/110.

NATT, Rev. John (1779–1843), of Oxford.

Diary, June, 1812–April, 1828.

Contents: kept while he was lecturer at St. Giles's Church, Oxford; texts and sources of sermons; church life and services; details about evangelical

sentiments of times, with notes on notable churchmen; Oxford happenings; public events.
Private: Rev. Dr. Sherwin Bailey, 10 Glengyle Terr., Edinburgh.

ORD, William (1781–1885).
Diaries, 1812–25 (with gaps). 6 vols.
Contents: journals of tours; through Oxfordshire and Derbyshire, July, 1812; Wales and Lancashire, July, 1821; Scotland, Sept., 1812; France and Italy, Sept., 1814–April, 1815, and May, 1815–April, 1816, also May, 1816–Jan., 1817; France, Rhineland, and Switzerland, June–Aug., 1825.
Northumberland Record Office: NRO 324/A/10–15. (Blackett Ord of Whitfield MSS.).

PIGGOTT, Harriett (1775–1846), of Chetwynd, Salop.
Diaries and travel journals, 1812, 1823–44, 1843, and 1845.
Contents: 1812, mainly accounts with some personal notes; 1823–44, social life and tours through England, France and Scotland; 1843, a visit to Clifton and Bath; 1845, a visit to her family in Shropshire; social life, especially in London and Paris; travel notes.
Oxford, Bodleian Library: Piggott coll. e.1–2, f.3–4, g.1–21.

POPE, William, of Down St. Mary, Devon, a farmer.
Diaries, 1812–13. 2 vols.
Contents: very brief and irregular entries re farming matters and financial transactions; accounts of disbursements; entered in "The Exeter Pocket Journal".
Devon Record Office: MSS. 1791 M/F 3–4.

POWELL, Catherine (née Kingdon).
Diaries, Sept.–Nov., 1812, Feb–April, 1819, and 1839–43.
National Library of Wales: MSS. 13271–685/6–8.

PRIDEAUX, Henry, a soldier.
Diary–autobiography, 1812–15. 1 vol.
Contents: reminiscences about his life in Plymouth.
Plymouth Central Public Library: MSS. coll.

SPENCER-STANHOPE, Rev. Charles, Vicar of Cawthorne, Yorkshire and Weavertham, Cheshire.
Diaries, 1812 and 1820–74 (with gaps). 48 vols.
Contents: entries of a typical country-gentleman parson; appointments, daily activities.
Sheffield City Library: Spencer-Stanhope Papers, MSS. 60640.
A.M.M. Stirling, *Annals of a Yorkshire House*, 2 vols. (London, 1911).

WALKER, Caroline Wyvill, of Walterclough in Southowram, Near Halifax, Yorkshire.
Diaries, Feb., 1812–April, 1830 (with gaps). 15 vols.
Contents: comment by the diarist, a spinster lady, on her personal life,

preoccupied with search for possible husband with suitable social standing ; her family ; local society.

Halifax Central Public Library: MS. SH/AB/21.

Transactions of Halifax Antiquarian Soc., 1908.

WHITE, Rev. Joseph Blanco (1775–1841), of Liverpool.

Diaries, 1812–39 (with gaps).

Contents: theological studies at Oxford ; friendship with Arnold, Newman, Whately ; work in Church of England, and tutorial work ; the humanitarian movement ; journal of a tour to the Trossachs, Scotland.

Oxford, Manchester College Library: MS. coll.

Liverpool University Library: Blanco White Papers.

Life of Rev. Joseph Blanco White, ed. J. H. Thom, 3 vols. (London, 1845).

1813

ANON.

Diary, 1813, with one undated descriptive narration.

Contents: journal of a tour from Southampton to the Isle of Wight, with colour sketches. Descriptive narrative of tour from Coventry through Warwick, Stratford, Winchester, Southampton, etc.

Private: Godfrey Meynell, Meynell Langley, Derbyshire.

ANON., (W. M.).

Diary, c.1813–33 (with gaps). 1 vol.

Contents: journal of visits and tours made in England: Beeston Castle, Tarporley, Ashton Hayes (Cheshire), Lake District, and the Wye Valley.

Cheshire Record Office: MS. DDX 224.

ANON., a soldier.

Diary, May, 1813. 2 sheets.

Contents: journal of the march of Major-General George Anson's Brigade of Light Cavalry from Braganza.

Hertford County Record Office: MS. Ref. AR 962.

ANON., an official in Portsmouth Dockyard.

Diary, May–Dec., 1813. 4 sheets.

Contents: contains references to launching, docking, etc. of ships ; dockyard events, fire, accidents, pelf ; details of the workers ; some personal affairs and happenings in the town.

Portsmouth City Record Office: MS. Ref. 4A.

ANON.

Diary, 1813. 1 vol.

Contents: journal of a Continental tour.

Scottish Record Office: GD 153/92.

ANON.

Diary, 1813.

Contents: journal of tour from Glasgow to Lake District and north of England; notes on scenery and beauties.

National Library of Scotland: MS. 3382.

ANON.

Diary, 1813.

Contents: tour in Scotland and north of England; notes on scenery and beauties.

National Library of Scotland: MS. 2540.

ANON., (a curate of Ormskirk, Lancashire).

Diary, June, 1813–Dec., 1815.

Contents: death of his father at Thornton, Cheshire; proposal of marriage to Miss Maria Beezley; visits; reading; botanical observations; personal opinions.

Liverpool Record Office: Arch. MS. 920 MD Acc. 331A. (Purchased 1957).

ANON.

Diary, Jan–March, 1813.

Contents: written in Edinburgh, probably by a lady; domestic and religious notes; with Dickson family.

National Library of Scotland: MS. 1658.

ASHBROOK, Lady Emily Theophilia (née Metcalfe), wife of Henry Flower, Viscount Ashbrook.

Diaries and travel journals, c. 1813–80. 57 vols.

Lincolnshire Archives Office: Monson Papers 14/15.

BROUGHAM, Eleanor Syme (1750–1837), of Brougham Hall, Northumberland.

Diaries, Jan–March, 1813 and Jan–May, 1825. 2 vols.

Contents: weather, family affairs, short entries.

London, University College Library: Brougham Papers.

DICK, Elizabeth D. T.

Diary, 1813.

Scottish Record Office: GD 246/Box 45.

ELLIS, Sir Henry (1777–1869), antiquary and librarian.

Diary and memoranda, Aug., 1813–Jan., 1849.

Contents: early literary diary at Oxford; literary and antiquarian matters; business and administration while librarian of the British Museum.

London, British Museum: Add. MSS. 37037, 36653.

(1–19).

FINCH, Rev. Robert (1783–1830), of London.

Diaries, June, 1813–Jan., 1818, and 1829–30.

Contents: written in Portugal, London, Paris, Italy, and Greece; notes on architecture and engraving; classical interests; scholarly interests.

Oxford, Bodleian Library: Finch coll. MS. d. 19–21; e. 2–19; f. I.

HALE, William.

Diaries, 1813–20.

Contents: journals of tours, Isle of Wight and France.
Bristol Archives Office: MS. HB/J/2a, Arch. Acc. 15400.

HIBBERT, Sarah.
Diaries, 1813–39, 1843, and 1845–69. 23 vols.
Contents: family affairs only, mostly brief entries. Some diaries have press cuttings. Separate journals of tours to Wales and Liverpool Music Meeting (1823), York Music Meeting (1835), Paris (1843, 1845), Scotland (1850, 1855), and the Lake District (1853).
Gloucestershire Record Office: Dyrham Park MSS., D 1799.

HILL, Sir Rowland (1795–1879), of Birmingham and London, Secretary to the Postmaster General, 1854–64.
Diaries, 1813–23, 1846–55, and 1870–77. 11 vols.
Contents: early recollections of his life and schooldays; visits; work at his father's private school (Hazelwood); school events, abolition of corporal punishment; literary and scientific interests; later diaries concern his career in the Post Office, reforms made, intrigues of others; meetings with politicians of the day.
Haringey Borough Libraries, Bruce Castle Museum: MSS. 450 093/22324, 20004, 20619, 22325, 22321. (Some drafts of the above diaries plus diaries for 1839–43, 1846–50, 1851–55, 1861–65 are at Post Office Records, London, E.C.1.) (W.S.H. Ashmore, Controller of Libraries).
The Life of Sir Rowland Hill and the History of Penny Postage (London: De la Rue, 1880).
The Philatelic Journal of Great Britain 76,1 (March, 1966) –80,2 (June, 1970).

HOLTZAPFEL, Miss Charlotte (1800–1873), of London.
Diaries, 1813–16, 1817–20, and 1824–36. 12 vols.
Contents: records of a would-be fashionable daughter of a German merchant; affections and attachments for various beaux; secrets of a Regency coquette; domesticities of a Cockspur Street merchant.
Wigan Central Public Library: Edward Hall coll. M 895–902.

JONES, Capt. T. M. (Royal Marines), Cilgerran.
Diary, 1813.
National Library of Wales: MS. 1452.

KIRBY, John (c. 1800–1845), of Friar Lane, Leicester.
Diary, 1813–48. 1 vol.
Contents: family and local events, punctuated by biblical extracts and commentary thereon; continued by his daughters after his death.
Leicestershire Record Office: MS. DE619.

LOWTHER, William, Viscount later Earl of Lonsdale (1787–1872).
Diaries, 1813–1825 (with extensive gaps). 9 vols.
Contents: brief pocket diary comments on political, social, horsebreeding

and racing affairs; parliamentary elections; diary of travel, Edinburgh and Glasgow.

Cumberland & Westmorland Record Office: MSS. D/Lons/L.

MORGAN, Thomas, of The Hill, Abergavenny, Monmouthshire.
Diary, 1813–16.
Contents: journal of a Captain in the Royal Monmouth and Brecon Regiment of the Militia.
National Library of Wales: Baker-Gabb MS. 951.

MORRIS, George, a veterinary surgeon to the 25th. Light Dragoons.
Diary, Jan.–August, 1813. 1 vol.
Contents: journal of a voyage to India on the *Atlas*.
India Office Library: MSS. Eur. C. 166.

PARKE, T. James, later Baron Wensleydale (1782–1868).
Diary, 1813. 1 vol.
Contents: journal of a tour in North Wales, with B. Parke.
Northumberland Record Office: MS. ZRI 31/2/7 (Ridley of Blagdon MSS. NRO 138).

SPURRETT, Mrs. Eliza (née Stone).
Diaries, 1813, 1817–94 (with gaps).
Contents: notes written in pocket remembrancers and almanacks; travels and holidays, in England and Wales.
Leicester Museum: Dept. of Archives. (Acquired 1954).

STEWART, Mrs. T., of Bath, Somerset.
Diaries, July, 1813 and July, 1814.
Contents: travel notes, Durham to Bath, and Bath to Weymouth; local celebrations and events; Wellington's victories; places of interest.
Wigan Central Public Library: Edward Hall coll. (plus typescript).

TRAVERS, Captain T. O.
Diary, 1813–43.
Contents: journal of a captain in the Bengal Army.
Cambridge University Library: MSS. Add. 7395–7400.
(Copies)

TUCKER, Captain Thomas Edward, of 23rd. Regiment.
Diary, April, 1813–April, 1816.
Contents: brief details of movements of troops under Picton in Portugal during the Peninsular War.
Trans. Hist. Soc. West Wales X (1924), 86–114.

WILBRAHAM family, of Nantwich and Delamare House, Cheshire.
Diary, 1813 onwards. (Xerox copy)
Contents: brief family matters by George Wilbraham (1779–1852), George Fortescue Wilbraham (1815–85), and Roger William Wilbraham (1817–97).
Cheshire Record Office: DDX 210.

WOODBERRY, Lieut. George, a soldier of the 18th. Hussars.
Diary, Jan.–Sept., 1813.
Contents: journal with title "The Idle Companion of a Young Hussar during the Year 1813"; gives an account of service in the Peninsular campaign.
National Army Museum: MSS. 6807/267.

WRAXALL, Mr.
Diary, 1813.
Contents: tour in Scotland, notes on towns, topography, and scenery.
National Library of Scotland: MS. 3108.

1814

ANON.
Diary, 1814. 1 vol.
Contents: "Diary of a Summer at Rottingdean (near Brighton); a slight account of a summer holiday spent there by a young lady."
Brighton Public Library: MS. coll.

ANON.
Diary, 1814 and some brief engagement diaries, 1793, 1798, 1807, 1821, 1823–24, 1826.
Contents: journal of a journey to Yorkshire and Durham.
Kent Archives Office: MSS. U1127, F 14 (Smith Masters MSS.).

ANON.
Diary, 1814.
Contents: kept by a young woman of good family, a journal of travel in Germany, Switzerland, southern France; notes on scenery, architecture, inns, and persons.
Oxford, Bodleian Library: Eng. misc. d. 226.

ANDERSON, William (b. ca. 1765), a solicitor.
Diary, May–July, 1814. 1 vol.
Contents: narrative journal of a journey from Edinburgh to Dresden.
Edinburgh Central Public Library: MS. qYDA 1820 A55 (Edinburgh Room).
James Maclehose, *Scottish Historical Review* II (1914),, 376ff.

BAYARD, Maria (1789–1875), of New York.
Diary, Oct., 1814–May, 1815.
Contents: journal of a tour in England, Scotland, and France; a Grand Tour in England and Scotland, with usual notes on antiquities and sights.
New York Public Library: MSS.

BLACHFORD, B. P.
Diary, 1814.
Hampshire Record Office: 8M57/164.

COLFOX, Hannah (née Abbott) (1798–1893), of Bridport, Dorset.
Diary, March–June, 1814. 1 vol.
Contents: journal of a visit to London, 1814.
Dorset County Record Office: MS. D43/F15.

COTTESLOE, Sir T. F. Fremantle, 1st Baron (1798–1890), of Swanbourne House, Bucks.
Diaries, Sept., 1814–Jan., 1815 and 1837–86. 51 vols.
Contents: brief accounts of daily activities, including magistracy and County business.
Buckinghamshire Record Office: Fremantle coll. Box 93.

DRURY-LOWE, Mrs. Ann (née Steer) (d. 1849), of Locko Park, Spondon, Derbyshire.
Diaries, 1814, 1815, 1835, and undated.
Contents: brief entries by the wife of William Drury-Lowe.
University of Nottingham Library: Drury-Lowe coll., MSS. Dr F5–8.

ELLIOT, Lady.
Diary, 1814.
Contents: journal of tours to the Lakes and Ireland.
Private: G. J. Yorke Esq., Forthampton Court, Tewkesbury, Glos.

[?]HANSON, J. O.
Diary, March–June, 1814.
Contents: travel journal, from Smyrna to Greece and Venice; extensive notes on antiquities, towns, trade, prices, etc.
London, British Museum: Add. MSS. 38592.

HOLLAND, 4th. Lord.
Diary, 1814–56.
London, British Museum: Add. MSS. 52080–52102 (Holland House MSS.) (Acquired 1963).

KERSHAW, William, purser.
Diary, Aug., 1814–April, 1816.
Contents: voyage of the East India Company's ship, *Cuffnells* to India and China, and return to St. Helena; life on shipboard; notes on India and China; conversation with Napoleon at St. Helena.
Arthur Ponsonby, *More English Diaries* (London, 1927), pp. 183–189.

LIND, Francis M., a soldier.
Diaries, 1814 and 1854–76. 9 vols.
Contents: journal of a voyage to Bengal, 1814; later volumes include service in New Zealand and India, especially an account of the Indian Mutiny at Benares.
National Army Museum: MSS 5105/70 and 76.

LINDSAY, Lady Charlotte (d. of Lord North, 1732–1792), Lady of the Bedchamber to Charlotte, Princess of Wales.
Diary, Aug.–Dec., 1814. 1 vol.

Contents: journal of a tour to the Continent, written at Nice.
Oxford, Bodleian Library: Eng. misc. d. 226.

MACREADY, Edward Nevil, soldier of the 30th. Foot.
Diaries, 1814–30 (with gaps). 3 vols.
Contents: journals include accounts of the expedition to Holland, 1814, the Waterloo campaign, 1815, and some fighting in India 1819–20.
National Army Museum: MSS. 6807/209.

MANNOCK, Catherine Power.
Diary, 1814–19. 1 vol.
Contents: diary with some sketches.
Ipswich & East Suffolk Record Office: MS. S1/13/2.4.

MAXWELL, Marmaduke William Constable.
Diary, 1814.
Contents: journal of a tour of the Highlands.
East Riding of Yorkshire County Record Office: Coll. DDEV/61/2.

MILLS, Mrs. Catherine, wife of Rev. Francis Mills (d. 1852).
Diaries, 1814, 1828–34, and 1842–46. 9 vols.
Contents: the early volume is a journal of a visit to Ireland.
Stratford, The Shakespeare Birthplace Trust: DR 240/3/3–11.

PIERCE, Captain Nathaniel (1795–1823), of Newburyport, Mass.
Diary, Nov., 1814–July, 1815.
Contents: capture at sea by British and imprisonment in Dartmoor; notes on daily activities of the American prisoners; weather, food, treatment, *Essex Inst. Hist. Colls.* LXXIII (1937), 24–59.

SHIFFNER, Sir George (1762–1842), 1st. Bart., of Coombe House.
Diaries, 1814–26, 1784–37, and 1829. 14 vols.
Contents: journal of travels, 1814–26; notes on places visited, tabular statement of stages, inns, miles, posting and expenses; travel in 1829 to France, Switzerland, Germany, and Belgium; also earlier diaries with brief notes of engagements and activities.
East Sussex Record Office: Shiffner Arch., 818–830, 832.
Francis W. Steer, ed., *A Catalogue of the Shiffner Archives* (Lewes, 1959).

SHIFFNER, Henry (1789–1859), 2nd. Bart., a Vice-Admiral.
Diaries, 1814–15. 3 vols.
Contents: journal kept aboard H.M.S. *Leda*, includes account of a remarkable swarm of bees in the Bay of Bengal; cheapness of poultry and pigs there; coursing after hares; journal of journey to Paris via Dieppe and Rouen; sightseeing.
East Sussex Record Office: Shiffner Arch., 833–834, 3154.
Francis W. Steer, ed., *A Catalogue of the Shiffner Archives* (Lewes, 1959).

SOUTHCOMB, Sarah (née Hamilton) (c. 1789–1860).
Diaries, Jan., 1814–March, 1816. 2 vols.

Contents: innermost thoughts and feelings of a religious nature; family events; local events; one of the volumes gives an account of the illness, treatment and ultimate death of her brother who was accidentally shot when out shooting.
Private: Miss Viola L. Southcomb, Pennington, Lymington, Hants., SO4 8GX.

TISDALL, James Thomas Townley (1792–1850).
Diaries, Autumn, 1814, 1819–20, 1820 (with gaps). 4 vols.
Contents: journals of tours in France, Switzerland, Rhineland, Belgium, and Holland; topography and social notes.
Nottingham University Library: Marlay coll. MSS. My 1784–1787.

VAUGHAN, Anna Maria (née Maxse) (1783–1847), of Dorking, Surrey.
Diary, Sept.–Nov., 1814. 1 vol.
Contents: journal of travel in France and Switzerland.
West Sussex County Record Office: Maxse MS. 26.

WINN, Louisa (1799–1861).
Diary, 1814–36. 20 vols.
Contents: journal of a spinster.
Private: Rt. Hon. The Lord St. Oswald, Nostell Priory, Wakefield, Yorkshire.

1815

ANON.
Diary, 1815. 1 vol.
Contents: journal of a visit to Dresden, Germany.
Scottish Record Office: GD 1/395/16.

BACKHOUSE, J.
Diary, 1815–20.
Contents: journal of the journeys of a grocer.
Kendal Public Library, Westmorland: MSS.

BAILEY, Hinton Richard, of Pittleworth, Hampshire, farmer.
Diaries, 1815–67. 2 vols.
Contents: almost entirely a record of harvesting, weather, prices, cost of labour, and other farming details; diarist farmed at Little Somborne, Wallop, and Pittleworth.
Winchester Public Library: MS. SH15.4.

BINGHAM, Lieut-Col. Sir George Ridout, K.C.B.
Diary, Aug.–Oct., 1815. 1 vol.
Contents: journal of the passage to St. Helena escorting Napoleon; Napoleon's behaviour and conversation recorded.
Dorset County Record Office: MS. MR/43.
Holland Rose, *Life of Napoleon* (London: Bell, 1902).

BODDINGTON, Samuel (1766–1843), of London, a fishmonger and merchant.
Diary, Aug., 1815–March, 1843. 1 vol.
Contents: matters social, family, domestic, business, and his travels.
London, Guildhall Library: MS. 10,823/5C.

BOWEN, John (1785–1854), of Bridgwater, Somerset.
Diary, Oct., 1815–May, 1816. 1 vol.
Contents: journal of a journey while moving an iron bridge from Calcutta to Lucknow.
Somerset Record Office: MS. DD/CLE.

BROWN, John, a Methodist.
Diaries, 1815–19. 4 vols.
Contents: life and work of a young Methodist preacher.
London, Methodist Book Room: MSS.

BRUCE, Robert, advocate; later sheriff of Argyll.
Diary, July–Aug., 1815.
Contents: journal of a Continental tour with Sir Walter Scott and others; tourist's notes, with some literary interest.
National Library of Scotland: MS. 991.

CALDWELL, Margaret Emma (later wife of Sir Henry Holland).
Diary, Jan., 1815–July, 1817.
Contents: domestic matters; home at Linley, Staffs.; visits to London, Vauxhall, etc.; views on Waterloo, Napoleon, Sidney Smith, etc.
Private: Col. A. C. Barnes, D.S.O., O.B.E., Foxholme, Redhill Road, Cobham, Surrey.

COCKBURN, Sir George (1772–1853), admiral.
Diary, Aug.–Oct., 1815.
Contents: notes kept while he was taking Napoleon to St. Helena; conversations with Napoleon about his military and political life; Napoleon's social behaviour.
Buonaparte's Voyage to St. Helena (Boston, 1833); *Napoleon's Last Voyage* (London, 1888); *Napoleon Banished* (London: Miniature Books, 1955), pp. 23–44.

GAGE, John.
Diary, 1815. 1 vol.
Contents: journal of a visit to Holland and Belgium.
West Suffolk Record Office: MSS. Acc. 449/5/14.

GREENE, Edward, Lieutenant in Royal Artillery.
Diaries, 1815–16. 2 vols.
Contents: journal kept during his military service in Flanders; appears to have been in close touch with the Prussian army; he was not at Waterloo.

Berkshire Record Office: MSS. D/EE/F85, 1,2. (Miss A. Green, County Archivist).
The Families of Ewen of East Anglia and the Fenland (London, 1928).
GURNEY, Priscilla (1785–1821), of Earlham, Norfolk.
Diaries, Feb., 1815–March, 1820 (extracts).
Contents: Quaker religious life and travels; Norfolk, Ireland, France and England; meetings; travel notes and scenery; introspection and prayers.
London, Friends' Society Library: Box I.
HENNELL (later Mrs. Bray), Caroline (1805–1902), of Coventry, Warwick.
Diary and commonplace book, 1815–June, 1902.
Contents: wife of Charles Bray of *Coventry Herald*, the intimate friend of George Eliot; interesting for Eliot, Spencer, and their circle; jottings, cuttings, poems, anecdotes, and early autobiography.
Coventry City Library: MS. C and W.
HOBHOUSE, H. W. (1791–1868), in service of the H.E.I.C., later a country gentleman.
Diaries, Aug–Sept., 1815, Oct., 1816–Aug., 1817, and Dec., 1818–June, 1820. 6 vols.
Contents: journals of journeys to India, the near East, Greece, and several European countries; much topographical description.
Wiltshire Record Office: MSS. 112/4.
LEGGE, Lady Caroline, Lady-in-Waiting to the Duchess of Gloucester.
Diaries, 1815–20, 1827, 1828, 1836, and others undated. 16 vols.
Contents: mostly brief entries; five travel diaries: Germany and Italy.
Greater London Record Office (S.E.1): MSS. F/LEG, 868–883.
LEIGHTON-CATHCART-DALRYMPLE, Lieut.-Colonel, of the 15th. Hussars.
Diary, May-Sept., 1815. 1 vol.
Contents: journal of his service with the 15th. Hussars.
National Army Museum: MSS. 7207-22/20.
MAITLAND, Sir Frederick Lewis, Rear Admiral.
Diaries and logs, 1815–30.
Private: Adam Maitland, Armstown, Kirkendbright. [Enquiries to National Register of Archives (Scotland)].
MUSGRAVE, Rt. Rev. Thomas (1788–1860), Archbishop of York, 1847–60.
Diaries, June–July and Sept.–Oct., 1815. 2 vols.
Contents: an account of his Grand Tour of Europe; Brussels during Waterloo.
University of York, Borthwick Institute of Historical Research: MSS. MUS 1.
PALMER, Miss, of Norfolk.
Diaries, 1815–22.
Norwich Public Library: MSS.
Friends of National Libraries, 1951–52.

PRINGLE, Alexander.
Diaries, 1815 and 1818. 3 vols.
Contents: journal of a tour in France, Holland, and Switzerland in Autumn of 1815 ; later volume treats of tour in Italy and France.
Scottish Record Office: GD 246/25/4, and Box 47.

RAMSEY, Mrs. William (née Dryden), of Canons Ashby, Northants.
Diary, 1815. 1 vol.
Contents: brief entries in the Ladies Daily Companion.
Oxford, Bodleian Library: MS. Dep. a. 29.

SALTON, Gilbert.
Diary, 1815. 1 vol.
Contents: brief entries in the *Ladies Daily Companion.*
Scottish Record Office: GD 9/354.

SEYMOUR, Sir George Francis, sometime C-in-C of the Royal Navy.
Diaries, 1815–70.
Warwickshire Record Office: MSS. CR114A/373/381.

SHARPLES, Joseph, of Hitchin, Hertfordshire.
Diary, 1815–67.
Contents: Quaker life and work ; religious interest ; Hitchin.
Private: Mrs. Francis Ransom, Gosmore, Hitchin.

SLANEY, Robert Aglionby (1791–1862), of Walford Manor and Hatton Grange, both in Shropshire, barrister and M.P. for Shrewsbury.
Diaries (i) April, 1815–Dec., 1817, April, 1825–Jan., 1826, 1835, 1850, and undated (5 vols) ; (ii) 1818–49 (9 vols).
Contents: (i) journals of daily activities, 1815–26 ; travel in Holland, June–July, n.d. ; in Ireland, July–Sept., 1835 ; brief tour of the Lakes, Aug., 1850 ; (ii) entries of a social and political nature, reflecting his advocacy of rural and economic reform ; (iii) travel abroad, 1861–62.
(i) Birmingham University Library: MSS. 9/v/2. 1–5
(ii) Shrewsbury Public Libraries: Morris-Eyton coll. MSS. 1–9.
(iii) Salop County Record Office: MSS. coll.

SOMERSET, Edward, Lord, an officer of the Cavalry Brigade.
Diary, 1815–17. (Typed Transcript).
Contents: journal of the Napoleonic Wars ; includes Waterloo, where he commanded a brigade, and the occupation of Paris.
National Army Museum: MSS. 6807/344.

STARKE, Col. R. J., of Laugharne Castle, Carmarthenshire, landowner.
Diary, 1815. 1 vol.
Carmarthen County Record Office: MSS. Acc. 4326.

STEWART, J. A.
Diary, 1815. 1 vol.
Contents: journal of travels in Germany, Austria and Italy.
Scottish Record Office: GD 46/15/127.

C

WALCOTT, Capt. E. Y., officer in the Royal Artillery.
Diary, 1815. (Typescript).
Contents: journal relating to his experiences in the Waterloo campaign.
National Army Museum: MSS. 6705/45/4.
WALKER, Colonel.
Diary, 1815. 1 vol.
Contents: description of tour in southern provinces of Ceylon with reference to condition of roads, villages, and general topography.
Scottish Record Office: GD 46/20/1.
WINN, John (d. 1817, in Rome).
Diary, 1815–17.
Contents: journals of Continental travel.
Private: Rt. Hon. Earl St. Oswald, Nostell Priory, Wakefield, Yorkshire.
YEARDLEY, Mrs. Elizabeth (d. 1821), of Bentham.
Diary, Feb., 1815–July, 1821 (with gaps).
Contents: Quaker religious life and worship; perpetual concern for her husband; meetings; introspection and selfbelittlement; family affairs; prayers; "sinfulness"; business affairs; missionary's life.
London, Friends' Society Library: Box. R.

1816

ANON.
Diary, 1816. 1 vol.
Contents: journal of a tour in Europe.
Carmarthen County Record Office: Cawdor MSS. 1/244.
ANON., (A. C.—).
Diary, 1816. 1 vol.
Contents: journal of a tour on the Scottish Border country.
Edinburgh University Library: MS. La.II.378.
ANON.
Diary, 1816. 1 vol.
Contents: journal of a Continental tour.
Scottish Record Office: GD 152/92.
ANON.
Diary, 1816.
Contents: journal of a tour through the Netherlands, Holland, and parts of France.
Lincolnshire Archives Office: Monson Papers 7/20.
ANON.
Diary, 1816.
Contents: journal of a tour from Brighton to Weymouth; coloured maps; scenery.
London, British Museum: Add. MS. 31337.

ANON.
  Diary, 1816.
  Contents: three journals of a journey to Wales.
  Private: Betts-Doughty MSS. (Present location unknown).
ARATOON, Carapiet Chater (d. 1857).
  Diaries, July–Oct., 1816 and Feb.–April, undated (extracts).
  Contents: journal of a Baptist missionary in Surat, India.
  London, Baptist Missionary Society: MS IN/1.
ATTWOOD, Samuel, of Basingstoke, a tailor.
  Diaries, 1816–70.
  Hampshire Record Office: MSS. 8M62/27.
BEAMONT, William (1797–1889), of Warrington, Lancashire, solicitor.
  Diaries, April, 1816–Nov., 1886 (with gaps) 14 vols; and travel journals,
  1825–42 (with gaps) 7 vols.
  Contents: historical and antiquarian interests; local topography; effects
  of industrialism; local institutions and municipal affairs; public affairs;
  his business; tour to Scotland, Ireland, Harrogate, Lake District and
  France.
  Warrington Municipal Library: 284–287, 293–294, 296–300, 701–703.
BELL, J. T. of Lincoln, town clerk.
  Diary, 1816–18.
  Lincolnshire Archives Office.
BROUGHAM, William, 2nd. Baron (1795–1886), of Petersham, politician.
  Diaries, 1816–17, 1827, 1835–40, 1844–77. 26 vols.
  Contents: a student's journal, Nov., 1816; journals of travel in Italy &
  Sicily, Aug–Sept., 1827, in Germany, Aug–Oct., 1835, and in Germany
  & Switzerland, July–Sept., 1837; remainder are family diaries, notes on
  weather, occasional political references, etc.
  London, University College Library: Brougham Papers.
BROWNLOW, Canon John, of Harvington, Worcestershire.
  Diary and memoranda, c. 1816–83 (Typescript).
  Contents: apparently part recollection and part diary kept from day
  to day.
  Warwickshire County Record Office: Throckmorton MSS., Folder 41.
BULTEEL, Miss (later Mrs. A. G. Stapleton), of Flete, Near Yealampton,
  Devon.
  Diaries, 1816–55.
  Plymouth Public Library: MSS. Acc. 381.
COWBURN, William and Catherine Rebecca (née Smith), his wife.
  Diaries, 1816 and 1827. 2 vols.
  Kent Archives Office: MSS. Smith-Masters U 1127 F 10,11. (Deposited
  1965)
DASHWOOD-KING, Sir John, 4th. Bart. (c. 1766–1848), of West Wycombe
  Park, Buckinghamshire.

Diaries and Memo-books, 1816–27 and 1820.

Contents: personal and estate matters; appointments, etc; 1820 volume has brief daily memoranda.

Oxford, Bodleian Library: MSS. D.D. Dashwood F.4. (Acquired 1950).

Buckinghamshire Record Office: Dashwood coll., D/D/18/13.

DOUGLAS, W.

Diary, 1816–17. 1 vol.

Contents: journal of travel, entitled "Through Europe in the Wake of Napoleon".

Edinburgh University Library: MS. Dc.5.113.

ELPHINSTONE, Captain Thomas R.N. (?1774–?1820).

Diary and autobiography, 1816.

Contents: diarist titles it: "places that I have passed my Christmas Days since the year 1774".

Devon Record Office: Langley Papers, ZI.

GOULBURN, Henry (1784–1856).

Diaries, 1816–49 (1823 missing). 33 vols.

Personal account books, in diary form, 1850–51, 1854, and 1856. 4 vols.

Contents: the diaries proper deal with personal and domestic accounts; notes on family matters.

Surrey Record Office: Goulburn MSS. Acc. 319. LL/L, Acc. 426/16/1.

HARPER, Captain John, R.N.

Diary, 1816–18.

Contents. private reflections of the commanding officer of H.M.S. *Wye*.

London: Public Record Office: MS. 30/26/122. (Presented 1952).

MACLEOD, John (d. 1823), sometime A.D.C. to the Governor of Bombay.

Diaries, 1816–21. 5 vols.

Contents: journal of his route to survey passes of Western & Northern Ghauts during Pindaree Incursions; April–June, 1817, from Mazaon to Panwell and to Poona: observations on locals, skirmishes; journal kept during Maharatta War, pursuits and seiges; tour in the Dekhan, 1818, shooting tigers, people met, pagodas described; hog hunting etc. in another tour of Dekhan Nov., 1820–Jan., late 1821 in Poona, Doulatabad, Dhoolia, etc.

India Office Library: MSS. Eur. B.7.

McMILLAN, Rev. Samuel.

Diary, Dec., 1816–Oct., 1863 (with gaps). 1 vol.

Contents: mainly a diary of his activities in Aberdeen where he was a minister.

University of Glasgow: MS. Gen. 1264.

MITFORD, Charles (1785–1831), of Tillington, Sussex.

Diary, 1816. 1 vol.

Contents: journal of travel in France, Belgium, Germany, Switzerland.

West Sussex County Record Office: Mitford MS. 33.

MOUNT, William.

Diary, 1816–17. 1 vol.

Contents: an account of his journey to the Continent.

Berkshire Record Office: MS. D/EMt F13.

SOAME, Mrs., of Thurlow, Suffolk.

Diary, Jan–Dec., 1816.

Contents: card-playing; home life and social; a visit to Beverley, York-shire, entered in Gedge's Own Memorandum Book.

Bury St. Edmunds Public Library: Muniment Room.

WILLIAMS, Mrs. Hannah, wife of Peter Bayly Williams, of Llanrug, Caernarvonshire.

Diary, 1816–17.

Contents: domestic; with an account of a journey from Llanrug to Cardiganshire and Carmarthenshire.

National Library of Wales: MS. 856A (Ty Coch MS. 42).

1817

ANON., an army officer.

Diary, 1817–18. 1 vol.

Contents: journal kept by an army officer in the Dekkan.

India Office Library: MSS. Eur. D. 465.

ANON., a soldier.

Diaries, c.1817, 1824, 1825. 6 vols.

Contents: journal intermittently kept while serving in India and Burma during the First Burma War (1824–25).

National Army Museum: MSS. 6807/337.

ANON., (an inhabitant of Shalborne).

Diaries, 1817–33. 4 vols.

Contents: personal interests; gardening at Shalborne; some weather notes; recipes; schooling fees received, etc.

Private: Vol. I with E. G. H. Kempson, Marlborough College, Wiltshire; Vols. II–IV with George Smith, Esq., The Old House, Great Bedwyn, Near Marlborough, Wiltshire.

ANON.

Diary, 1817–19. 1 vol.

Contents: journal kept in Byrom's system of shorthand.

London University Library: Carlton MSS. 20/9.

ABBOT, Philip.

Diaries, 1817 and 1821.

Contents: journals of various travels and visits in England, Scotland and France.

London, Public Record Office: MSS. 30/9 12/9 (Colchester Papers).

BROWNCKER, Elizabeth Maria.
Diaries, July, 1817–May, 1818, Sept., 1819, and one undated.
Contents: journal of a tour in France; a tour in Wiltshire; a holiday in the Isle of Wight; in Cheltenham.
Oxford, St. Hilda's College Library: MSS.

BUCHANAN, Harriett Flora Macdonald.
Diary, 1817. 1 vol.
Scottish Record Office: GD 47/1279.

BURGOYNE, Sir John Montagu (1796–1858), 9th. Bart., of Sutton Park, Bedfordshire.
Diaries, Feb., 1817, Aug., 1819, Oct., 1822, July, 1824–July, 1831, Aug., 1831–Dec., 1839; also a fair copy of a journal, Aug., 1819–April, 1820.
Contents: journals of two European tours, 1819, 1822; military diary kept in Ireland with the Grenadier Guards in which the diarist was a Colonel; some family references; royalty and current affairs; a stay at Brighton.
Bedfordshire Record Office: MSS. X 143/16–19.

COKE, D'Ewes, of Brookhill, Pinxton, Derbyshire.
Diaries, 1817 and 1839.
Contents: private matters.
Derby Central Library: Brookhill MSS.

COWAN, Charles (1801–1889), of Penicuik and Murrayfield, a member of papermaking family and M.P. for Edinburgh, 1847.
Diaries, May–July, 1817, and Jan., 1842–Dec., 1846. 2 vols.
Contents: early journal of travels to and residence in Geneva; later volume gives details of life in Edinburgh, with particular reference to papermaking.
Edinburgh Central Public Library: Edinburgh Room, MSS. YDA 1820 C87.

DE BRUYN, J. C. (d. 1817).
Diary, July–Sept., 1817.
Contents: journal of a Baptist missionary at Chittagong describing his work among the Moghs; diarist was stabbed by a boy he had taken into his family.
London, Baptist Mission Society: MS. IN/2.

DE COETLOGON, Charles Frederick, son of Charles Edward de Coetlogon, a writer and divine, of Ashford, Middlesex and Grosvenor Place, S.W.1.
Diaries, 1817–18, 1822–23, 1826–28, 1831–32, 1835. 11 vols.
Contents: his health; weather; domestic matters; philosophy.
Greater London Record Office (Middlesex Records): MSS. Acc. 268/1–11.

ELERS, Captain George. (et al.).
Diaries, 1817–39.
Contents: some definitely by him, others by diarists with an Elers-Speidell connection.
Lincolnshire Archives Office: Monson coll. 14F.

HALL, Capt. Basil, an army officer.
Diary, August, 1817. 13pp.
Contents: notes of an interview with Bonaparte at St. Helena.
National Army Museum: MSS. 6807/391.
HAMMOND, Lord Edmund.
Diaries, 1817, 1826, 1829–31.
Contents: journals of travel in Europe; Switzerland, 1817 and 1826;
Brussels, Aix, Frankfurt, Leipsic, Vienna, 1829–31.
Private: Col. A. C. Barnes D.S.O., O.B.E., Foxholme, Redhill Road,
Cobham, Surrey.
HATHERTON, E. J. Littleton, 1st. Baron (1791–1863), politician.
Diaries, 1817–62. 93 vols.
Contents: mostly brief entries; political matters, etc.
Staffordshire Record Office: MSS. D260/M/F/3/26/1–93.
HIGGINSON, James (1760–1835), of Barrow, Cheshire, farmer.
Diary, Oct., 1817–Jan., 1819. 1 vol.
Contents: daily accounts of work on farm and personal activities.
Cheshire Record Office: MS. DDX 106.
HILL, Matthew Davenport (1792–1872), prison reformer.
Diary, March, 1817–March, 1818.
Contents: literary reading and studies; journalistic work; social and
private life; visits to London (meetings with other reformers, Romilly,
Howard, etc.).
Oxford, Bodleian Library: MS. Eng. Misc. e.88.
HUNTINGFORD, Henry (c. 1786–1867), of Winchester, Hampshire.
Diaries, April–Nov., 1817. 8 vols.
Contents: journals of a tour on the Continent: Holland, Germany, France,
Italy, and Switzerland; detailed remarks on daily events.
Oxford, Bodleian Library: MSS. Eng. misc. e.540–7.
JERSEY, Sarah Sophia, 5th. Countess (1785–1867).
Diary, 1817. 1 vol.
Contents: journal of a trip to Italy, when she met Byron; notes on
Italians and their customs.
Greater London Record Office (Middlesex Records): Jersey Papers.
JOHNSTON, Mrs. Jane.
Diaries, 1817 and 1819–40. 23 vols.
Contents: social engagements, family and other day-to-day trivia.
Hertford County Record Office: MSS. Ref. 16195–16217.
KENNAWAY family, of Exeter, Devon.
Diaries, 1817–75 (with gaps).
Contents: slight; only occasional entries.
Exeter City Record Office: MSS. 58/9, Box 30.
KER PORTER, Sir Robert.
Diary and notebooks, 1817–20.

Contents: journals of travels in Russia, the Caucasus, Persia, and Mesopotamia.

London, British Museum: Add. MSS. 53791–53799. (Purchased 1966).

KERR, William, 6th. Marquess of Lothian (1763–1824), Lord Lieutenant of Midlothian and Roxburghshire.

Diary, 1817–20. 1 vol.

Contents: a timetable of a Continental tour; some anecdotes, poems and jottings.

Edinburgh Central Public Library: Scottish Dept., MS. XDA 816 L88.

LISTER, Ann, of Shibden Hall, near Halifax, Yorkshire, spinster.

Diaries, March, 1817–Aug., 1840. 24 vols.

Contents: detailed entries about local life, social and economic conditions at time of industrial change and development, local politics; accounts of her travels in France, Germany, Spain, Scandinavia and Russia; descriptions of the places visited and observations on societies.

Halifax Central Public Library: MSS. SH/ML. (Frederick U. Batchelor, Archivist).

Trans. of Halifax Antiquarian Society, 1950 and 1970.

MATTHEWS, John, of Orston, Nottinghamshire.

Diaries, 1817–31.

Private: Canon Bartlett MSS. (Present location unknown).

MITFORD, John (d. 1859), poet.

Diary, 1817–21.

Contents: journal of tours in Europe.

Cambridge University Library: Add. MS. 7495–7497.

PEASE, John (1798–1868), of Darlington, industrialist and a Minister of the Society of Friends.

Diaries, 1817–45. 11 vols.

Travel diaries, 1833–34, 1843–45. 3 bundles of loose sheets.

Contents: diaries of a personal kind; religious journeys made in Ireland, 1833–34, and in America, 1843–45.

Durham County Record Office: MSS. D/Ho/F 96–106, 114, 116.

PENNANT, David (d. 1841), artist.

Diary, April, 1817–April, 1819.

Contents: journal of tours mainly of exhibitions, museums, and mineralogical collections in England.

Yale University Library: Connecticut MS.

RAYMOND, Rev. Gregory (d. 1863), Rector of Symondsbury, Dorset.

Diaries, 1817–32, 1837, 1840–43. 41 vols.

Contents: brief accounts of social and sporting activities.

Dorset County Record Office: MSS. KW513.

RENNIE, George (1791–1866), brother of Sir John Rennie, and a civil engineer.

Diary, June–Dec., 1817. 1 vol.

Contents: journal of a visit to Portugal, Spain, southern France; notes on buildings and monuments; sketches and accounts.
Oxford, Bodleian Library: MS. Eng. Misc. e.203. (Purchased 1933).
ROBSON, William (1797–1881), of Darlington, mercer.
Diary, Jan., 1817–81.
Contents: his work as shopkeeper; Quaker religious life and observances and customs; family and social life; his reading (general) and criticisms.
London, Friends' Society Library. (Typed copy)
Journal Friends' Hist. Society XIX (1922).
ROSCOE, Margaret.
Diaries, 1817–19 and 1822–24.
Liverpool Record Office: Archives 920 ROS 5827 Acc. 06.
SCROPE family, of Danby, Yorkshire.
Diary, June–July, 1817.
Contents: journal of a tour to North Wales.
North Riding of Yorkshire County Record Office: MS. Z PT V 2.
SMITH, Colonel.
Diary, 2-24 July, 1817. 1 vol.
Contents: journal of a journey to Edinburgh; engravings; cuttings from contemporary newspapers and magazines; original drawings; "notices of what we saw upon this journey to serve as a rough guide to our friends who may hereafter visit the Scotch capital".
Edinburgh Central Public Library: Edinburgh Room, MS. YDA 1862.817.
SMITH, Richard (1784–1824), of Manchester.
Diary, Jan., 1817–July, 1824. 7 vols.
Contents: daily occupations and work as cotton spinner; journeys to Philadelphia; residence at Leek (Staffs.) and Quaker religious life there; voyage to Gambia, trading, residence Bathurst and Berkou; travels and Quaker ministry; notes on American life; visits to Indians and Negro settlements.
London, Friends' Society Library: Cupboard 5.
Journal Friends' Hist. Society, XIII (1916) and XIV (1817).
THARP, John (1769–1851), of Chippenham Park, Cambridgeshire, a Captain in the Horse Guards Blues.
Diary, May–July, 1817. 33 pp.
Contents: journey with wife and family to Paris and Baden.
Cambridgeshire Record Office: MS. R55/7/21/1.
TYLER, C. H.
Diary, 1817–24. 1 vol.
Kent Archives Office: Roper of Linstead MS. U 498/F7.
WEST, Katherine.
Diary, 1817.
Contents: journal of travels.
London, British Museum: Add. MS. 52498.

c*

WILKINSON, John Walter, Assistant Commissary-General of Stores to the Army, and Spanish Vice-Consul at Portchester.
Diary, 1817–40. 1 vol.
Essex Record Office: MS. D/DJG Z23.
WILLIAMS-WYNN, Frances ("Fanny") (1773–1857), daughter of 4th Baronet, of Wynnstay, Rhuabon, Denbighshire.
Diaries, 1817 and 1833–40.
Contents: first is a journal of a tour in France, Switzerland, Germany, and Belgium ; later ones are of tours in France, Belgium, Holland, Germany, Denmark, Switzerland and Italy ; including some original sketches and some engravings.
National Library of Wales: MSS. 2779–2783.
Abraham Hayward, *Diaries of a Lady of Quality: 1797–1844* (London, 1864).

1818

ANON., (of London).
Diary and commonplace book. July, 1818–Dec., 1824.
Contents: sporting events ; theatre, court, political gossip, polling in provinces, and civic life, mainly in city of London.
London: Guildhall Library: MS. 3730.
ANON.
Diary, 1818.
Contents: journal of tour from Ireland to Scotland: Dublin, Belfast, Glasgow, Perth, Edinburgh, Manchester, Shrewsbury, Holyhead ; notes on towns, scenery, etc.
National Library of Scotland: MS. 2795.
ANON.
Diary, 1818. 1 vol.
Contents: journal of foreign travel: France, Germany, and Italy.
East Sussex County Record Office: Ashburnham arch. MS. 3995.
Francis W. Steer, ed., *The Ashburnham Archives* (Lewes, 1958).
ANON., (Edinburgh citizen).
Diary, May, 1818–Dec., 1839 (gaps). 1 vol.
Contents: recording his visit to London and return to Manchester in 1818, and later notes of preachers and sermons.
National Library of Scotland: MS. 166.
ANDERSON, John.
Diary, 1818.
Contents: journal of tour in the Highlands ; notes on scenery and beauties.
National Library of Scotland: MS. 2509.
ARROWSMITH, Mrs. Louisa (née Lee), of Totteridge Park, Totteridge, Herts.

Diaries, 1818–20, 1822–32, and 1836–37. 17 vols.
Contents: country and town life, gardens, contemporary national events, journeys, etc.; brief entries, but lively.
Hertford County Record Office: MSS. Ref. 70150–70168.
BANKS, John Cleaver, of London.
Diary, Jan–Sept., 1818.
Contents: scrappy record of share dealings, social contacts, and tour of Italy.
Wigan Central Public Library: Edward Hall coll.
BARNES, Thomas.
Diary, Aug–Dec., 1818. 1 vol.
Contents: journal of a journey to the interior of the island of Sumatra; topographical details, information on people, difficulties encountered.
India Office Library: MSS. Eur. D. 199.
BERNARD, Charles, of Frampton-on-Severn, Gloucestershire.
Diary, 1818–19.
Contents: detailed journal of country life; weather; church attendance; sermons; visits to other towns and cities; local families; notes on reading (mainly historical).
Private: V. E. Scott Esq., Kyneton House, Thornbury, Glos.
BLUNDELL, William.
Diaries, March, 1818, Jan., 1834–June, 1854 (with gaps).
Contents: journal of tour (1818), from Acton Burnell, Salop, to France, Germany, and the Netherlands.
Lancashire Record Office: Blundell MSS.
CARTER, Maria (second daughter of Joshua Carter), of Allington, Dorset.
Diaries, 1818–34. 18 vols.
Contents: personal matters; visits made and paid; books read; births, deaths, marriages, illnesses in her family; occasional glimpses of royalty; political comment.
Dorset County Record Office: MS. D.43.
M. B. Weinstock, "Portrait of a Bridport Lady", *Dorset Year Book*. 1960–61.
CLARKE, John, of Coventry, silkman.
Diary, June, 1818. 1 vol.
Contents: brief journal of the mayor of Coventry at the time of the Coventry election of June, 1818, when there were riots.
Coventry Corporation Archives: MS. A. 158.
COLFOX, Harriett (1783–1851), of Bridport, Dorset.
Diary, Dec., 1818–May, 1819. 1 vol.
Contents: journal of a visit to London.
Dorset County Record Office: MS. D 43/F 11.
DARROCH, Duncan, of Gouroch, Renfrewshire.
Diary, 1818–24.

Contents: personal matters; memoranda; accounts, etc; interests of the son of Maj-Gen. Duncan Darroch.
Scottish Record Office: MSS. coll. (Acquired 1952).

De la BECHE, Sir H. T. (b. 1796), of London, geologist.
Diaries, 1818–20, and 1829.
Contents: early tours in England and Wales, France, Switzerland, and Italy, with personal observations, as well as geological notes.
Cardiff, National Museum of Wales. MS. in Dept. of Geology.

DICKINSON, Anne (1789–1870), wife of the founder of the papermaking and stationery business.
Diaries, 1818–29 and 1841–48. 13 vols.
Contents: matters of local interest in Hertfordshire; visits to towns in the area, etc.
London, Bedford College Library, University of London: MSS. (Presented 1955).

ELGEE, John, a soldier of the 34th. Regiment.
Diaries, Sept., 1818–Dec., 1822. 2 vols.
Contents: journals kept in India while serving with the 34th. Foot from the moment of landing at Madras.
National Army Museum: MSS. 7108–6/1–2.

EVANS, Robert (1773–1849), of Griff, Nuneaton, Warwickshire.
Diaries, April, 1818–Jan., 1843 (with gaps).
Contents: his work as an estate agent; private affairs; diarist is the father of George Eliot, novelist.
Private: Charles H. Evans, Esq., Librarian, Charterhouse, Godalming, Surrey.

HENNIKER, Hon. John, (later 4th Baron Henniker).
Diary, Oct., 1818–Aug., 1819. 1 vol.
Contents: journal of a tour in Italy in a calèche; written at Messina, 10 Aug., 1819.
Ipswich Public Library: MS. S1/2/501.1.

HICKS, P. Thomas.
Diary, June–Aug., 1818.
Contents: journal of journey through North Wales and Ireland; from Kidderminster to Holyhead, Dublin, Kilkenny, Fermoy, Mallow, Killarney.
Dublin, Trinity College Library.

JACKSON, Rev. Jeremiah, of Wisbech, Cambridgeshire.
Diary, 1818–57. 65 notebooks.
Contents: clerical affairs; local events; work at Wisbech G.S. where the diarist taught; Fens drainage; agricultural riots.
Wisbech Museum, Cambridgeshire: MSS.

MASTER, Rev. Robert Mosley.
Diary, 1818–19.

Contents: journal of a tour in Egypt, Palestine, and Greece; transcript, with original sketches.

London, British Museum: Add. MS. 51313 (Moffit coll.).

PEACOCK, Thomas Love (1785–1866), novelist.

Diary, July–Sept., 1818.

Contents: journal kept at Marlow; reading and critical thoughts; social, literary affairs; modern classics; correspondence with Shelley.

London, British Museum: Add. MS. 36815.

PERRY, John (1781–1844), of Ipswich.

Diary, May, 1818–Dec., 1842.

Contents: Quaker life and ministry; business affairs and misfortunes; shopkeeping; bankruptcies, general social and political life in Suffolk; travels on business and religion.

London, Friends' Society Library: Box. T.

SABINE, Sir Edward (1788–1883), soldier and scientist, President of the Royal Society.

Diary, April–Oct., 1818. 1 vol.

Contents: kept while acting as astronomer to the Arctic expedition in search of the North-West Passage commanded by (Sir) John Ross in the ship *Isabella.*

Plymouth Public Library: Dept. of Archives & Local History, 920 SAB.

SMITH, Mrs. of Knutsford, Cheshire.

Diaries, 1818–21. 14 vols.

Warrington Municipal Library: MSS.

THOMAS, David (1756–1840), of Llwynywermwd, Llanycrwys, Cardiganshire.

Diary and account book, 1818–36.

Contents: journal of a farmer; farming activities; receipts and payments etc. (some entries in Welsh).

National Library of Wales: MS. 4560D.

THROCKMORTON, Frances ("Fanny") (d. 1825).

Diary, Aug., 1818–Feb., 1825.

Contents: mostly brief entries up to a month before her death in Paris.

Warwickshire Record Office: Throckmorton MSS., Drawer 7.

VERLING, Dr. James (d. 1858), military surgeon.

Diary, July, 1818–Sept., 1819.

Contents: journal kept at St. Helena, while in attendance upon Napoleon and household; gossip and complaints of the French household; military and literary conversations with the Bertrands and Montholon; hears reports of Napoleon's health and habits, but prevented from actually attending upon him; narrative of the entourage.

Paris, Archives Nationales: MS.

Oxford, Bodleian Library: Curzon coll. 1 (copy made by A. E. Ross in 1911).

WILKINSON, George Hutton, of Harperley Park, Witton-le-Wear, Co. Durham.

Diaries, 1818–56 (with gaps). 36 vols.

Contents: include cash accounts, and separate journals of an Italian tour (1818–19) and European tours (1846, 1851).

Durham County Record Office: MSS. D/X 99/2–35. (Dr. W. A. L. Seaman, County Archvist).

[?] WILLIAMSON, Samuel (1792–1840), landscape painter.

Diary, April, 1818–Oct., 1820. 1 vol.

Contents: journal of travel notes of an artist in Italy, Greece, and Turkey ; guidebook detail ; contacts with Kinnaird ; some adventures ; accompanied by Rev. Henry V. Elliott and Edward B. Elliott.

Wigan Central Public Library: Edward Hall coll.

1819

ANON.

Diary, c. 1819.

Contents: dates of deaths etc. ; copies of the will of Martha Williams Hamilton ; several entries relating to families named Baker and Burke.

Oxford, Rhodes House Library: MS. West Indies S. 24. (Presented 1964).

ANON., (of London).

Diary, July–Aug., 1819. 1 vol.

Contents: journal of pleasure and business trip to Dublin and back ; acute observation and dry humour.

Wigan Central Public Library: Edward Hall coll.

ANON.

Diary, Jan., 1819–Jan., 1820. 1 vol.

Contents: journal of an unknown young woman from the Manchester area.

Manchester Public Libraries: Arch. Dept., MS. MISC/339.

ASPLIN, Jonas, of Wakering and Raleigh, Essex, physician.

Diaries, 1819–28.

Contents: mostly personal matters.

Montreal, McGill University Library: Osler coll.

Colchester Borough Library: local coll.

BONTINE, Robert Cunninghame.

Diaries, 1819.

Contents: journals recording travels on the Continent.

Scottish Record Office: GD 22/Section 1/568.

CATHCART, Lady Mary.

Diary, Oct–Nov., 1819. 1 vol.

Contents: journal of her travels on the Continent.

Private: Lord Cathcart, 14 Eaton Mews, London, S.W.1.

EYTON, T.
Diary, Sept–Oct., 1819. 1 vol.
Contents: journal of a Continental tour: Switzerland, Rhineland, Belgium ; drawings ; scenery ; buildings ; beauties.
Oxford, Bodleian Library: Add. MS. B94.

FOX, John.
Diary, 1819–43.
Contents: journals of walking tours in England ; Devonshire ; sightseeing ; comments on people and his own affairs ; inns and innkeepers.
Private: Sir John Fox (in 1927). (Present location unknown).
Arthur Ponsonby, *More English Diaries* (London, 1927), pp. 17–19.

GROVE, William Chafyn (1786–1865), of Zeals House, Wilts., country gentleman.
Diaries, 1819, June, 1823–Oct., 1839, Jan., 1864–Nov., 1865 (with gaps). 15 vols.
Contents: fairly brief details of daily life ; many deal with time spent abroad, mostly in Western Europe, but also Egypt (1864) and Australia and India (1854–55).
Wiltshire Record Office: MSS. 865.

JONES, Captain Jenkin, R.N.
Diaries, May–June, 1819 and 1836.
Contents: journals of tours in England and Wales ; notes relating to his social and literary interests.
National Library of Wales: MS. 785A.
Trans. Hist. Soc. West Wales, I (1911), 97–114.

MADDEN, Sir Frederick (1801–1873), palaeographer and assistant keeper of Manuscripts in the British Museum, 1828–37, head of that Dept., 1837–66.
Diaries, 1819–72. 43 vols.
Contents: giving an exact account of his work and reading day by day, and of his private occupations ; containing also many notes on palaeographical and antiquarian questions ; comments upon the scholarly and literary worlds of his day.
Oxford, Bodleian Library: MSS. Eng. hist. c. 140–182.

MITFORD, Mary Russell (1787–1866), author, of Reading and Three Mile Cross, Berkshire.
Diary, Jan., 1819–March, 1823. 1 vol.
Contents: private journal of home life with her parents ; visits, her reading ; some references to her early works, *Foscari, Julian,* and *Our Village.*
London, British Museum: Add. MSS.
Reading Public Library: B/TU/MIT is photostat copy.
Vera Watson, *Mary Russell Mitford* (London, 1951).

NORTHCOTE, Mrs. (wife of Sir Stafford Northcote).
Diary, 1819–23.

Devon Record Office: Northcote–Iddesleigh MS. 3807/C20/1. (Typescript)

O'DONOVAN, Richard (c. 1780–c. 1830), of 6th. Dragoons, major-general. Diaries, 1819–23. 2 vols.
Contents: brief entries of farming in South Wales and estates in Ireland; visits to London, Bath, and Bristol; annual lists of stock given.
Bath Municipal Libraries: MSS. 1253–1254.

OLIPHANT, James, Ensign in the Madras Engineers. Diary, c. 1819. 1 vol.
Contents: journal of seige of Nowah.
Oxford, Bodleian Library: MS. Eng. misc. c. 326. (Russell of Swallowfield Papers).

ROLLS, John (1776–1837), gentleman of leisure residing in various places. Diaries, May–Dec., 1819, Jan–July, 1820, Sept., 1820–Sept., 1821, Jan.–Aug., 1822. 4 vols.
Contents: general account of travel arrangements, people met, letters written, tasks performed.
Monmouthshire Record Office: Rolls MSS. D361. F/P3.

ROUND, C. G., of Birch Hall, Essex. Diaries, 1819–67 (with gaps). 13 vols.
Essex Record Office: MSS. D/DR F60–72.

ROUND, John, of Danbury Park, Essex. Diaries, 1819–49. 30 vols.
Essex Record Office: MSS. D/DRh F25/1–30.

SANDERS, Benjamin, of Bullington, Hants. Diary, June–July, 1819. 1 vol.
Hampshire Record Office: MSS. 133.M71 F1.

SEEBOHM, Benjamin, of Bradford, Yorkshire, a wool merchant and Quaker minister. Diary, May 1819–June, 1821. 1 vol.
Contents: Quaker meetings; journey through France, Belgium, and Holland to Germany; much interesting detail; pen sketches.
Hertford County Record Office: MS D/E Se F37.

SHORE, Hon. Frederick John (1799–1837), Bengal Civil Service. Diaries, Jan., 1819–March, 1837. 3 vols.
Contents: include his experiences as joint magistrate of Dehra Dun (1822–25), as Assistant to the Commissioner in Kumaun (1825–29), as officiating Judge of Furruckabad and as Agent to the Lieut-Gov. in N–W Provinces (1835–37); involvement in judicial campaigns against Thugee in 1830's.
India Office Library: MSS Eur. E 307.

SORBY, Edwin (1792–1864), of Orgreave, near Rotherham, farmer and colliery owner. Diaries, 1819–63. 46 books.

Contents: personal activities on the farm and as colliery owner; chiefly local in interest; colliery details.

Sheffield City Libraries: Special collections, Misc. Documents, 1326–41.

TURNER, Eleanor Frewen (b. ca. 1790).

Diary, 1819–24.

Contents: mainly religious and self-analytical.

Leicestershire Record Office: MS. DG6/C/83.

TWINING, Richard (1749–1824), tea merchant.

Diary, July–Aug., 1819. 1 vol.

Contents: journal of a tour through the south of England and in France (Havre, Rouen, Paris); notes on meals, sights and antiquities.

London, British Museum: MS. 39936.

VERULAM, James Walter Grimston, 1st. Earl, of Gorhambury, St. Albans, Hertfordshire.

Diaries, 1819–29 and 1832. 12 vols.

Contents: fairly full entries, though the mid-year period (London season) is not always covered; personal, political, sporting, and social matters.

Hertford County Record Office: MSS. AR 942.

WILKINSON, Mary Georgiana.

Diaries, Sept.–Oct., 1819. 2 vols.

Contents: child's diary of daily routine; journal of a visit to Germany.

Nottinghamshire Records Office: MSS. DDW 170, 171.

WILLIS, Robert, later Professor of Natural Experimental Philosophy, Cambridge.

Diary, 1819–21.

Contents: deals mainly with work on improvement to a harp pedal.

Cambridge University Library: Add. MS. 7574.

WYTHE, John, of Chandos Lodge, Eye, Suffolk.

Diary-fashion memoranda, 1819–31. 1 vol.

Contents: accounts relating to estate of his brother, Thomas; includes electioneering at Eye, 1831; accounts of Wythe family.

Ipswich and East Suffolk Record Office: MS. SI/8/2.3.

1820

ANON.

Diary, Aug.–Oct., 1820. 1 vol.

Contents: journal of a journey to Dresden.

Edinburgh University Library: MS. Dk.3.34.

ANON.

Diary, 1820. 1 vol.

Contents: journal of a visit, from Cambridge to Paris.

Hampshire Record Office: MS. 8 M57/162.

ANON., a soldier of the 11th. Light Dragoons.

Diary, 1820.

Contents: a long and detailed journal of a voyage to India; the writer had previously served with 5th. Dragoon Guards and the 10th. Hussars.
National Army Museum: MSS. 6807/213.

ANON., an army officer.
Diary, c. 1820–39 (with gaps).
Contents: journal of an officer sailing to and serving in India; mostly deals with social and sporting matters.
National Army Museum: MSS. 6907/15.

ANON. [? Hardwicke of Wimpole].
Diary, c. 1820.
Contents: journals of tours in England.
Private: G. J. Yorke Esq., Forthampton Court, Tewkesbury, Glos.

ANON.
Diary, 1820.
Contents: journal of a tour to the Wye Valley.
Cambridge University Library: Add. MS. 2702.

ANON.
Diary, Aug.–Dec., (?1820). 1 vol.
Contents: private log of voyages between Hamburg and Berlin on paddle-barge *Kurrier*; technical details of early steamboats; some personal items.
Wigan Central Public Library: Edward Hall coll.

ANON., a medical student from Sheffield.
Diary, Sept., 1820–June, 1821. 1 vol.
Contents: notes about medical literature and lecturers; Unitarian interests; student life in London.
Manchester, Chetham's Library: MS. 27890.

BOSANQUET, Rev. R. W.
Diary, 1820–40.
Contents: journal deals principally with foreign travel, family visits, and parochial work in the north of England; occasional references to farming.
Private: C. C. Bosanquet Esq., Christ Church, Oxford.

COKE, Colonel John, of Debdale, Nottinghamshire.
Diaries, 1820–87 (with gaps). 11 vols.
Private: Mrs. R. Coke-Steel, Trusley Old Hall, Sutton-on-the-Hill, Derbyshire.

De GREY, Henrietta Frances (née Cole) (1784–1848), of Wrest Park, Bedfordshire.
Diaries, 1820, Sept.–Oct., 1821, 1822, 1843, 1845. 1 vol. and 48 loose sheets.
Contents: national affairs, court and social matters; the 1821 journal contains meditations and exhortations addressed to her daughter.
Bedfordshire Record Office: MSS. L 32/110, 112.

DISRAELI family, (possibly the later Lord Beaconsfield).
Diaries and memoranda: 1820, 1824, 1826, 1833, 1836–37.
Contents: journals of studies, 1820; journey to the Rhine, 1824; Continental tour, 1826; and memoranda.
National Trust, Hughendon Manor, near High Wycombe, Buckinghamshire: Hughenden Papers, A II, III a–c.

FILMER family, of East Sutton Place, Kent.
Diary, 1820. 1 vol.
Contents: few entries.
Kent Archives Office: Filmer MSS. U120, F27/2.

FitzWILLIAM, (?2nd.) Earl.
Diary, 1820.
Contents: two pages only in his hand.
Sheffield City Libraries: Arch. coll., Wentworth Woodhouse Muniments.

HORNER, Thomas.
Diary, 1820.
Contents: sketch of a ramble in South Wales.
Swansea Central Public Library: MSS. coll.

HUNT, Henry (1773–1835), radical politician.
Diary, June, 1820–March, 1821. 1 vol.
Contents: journal kept while in prison after Peterloo; prison conditions and treatment; appeals to prison commissioners and county magistrates against harsh treatment in Ilchester jail.
Manchester Central Library: Arch. Dept., MS. 923. 2 H102.

[?]LEGGE, Charles, R.N., brother of William, 4th. Earl of Dartmouth.
Diary, 1820. 1 vol.
Contents: private reflections.
Greater London Record Office (S.E.1.): MS. F/LEG/967.
(Head Archivist).

LEMPRIERE, Captain George Ourry, of Pelham Place, Alton.
Diaries, 1820. 2 vols.
Contents: journal of his travels in Switzerland, Germany, Prussia, Holland, and France; also, an undated account of Paris and a journey to Brittany.
Hampshire Record Office: MSS. 5M52/59, 60.

LUCKHAM, Levi.
Diary, 1820–21 (extracts). 1 vol.
Contents: journal of a journey to France via Guernsey; visits to Toulouse, Lyons, and Paris.
Dorset County Record Office: MS. D97/2.

MANSFIELD, Winifred.
Diary, 1820.
Hampshire Record Office: MS. 8M57/16.

MILL, John Stuart (1806–1873), economist.
Diaries, 1820, 1831, and 1832.

Contents: (i) June–Oct., 1820, tour through the south of France, Toulouse, Orleans, and Paris; tourist's notes, society, visits, music; kept in letters. (ii) one volume journal of a tour through Yorkshire and the Lake District, including a visit to Wordsworth. (iii) journal of a walking tour with Henry Cole in the south of England, July–Aug., 1832.

(i) London, British Museum: Add. MS. 31909.

(ii) Oxford, Bodleian Library: MS. Don. d.26 (Presented 1932).

(iii) Whereabouts unknown; see Matthews, *British Diaries*, p. 199.

Anna J. Mill, "John S. Mill's . . . Wordsworth", *MLR* XLIV, 1949, 341–350, deals with (ii) above.

MOORCROFT, William (d. 1825), official of East India Company in Bengal.

Diaries, Feb., 1820–Aug., 1825.

Contents: journals of travels, to Bokhara via Kabul, Sreenugur to Nahn, Joalamookhu to Lahore, Leh to Dras and Kashmir etc.

India Office Library: MSS. Eur. C. 40–43.

H. H. Wilson, ed. *Travel in the Himalayan Provinces etc.* 2 vols. (London, 1841).

NEWMAN, William (1773–1835), of Stepney, London.

Diary, 1820–25.

Contents: religious journal; life and work of a Baptist in East London.

Oxford, Regent's Park College: Angus Library.

NUGENT, Emma.

Diaries, 1820, 1822, and 1824. 4 vols.

Contents: tour journals, 1820 (in Italian), through Holland, 1822.

Buckinghamshire Record Office: Freemantle coll., Box 140.

RUSSELL, Sir Henry (2nd. Bart.).

Diaries, Dec., 1820–May, 1821; May–July, 1827; May–June, 1828, and Aug.–Oct., 1838.

Contents: travel from India to England with visit to St. Helena, 1820–21; tour through Flanders and Holland, 1828; and journal of an excursion to Paris, 1838.

Oxford, Bodleian Library: MS. Eng. Misc. c. 329. (Obtained 1952).

SALT, Henry, Consul-General in Egypt, 1812–24.

Diary, 1802–21.

Contents: journal of Ismail Pasha's expedition to Sennar.

London, British Museum: Add. MS. 54195. (Presented 1967).

SHILTON, Richard Phillips, of Southwell, Nottinghamshire.

Diary, March, 1820–May, 1834.

Contents: brief notes on weather and local events in Notts.; country life and work.

Nottingham Public Library: MS. M 457–458.

STANLEY, Louisa Dorothea (1799–1877), of Alderley Park, Alderley, Cheshire.
Diaries, Dec., 1820–Dec., 1821 and April–May, 1847. 2 vols.
Contents: two personal diaries, including comments on the weather etc.
Cheshire Record Office: MS. DSA 129/1,2.
Nancy Mitford, *The Ladies of Alderley etc.* (London, 1938).
Nancy Mitford, ed. *The Stanleys of Alderley, Their Letters etc.* (London, 1939).

STEVENS, Eliza Hope (later Plunkett).
Diary, Oct., 1820–June, 1821. 1 vol.
Contents: journal of educational progress of a child under supervision of her mother, Sarah Stevens. Detailed reports on child's work–mainly censorious.
Hertfordshire Record Office: MS. 86326

TISDALL, Catherine Anderson Louisa (1796–1882), later wife of Col. George Marlay.
Diary, 1820. 1 vol.
Contents: journal of a tour of the Continent with her mother, Lady Charleville.
Nottingham University Library: MS. My 2175.

WYNDHAM, William.
Diary, 1820–48.
Contents: mostly fox-hunting activities.
National Trust: Philipps House, Dinton, Wilts.

1821

ANON.
Diary, July–Aug., 1821. 1 vol.
Contents: journal of a voyage of exploration of the River Ganges upstream to Patna.
India Office Library: MSS. Eur. E 271.

ANON.
Diaries, 1821, 1828, and 1829. 4 vols.
Contents: journals of Continental tours.
Scottish Record Office: GD 24/1/1035.

BARRETT, Richard (member of the Burney family).
Diaries, 1821 and Nov., 1834–Sept., 1837.
Contents: brief notes written when he was eight, 1821, on his games, family, and nursery rhymes; later, notes on his work as a teacher; his reading and lessons; religious life; versemaking.
New York Public Library: Berg coll.

BLATHWAYT, Colonel George William (1797–1871), of Dyrham Park, Gloucestershire.

Diaries, 1821–23, and 1828. 4 vols.

Contents: brief entries of personal nature.

Gloucestershire Record Office: Dyrham Park Arch. D 1799. F 216–219. (Deposited 1961).

BROMLEY, Rev. Walter Davenport and his wife, Caroline.

Diaries, 1821–29. 2 vols. each.

Manchester, John Rylands Library: Bromley Davenport Muniments, MS. Vol. 14.

CLOWES, Admiral Thomas Ball (1787–1864).

Diary, 1821–23. 1 vol.

Contents: journal kept while in command of H.M.S. *Rose* in the Levant; some sketches and poetical commonplace book.

National Maritime Museum: JOD 73, MS. 59/0.

DAUBENY, Rev. James.

Diary, Aug–Oct., 1821. 1 vol.

Contents: journal of a journey to France; account of expenses incurred.

Oxford, Bodleian Library: Sherard MS. 263. (Deposited 1957)

ELD, George (1791–1862), of Foleshill, antiquary, farmer, mayor.

Diaries, June, 1821–Aug., 1826, and May, 1843–47.

Contents: (i) details of the working of a farm at Hawkesbury; sowing, harvesting, mowing, etc.; details of servants hired and wages paid 1819–29; (ii) records of his executorship of Hawkesbury Hall; running of the farm; personal encounters with members of the family, servants, neighbours, the Manor Court at Oldbury; the colliery; meals.

Coventry Corporation Archives: A. 159 and 221.

FISK, Rev. J. (or G.?), vicar of Walsall.

Diary, June, ?1821. 1 vol.

Contents: journal of a tour in the Wye Valley.

Oxford, Bodleian Library: MS. Eng. misc. d.617.

FLETCHER, Angus.

Diary, 1821–22.

Contents: journal of a tour in Holland, Switzerland, and Italy.

Edinburgh University Library: MS La.III.574.

GRIFFIN, John.

Diary, 1821–25.

Contents: journals of various tours.

London, British Museum: Add. MSS. 47770–47772. (Franklin Papers).

HOLDEN, Robert, of Darley Abbey, Derbyshire, and Nutthall Temple, Notts.

Diaries, 1821–35 (with gaps). 11 vols.

Contents: private matters.

Nottingham University Library: Drury Lowe MSS. Dr/F/17–27.

KINGSCOTE, Emily Frances (d. 1858), later wife of Sir John Kennaway (m. 1831), High Sheriff of Devon.

Diary, 1821. 1 vol.
Contents: brief daily entries ; matters personal and social.
Devon Record Office: MS. B961 M add./ F 40.
LINANT de BELLE FONDS, Louis Maurice Adolphe.
Diary, 1821–22.
Contents: journal kept in Egypt.
Oxford, Ashmolean Museum: Griffith Institute MS coll. (On loan).
LUTTRELL, John Fownes (the younger).
Diary, 1821–37.
Somerset Record Office: MSS. DD/L.
MAMMATT, Edward, of Ashby de la Zouch, a solicitor's clerk.
Diary, 1821. 1 vol.
Contents: daily events ; walks, pastimes ; visits.
Leicestershire Record Office: MS. DE41/1/157.
MANSON, William, lighthouse-keeper.
Diary, March–Oct., 1821. 1 vol.
Contents: journal kept at Pentland Skerry.
National Maritime Museum: JOD 60, MS57/070.
MARKHAM, Thomas, of Nash.
Diary, 1821.
Contents: personal interests ; account book.
Glamorgan County Record Office: Carne of Nash MS. F 13.
MEYRICK, Llewellyn, of Queen's College, Oxford.
Diary, summer 1821.
Contents: journal of journey from London through St. Albans, Dunstable,
Northampton, Coventry, Lichfield, Shrewsbury, etc. ; notes on the towns,
scenery, buildings.
London, British Museum: Add. MS. 28802.
RAWSON, Mrs. William, of Savile Green, Halifax.
Diary and account book, 1821–27.
Halifax Central Public Library: Sutcliffe of Ovenden Papers.
ROBINSON, Lieut.
Diary, c. 1821.
Contents: notebook of H.M. Brig *Carnation*.
East Riding of Yorkshire County Record Office: coll. DDHV/74/1.
ROGERS, Sarah (1772–1855), sister of the poet.
Diaries, July–Oct., 1821 and Aug., 1827.
Contents: tour on Continent with her niece, Martha, and her brother,
Samuel Rogers ; Paris, Switzerland, and back, 1821 ; scenery, beauties ;
then a few leaves of a journey through Belgium to Spa.
Oxford, Bodleian Library: MS. Eng. Misc. e.230. (Obtained 1938).

1822

ANON.
Diary, 1822.
Contents: private Notes of a Wakefield bookseller.
York Minster Library: MS. F4.

ANON., (the curate of Great Burstead, Essex).
Diary, 1822. 1 vol.
Contents: brief entries regarding parochial matters, church services, parish meetings and personalities; expenditures on clothes; appointments kept, etc. In printed vol. *The Ladies Diary or Complete Almanack 1822 ... designed for the Use of the Fair Sex.*
Private: Lord Kenyon Papers, D/Dke Box 6 MS. F13. (Deposited at Messrs. Rooper and Whately, Solicitors, 17 Lincoln Inn Fields, London W.C.2, in 1940.)

ANON.
Diary, 1822-24.
Contents: journal of foreign travel in Italy, Turkey, Greece, and Africa.
East Sussex Record Office: Ashburnham arch., MS. 3997.
Francis W. Steer, ed. *The Ashburnham Archives* (Lewes, 1958).

ANON.
Diary, Aug., 1822.
Contents: journal of a visit to Oxford, Cheltenham, Bath, Wells and Salisbury by an unidentified lady.
Oxford, Bodleian Library: MS. Sherard 263, fols. 93-99. (Deposited 1957).

ANON.
Diary, 1822-25.
Contents: a journal of an unidentified huntsman from Brocklesby, Lincolnshire.
Lincolnshire Archives Office: MS. coll.

ALEXANDER, Captain T., R.N.
Diary, 1822-24.
Contents: journal in India, Persian Gulf, etc.
Cambridge University Library: MS. Acc. 7223.

BAKER, Lieut. George, a soldier.
Diaries, 1822-23. 3 vols.
Contents: journals of journey from Ceylon to England, on sick leave from the army; conditions of sea travel; the Red Sea; visit to the Pyramids; quarantine in Alexandria and Malta because of the bubonic plague; vivid pictures of travel by land and sea.
Oxford, Rhodes House Library: MSS. Afr. s. 1091 Box 1.

BRANFILL, Eliza, of Upminster, Essex.
Diaries, 1822–72. 44 vols.
Essex Record Office: MSS. D/DRu F12.

CHICHESTER, Sir Charles (1795–1847), sometime Governor of Trinidad.
Diaries, Aug., 1822–Feb., 1838. 16 vols.
Contents: voyage to Nova Scotia; accounts of people and places; Newfoundland; fighting in Carlist War in Spain, 1835–37; returns to North America; political comment; leave in England; visits South America and West Indies; life in Canada; towns visited.
East Riding of Yorkshire County Record Office: MSS. DDCH/70–85 (Loan).

CHICHESTER, Lady, wife of Sir Charles.
Diaries: Aug., 1822–76 (with gaps). 7 vols.
Contents: travels on the Continent; travel conditions; meets Washington Irving; later volumes include some kept in South America and the West Indies.
East Riding of Yorkshire County Record Office: MSS. DDCH/86–92.

COCKBURN, Jane.
Diary, 1822–24.
London, British Museum: Acc. MS. 48339. (Obtained 1952).

CULLHAM, Susanna Arethusa (later Gibson) (b. 1814).
Diaries, 1822–24, 1829–30, and 1832. 3 vols.
Contents: small girl's journal of a trip to the Continent, 1822–24; journal of a tour on the Continent; and of a cruise.
West Suffolk Record Office: MSS. E2/44/52–58, 61.

FRANKLEN, Richard.
Diary, 1822.
Contents: journal of a journey to Scotland and England.
Glamorgan County Record Office: Clemenstone MSS.

GRAY, Margaret, daughter of Jonathan Gray.
Diaries, 1822 and 1823–25. 2 vols.
Contents: journal of a tour of the Isle of Man, 1822; tours of the Lake District, Cambridge, and London.
York Public Library: Gray's Court Papers, T/7–8.
Mrs. Edwin Gray, *Papers and Diaries of a York Family: 1764–1839* (London: Sheldon Press, 1927).

JOHNSTON, Archibald, surgeon.
Diary, 1822–23.
Contents: journal of the voyage of the *Lonach* from London to Batavia and Singapore via the Cape of Good Hope.
Oxford, Rhodes House Library: MS. Africa, r.1.

LANE, John Rayner.
Diaries, 1822–71. 4 vols.

Contents: personal matters ; farm business at Cutler's Farm, Castlemorton, Worcestershire.

Private: H. J. C. Lane Esq., Clerkenleap Kempsey, Worcester.

LOCKHART, Mrs. Sophia (d. 1837), and her husband, John Gibson Lockhart (1794–1854).

Diaries, Jan., 1823–53.

Contents: mostly kept by Mrs. Lockhart until her death ; brief memoranda of work and engagements ; literary and social life in Scotland ; meetings with famous writers, and some comments on dinners and diners (Scott, Dickens, etc.).

National Library of Scotland: MSS. 1585–1613.

MACDONALD, Rev. John.

Diaries, 1822–24.

Contents: journals on two visits to Island of St. Kilda.

Scottish Record Office: GD 95/11/12.

MITCHELL, James, Surgeon R.N.

Diary, 1822–23.

Contents: journal of a voyage to New South Wales returning via Batavia and the Cape of Good Hope.

Edinburgh University Library: MS. Dc.7.123.

NEWCASTLE, Henry Pelham Pelham-Clinton, 4th. Duke of (1785–1851), of Clumber Park, Notts.

Diaries, 1822–50. 8 vols.

Contents: general interests, and family ; local electioneering ; matters parliamentary and political.

Nottingham University Library: MSS. Ne2 F 1–8.

OWENS, Rev. Owen, of Rhesycae, Flintshire.

Diaries, 1822–23, and 1835.

Contents: entries in English and Welsh, by a Congregational minister.

National Library of Wales: MSS. 6085–7A.

SAUNDERS, Captain James (d. 1830), of Stratford-upon-Avon, antiquary.

Diary, Oct.–Nov., 1822. 1 vol.

Contents: account of his election and proceedings as mayor of Stratford-upon-Avon.

Stratford-upon-Avon, Shakespeare's Birthplace Trust Library: Wheler coll. 106.

TREBECK, George.

Diaries: June, 1822–Oct., 1824. 3 vols.

Contents: journals of travels in India etc.: Tashqurghan to Qunduz ; the borders of Kashmir and Tibet, Kebul ; Leh to Yarkhund, etc.

India Office Library: MSS. Eur. C41, D255, F35.

WALKER, Miss Anna Louisa (b. 1796), daughter of General G. Townshend Walker.

Diary, July–Aug., 1822. 1 vol.

Contents: journal kept during sojourn of the Continent in company of her father; shrewd comment on her father and on the things and places she saw.
Wigan Central Public Library: Edward Hall coll.
WALKER, Mrs. Helen, second wife of General G. Townshend Walker.
Diary, April, 1822–Jan., 1824.
Contents: travel on the Continent; society en route; her husband and her devotion to him; the General living on his laurels; apt comment on his first wife's diary.
Wigan Central Public Library: Edward Hall coll.
[?]WHARNCLIFFE, 1st. Baron.
Diary, 1822.
Sheffield City Library: Wharncliffe Muniments.
WILSON, Robert (1772–1837), of Hawick.
Diary or notebook, beginning 1822 (account & extracts).
Contents: notes on his reading and on local excitements and events.
Trans. Hawick Archaeol. Soc. (Sept. 1910).
WOLLEY, Thomas Lamplugh (b. 1806), of Clifton, Bristol. (?) an army officer.
Diaries, May, 1822–Feb., 1833. 4 vols.
Contents: travels in England, Oxford, Plymouth, Portsmouth; visit to the court of Weimar, Dresden, Berlin; later travels on the continent; stationed on the Isle of Man; Ireland; record of his flirtations.
Greater London Record Office (Middlesex Records): MSS. Acc. 611/1–4.

1823

ANON., (of Edinburgh).
Diaries, Feb., 1823–Dec., 1847. 4 vols.
Contents: a discursive account of contemporary events in Edinburgh and elsewhere; diarist has interest in public finance and government; extensive copying from newspapers of the time.
Edinburgh Central Library: Edinburgh Room, MSS. YDA 1862–823.
D. G. Moir, ed. *Book of the Old Edinburgh Club* 29 (1956), 143–184, and 30 (1959), 142–159.
ANON.
Diary, Sept., 1823.
Contents: a Scotsman's travel to eastern Scottish borders; high-flown sentiments on Melrose and Dryburgh abbeys, etc.
Wigan Central Public Library: Edward Hall coll.
ANON.
Diary, Jan., 1823–June, 1825. 1 vol.
Contents: journal kept by a farmer's wife living on the borders of

Warwickshire and Leicestershire.
Birmingham University Library: MS. 10/iii/15.

ANON.
Diary, 1823. 1 vol.
Contents: journal of tour in Glamorganshire and Monmouthshire; illustrated with notes on scenery, towns, beauties.
Cardiff Public Library: MSS.

ARBUTHNOT, Mrs.
Diary, 1823.
Private: Duke of Wellington, Reading, Hants.

BACON, Major Francis D'Arcy, of the Light Dragoons.
Diary, 1823-25.
Contents: journal of travels and wanderings, northern Germany, Russia, Persia, Near East, Greece and the Islands; account of the rescue of Edward John Trelawny from the chieftain Odysseus on Mount Parnassus; some notes on foreign policy, and drawings.
Oxford, Bodleian Library: MS. Don. e.13. (Obtained 1935).

BAYLEY, Francis (1803-1893), judge.
Diary, 1823-24.
Contents: journal of journey to France, Germany, Russia, Finland, Sweden, and Channel Islands; literary and historical interests.
Private: Leonard Clark Esq., 6 Ashwood Villas, Headingley, Leeds, Yorkshire.

CROOME, Margaret Anne, of Bourton-on-the-Water, Glos.
Diary, 1823, 1829. 1 vol.
Contents: personal affairs.
Gloucestershire Records Office: MS. D 1183.

CUNNINGHAM, John, Surgeon, R.N.
Diary, 1823-25. 1 vol.
Contents: journal kept during a voyage in the Pacific.
National Maritime Museum: JOD 21, MS. 9839.

DAUBENEY, Mrs. Margaret.
Diary, 1823-39.
Private: Captain R.D.R. Troup, Hountwell, Henley, Alton Pancras, Buckland Newton, Dorset.

DOUIE family.
Diary, 1823.
Contents: a record of a visit to Edinburgh, with description of Sir Walter Scott in the Law Courts.
Private: D. L. Douie Esq., 12 Charlbury Road, Oxford.

GOSSIP, Leah.
Diary, Oct-Dec., 1823.

Contents: journal kept during a holiday at Papplewick Hall, Nottinghamshire; social notes.

Trans. Thoroton Soc., XXXV (1931), 117–148.

GULSTON, Miss Eliza, of Carmarthen.

Diaries, 1823–27.

Contents: journals kept by the daughter of a landowner.

Carmarthen County Record Office: Derwydd MSS. H38–40.

HALE, Robert H. Blagden (1780–1856), M.P.

Diaries, 1823 and 1826–55 (some gaps).

Contents: journal of a Continental tour, 1823; brief entries thereafter of some public interest.

Gloucestershire Record Office: Hale (Alderley) MSS. (Deposited 1954).

HOLLAND, Samuel (1803–1892), pioneer of the North Wales slate industry, and M.P. for Merioneth.

Diary, Jan., 1823–May, 1824.

National Library of Wales: Holland MSS., 4987B.

HOWELL, John, of Albrighton, Shropshire, a farmer.

Diary, 1823–45.

Contents: farm matters.

Salop County Record Office: MSS. coll.

(JACKSON, William?).

Diary, 1823–25.

Contents: journal kept while in South America.

Scottish Record Office: GD 233/31.

KEMP, Grover, of Brighton.

Diaries, Dec., 1823–Feb., 1859 (occasional entries). 2 vols.

Contents: his conversion to Quaker faith; Friends' meetings in Sussex; visits from travelling friends; religious reflection and experiences; a visit to the West Indies, 1857–58.

London, Friends' Society Library: MSS. S.86–87.

LE GRICE, Rev. Charles V., of Trereife, near Penzance, Cornwall, landowner and cleric.

Diary, May–Sept., 1823. 1 vol.

Contents: journal of travel on the Continent: via Exeter and Southampton to France (Rouen and Paris), Geneva, Switzerland, Germany, and Holland.

Cornwall County Record Office: MS. DD.X 20/44.

POWELL, Charles.

Diary, 1823. 1 vol.

Contents: journal of a tour of Kent made when the diarist was sixteen years of age; gives a glimpse of Kent in the reign of King George IV.

Kent Archives Office: MS. U934 Powell, F8.

F. Hull, "A Kentish Holiday: 1823", *Archælogia Cantiana* LXXXI (1966), 109.

RICHARDSON, Eliza, (later Mrs. John Obadiah Westwood).
Diary, summer 1823. 1 vol.
Contents: notes on a pleasant journey made into Oxfordshire with her father.
Oxford, Bodleian Library: MS. Dep. d.145. (Deposited 1960).
RODD, Francis Hearle (1766–1836), of Trebartha Hall, Northill, Cornwall, landowner and squire.
Diaries, 1823 and 1827. 2 vols.
Contents: personal, family and local events.
Cornwall County Record Office: MSS. AD.360/19–20.
Bryan Latham, *Trebartha, The House By The Stream* (1971).
SHARPE, Catherine (1782–1853), of London.
Diaries, 1823–30, 1835, and 1836. 3 vols.
Contents: journals of travel; Paris, 1828; Switzerland, Milan, and Le Havre, 1835 and 1836; retrospective notes on her life up to 1823; social matters, 1823–30.
London, University College Library: Sharpe Papers 65–67.
SHIRLEY, John Evelyn.
Diaries, 1823–45, 1846–54, 1855–57. 3 vols.
Warwickshire Record Office: MS. CR229/174–176.
SHORT, (?——), of Kenn, profession unknown.
Diaries, 1823–24. 2 vols.
Contents: travel journals of the Grand Tour: fairly detailed descriptions of places visited: London, Calais, Paris, Versailles, Lyons, Turin, Rome, Naples, Pisa, Venice, Milan, Genoa, Como, Geneva, Lausanne, Basle, etc.
Devon Record Office: MSS. 1311 M/6/13.
SMITH, Joseph, of Rothwell Haigh Farm, Yorkshire.
Diary, March–May, 1823.
Contents: farming matters; sowing, ploughing, going to market.
Private: Clifford Webster Esq., British Records Association, Charterhouse, Charterhouse Square, London, E.C.1.
TAYLOR, Sir Henry (1800–1886), civil servant, dramatist, poet.
Diaries, 1823–24, 1826, 1837.
Contents: notes on his reading, criticism, reflections, April, 1823–Aug., 1824; journal of travels in the Low Countries with Robert Southey, June, 1826; finally, a diary recording spiritual reflections, 1837, from which sections were later removed by Taylor.
Oxford, Bodleian Library: MSS. Eng. Misc. f.57, e.191, f.56.
[?]TYRELL, Sir John.
Diary, 1823. 1 vol.
Contents: many brief entries relating to family and estate matters; dates of death; wages paid to coachmen; acreage of various fields on Runwell estate; notes on timber and coal; acreage of wheat.

Private: Lord Kenyon, D/DKe Box 6. (Deposited at Messrs. Rooper and Whately, Solicitors, 17 Lincoln's Inn Fields, London W.C.2, in 1940).

WESTCAR, Henry.
Diary, 1823–24 (Transcript only; by W. R. Dawson).
Contents: journal describing travels in Egypt.
London, British Museum: Add. MS. 52283. (Presented 1963).

1824

ANDERSON, Captain James, R.N., of the Hollam Estate.
Diary, 1824–34 and 1837–40. 1 vol.
Contents: journals of farming matters.
Portsmouth Record Office: Hewett coll., 16/A/155.

ANON.
Diary, 1824–34. 1 vol.
Contents: farm matters, giving details of work done each day; rotation of crops; annual values and amounts of wool sold.
Berkshire Record Office: Wilder Papers, D/EWi/E17.

ANON.
Diary, 1824–25. 1 vol.
Contents: journal of a voyage up the Nile from Cairo; list of birds seen during the voyage, etc.
East Sussex Record Office: Ashburnham arch., MS. 4003.

ANON.
Diary, June–Nov., 1824. 1 vol.
Contents: notes of an Oxford student while travelling in Europe in the family of Colonel Roberts.
Toronto Public Library, Canada: Henry Scadding coll.

ANON.
Diary, 1824. 1 vol.
Contents: journal of foreign travel in Europe and the East.
East Sussex Record Office: Ashburnham arch., MS. 3999.

ANON., (young married woman).
Diary, 1824.
Contents: journal of young married woman, [?] Betty Barrett, from Leeds, who visits London.
East Riding of Yorkshire County Record Office: DDX/94/190.

ARNOLD, Dr. Thomas (1795–1842), of Rugby.
Diaries, 1824, 1825 summer, 1826–27, 1828 and 1829.
Contents: journals of tours: in Scotland, France, Italy, Switzerland, and Germany; notes mostly on scenery; some social life and visits; reflections; brief extracts.
Leeds University Library (Brotherton): MSS. (on loan).

Arnold's Travelling Journals, ed. A. P. Stanley (London, 1852), pp. 3–135.
(Documents do not include diaries of 1824 and 1829).

BANNERMAN, Sir Alexander (1769–1840), of Elrick, Scotland.
Diaries, 1824–39. 7 vols.
Contents: random reflections on current events; frank notes on the people
of Aberdeen and environs; local society; eccentrics in the neighbourhood.
National Library of Scotland: MSS. 1685–1691.

BURTON, R.
Diary, April–May, 1824.
Contents: a journey into the Batak country of Sumatra in the company of
Ward; reaches Silinduny; illness; observations on country, its language
and people.
India Office Library: MSS. Eur. E. 108 (fols 268–380).

CARLOS, E. J.
Diary, 1824.
Contents: narrative of a tour in the West of England.
Present location of MS. unknown.

CHALONER, Robert, of Guisborough, Yorkshire, M.P.
Diary, 1824. 1 vol.
Contents: journal of a tour through Germany, Switzerland, and France;
not very detailed.
North Riding of Yorkshire County Record Office: MS. ZFM, bundle 319.
(M. Y. Ashcroft, County Archivist).

DENISON, John Evelyn (later Viscount Ossington) (1800–1873), of
Ossington House, Notts., Speaker of the House of Commons (1857–72)
and M.P. (1823–73).
Diaries, personal ones, Feb., 1824–61 (with gaps);
Speaker's diaries, April, 1857–71.
Contents: travels to France, Belgium, Switzerland; correspondence; his
reading; parliamentary affairs; visits to Italy and Scotland.
Nottingham University Library: Ossington coll., MSS. OSD 1–8, 11–16.
(Mrs. M. A. Welch, Keeper of Manuscripts).
Viscount Ossington, *Notes from My Journal when Speaker of the House
of Commons* (London, 1900).

FIELD, R., of London.
Diary, Jan., 1824–Dec., 1825.
Contents: religious and private affairs of a diarist who seems to have
been a customs officer at London Docks.
Private: Mrs. J. Webb, Chislehurst, Port Hill Road, Shrewsbury.

GLASSFORD, James, an advocate.
Diary, Sept., 1824.
Contents: brief journal of a tour in Ulster.
Edinburgh University Library: MS. La. III. 576.

GLYNNE, Henry (younger son of Sir S. R. Glynne, 8th. Baronet).
Diary, 1824.
Contents: personal memoranda ; visits ; activities of brothers and sister.
National Library of Wales: Glynne of Harwarden MS. 26.

GLYNNE, Mary (later Mary Lyttleton).
Diaries, 1824–25, 1827–29, 1831, and 1837.
Contents: notes on personal and domestic affairs ; events of a visit to
Paris in 1829.
National Library of Wales: Glynne of Harwarden MS. 27–33.

HAY, Robert (1799–1863), of Linplum, Haddington, Egyptologist.
Diaries, March–Nov., 1824 ; Jan., 1826–July, 1827, and 1830.
Contents: journal kept in Egypt and Mediterranean, Greece, etc ; travel
notes on social life and scenery ; historical, antiquarian, and archaeological
sketches.
London, British Museum: Add. MSS. 31054.

JONES, Marianne (later Mrs. Jones-Bateman), Pentremawr, Abergele.
Diaries, 1824–44.
Contents: accounts of tours in Wales, England, Scotland, and Ireland ;
some on the continent of Europe ; illustrated with engravings and original
sketches.
National Library of Wales: MSS. 3594–3599B.

LEADLEY, J. Watson.
Diary, Oct., 1824–June, 1839 (extracts).
Contents: abstracts of voyages made ; Liverpool-Lima-London ; Liverpool-
Lima-Valparaiso-Lima-England.
Liverpool Record Office: MS. GQ 558.

PARKER, Charles Stewart.
Diary, 1824.
Contents: journal in the West Indies.
Liverpool Record Office: Arch. 920 ParIII.

POWYS, Eleanor (daughter of 2nd. Lord Milford).
Diary, July–Oct., 1824.
Contents: journal of a tour through France, Low Countries, Germany,
Switzerland, and Italy ; notes on scenery, towns, buildings, etc.
Oxford, Bodleian Library: MS. Eng. Misc., g.14.

RICHMOND, Capt. J.
Diary, 1824–25. 1 vol.
Contents: pocket book with brief description of voyage from Calcutta to
London.
Scottish Record Office: GD 226/18/294.

ROBSON, Elizabeth (1771–1843), of Liverpool.
Diary, with preceding autobiography, 1824–37.
Contents: Quaker ministry ; her inner life and public work and travels,
including a visit to the U.S.A.

D

London, Friends' Society Library: Cupboard 7.

SEMPILL, Hon. Maria Janet.

Diary, 1824–25.

Contents: journal kept at Caen, France.

Scottish Record Office: GD 250/13.

SHARPE, William (1804–1870), of London, a solicitor.

Diaries, 1824, 1834–51, 1837, 1840, and 1852. 5 vols.

Contents: personal and social matters with some sections obliterated (apparently by Sharpe), 1834–51; travel journals to Isle of Wight, Ireland, and Le Havre.

London, University College Library: Sharpe Papers 89, 90, 93–5.

SHIRLEY, Horatio Henry.

Diary, 1824–79.

Warwickshire Record Office: MS. CR 229/117.

SHORE, Charlotte Mary (née Cornish), of near Salcombe, Devon.

Diaries, 1824 (while unmarried) and 1831. 2 vols.

Contents: journal of a voyage to India.

Exeter City Record Office: MSS.

SMITH family.

Diary, July–Sept., 1824. 1 vol.

Contents: journal of a family trip to Paris by an English family who had lived in Boulogne and were leaving France.

Birmingham University Library: MS. 6/vi/17.

STANLEY, Hon. William Owen (1802–1884), landowner, M.P., of Penrhos, Anglesea.

Diary, Aug–Oct., 1824. 1 vol.

Contents: journal of a tour in Sicily with his uncle George, 2nd. Earl of Sheffield.

Cheshire Record Office: MS. DSA 105/1.

STEWART, John, of Dalguise.

Diaries, 1824–41, and 1843–51. 13 vols.

Contents: all kept at Capetown.

Scottish Record Office: GD 38/1/1256–1258.

TURNER, Lady.

Diaries, 1824–30 (with gaps).

Contents: two pocket diaries, chiefly concerned with the London season; four diaries of Continental tours, 1828, 1829, 1830: Brussels, Munich, Innsbruck, Geneva, Rome, Naples.

North Riding of Yorkshire County Record Office: Kirkleatham Hall Arch. 11782–11785. (Deposited 1956).

WHARNCLIFFE, John Stuart Wortley, 2nd. Baron (1801–1855), of Wortley Hall, Sheffield, Yorks.

Diaries, 1824–25. 3 vols.

Contents: journal of his American tour; entries in some detail.

Sheffield City Libraries: Dept. of Local History and Archives, Wharn-cliffe Muniments 450–452.

WILSHIRE, William (c. 1805–1867), of The Frythe, Welwyn, Herts., attorney, barrister, M.P., gentleman.
Diaries, Feb–April, 1824 and Aug–Sept., 1833. 2 vols.
Contents: early diary is of studies as undergraduate at Wadham College, Oxford; later volume is of a pleasure journey in France and Italy.
Hertford County Record Office: MSS. 60152, 60154.

WORSLEY, William, of Hovingham, Yorkshire.
Diary, 1824.
Contents: journal of an Italian tour.
Private: MS. is at Hovingham Hall. (Information: Archivist, North Riding of Yorkshire C.R.O.)

WRIGHT, [? ——].
Diary, 1824–53.
Stafford, William Salt Library: MSS.

1825

ANON.
Diary, 1825. 1 vol.
Contents: notebook with daily entries.
Scottish Record Office: GD 246/Box 45.

ANON.
Diary, Sept., 1825–Sept., 1826.
Contents: journal of proceedings of the Brig *Enterprize*, on a voyage from London to Vigo Bay and back; notes on salvage of sunken Spanish vessels by means of a diving bell.
London, Public Record Office: 30/26/49.

ANON.
Diary, 1825. 1 vol.
Contents: tour into North Wales via mid-Wales, illustrated and with notes on scenery, beauties, buildings, etc.
Cardiff Public Library: MSS.

ANON.
Diary, 1825.
Contents: small diary containing a few notes.
Surrey County Record Office: Goulburn Papers.

ANON.
Diary, June–Aug., 1825.
Contents: journal of a tour in Normandy and Picardy; notes on scenery, churches, etc; diary has been ascribed to John Earle.
Oxford, Bodleian Library: MS. Eng. Misc. e.234.

ANON.
> Diary, 1825. 1 vol.
> Contents: journal of foreign travel in Asia Minor and Greece.
> East Sussex Record Office: Ashburnham Arch., MS. 3999.

ANON., [?] the Wilberforce family.
> Diaries, 1825, 1827. 2 vols.
> Contents: brief entries.
> West Sussex County Record Office: Wilberforce MSS., 36, 37.

[?]——, Lydia Ann, (may have married a Rev. Oakley).
> Diary, Sept., 1825–Jan., 1826. 1 vol.
> Contents: personal affairs of a young lady at home.
> Dorset County Record Office: MS. D320.

ANDERSON, W., a soldier of the Light Infantry.
> Diary, 9-25 Dec., 1825. 1 vol.
> Contents: journal kept at the seige of Bhurtpore; list of seige ordnance etc; plans of seige and batteries.
> India Office Library: MSS. Eur. A.9.

ASHBURNHAM, Bertram, 4th. Earl of (1797–1878).
> Diaries, 1825–77 (with gaps). 21 vols.
> Contents: mostly diaries of the printed almanack type, with brief entries; early shooting experiences; game kept in East Anglia; a visit to Wales, 1842; Scottish travels, 1848.
> East Sussex Record Office: Ashburnham Arch., MSS. 956–974, 2507, 4004.
> Francis W. Steer, ed. *The Ashburnham Archives* (Lewes, 1958).

CASWALL, Miss——, sister of George Caswall of Sacombe.
> Diary, 1825–30. 1 vol.
> Essex Record Office: MS. D/DRh F26.

COKE, Edward T.
> Diary, 1825–32 (with gaps).
> Contents: journal of a Lieutenant touring in France, Germany, Belgium, and Holland; notes in Rangoon, Burma; later diaries deal with a journey to U.S.A. and Canada.
> Private: Mrs. R. Coke-Steel, Trusley Old Hall, Sutton-on-the-Hill, Derbyshire.

CONSTABLE, Rev. John, vicar of Ringmer.
> Diaries, 1825–52. 2 vols. (typescripts).
> East Sussex Record Office: Monk-Bretton MSS. 1605–06.

CULLUM, Mary Anne (Eggers).
> Diary, 1825–26. 1 vol.
> Contents: journal of a tour in Italy.
> West Suffolk Record Office: MS. E2/44/59.

DORVILLE, Anne (b. 1765), of Clapham, London.
> Diary, Nov., 1825–March, 1837. 1 vol.

Contents: record of domestic and religious matters; some holidays; after twenty years of establishment, she left Clapham in 1833, her mistress having died of cholera, to live alone in Hammersmith.

Oxford, Bodleian Library: MS. Eng. Misc. d. 352. (Presented 1953).

FIELDING, Rev. Henry, prison chaplain.

Diary, 1825–27 (extracts).

Contents: work among prisoners at New Bailey Prison, Salford, Lancashire; brief notes.

Trans. Lancs. & Cheshire Antiq. Soc., XLV (1928), 21–31.

GLYNNE, Sir Stephen Richard, 9th. Baronet, of Harwarden.

Diaries, 1825 and 1840–74 (with gaps).

Contents: notes of his personal activities; tours in Spain, France, Wales; railways; prices; charities; some notes on W. E. Gladstone.

National Library of Wales: Glynne of Harwarden MSS., 34–41, 43–54.

ISHAM, Sir Justinian.

Diary, 1825–43.

Northamptonshire Record Office: MSS. coll.

KEATING, Sir H.S.

Diary, 1825–31.

Contents: journal of travels in Madagascar, Greece, North America, etc.

Cambridge University Library: Add. MS. 3819.

MOORE, Thomas (1779–1852), Irish poet.

Diary, Oct–Nov., 1825.

Contents: journal of a visit to Sir Walter Scott at Abbotsford, Scotland.

National Library of Scotland: MS. 911/60–62. [Moore's other diaries have been published; Lord John Russell's edition in 1853–56, and J. B. Priestley's edition in 1925.]

PARKER, T. B.

Diary, 1825–26.

Contents: journal of a tour in Russia.

Salop County Record Office: Leighton of Sweeney coll.

PEARSON, T. J. H., a soldier.

Diaries, Nov., 1825–June, 1827 and Nov., 1838–Nov., 1843.

Contents: early three volumes kept at Bhurtpore, and later ones include the First Afghan War.

National Army Museum: MSS. 5910/152.

READE, Edward Anderton (1807–1866), Anglo-Indian official.

Diary, with autobiographical introduction, 1825–31. 5 vols.

Contents: personal matters; summary of events.

Oxford, Bodleian Library: MSS. misc. d. 260–264.

Bodleian Library Record, v. I (1939–41), 72–73. (Presented 1938).

ROGERS, Mary (niece of Samuel Rogers, poet).

Diary, 1825. 1 vol.

Contents: journal of a tour to Paris with her aunt Sarah and her uncle Samuel; tourist's notes.

Oxford, Bodelian Library: MS. Eng. misc. e. 231. (Purchased 1938).

ROLLS, John Etherington Welch (1807–1877), of the Hendre, Llangattock-vibon-avel, near Monmouth.

Diaries, 1825–69 (with gaps). 34 vols.

Contents: mostly diarist's interests in yachting, theatre, hunting, and other activities.

Monmouthshire Record Office: Rolls MSS. D361 F/P3.

RUSSELL, Sir James, of Ashiesteel, general.

Diaries, Jan–Oct., 1825 and 1839–Nov., 1858.

Contents: notes on his military life and travels; Persia, India, Turkey; domestic and social life in Scotland; visits.

National Library of Scotland: MSS. 3224–3331.

SHARPE (nee Reid), Lucy (b. 1814), of London, wife of William Sharpe.

Diaries, 1825–27, 1834, 1836, and 1844. 5 vols.

Contents: travel journals, to Holland and France, 1825–27, to visit an uncle in York, 1826, to Scotland, 1834, to Holland, 1836, and to Devon and Somerset, 1844.

London, University College Library: Sharpe Papers Nos. 112–116.

WILLIAMS, Rev. Peter Bayley (1765–1836), of Llanrug and Llanberis, Caernarvonshire.

Diary, 1825.

Contents: notes of an Anglican minister and antiquary in Wales; his parishioners; family affairs; tithes; farming; visits to Holyhead and Liverpool; weather, etc.

Bangor, University College: Bangor MS. 1633.

1826

ANON.

Diary, 1826–39. 1 vol.

Contents: journal of travels in Italy, Germany, and Sweden.

Scottish Record Office: GD 18/2122.

ANON.

Diary, 1826.

Contents: journal of a tour in Belgium, etc.

London, British Museum: Add. MS. 52499.

ANON., (an army officer).

Diary, 1826–28.

Contents: journal of an officer serving in Portugal under Sir William Clinton; Manoelite troubles, etc.

Private: Miss E. M. Allen, Inchdene, Woodchester, Stroud, Gloucestershire.

ANON., [?] Rector of All Souls', London, and of Mortimer St., London.
Diaries, 1826–44. 2 vols.
Contents: records of almost annual Continental tours undertaken by a
clergyman of taste and culture; guide-book itinerary of churches and
castles; customs; societies, etc.
Wigan Central Public Library: Edward Hall coll. M. 932.

ANON., (a Yorkshire gentleman).
Diary, July–Aug., 1826.
Contents: journal of a tour in Scotland; to Edinburgh and central and
southwest Highlands; illustrated with sketches of landscapes, people met,
and architecture.
Glasgow, Mitchell Library: MS. B. 240800.

ANON.
Diaries, 1826–27. 2 vols.
London, British Museum: Add. MSS. 52251–52252. (Holland House
Papers) (Acquired 1963).

BEST, Mawdistley Gaussen.
Diaries, 1826–1902. 50 vols.
Contents: mostly small printed Letts diaries; partly in the form of re-
collections; account of part in Indian Mutiny and Crimean War.
Kent Archives Office: Best MSS. U480 acc. 717, F56–57.

CHAMIER, Captain Frederick (1796–1870), R.N., author.
Diary, 1826–27. 1 vol.
Contents: journal kept while in command of H.M. Brig *Britomart*, re-
turning to England after cruising in West Indian and South American
waters.
National Maritime Museum: JOD 52, MS. 57/021.

CRYER, John, of Rotten Row, Wakefield, Yorkshire, a bookseller.
Diaries and scrapbook, c. 1826–63. 15 vols.
Contents: only part is straight diary; miscellaneous pieces of information
on contemporary and historical events.
Wakefield Public Library: MSS. 84.

DASHWOOD, G. H., of West Wycombe, Buckinghamshire.
Diary, 1826–28.
Contents: family matters.
Oxford, Bodleian Library: MS. D.D. Dashwood (Bucks.) e.4. (Acquired
1950).

ELMHIRST, Anna Francis (née Walker) (c. 1805–1858), wife of William
Elmhirst, of Round Green, Worsborough, Yorks.
Diaries, 1826 and 1843–53. 11 vols.
Contents: detailed entries of daily life.
Sheffield Public Libraries: Dept. of Local History and Archives, Elmhirst
MSS. 1182.

GOULBURN, Henry ("Harry") (1813–1843).
Diaries and personal account books, 1826–43 (with gaps). 13 vols.
Contents: comments on the political situation; family matters; personal observations.
Surrey Record Office: Goulburn MSS. Acc. 319. III/7–9.

GRAINGER, John, of Holm Cultram, a yeoman farmer.
Diary, July, 1826–June, 1830. 1 vol.
Contents: farming and personal affairs; parish matters, etc.
Cumberland and Westmorland Record Office: MS. DX/74/5.

GREY, Thomas (1810–1826), of Liverpool, son of Lord Grey, the Prime Minister.
Diary, Jan–May, 1826. 1 vol.
Contents: brief notes of a young boy; family interest.
Private: Grey family.
Arthur Ponsonby, *English Diaries* (London, 1923), p. 422.

HASSAL, John Satterfield, of Liverpool and New York.
Diaries, 1826–27 and 1829–36.
Contents: entries by resident of Liverpool who moved to New York in 1834.
Liverpool Record Office: Arch. MD 219/2–11.

HEYWOOD, Robert (1786–1868), of Bolton, Lancs., manufacturer.
Diaries, April, 1826–July, 1858 (with gaps). 6 vols.
Contents: journal of travels to Italy, America, Russia, Egypt, France, Switzerland, and Ireland.
London, Dr. William's Library: MSS. 28. 157–161, 28. 163–164.

LE GRICE (? Rev. Charles V.) (d. 1858), cleric and landowner, of Trereife, near Penzance, Cornwall.
Diaries, July–Oct., 1826 and May–Oct., 1829. 2 vols.
Contents: travel diary in summer of 1826, Truro, Monmouth, Wales, Scotland, York, East Anglia, and London; later one is of travel from Penzance, Falmouth, Plymouth, Portsmouth, Southampton, London, Bristol, S. Ireland, Liverpool, Oxford, London, and Exeter.
Cornwall County Record Office: MSS. DD.X. 20/40 & 41.

MASSINGBERD, Rev. Francis Charles (1800–1872), Chancellor of Lincoln Cathedral 1863–72.
Diary and notebooks, 1826–66.
Contents: activities of a devoted parish priest; South Ormsby parishioners; admiration of Gothic revival; association with John Keble; organization against Catholic emancipation in 1829; moderate High Church views; illness and travel abroad.
Lincolnshire Archives Office: Massingberd papers.

MAXWELL, William Constable, 10th. Lord Herries.
Diaries and tour journals, 1826–76 (with many gaps).
Contents: social events; hunting and shooting; visits; weather; family

affairs; assize attendance; estate and farm matters; railway proposals; church matters (R.C.); Continental tours, France, Italy, Austria, Switzerland; Scottish holidays.
East Riding of Yorkshire County Record Office: MSS. DDEV/ 61/3–32.

MONRO, David.
Diary, 1826. 1 vol.
Contents: journal of a tour in France and Switzerland.
Scottish Record Office: GD 71/478.

PAYNE, Robert, of Barford, Northumberland.
Diary, 1826–30 (extracts).
Contents: notes referring to farm work and country social life and events.
Proc. Soc. Antiqs. Newcastle-upon-Tyne, 4th. ser., VII (1937–38), IX (1939–42).

PHILIPS, John, F.R.S.
Diary, July–Aug., 1826.
Contents: journal of a tour in Scotland by diarist and three companions studying geology of the country; almost exclusively made up of geological observations.
Glasgow, Mitchell Library: MS. S.R. 183, 240800.

PINDER, J.
Diary, May–Oct., 1826.
Contents: journal and abstract of a journal on a voyage from Liverpool to Maranhao and Demeraray and back to London on the ship *Crown*.
Liverpool Record Office: MS. KF 49.

SKELTON, Joseph, of Crookes, Sheffield, [?] manual worker.
Diaries, 1826–30, 1833–36, and 1840–48. 5 vols.
Contents: brief notes of local events; births, deaths, marriages.
Sheffield City Libraries: Dept. of Local History and Archives, misc. doc. 2064.

TAYLOR, J., of Sutton-on-Trent.
Diary, 1826–93 (with gaps). 1 vol.
Contents: family and local events.
Nottinghamshire Records Office: MS. DD 164.

WALDIE, John.
Diaries, 1826–27, 1859–60, and 1860–62. 3 vols.
Contents: first journal includes a tour of Scotland; later ones include visits to English collieries, comments on the coal trade, etc.
Scottish Record Office: GD 1/378/30–32.

WEBB, Thomas William (1807–1885), of Tretire, Herefordshire.
Diary, 1826–40.
Contents: details of a student's studies in natural science; diarist's astronomical studies.
Herefordshire Public Library: MS. Local coll. 920.

D*

[?] WEDGEWOOD, Thomas.
  Diary, Dec., 1826–March, 1828.
  Contents: journal of an officer serving in Portugal under General Sir
  William Clinton; military duties; social life; Portuguese scenery and
  society.
  Private: Miss E. M. Allen, Inchdene, Woodchester, Stroud, Gloucester-
  shire.

WIX, Edward (1802–1866), of Newfoundland.
  Diaries, June, 1826. 2 vols.
  Contents: chief author may well be Wix, a member of Trinity College,
  Oxford, afterwards Archdeacon; one copy is marked in his name, and the
  other "F.B. from E.W. . . ." and "Fanny Browne from a sincere and
  affectionate friend, June 11th, 1826". The headings appear to be the same
  in the two volumes, and the entries independent.
  Oxford, Balliol College Library: MSS. 435 (Acquired 1887).

WOLLEY, Mr. [——] (d. Aug., 1826), of Clifton, near Bristol.
  Diary, 1826. 1 vol.
  Contents: pocket journal kept up to his death, and continued spasmodi-
  cally by his widow. The family let their house at Clifton and lived in
  Boulogne; weather; arrival of pacquets recorded; weekly cash account.
  In March he returned to England staying in London and Bristol. In July
  the family moved to Brussels, Liege, Aix, Namur, and back to Brussels
  where diarist died.
  Greater London Record Office (Middlesex Records): MS. Acc. 611/5.

1827

ANON., of Llanelly and later of Richmond, Surrey.
  Diary, 1827–31 (with gaps). 1 vol.
  Contents: journal of journeys in France, Belgium, Holland, and
  Germany; some personal matters while at home.
  Scottish Record Office: GD 35–171.

ANON.
  Diary, 1827. 1 vol.
  Contents: journal of tours in England and Scotland.
  Private: Sir John Laurie, Bart., C.B.E., D.S.O., Maxwelton, Moniave,
  Dumfries.

ANON.
  Diary, 1827. 1 vol.
  Contents: few entries in Marshall's *Gentleman's Pocket Book*, with
  miscellaneous printed information.
  Liverpool Record Office: Tarleton Papers, 65.

ANDERSON, Sir Charles John Henry (1804–1891), of Lea by Gainsborough,
  Lincs., last baronet and landowner.

Diaries, 1827–Oct., 1844.

Contents: include a tour abroad with Samuel (later Bishop) Wilberforce, 1827, to Switzerland, Germany, and Italy; local matters and politics (Tory); sports, hunting, shooting, and cricket; farming and stock sales; magistrates' meetings; yeomanry; local societies (architecture and archaeology); visits to Wilberforce and family estates.

Lincolnshire Archives Office: MSS. And. 5/2/2. (Acquired 1955).

Francis Hill, "Squire & Parson in Early Victorian Lincolnshire", *History* 58, No. 194 (Oct., 1973), 340f.

BLACKETT, Sir Edward (sixth baronet).

Diaries, 1827–41, 1847–58, 1864–68, and 1873–75.

Northumberland Record Office: Blackett (Matfen) MSS., ZBL 266. (Acquired 1963).

CURLING, Edward Spencer.

Diary, 1827–37.

Contents: journal of Continental travel; apparently a government official; brief account and quotations.

Notes & Queries, 2nd. ser., X (1860), 266.

DOUGHTY, Sir Edward.

Diary, 1827–28.

Private: Capt. J. B. E. Radcliffe, M.C., Rudding Park, Harrogate, Yorkshire.

FECTOR, J. M.

Diary, 1827.

Contents: journal of a tour through parts of Scotland.

Private: Sir John Laurie, Bart., C.B.E., D.S.O., Maxwelton, Moniave, Dumfries.

GREGOR, Gordon William Francis (1789–1865), landowner, of Trewarthenick, near Truro, Cornwall.

Diaries, 1827, 1829, 1830–32, 1851, 1857, 1859–60, and 1863. 8 vols.

Contents: mostly brief jottings, letters sent, the weather, some accounts; commonplace book on business affairs.

Cornwall County Record Office: MSS. DD.G 1953/1–8.

HOWICK, Henry George Grey, Viscount (1802–1894), of Howick Hall, Northumberland, statesman.

Diaries, Aug., 1827–July, 1871 (with gap 1830–33). 28 vols.

Contents: political and personal comment.

Durham University, Dept. of Palaeography: MSS. C2/1–C3/22.

LAPIDGE, Charles H., of Hampton Wick, Middlesex, ex-naval officer.

Diary, Feb., 1827–March, 1829.

Contents: irregular and scrappy entries of little value.

Wigan Central Public Library: Edward Hall coll.

LAURIE, Admiral Sir Robert.

Diary, 1827–31.

Private: Sir John Laurie, Bart., C.B.E., D.S.O., Maxwelton, Moniave, Dumfries.

LLOYD, Captain.
Diary, 1827.
Contents: journal of a tour made through parts of England and Wales.
National Library of Wales: MS. 786A.

MAKERSY, Lindsay, of Edinburgh, accountant.
Diary, Feb., 1827–June, 1834. 1 vol.
Contents: social events, including a dinner when Scott acknowledged *Waverley*; social life in Edinburgh; public events and local politics; lectures and amusements; theatres; his business.
National Library of Scotland: MS. 192.

MARTIN-LEAKE, (——), a female member of household at Marshalls, Standon, Hertfordshire.
Diaries, 1827–60. 34 vols.
Contents: commonplace events: family, walks, church, calls, dinner, weather etc; brief entries in printed diaries.
Hertford County Record Office: MSS. 85809–85842.

MOORSOM, Sir Robert, admiral.
Diary, 1827.
Contents: journal kept while serving in Canada.
National Maritime Museum: Moorsom papers.

MORAN, Edward Raleigh, of "The Globe", journalist.
Diary, Jan., 1827–36. 1 vol.
Contents: anecdotes and reminiscences; Dublin and Ireland, with visits to London and Paris; literary antiquarian; social notes; journalism; his dreams; law cases; literary friends and anecdotes.
London, British Museum: MS. Egerton coll. 2156.

OWEN, Sir Richard (1804–1892), K.C.B., F.R.S., Conservator of Hunterian Museum, Royal College of Surgeons of England; anatomist.
Diary, 1827–30. 1 vol.
Contents: journal and notes of his life and work as Assistant Conservator at the R.C.S.
London, Royal College of Surgeons Library: MS. Add. Owen.

PAMPLIN, W., of Battersea, Surrey.
Diary, 1827–41.
Contents: private notes kept at Battersea.
Private: Rev. D. H. Ruddy, M.A., Longworth Rectory, Abingdon, Berkshire.

PARKER, George.
Diary, 1827–33.
Liverpool Record Office: Arch. 920 PAR II.

PARSONS, John.
Diaries, 1827 and 1831.

Oxford, Bodleian Library: MS. d.d. Parsons d. 1–3. (Acquired 1953).

RAMSAY, Lord George.

Diary, 1827. 1 vol.

Contents: journal kept during a tour of France, Switzerland, Italy, Austria, Germany, and the Netherlands.

Scottish Record Office: GD 45/26/86.

RUDDY family.

Diaries, several from 1827 onwards.

Private: Rev. D. H. Ruddy, M.A., Longworth Rectory, Abingdon, Berkshire.

SANDWICH, Lord.

Diaries, 1827 and 1841–65.

Contents: pocket diaries; as a boy at Eton in 1827.

Private: Lord Hinchingbrooke, Mapperton, Dorset.

SMITH, Frederick Culling, aide-de-camp.

Diary, 1827. 131 fols.

Contents: sea journey from Falmouth to Lisbon; expedition with Sir H. F. Bouverie; his service in Portugal, and notes on political events at home and in Portugal.

University of Leeds, Brotherton Library: MS. 36.

TARLETON, Thomas.

Diary, 1827–31.

Contents: life in India; manuscript apparently compiled from his letters.

Liverpool Record Office: Tarleton Papers, 63.

WALKER, Lieutenant Bethune James.

Diary, 1827.

Contents: naval journey of a voyage in H.M.S. *Astrea.*

Private: Walker-Morison MSS. (Present location unknown).

WHITWELL, Thomas (1814–1828), of Darlington, Co. Durham.

Diary, Sept., 1827–Jan., 1828 (extracts).

Contents: notes of a schoolboy on his schooling and sports; some notes on Quaker meetings.

Journal Friends' Hist. Soc., XXIV (1927), pp. 21–30.

WOODS (presumed WOOD), H. H.

Diaries, 1827–28 and 1842.

Contents: earlier journal is of a tour of Switzerland; later volume is of a European tour, the Low Countries, Germany, Central Europe, Italy, Greece, and Constantinople.

Hampshire Record Office: MSS. 4M57/16, 4M51/395, 396.

1828

ANON.

Diary, April–May, 1828. 1 vol.

Contents: journal of a holiday in Dorset and Devon by a recently

widowed woman ; some interesting social comment.
Devon County Library: MSS.
ANON.
Diary, Dec., 1828–Dec., 1829. 1 vol.
Contents: concern with the activities of M. T. Sadler, M.P. for Newark
and Aldborough ; contains an account of the Newark election of 1829.
Leeds Public Libraries: MS. 923.25 A15L.
ANON.
Diaries, 1828–69. 6 vols.
Contents: notes of the consulate general ; calendar of documents relating
to Algiers.
London, Public Record Office: MSS. F.O. 113, Misc.
ALLEN, Ebenezer Brown (1804–1880), cleric.
Diaries, 1828–80. 4 vols.
Contents: social life ; an interest in Dukes ; personal reflections of man
who lived in a variety of places: Clapham, Durham, Goodshaw and
Bacup (Lancs.), Chatham, and London.
York City Libraries: Arch. Dept., Acc. 100.
ANGIER, John (b. 1764), of Coton, Cambs., a farmer.
Diary, Oct., 1828–Sept., 1831. 1 vol.
Contents: brief notes on farming ; naturalist and domestic memoranda ;
not used daily.
Cambridgeshire Record Office: MS. R58/9/4/2.
AYRE, Burrell, of Liverpool and Stoneham, Herts.
Diary, 1828–34. 1 vol.
Contents: sea journal of voyages at different seasons.
Cheshire Record Office: MS DWS 23/1.
BAWER, George, of Sheffield, wine and spirit merchant.
Diary, Jan., 1828–Dec., 1829. 168 pp.
Contents: record of his personal history, business details, and local events ;
chiefly interesting for prices of wine.
Sheffield City Libraries: Sheffield coll. B.B288 S.
BUCKINGHAM, Richard, 1st. Duke (1797–1861), of Stowe, Bucks.
Diary, Aug–Nov., 1828. 53 pp.
Contents: journal describing travel in Switzerland, Germany, and France.
Buckinghamshire Record Office: MS. D/54/44.
COCKERELL, Maria.
Diary, 1828.
Contents: journal of travels on the Continent.
Herefordshire Record Office: MSS.
GUTHRIE, Robert, R.N., surgeon.
Diaries, 1828–29, 1829–32. 2 vols.
Contents: journals kept in H.M.S. *Undaunted*, in which Lord William
Benbrick booked a passage to India.

National Maritime Museum: JOD 16, 17, MSS., 54/Oll a & b.

LEVER, Charles James (1806–1872), novelist.
Diary, 1828.
Contents: kept by him during his stay at Gottingen University; student life at the university; extracts in prose and poetry from French and German literature; pencil drawings of scenery and castles on the Rhine.
Dublin, Royal Irish Academy: MS. SR. 3. B. 52.

LYELL, Charles, banker.
Diary, 1828–29.
Contents: brief entries by father of Sir Charles Lyell (1797–1875).
India Office Library: MSS. Eur. C. 209.

[?] MACLANE, E.
Diary, Sept., 1828–May, 1830. 1 vol.
Manchester Public Libraries: Arch. Dept., MS. 942.72 R010.

MARGRATH, Edward (d. 1855), secretary of the Athenaeum Club.
Diary, 1828.
Contents: tour through Burgundy, Dauphiny, Savoy, Piedmont, northern Italy, Carinthia, and Tyrol; return via Switzerland and Paris.
London, Athenaeum Club.

MONTEITH, Col. W. (1790–1864).
Diary, Aug., 1828–June, 1829.
Contents: journal of a tour through Azerdbijan and the shores of the Caspian Sea.
India Office Library: MSS. Eur. B. 25.
Journal of the Royal Geog. Soc. Vol. III (1833), 1–58.

MOORSOM, Capt. William Scarth (1804–1863), railway engineer.
Diaries, July–Sept., 1828. 2 vols.
Contents: journal from Halifax, Nova Scotia, via Portland, New York, Philadelphia, Rochester, and Niagara; another of journey from Kingston, Ontario, to Nova Scotia.
India Office Library: MSS. Eur. E. 299. (On Loan).

PARSONS, Christopher (1807–1882), of North Shoebury Hall, Southend, gentleman.
Diaries, 1828–82. 55 vols.
Contents: Private and local interests in brief entries; usually there is little more than a note on the weather under each printed date; notes on natural history; personal engagements.
Southend-on-sea Central Public Library: MS. 63/921. (L. Helliwell, Borough Librarian).

RODD, Rev. Edward (1768–1842), Rector of St. Just-in-Roseland (1836–42) and squire of Trebartha, Northill, Cornwall.
Diary, 1828. 1 vol.
Contents: personal and family matters.

Cornwall County Record Office: MSS. AD.360/21.
Bryan Latham, *Trebartha, The House By The Stream* (1971).
RODD, Col. Francis (1806–1880), squire of Trebartha, Northill (1842–80).
Diaries, 1828, 1834, 1866. 3 vols.
Contents: first journal kept at Cambridge University; for middle one he was in London; finally one kept at Trebartha.
Cornwall County Record Office: MSS. AD.360/22–24.
Bryan Latham, *Trebartha, The House By The Stream* (1971).
RUSHOUT, Hon. Anne (?1791–1845), daughter of Baron Northwick, Northwick Park, Worcs.
Diaries, 1828–52 (with gaps). 20 vols.
Contents: early volumes are of a spiritual nature; later ones give accounts of travels in the British Isles, the Channel Islands, and abroad.
University of London Library: MSS. 682.
Private: Geoffrey Bright Esq., Hereford. (1 undated volume).
Geoffrey Bright, *Trans. Radnorshire Soc.* XXVIII (1958), 7–10.
STANLEY, [?] John Thomas.
Diary, July–Sept., 1828.
Contents: tour from Bordeaux; journey to the Pyrenees; tourist's notes on scenery, etc; personal experiences.
Manchester, John Rylands Library: Eng. MS. 1090.
STURT, Charles, explorer of central Australia.
Diaries and letters, 1828–29, 1829–30, and 1844–46. 2 vols.
Contents: journals of his three expeditions of discovery into the interior of Southern and Central Australia.
Oxford, Rhodes House Library: MSS. Austr. S. 4–9.
Geoffrey Dutton, *The Hero as Murderer: the Life of Edward John Eyre* (London, 1967).
TROTTER, Henrietta (née Skerne), of Bishop Auckland, Co. Durham.
Diaries, 1828–29, 1843–54, and n.d. 3 vols.
Durham County Record Office: MSS. D/X 277/1–3.
WILDMAN, Abraham (d. 1870), of Keighley, Yorkshire, wool comber, poet.
Diary, Jan–April, 1828. 26 pp.
Contents: journal of a working man on his hilarious course towards improvident marriage on nothing but hope; radical sympathies; some versifying.
Wigan Central Public Library: Edward Hall coll.

1829

ANON.
Diary, 1829.
Contents: journal of a tour of France and Italy.
East Riding of Yorkshire County Record Office: MS. DDLA/38/11.

ANON., (of Birmingham).
Diary, 1829–37.
Contents: notes of Birmingham manufacturer; business, social, domestic.
Midland Antiquary, IV (1885), 131–132.

ANON.
Diary, 1829.
Contents: journal of a Continental tour.
East Riding of Yorkshire County Record Office: MS. DDLA/38/12.

ANON., an officer.
Diary, 1829.
Contents: journal of a regimental officer.
India Office Library: MSS. Eur. A. 29.

ANON.
Diary, 1829.
Contents: journal of voyage from Leith to the Cape of Good Hope.
Scottish Record Office: GD 38/1/1228.

ANON.
Diary, June, 1829–Feb., 1830. 252 pp.
Contents: tour made from Tottenham, Middlesex, to Scotland, the Lakes,
and Derbyshire; scenery, buildings, topography.
St. Andrews University Library, Scotland: MS. DA625. J7E29.

APLIN, Capt. Christopher D'Oyley, a soldier.
Diary, Dec., 1829–Oct., 1831.
Contents: journal kept in India while serving with the Bengal Native
Infantry.
India Office Library: MSS. Eur. B. 208.

BRANDLING, Charles John (1797–1856), of Gosforth.
Diary, 1829–30. 1 vol.
Contents: journal of a visit to France and Italy.
Northumberland County Record Office: Brandling of Gosforth MSS.
NRO 233, ZBG 23.

BROOKS, John Thomas (1794–1858), of Flitwick Manor House, Bedford-
shire, Deputy Lieutenant of the County.
Diaries, 1829–58 (with gaps). 4 vols.
Contents: family and local matters; some religious concerns.
Bedfordshire Record Office: MSS. LL 17/280/1–5, 17/281–283.

BROWSE, Nicholas, of West Combe, Stoke Fleming, Devonshire.
Diaries, May–July, 1829 and Aug–Dec., 1830. 2 vols.
Contents: farming details.
Exeter City Record Office: MSS.

COLE, Lady Frances, wife of Sir Galbraith Lowry Cole, and younger
daughter of the Earl and Countess of Malmesbury.
Diaries, Jan., 1829–Oct., 1833. 2 vols.

Contents: kept when she was with her husband at Cape Colony; mostly travel notes.

London, Public Record Office: MSS. 30/43/114–115. (Acquired 1936–38).

CONSTABLE, Lady Clifford.

Diaries, June–Aug., and June–Sept., 1829 (? two versions of the same tour).

Contents: tour of Belgium, and Belgium and Germany. There is a further travel journal without date.

East Riding of Yorkshire County Record Office: MSS. DDCC/150/278, 279, 281.

COZENS, Miss E. (? Elizabeth) "Lisinka".

Diary, Oct., 1829–Jan., 1833 (with gaps). 1 vol.

Contents: journal of stay at Cape Colony with Sir Lowry and Lady Cole.

London, Public Record Office: MS. 30/43/121.

FINLAY, George (1799–1875), historian.

Diary, June, 1829–46.

Contents: account and quotations; notes on political and social affairs in Greece.

English Hist. Rev., XLI (1926).

GALTON, Samuel Tertius.

Diaries, 1829–44. 15 vols.

Contents: social, family news, short journeys; written in his own shorthand (key available). Transcript by L. M. Carey.

London, University College Library: MSS. Galton II, 81.

GREEN, Edward Humphreys (1799–1868), assumed name De Freville in 1850; of Hinxton Hall, Cambs., landowner and Major in the Cambridgeshire Militia.

Diaries, Jan., 1829–Jan., 1868 (with gaps). 30 vols.

Contents: little more than itineraries and notes of appointments; much foreign travel, particularly in France, but later more matters concerning relatives in Hinxton.

Cambridgeshire Record Office: MSS. R57/24/13(d)3.

GROSS, Samuel (d. 1836), of Pettistree, Suffolk, yeoman farmer.

Diary, 1829–32.

Contents: personal and farming affairs; family and local matters; farming at Pettistree and Whitton, Suffolk.

Ipswich Public Library: MS. S1/8/3.1.

HÉKÉKYAN BEY, Joseph (b. 1807), engineer.

Diary, May, 1829–Jan., 1830, and autobiography (1807–41).

Contents: tour through England; architectural and engineering notes; bridges, canals, roads, harbours; applicability to Egypt.

London, British Museum: Mdd. MS. 27448.

JACSON, Rev. Roger (b. 1753 or 1754), of Bebington, Wirral Peninsular, Cheshire.
Diary, March, 1829–Oct., 1837. 12 vols. Diary and accounts, 1847–55.
Contents: personal and domestic events at Bebington and at Barton, near Preston ; chiefly local interest.
Lancashire County Record Office: MSS. DX 267–278.

LEYLAND, John (1813–1883), of Hindley, Lancashire, gentleman.
Diaries, Sept., 1829–Sept., 1882. 2 vols.
Contents: local events and personalities ; much about travels in England and Continent, especially to cathedral cities ; church antiquities.
Hindley, Lancashire: Leyland Free Library.

LLOYD, Edward Harvey.
Diaries, 1829–69.
National Library of Wales: Aston Hall MSS. 4799–4820.

LOVEJOY, George (1808–1883), of Reading, Berks., bookseller.
Diary, July, 1829–May, 1834. 1 vol.
Contents: record of his early struggles to establish himself in business— he was proprietor of the Southern Counties Library ; his courtship of Martha Wilkinson of Wallingford whom he married in September, 1834.
Reading Public Library: MS. R/TU/LOV.

LYALL family.
Diaries, 1829–81. 11 vols.
Bedfordshire Record Office: Lyall Papers.

MacDONALD, Sir John.
Diary, 1829–30 (extracts).
Contents: private matters.
London, Public Record Office: MS. 30/9/4 Part 1–5.

MARTIN, Rev. Robert.
Diary, 1829–34 (with gaps).
Contents: journal of tours made when he was an undergraduate on vacation ; Wales, Ireland, Isle of Man, Scotland, Derbyshire, Isle of Wight, Channel Islands, etc.
Leicestershire Record Office: MS. DG6/C/13.

MENDELSSOHN, Felix Bartholdy (1809–1847), composer.
Diaries and notebooks, May, 1829–May, 1847. 10 vols.
Contents: brief diary entries mostly ; drafts of music ; verses ; accounts ; memoranda noting contents of programmes, lists of books ; addresses.
Oxford, Bodleian Library: MSS. Mendelssohn g. 1–10.

MORRIS, Lewis, of Carmarthen, S. Wales, lawyer.
Diaries, 1829, 1834–36, and 1855.
Carmarthenshire County Record Office: Museum 297–300, 306.

MURPHY, Thomas, docker.
Diary, 1829–79 (selections).

Contents: notes on working conditions, wages, holidays, ship launchings, general events.

Life and Letters Today, XXX (1941), 7–18.

PARKER, John Oxley, of Woodham Mortimer, land-agent.
Diaries and day-books, 1829–98. (microfilm)
Essex Record Office: T/B 225.
The Oxley Parker Papers: from the Letters and Diaries of an Essex Family of Land Agents in the Nineteenth Century (Colchester: Benham, 1964).

PENN, William, of Clifford, Stratford-upon-Avon.
Diary, Jan., 1829–Dec., 1833. 1 vol.
Contents: mainly business matters, many of which took the diarist to Birmingham.
Birmingham University Library: MS. 13/i/12.

RAMSAY, Col., a soldier.
Diaries, 1829.
Contents: books kept on voyage of the ship *Pallas* from Spithead to Calcutta.
Scottish Record Office: GD 45/5/18.

SALVIN, Edward John (1810–1829), of Croxdale Hall, Co. Durham.
Diary, 1829 (part only). 1 vol.
Contents: part of a journal written when diarist was in George Stephenson's office, working as an assistant to the railway builder in Liverpool.
Durham County Record Office: MS. D/Sa/F/313. (Deposited 1964).

SCOTT, Samuel.
Diary, 1829.
Contents: journal of private interests; this MS. is included among diaries of his cousin, John Barber Scott of Bungay.
Ipswich Central Library: MS.

SHAW, George (b. 1810), of Saddleworth, Yorkshire, architect, antiquarian, woollen manufacturer.
Diaries, Jan., 1829–Aug., 1835 and July–Aug., 1848. 4 vols.
Contents: records of daily events and journeys made in some detail; notes on his father's business, textile manufacturing; his reading; drawing and painting; walking tours in Lancashire, Derbyshire, and Cheshire; Scottish business trips; scenery and architecture, halls and castles; family events.
Saddleworth Central Library, Yorkshire: Irad Hewkin coll. MS. 49, 50.
Manchester Central Library: Reference Library has 1848 volumes and some covering 1829–35, MS. 927.2 S15.

SHEPPARD, Mrs. Susan (1810–1896), of Frome, Somerset.
Diaries, 1829–32 (with gaps). 4 vols.

Contents: journals of holiday tours in Lake District, Wales, Cornwall, and Scotland ; travel conditions.

Private: M.S. Money-Kyrle Esq., 70 Belmont Road, Hereford.

THOMAS, Edward (1805–1862), of Sandon, Staffs., schoolmaster and parish clerk.

Diaries, 1829–62 (with gaps). 19 vols.

Contents: little written about the school ; religiosity ; references to local and national affairs ; longwinded.

Staffordshire Record Office: MSS.

1830

ANON.

Diary, 1830–42. 1 vol.

Contents: journal of farming matters at Hengrove Farm, near Margate.

Kent Archives Office: MS. U.36, E144 (Smithett Estate).

ANON.

Diary, June, 1830–Feb., 1831. 56 fols.

Contents: notes on fishing in the Thames.

Oxford, Bodleian Library: MS. Eng. Misc. e. 89.

ANON.

Diary, 1830.

Contents: log of *Madagascar* cruise.

Plymouth Public Library: MS. Acc. 216.

ANON.

Diary, 1839–43. 1 vol.

Contents: diary from the British vice-consulate in North Africa.

London, Public Record Office: MS. F.O. 635.

ANON.

Diary, April–June, 1830 and April–June, 1836. 1 vol.

Contents: journal of two voyages made as a passenger ; from Demerara, British Guiana, to London on the ship *Reliance*, 1830 ; from Port Glasgow to Demerara on the ship *Leguan*.

National Maritime Museum: JOD 77, MS60/0.

BAKER, Colonel George.

Diary, March, 1830–July, 1835 (with gaps).

Contents: journal kept while diarist was British representative on the Greek Boundary Commission ; statistical notes on Malta ; letters written and received ; sketch-map of the Dardanelles showing gun batteries ; visits, Athens, July–Aug., 1835.

Oxford, Bodleian Library: MS. Dep. e. 52–59 and c. 270d. (Acquired 1966).

BEST, James John, Lieutenant in the 62nd. Regiment of Foot.

Diary, 1830–Jan., 1831. 1 vol.

Contents: journal of a voyage to India in the East India Company ship *Henry Porcher*, under Captain G. J. Redman; from June onwards notes on his life and military duties.

National Maritime Museum: JOD 50, MS56/007.

CURZON, Hon. R.

Diary, 1830.

Private: formerly owned by the late Hon. Clive Pearson of Parham, Sussex.

LAW, Elizabeth (later wife of 2nd. Lord Colchester).

Diary, 1830.

Contents: journal of tour of the West Country; included a list (in French) of semi-precious stones and their influences.

London, Public Record Office: MS. 30/9 3 Part II (Colchester Papers).

MAXSE, Lady Caroline Fitzhardinge, (née Kingscote) (d. 1886), of Dunley Hill Dorking, Surrey.

Diaries, 1830–84. 43 vols.

Contents: not detailed.

West Sussex County Record Office: MSS. Maxse 90–132.

M[ELLISH], R. C., of Hodsock Priory, Nottinghamshire.

Diary, 1830. 1 vol.

Contents: narrative journal of a journey from Constantinople to Semlin.

Nottingham University Library: Mellish coll., Me 185–124. 10

PARSONS, William (1809–1881), of Nottingham, solicitor and member of the borough council.

Diaries, 1830–71. 8 vols.

Contents: mainly personal and family matters.

Nottingham University Library: Parsons coll. (uncatalogued).

PRICE, Henry Edward (1824–c. 1908/9), of Islington and various addresses, Warminster, Bristol, and America, a cabinet maker.

Diary, c. 1830–1904. 1 vol.

Contents: begins in the style of reminiscence with his childhood; his working life; a visit to America, 1842–48; household expenditure, and day-to-day accounts.

London, Islington Central Library: MS. YX PRI 66342.

British Association for American Studies have microfilmed MS. E. A. Willats, *Islington Gazette* (17 June, 1966), (24 June, 1966).

PRINCE, Miss Elizabeth W. (b. 1805), of Liverpool.

Diary, May, 1830–April, 1931. 96 pp.

Contents: religious life of a Sunday school teacher, which develops into a thwarted romance; sermons by Rev. Charles Swain, her unfortunate affection for whom was wasted; included a trip to Wales.

Wigan Central Public Library: Edward Hall coll.

RATHBONE, Miss Kate F. P., of Dunsinea, near Dublin.

Diary, c. 1830–c. 1840. 40 pp.

Contents: diarist was favourite niece of Sir William Rowan Hamilton, the mathematician; notes of his lessons to her in algebra and astronomy; expenses.

Private: F. E. Dixon Esq., 15 Morehampton Road, Donnybrook, Dublin.

RIDLEY, Matthew White, 4th. Bart. (1807–1870), of Blagdon.

Diary, 1830. 1 vol.

Contents: two journals of travels in Germany and Italy.

Northumberland County Record Office: Ridley of Blagdon MSS., NRO 138, ZRI 32/5.

ROLLS, Martha (d. 1858), wife of John Rolls.

Diaries, 1830 and 1840. 2 vols.

Contents: earlier one contains very brief entries; family matters, husband's illness, etc.; visits to the opera or play; later volume is barely used.

Monmouthshire Record Office: Rolls MSS. D361 F/P3.

ROUMIEU, J. F., of London.

Diaries, 1830–32.

Contents: accounts of his life and society in London.

Derbyshire Record Office: 104M/E71–74.

SAUNDERS, William Wilson, (1809–1897), F.R.S., of Wandsworth and Reigate, a naturalist.

Diaries, Aug., 1830– July, 1840 (with gaps). 8 vols.

Contents: early journal of a voyage from England to Calcutta aboard the *Duke of Bedford*; occasional observations of birds and insects, charts; meteorological observations for April, 1833 and subsequent times in later years; many misc. sheets torn from later pocket diaries.

Buckinghamshire Record Office: Saunders MSS. (On loan).

SCOTT, Charles (d. 1841), of the Foreign Office.

Diaries, Sept., 1830–Sept., 1841 (with gaps).

Contents: mostly notes on social engagements; European and Asiatic travels; dinners with Lockhart.

National Library of Scotland: MSS. 1614–1622.

TORR family, of Wreyland, Devonshire.

Diaries, 1830–80.

Contents: small rough notebooks giving details of journeys to Europe.

Exeter City Record Office: 4 box files.

TOWNSEND, Joseph, of Wood End, Great Marlow, Bucks., a farmer and surveyor.

Diaries, 1830–31. 2 vols.

Contents: brief daily entries; some references to activities in connection with parliamentary enclosures.

Buckinghamshire Record Office: Townsend Papers D.85.

VIGNOLES, Charles Blacker (1793–1875), civil engineer.

Diaries, 1830–62. 10 vols.

Contents: notes on the building of the Dublin and Kingston Railway,

and other railway and engineering projects in the British Isles and abroad.
London, British Museum: Add. MSS. 35071, 34528–34536.
Olynthus J. Vignoles, *Life of C. B. Vignoles* (London, 1889).
WESTMACOTT, George Edward (d. 1841).
Diary, 1830. 533pp.
Contents: journal of travels in India: accounts of places visited, anecdotes; notes on historical, literary, and natural history matters; customs of the country: Saharanpore, Mussooree, Landoor, Ambala, the unsettled state of Oude.
India Office Library: MSS. Eur. C. 29.
WILBERFORCE, Rt. Rev. Samuel (1805–1873), Bishop of Oxford.
Diaries, 1830–73.
Contents: notes on his parish work at Brighton, and on his work and administration as bishop of Oxford; his travels, visits, reading, sermons, ecclestiastical disputes, conversations with Gladstone; his visits to court; brief and hurried jottings which are best on his domestic life.
Oxford, Bodleian Library: MSS. Wilberforce Dep. c. 186. (Deposited 1956).
A. R. Ashwell, *Life of Samuel Wilberforce*, 3 vols. (London, 1880).
WILKINSON, Martha (Mrs. George Lovejoy), of Wallingford, Berks.
Diaries, Nov., 1830–Aug., 1834. 2 vols.
Contents: record of uneventful family life during her engagement to George Lovejoy of Reading, a bookseller, whom she married in Sept., 1834.
Reading Public Library: MSS. coll.

1831

ANON.
Diary, 1831.
Contents: journal kept while resident in Scotland.
Scottish Record Office: GD 38/1/1228.
ANON.
Diaries, 1831 and 1835.
Northumberland Record Office: Blackett (Matfen) MSS. ZBL 266. (Acquired 1963)
ANON.
Diary, 1831. 1 vol.
Contents: possibly kept by a member of the Twisden family.
Kent Archives Office: MS. Twisden U49 F20.
ALNUTT, Mrs., of Sevenoaks, Kent.
Diary, 1831–32.
Contents: domestic and topographical; Sevenoaks and Kent.
Sevenoaks Public Library: MS. L. 770.

BENSON, Edward White (senior).
Diaries, 1831–41. 3 vols.
Contents: diarist was the father of Archbishop Benson.
Oxford, Bodleian Library: MSS. Benson coll. 1/64–66.

BORRODAILE, Ann (b. 1812), married Richard Sale.
Diary, July–Oct., 1831. 1 vol.
Contents: journal of a journey from London to Workington and back.
Manchester Public Libraries: Arch. Dept., MS. 942 B270.

BUTTERWORTH, Edwin.
Diary, 1831–36.
Contents: journal of excursions in Lancashire to collect historical information.
Manchester Public Library: Dept. of Local History, Giles Shaw MS.

COKE, Edward, of the 45th. Regiment.
Diaries, 1831–32. 3 vols.
Contents: diarist in Bengal (India) and Cape of Good Hope, South Africa.
Private: Mrs. R. Coke-Steel, Trusley Old Hall, Sutton-on-the-Hill, Derbyshire.

COOKE, Miss Isabella (d. 1904), daughter of Sir William Bryan Cooke of Wheatley.
Diaries, June, 1831, 1839–40, July, 1855–March, 1861. 3 vols.
Contents: journal of a visit to Edinburgh, 20–27 June, ascribed to this diarist; journal of journey to Madeira, Spain, and Portugal, 1839–40; final volume has entries on personal and social life.
Northumberland County Record Office: Middleton of Belsay MSS. NRO 79, ZMI B33/41–43.

DOYLE, Sir Charles William.
Diary, 1831.
Contents: journal of a voyage to Canada.
Oxford, Bodleian Library: MS. North d. 63 (ff3–28).

FERGUSON, G.
Diary, Oct.–Dec., 1831.
Contents: small pocket-book, less than half-filled with entries.
Cambridge, Trinity College Library: MS. Add. d. 77. (Acquired 1969).

FITZGIBBON, Mary, second wife of Lieut. Richmond Allen FitzGibbon (c.1805–1871).
Diaries, 1831–61.
India Office Library: MSS. Eur. B. 205.

FOX, George Townshend IInd., of Durham.
Diary, 1831–37. 1 vol.
Contents: journal kept in America.
South Shields Central Library: Fox coll.

FRASER, C., an official in Revenue Dept. at Sangor, India.
Diary, Jan., 1831–Jan., 1833.
Contents: journal of itineraries from Sangor, to Agra, the hills Mansooree; people met; notes on temperature.
India Office Library: MSS. Eur. E. 97.

GROSS, Samuel Chilton (d. 1844), of Alderton, Suffolk, yeoman farmer.
Diary, 1831–42. 1 vol.
Contents: farming and personal matters; chiefly concerned with farming at Alderton and Hollesley, Suffolk; local events.
Ipswich and East Suffolk Record Office: MS. SI/8/3.2.

HALFORD, Sir Henry, Bart. (1766–1844), of Mayfair, London, and Wistow Hall, Leicestershire, a physician.
Diaries, Nov., 1831–May, 1834. 3 vols.
Contents: accounts of his professional and social life; reminiscences; little personal information.
Leicestershire Record Office: MSS. DG 24.
J McAlpine and R. Hunter, *George III and the Mad Business* (London, 1969). W. Munk, *The Life of Sir Henry Halford* (London, 1895).

HILL, H.
Diary, Aug.–Sept., 1831.
Contents: brief notes of a tour in Ireland, visiting Cork.
Journal Cork Hist. & Archaeol. Soc., XXXVIII (1933), 30–37.

HIRST, Samuel, of Kellington, near Knottingley, Yorkshire.
Diary, 1831–80.
Contents: farming notes; his work as farmer and valuer.
Private: Mark Poskitt Esq., The Firs, Kellington, Yorkshire.

HOBHOUSE, Charlotte.
Diary, 1831–46.
Private: Sir Charles C. Hobhouse, Pondsmead, Oakhill, Somerset.
Wiltshire Record Office: (on loan).

KEITH, Mrs. Margaret E.J.C.A., of Ravelston.
Diary, Jan., 1831–Aug., 1847. 479 fols.
Contents: her religious life and thoughts; prayers; family life and friends; domestic work.
National Library of Scotland: MS. 984.

MALCOM, Sir John, a Major-General.
Diary, 1831.
Contents: journal of a journey from Alnwick to London.
India Office Library: Home Misc. 735/6.
Kaye, *Life and Correspondence of Major-General Sir John Malcolm* (London, 1856).

MILLS, Henry (1815–1906), of Barford.
Diaries, 1831, 1864, 1876–77, and 1888.

Contents: journal of tour in Wales, 1831; journey along the Fosse, 1864; some foreign tours in later years.

Stratford, The Shakespeare Birthplace Trust: DR 240/14–16.

NAYLOR, William Todd, of Liverpool.

Diary, in letter form, 16 Aug.–21 Sept., 1831. 1 vol.

Contents: voyage from Liverpool to New York in the ship, *Canada*; the letters were addressed to his mother.

Private: E. N. Constant Esq., Througham Place, Beaulieu, Hampshire.

Liverpool Record Office: Arch. 920 MD 147 Acc. 624 (Todd Naylor Papers). (Photostat copy)

PARKER, William, of Handthorpe, Grimsthorpe, Lincs.

Diaries, 1831–58. 3 vols.

Contents: journal of a diarist who was a magistrate, was on the board of guardians, Bourne drainage board, and a commissioner for the Blacksluice; notes on his stewardship of the Duke of Ancaster's estate.

Lincolnshire Record Office: Parker MSS., 32/2–4.

PATERSON, Lady Margaret, of Baring Place, Heavitree, Exeter.

Diary, 1831–35.

Contents: details about the family and the locality.

Exeter City Record Office: MS.

PATTISON, Rev. Mark (1813–1884), of Lincoln College, Oxford.

Diaries, June, 1831–April, 1884.

Contents: (i) student's diaries, June, 1831–79 (with gaps), records what he read and wrote initially; these form the basis of his published memoirs; also commonplace book and literary criticism; rest are largely engagement books; (ii) study journal, June, 1833–Oct., 1834, a record of his studies; (iii) accounts and diary, Sept.–Oct., 1855, an account of a tour in France and Germany; (iv) private diaries, March, 1843–April, 1884 (some overlapping), a consistent record of his reading and studies; critical opinions; notes on his literary friends and booksellers, Oxford academic and clerical life, Oxford social life, his own critical writings and literary journalism, his health and aspirations; travels abroad.

Oxford, Bodleian Library: Pattison coll. 1–32, 113, 115, 128–137.

PETTERAM, J., of London.

Diaries, 1831–35.

Contents: notes of a clerk.

Oxford, Bodleian Library: MSS. Lyell 38–9.

ROBINSON, Thomas.

Diaries, May, 1831–April, 1838. 14 vols.

East Riding of Yorkshire County Record Office: DDKV/74/2–15.

SALMON, J. D.

Diary, 1831.

Contents: record of a tour in the Orkney Islands.

Norwich Museum: MS.

112   *British Manuscript Diaries*   [1832

SHORE, Emily (1819–1839), of Brook House, Potton, Beds.
Diaries, July, 1831–June, 1839. 12 vols.
Contents: journal kept by a young girl; family and local matters.
Bedfordshire Record Office: MSS. CRT 180/32
Emily Shore's Journal (London: Kegan, Paul, Trench, Trubner, 1891).
D. Kitchener, *Bedfordshire Magazine*, III, 249
SIMMONDS, Peter.
Diary, 1831. 1 vol.
Contents: journal kept aboard H.M. Packet, *Mutine*, on a voyage from
Falmouth, Cornwall, to Jamaica.
National Maritime Museum: JOD 35, MS56/023.
TRAILL, Anne ([?]née Robertson).
Diary, 1831. (see also p. 20).
Contents: journal of a tour to Scotland.
Liverpool Record Office: Arch. 920 Par III.
WATERS, James.
Diary, 1831.
Contents: journal of travels.
London, British Museum: Add. MS. 52500. (Acquired 1964)
WILMORE, Miss Louisa E. (d. 1839), of Worcester and Clifford Place,
Hay-on-Wye.
Diary, 1831–37 (with prior autobiographical memoranda from 1814).
67 pp.
Contents: religious life of an invalid young lady, who later became the
wife of Rev. Edward Foley; mainly a record of the deaths of relatives
and friends; notes on accidents and God's providences; weather; excur-
sions; family matters.
Wigan Central Public Library: Edward Hall coll. M962.
WILSHERE, Charles Willis. (1814–1906), of Hitchen, Herts.
Diaries, Jan.–May, 1831 and Aug.–Sept., 1832. 2 vols.
Contents: full and connected entries: family, social, and religious
matters; books read, etc. Later journal of a leisure journey in France
and Switzerland (connected narrative).
Hertford County Record Office: MSS. 60153.

1832

ANON.
Diary, 1832–56 (with gaps).
Contents: personal jottings.
Worcester Record Office: MS. Ref. 705; 349 (Pakington MSS). (On loan
permanently since 1963).
ANON., a mariner.
Diary, Aug.–Nov., 1832. 1 vol.

Contents: journal of a voyage from Liverpool to Calcutta in the ship *Bland*, probably compiled by the captain.

India Office Library: MSS. Eur. D. 737/2.

ANON.

Diary, 1832–38. 1 vol.

Contents: entirely in shorthand ; Harding's system of shorthand.

University of London Library: Carlton MS. 17/7.

BADCOCK, Lieutentant-Colonel Lovell, of Andover, Hampshire.

Diary, July, 1832–April, 1834.

Contents: service in Portugal and Spain ; travel ; military life and war ; social and general conditions ; climate ; campaigns, attacks, bombardments of Peninsular War.

Rough Leaves from a Journal (London, 1835).

BAKER, Caroline Julia, wife of Colonel George Baker.

Diaries, Jan., 1832–May, 1836 (with gaps). 5 vols.

Contents: kept at various locations : in Balls Park, Hertfordshire, and Corfu, at Zacynthus ("Zante"), Nauplion ("Nauphlia"), Athens and London ; family news ; visits ; weather ; churches visited and sermons heard ; tourist's descriptions ; account of an earthquake at Piripimpi ; on voyage home, descriptions of Cadiz and Exeter.

Oxford, Bodleian Library: MSS. Dep. e. 60–64. (Acquired 1966).

BAKER, T. B. Lloyd, of Hardwicke Court, near Gloucester.

Diary, 1832–86 (with gaps).

Contents: personal affairs.

Private: Miss Olive K. Lloyd-Baker, C.B.E., Hardwicke Court, Gloucester.

Hardwicke Court MSS., Box 12 (b).

BARROW, Commander William, R.N., of London.

Diaries, 1832.

Contents: (i) 10 May–24 June, 1832 ; journal kept as Lieutenant on board H.M.S. *Belvedera* ; voyage around Cape Matapan ; eastern Mediterranean ; hints on seamanship ; (ii) 5 July–27 Aug., 1832, voyage from Plymouth, Malta, Marseilles, Dover.

Oxford, Bodleian Library: MSS. Eng. Misc. e. 85–86. (Acquired 1918).

BURTON, William, of Turnham Hill, near Selby, Yorkshire, gentleman farmer.

Diary, 1832–34.

Contents: notes on farming conditions, crops grown, when and how reaped, etc., labourers' wages, reference to meetings held concerning alteration of the Corn Laws ; personal and business expenditure.

Leeds City Archives (Sheepscar): GA/C/38.

CHATER, Elizabeth, of London.

Diaries, Jan.–Aug., 1832 and Jan., 1833.

Contents: personal details.

Exeter City Record Office: MSS.

CRAWSHAY, William IInd., of Cyfarthfa, Merthyr Tydfil, Glam.
Diary, 1832–55.
Contents: notes by the son of the uncrowned "Iron King".
National Library of Wales: Cyfarthfa Papers vols. 13, 14.

DELMÉ-RADCLIFFE, Frederick Peter, of Hitchen, Hertfordshire.
Diary, 1832–39.
Contents: notes on hunting; as used in his book on *The Noble Science*; local interest.
Hitchen Priory: MSS.

DENMAN, Miss Frances (1812–1890), of Russell Square, London.
Diary, July, 1832–April, 1833. 173 pp.
Contents: daily round of a charming young lady; domestic life and family anecdotes; visits to Isle of Wight, Midlands, Derbyshire; London life; her father was lord chief justice; useful material for biography of the chief justice.
Wigan Central Public Library: Edward Hall coll. M975.

DICKINSON, Frances Elizabeth (1814–1881), later married Frederick William Pratt Barlow.
Diaries, 1832–41 and 1846–81. 28 vols.
Contents: journal of mostly local interest by the daughter of John Dickinson (1782–1869) the stationery businessman.
University of London, Bedford College Library: MSS. coll.

DUNCAN, Mrs. Mary Lundie (1814–1839), of Cleish, Kinross.
Diary, Sept., 1832–Dec., 1838.
Contents: religious life, evangelism and introspection in Scotland; a desperately model religious life.
Memoir of Mrs. Mary Duncan, by her mother (New York, 1842), pp. 76–300.

HERFORD, Edward (1815–1896), of Manchester, public prosecutor.
Diaries, Jan., 1832–36, July, 1838–April, 1846, and March, 1857–March, 1858. 3 vols.
Contents: early life; young man of leisure; dances; gossip; references to political events and local reactions; later as prosecutor in cases against Chartists at Liverpool Assizes; remarks on Manchester borough council meetings; reference to work as founder of lyceums; comments on self-discipline; notes on local and church affairs; some interest in social life and references to municipal affairs. (Occasional shorthand).
Manchester Public Libraries: Arch. Dept., MSS. 923.4 H32.

HODGSON, Rev. John (1789–1845), of Hartbury, antiquary.
Diaries, July, 1832–Feb., 1844.
Contents: antiquarian studies and relations with Northumbrian antiquaries; his social life; religious work.
Northumberland County Record Office: Society of Antiquarians MSS. NRO93, ZAN M14/A13.

James Raine, *A Memoir of Rev. John Hodgson* (London, 1857).

JOHNS, Rev. Charles Alexander (1811–1874), authority on natural history, and sometime headmaster of Helston Grammar School.
Diary, 1832–37.
Contents: journal and notebook kept when the diarist was assistant master at Helston Grammar School.
Cornwall County Record Office: MS. Acc. 225 D.D.X.11.

LLOYD, Richard Thomas (d. 1904), of Aston Hall, Shropshire.
Diaries, 1832–98.
Contents: mostly family matters; including a tour of the Continent, 1838.
National Library of Wales: Aston Hall MSS., 4480–4501, 4702, 4727–4767.

LUCAS, William, of Hollowell House, Northants.
Diary, 1832. 1 vol.
Contents: weather reports; accounts; brief details of visits, etc.
Leicestershire Record Office: MS. DE 783/40.

MILLS, Rev. Francis (1759–1851), of Barford, Warwick.
Diaries, 1832–33 and 1835–36. 2 vols.
Stratford, The Shakespeare Birthplace Trust: DR 240/3/1–2.

NORCLIFFE, John.
Diary, 1832.
Contents: journal of a tour of France, Elba, Italy, Sicily, Malta, and Spain.
East Riding of Yorkshire County Record Office: DDHV/74/16.

PHILIPPS, Grismond, of Cwmgwili, Carms., landowner.
Diaries, 1832–49. 17 vols.
Carmarthen County Record Office: Cwmgwili MSS. 869–885.

SANDS, W., [?] of Atherstone.
Diary, April, 1832. 151 pp.
Contents: journal of travel; visits Henley-in-Arden, Stratford-upon-Avon, Woodstock, Oxford, Dorchester, Henley, Slough, and London; maps and engravings; train ride to London, Aug., 1851, in company of his father, account by W. Sands, Jr., aged 15.
Birmingham Reference Library: Cat. No. 259856.

THACKERAY, William Makepeace (1811–1863), novelist.
Diaries, 1832–63.
Contents: extensive notes by one of the century's foremost authors. [A diary for 1845 with a few notes of social engagements is in the Berg collection of New York Public Library.]
London, British Museum: Add. MSS. 46895–46905. (Acquired 1949).

THOMAS, M., of Newcastle Emlyn, Cardiganshire.
Diary, Jan.–March, 1832.
National Library of Wales: MS. 5154A.

THOROLD, Sir John Charles.
  Diaries, 1832 and 1833.
  Contents: journals of first and second Continental tours with a Mr. Yorke.
  Lincolnshire Archives Office: Thorold Deposits, MSS. 12/2/10–12.
TREDWELL, W., schoolboy.
  Diary, 1832–33. 44pp.
  Contents: daily jottings of an Oxford schoolboy.
  Oxford, Bodleian Library: MS. Top. Oxon. d. 383. (Acquired 1948).
VERDON family.
  Diary, 1932–40. 5 pp.
  Contents: family affairs in Sydney, Australia.
  East Riding of Yorkshire County Record Office: DDBH/27/4.
WARNER, A. W. and J. S. T.
  Diary and notes, Aug.–Sept., 1832.
  Contents: notes, scraps, remembrances, and account of a journey of pleasure; Liverpool, Chester, Malvern, Derbyshire; illustrations.
  Oxford, Bodleian Library: MS. Top. gen. f. 35. (Acquired 1948).
WELD, Charles (1812–1885), of Chideock Manor, Dorset.
  Diaries, 1832 and 1837–40. Loose papers.
  Contents: journal of travel in the Scottish Highlands, 1832; journal of travel in Italy, Sept., 1836–July, 1837; a list of events, 1837–40.
  Dorset County Record Office: MSS. D16/F19, F25.
WILLIAMS, John (d. 1841), of Town-end, Denbighshire.
  Diary, Jan., 1832–Nov., 1839.
  Contents: journal of business matters; book-keeper with Brown, Shipley & Co., in Liverpool.
  Cardiff Public Library: MS. 2. 937.
YOUNG, Catherine, became MACLEAR in 1835, (née Bellaire) (1797–1869), of Bedford.
  Diaries, Jan., 1832–Dec., 1835, and Jan.–Dec., 1846. 5 vols.
  Contents: family matters; local events.
  Bedfordshire Record Office: MSS. A.D. 1719–23.
  B.H.R.S. XL
YOUNG, Lieutenant Edward (d. 1842).
  Diary, 1832–41. 1 vol.
  Contents: journal kept in ships, H.M.S. *Jupiter, Talbot, Sparrowhawk, Princess Charlotte, Asia*; some sketches.
  National Maritime Museum: JOD 72, MS59/0.

1833

ANON.
  Diary, Sept.–Oct., 1833. 29 pp.
  Contents: a log of a voyage of the brig *Garland* from Liverpool to

Miramichi, New Brunswick.
Liverpool Record Office: MS. KZ 562.
ANON.
Diary, 1833–43. 1 vol.
Contents: a vice-consular journal kept in Morocco.
London, Public Record Office: MS. F.O. 636.
ANON.
Diary, 1833.
Contents: journal of a tour through Wales.
Private: Goldney MSS. (Present location unknown).
ANON.
Diaries, 1833 and 1834.
Contents: tours to Belfast, and through Clydesdale and Western Highlands; scenery and beauties.
National Library of Scotland: MSS. 2776.
ANON., of Hull, Yorkshire.
Diary, Jan.–Sept., 1833. 134 pp.
Contents: kept by a young girl, possibly related to William Etty, the painter; tour of the Midlands, Mid-Wales, North Wales, and back to Yorkshire; visits to relatives and friends; chatty and naive; many sketches; Etty was in the touring party; incomplete.
Wigan Central Public Library: Edward Hall coll.
ANON.
Diary, May–June, 1833. 1 vol.
Contents: journal of travel in Belgium and Germany.
West Sussex County Record Office: Maxse MS. 417.
ANON.
Diary, May–Nov., 1833. 63 pp.
Contents: journal of a young Irishman who made a sight-seeing tour in America: Boston, Philadelphia, Norfolk, Richmond, Washington, New York, Buffalo, Canada, New England, New York.
San Marino, California, Huntington Library: MS. HM 768.
ANON.
Diaries, 1833–69 (with gaps).
Contents: journals of tour in England, 1833–69, and in France, 1833–47.
Warwickshire Record Office: MSS. CR 136/A4 A5.
ANON.
Diary, 1833.
Contents: an official diary for the year, among the Egmont Papers.
London, British Museum: Add. MS. 47056–47075.
ALEXANDER, Rt. Rev. Nathaniel (d. 1840), Bishop of Meath.
Diary, 1833.
Contents: official visitations in his diocese; family matters; weather;

E

entries made at Dublin or Ardbraccan ; two pages a month.
Private: F. E. Dixon, Esq., 15 Morehampton Roard, Donnybrook, Dublin.

BEECROFT, Mrs., of Norwich.
Diary, 1833. 91 fols.
Contents: tour of Scotland and return ; visit to Mrs. Burns (Jean Armour), widow of poet ; hearsay about Scott.
National Library of Scotland: MS. 1674.

CHICHESTER, Robert, of Bishop's Tawton, Barnstaple, Devon.
Diaries, 1833–64 (with gaps) and 1871.
Contents: personal matters.
Private: Major C. Chichester, Hall, near Barnstaple, Devon.

COOPER, James Fenimore (1789–1851), American novelist.
Diary, June-Sept., 1833.
Contents: journal of travel ; notes kept in London.
Yale University, U.S.A.: MS. Za.

FitzJAMES, James, a midshipman.
Diary, Feb., 1833–Oct., 1834. 1 vol.
Contents: journal covering his service in the Mediterranean in H.M.S. *Madagascar* and H.M.S. *St. Vincent*, his return home and posting to the *Winchester*, and then to Captain Chesney's Euphrates Expedition.
National Maritime Museum: JOD 86, MS69/01.

FORBES, Professor E.
Diary, 1833.
Contents: journal kept in Norway.
Edinburgh University Library: MS. Dc.6.91.

FRY, Joseph (1777–1861), husband of Elizabeth Fry.
Diary, Aug., 1833–57.
Contents: account and extracts ; notes on Quaker religious life and travel.
Friends' Hist. Soc. Journal, XXVII (1931).

GIFFARD, Captain, H., R.N.
Diary, 1833–40.
Contents: a diary of events ; service on H.M. ships, *Volage* and *Cruiser*.
National Maritime Museum: JOD 38, 47. MS. 477/1, MS. 9753.

HINDMARSH, Henry, of Alnmouth.
Diary, 1833–39.
Newcastle-upon-Tyne Public Library: Arch. Dept. MSS.

HOLDEN, William Drury (became W. Drury–Lowe in 1849), of Locko Park, Spondon, Derbyshire.
Diaries, 1833–76 (with gaps). 52 vols.
Contents: (i) diaries of daily memoranda books, 1833–39, 1845–74, and 1876, (38 vols) ; (ii) pocket diaries, 1840, 1845–49, 1851–52, 1854, 1856,

1859, 1862–63, (13 vols); and (iii) one "journal" for 1843. Includes visits to Italy and purchase of pictures.
Nottingham University: Drury-Lowe coll. Dr/F/30–67, Dr/F/68–80, and Dr/F/85.

HOTHAM, Henry John.
Diaries, 1833, 1845, and 1851–52. 4 vols.
Contents: personal affairs and some tour journals; Aug.–Oct., 1851 in southern Germany, July–Oct., 1852, in Austria.
East Riding of Yorkshire County Record Office: DDHO/18/ 2–5.

HUNTER, George.
Diary, 1833–34.
Contents: personal accounts for journey to London.
Durham County Record Office: Londonderry MSS.

JARVIS, G. K.
Diaries, 1833 and 1852.
Contents: journal of a stay in Paris, 1833, and a tour in England in 1852; Coventry, Bath, London, and Paris again.
Lincolnshire Archives Office: 8/43.

KENNAWAY, Eliza (d. 1842), wife of William Richard Kennaway.
Diary, 1833–34. 1 vol.
Contents: detailed daily entries, personal and social, while living at Ghazeepoor, India, where her husband who was in the Bengal civil service was judge of Fultchpore.
Devon Record Office: MS. B961 M/ B3.

LAPIDGE, Miss Marianne (1819–1902), of Hampton Wick, Middlesex.
Diary, Jan.–Dec., [?]1833.
Contents: ingenuous record of the musical education of the diarist and her sister by a Mr. Williams; skilful recording of trivial dialogue; occasional domestic items.
Wigan Central Public Library: Edward Hall coll. M887, 839–841.

LAYCOCK, Thomas, a medical doctor.
Diary, 1833–57 (Microfilm).
Edinburgh University Library: Mic.M.82.

MILLS, Arthur (1816–1898), son of Rev. Francis Mills of Barford, Warwicks.
Diary, 1834.
Contents: journal of a foreign tour made in company of his brother, Henry.
Stratford, The Shakespeare Birthplace Trust: DR 240/3/13.

MITFORD, Frances, of Bath Somerset.
Diary, July–Oct., 1833. 1 vol.
Contents: journal of travel in France.
West Sussex County Record Office: Mitford MS. 34.

MITFORD, William Townley (1817–1889), of Pittshill, Tillington.
Diaries, Aug.–Oct., 1833, May, 1840–April, 1841, Aug.–Nov., 1842, Sept.–Nov., 1844, Aug.–Sept., 1847, Oct.–Nov., 1847, Sept., 1851–Jan., 1852, Dec., 1853–Feb., 1854. 8 vols.
Contents: journals of travel: France, 1833; Greece and the Mediterranean, 1840; northern Europe, 1842; central Europe, 1844; France and Spain, 1847; Germany, Switzerland, Italy, Egypt, 1851; Rome, 1853.
West Sussex County Record Office: Mitford MSS. 35–42.

PHILLIPS, John, first Principal of Bangor Normal College.
Diary and a notebook, 1833–36 and July, 1851–Dec., 1864.
Contents: diarist as a student in Edinburgh; entry into the ministry of Calvinistic Methodist Church; the later journal records the dates and places of meetings attended or arranged by him regarding his work as Principal.
National Library of Wales: MSS. 4254A, 4256C.

RASHDALL, Rev. John (1809–1869), curate in Exeter parishes 1835–47, Vicar of Dawlish, 1864–69.
Diaries, 1833–69.
Contents: daily record of events; calls, church matters, parish visits; family affairs; public events; clerical conferences in the south-west of England; spiritual matters; tours abroad, Italy in 1854.
Oxford, Bodleian Library: MSS. Eng. misc. e. 351–360. (Donated 1953).
Devon Record Office: MS. 444 2/2 1–5 (Typescript of 5 vols., 1835–47, 1847–69).

WALLER, Sir G. H.
Diaries, 1833–88.
MSS. not available to students.
Warwickshire Record Office: MSS. (On loan).

WATSON, H. R.
Diary, June–Oct., 1833.
Contents: journal of a tour from Demerara to Canada.
Liverpool Record Office: Arch. 920 Par III.

WILLIAMS, Rev. Thomas.
Diary, Aug.–Oct., 1833.
Contents: journal of a Continental tour.
National Library of Wales: MS. 1880 (Aberpergwm MSS.).

[?] WILLIAMS, Rev. William, of Wychwood.
Diary, June, 1833–Jan., 1834. 132 pp.
Contents: a travel journal written by the tutor of Guy, son of Lord and Lady Warwick, while on an extended tour of the Continent.
Wigan Central Public Library: Edward Hall coll., M998. (Presented 1954).

WOODS, Rev. G. H.
Diaries, 1833–34, and 1856. 2 vols.

Contents: journals of tours in Belgium, Germany, Switzerland and Italy.
West Sussex County Record Office: Add. MSS. 2726–7.
YOUNG, Sophia Agnes, sister of Alexander Young of Harburn, W.S.
Diary, 1833–35. 1 vol.
Contents: journal consisting mainly of social chit-chat.
Edinburgh Central Public Library: Edinburgh Room, MS. YDA 1820 Y76.

1834

ANON., army officer.
Diary, 1834–35. 1 vol.
Contents: journal of an officer on leave in Europe.
West Suffolk Record Office: MS. Acc. 353/3.
ANON.
Diary, Sept., 1834. 1 vol.
Contents: journal of a journey from Nottingham to Manchester via
Liverpool, and back again.
Nottingham Record Office: MS. DD. 109/1.
ANON., [S.G.B.]
Diary, Jan–Oct., 1834. 1 vol.
Contents: journal of an Englishman on a Mediterranean tour; visits to
Spain, Gibraltar, Tangier, Malta, Greece and the Islands, and Turkey.
Mostly written at Cadiz.
Oxford, Bodleian Library: MS. Eng. misc. e. 563.
ANON.
Diary, Nov., 1834–Sept., 1836 (intermittent). 57 pp.
Contents: notes of a man of culture and humour, a keen critic and patron
of the theatre; details of his children; sketches (including James Bruce
and Robert Owen, and theatrical figures); followed by a travel diary in
Sept., 1836, in which he acted as a tutor to a friend.
Wigan Central Public Library: Edward Hall coll.
ANON.
Diary, c. 1834–79.
Contents: notes by a nurse of the Throckmorton family.
Warwickshire Record Office: Throckmorton Papers.
ADAMS, E. Richards, of London and Beckenham, solicitor.
Diary, 1834–38. 272 pp.
Contents: family and personal events, church affairs, travel in and around
Kent; some shorthand.
Beckenham (Kent) Central Library: MS. L/B8/920.
ALLAN (formerly spelt ALLEN), Major-General, 34th. Bengal Infantry.
Diary, 1-30 Jan., 1834. 1 vol.
Contents: journal of travel from Bithur, near Cawnpore, to Morardabad,
Uttar Pradesh.
London, Public Record Office: MS. 30/2, 5.

BARNETT, Henrietta, widow of Lieut.-Gen. C. Barnett of Stratton Park.
Diary, April, 1834–April, 1838. 1 vol.
Contents: record of domestic events, weather, etc.
Edinburgh University Library: MS. Dk.5.26.

B(——), S. G. (see above–ANON)
Diary, 1834.
Contents: journal of a visit to Gibraltar and Malta.
Oxford, Bodleian Library: MS. Eng. misc. e. 563.

BAKER, Mrs. Barwick (formerly Mary Fenwick), wife of T. B. Lloyd Baker, of Hardwicke Court, near Gloucester.
Diary, 1834–1904.
Contents: personal notes entered in annual volumes both before and after her marriage.
Private: Miss Olive K. Lloyd-Baker, C.B.E., Hardwicke Court near Gloucester: Hardwicke Court MSS., Box 12 (a).

BEACH, William Hicks, of Witcombe.
Diary, 1834–37. 1 vol.
Contents: personal matters mostly.
Gloucestershire Record Office: MS. D 1866 F 14.

CHAMBERS, William Mellish.
Diary, 1834–35.
Contents: journal of a journey through Greece, Egypt, Palestine, Constantinople, the Balkans, Austria, Germany; notes on desert travel; an account of the character of Mohomet Ali and of the state of Egypt.
Nottingham University Library: Mellish coll., MS. M3 186–125.11. (Me 2 L4/5 appears to be in the same hand; travels in Near East).

CHARLES, David (1812–1878), of Trevecka; grandson of Thomas Charles of Bala.
Diaries, with autobiography and memoranda from 1830 onwards, 1835–48 and 1874–78.
Contents: regulations for study; earlier diary intermittently kept while at Trevecka; later diary contains occasional entries, observations, poems, etc., when diarist was secretary and registrar of University College, Aberystwyth, and held pastorates at Abercarn and Aberdovey.
National Library of Wales: MSS. 4799A–4801. (Acquired 1944).

DAUBENY, Charles Giles Bridle (1795–1867), Oxford Professor.
Diary, 1834–67. 233 leaves.
Contents: brief entries by the diarist who was Sherardian Professor of Botany and Sibthorpian Professor of Rural Economy; numerous letters and university notices are pasted in.
Oxford, Bodleian Library: MS. Sherard, 264. (Acquired 1957).

EDMUNDS, Jane (1825–1901), of Bala, housewife.
Diary, 1834–1900 (with gaps). 1 vol.
Contents: many aspects of life, especially religious matters; she moved

from Bala in 1859 to Bangor and thence to Caernarvon in 1866.
Caernarvon County Record Office: M/809.

[?] GOULBURN, Colonel Edward.
Diaries, Oct–Dec., [?] 1834, Sept–Nov., 1836. 2 vols.
Contents: notebook diary of a journey in France and Italy, most likely in 1834 ; another of a tour in France, 1836.
Surrey Record Office: Goulburn MSS. Acc. 319. II/9 G.

GREEVES, Charles (d. 1847), of Granby House, Harrogate, land agent and surveyor.
Diaries, May, 1834–Sept., 1835 and 1842–47. 2 vols.
Contents: earlier volume is journal of journey to America ; voyage from Liverpool with wife and two daughters ; stay in New York ; their life outside Philadelphia ; the return to Liverpool. Later volume records last years in Harrogate ; list of engagements, etc.
Harrogate Central Library: Arch. Greeves MSS. 322, 330 HB/GRE.

HIRST, James, of Huddersfield, Yorkshire, weaver.
Diary, 1834–83.
Huddersfield Central Library: Local coll.

HULME, John Rhodes.
Diary, 1834–38.
Contents: journal kept in Jamaica.
Staffordshire Record Office: MSS. coll.
Oxford, Rhodes House Library: Micr. W. Ind. 8.

KENNEDY, Miss [——].
Diary, 1834.
Contents: journey to England from Carlsruhe (with Mr. and Amelia Briggs) to her marriage with John Kennedy, Secretary of the Legation at the Court of Naples ; includes diarist's first trip in a railway from Manchester to Liverpool.
Liverpool Record Office: MS. 24299.

KNATCHBULL, Charles Henry.
Diaries, 1834–35, and 1835–36. 3 vols.
Contents: brief daily record of social life, 1834–35 ; account of some detail of his life at Meerut, India, 1835–36.
Kent Archives Office: Knatchbull U951 F22-3.

MACKENZIE, Keith William Stewart.
Diaries, 1834 and 1840–42.
Contents: first a journal of a tour in France, 1834 ; then journal which includes the attack on Canton.
Scottish Record Office: GD 46/15/133 and 46/6/86.

MARRIOTT, J., of Liverpool.
Diary, 8-27 Oct., 1834.
Contents: journal of a tour from Manchester by canal to London ; entitled, "A Journey to London with S. A. Marriott in search of health,

accompanied by Louisa and Margaret in search of pleasure, and followed by Tom Hobson in search of his wife"; details of London sights, including Parliament burning down, and buildings; return home in a coach via Birmingham.

Wigan Central Public Library: Edward Hall coll. M 997. (Acquired 1954).

MATTHEWS, Wilkinson, probably associated with Leyland, Lancs.

Diaries, Aug–Oct., 1834 and Aug–Oct., 1836. 40 fols.

Contents: first journal is of a tour through France and Italy; the second through Belgium, Germany, Switzerland, and Luxemburg; of general interest; scenery, towns, etc.

Lancashire Record Office: MSS. DDF/18.

MORLEY, 2nd. Earl of.

Diaries, March–Aug., 1834, Aug–Nov., 1839, and Oct., 1842–April, 1843.

Contents: journals of tours in Europe; some entries in the last volume are by the Countess of Morley.

London, British Museum: Add. MSS. 48261, 48262, Morley Papers.

NICHOLL, Thomas, of Redruth, Cornwall, a gardener.

Diaries, 1834–51. 2 vols.

Contents: always a note on weather each day; local happenings; references to teetotallers and to Methodism.

Cornwall County Record Office: MSS. DD.X 119/1–2.

PLYMLEY, (——).

Diaries, 1834–40.

Contents: journals of holidays abroad.

Salop County Record Office: MSS. coll.

PUGH, Charles (1798–1863), clerk in the High Court of Chancery of Barnard's Inn.

Diaries, 1834–63.

Contents: miscellaneous notes on reading, architecture, etc; and included some obituary notices which are indexed in vol. 8.

Oxford, Bodleian Library: MSS. Eng. misc. d. 465–73. (Acquired 1956–57).

REES, David Rice, of Llandovery, printer and bookseller.

Diaries and almanacs: 1834, 1836, 1839–40, 1843, and 1854. 7 vols.

Cardiff Public Library: MSS. 1. 651.

RISLEY, Rev. William Cotton, sometime vicar of Deddington, Oxfordshire.

Diaries, 1834–69. 44 vols.

Contents: local events; church matters and visits; weather; weddings, funerals, and anniversaries of his family and the parish; his activities as magistrate; letters written and received; reports nearly everything and that without much vitality.

Oxford, Bodleian Library: Risley Papers c. 66–72. (Acquired 1960).

SMITH, Major George, of the Royal Horse Guards.

Diary, 1834. 1 vol.

National Army Museum: MS. 6306/40.

SOMERSET, Lady Georgina Seymour, wife of 12th. Duke.
Diary, Aug–Nov., 1834. 1 vol.
Contents: journal of tour of Germany.
Buckinghamshire Record Office: Ramsden coll.

STEVENSON, John, of Hampstead, London.
Diary, 1834–40.
Contents: current events and local affairs at Hampstead; his work as keeper of Hampstead Heath; local interest.
Hampstead Public Library, (N.W.3): MS. H920.STE.

TAYLOR, William.
Diary, July, 1834–Jan., 1836.
Contents: records of an official in the Bredalbane household; inventories, payments, and receipts; the daily business of a steward.
Harvard University, U.S.A.: Houghton Library, Eng. MS. 578.

WALKER, John G.
Diary, 1834–38. 1 vol.
Contents: journal kept in shorthand, with key to system enclosed and transcript of one section.
University of London Library: Carlton MSS. 3/7.

WALLER, John Green (b. 1813), artist and archaeologist.
Diary, Jan., 1834–March, 1838.
Contents: student life at Royal Academy; burning of the Houses of Parliament; visits to London sights; pungent notes on Turner, Etty, Horsley, etc; written in Mavor's shorthand.
Private: W. J. Carlton Esq., 37, The Avenue, Andover, Hampshire.

WHITE, Frederick, a magistrate in Jamaica, West Indies.
Diary, Aug., 1834–Feb., 1835. 280 pp.
Contents: journal of a magistrate.
Oxford, Rhodes House Library: West Indies MS. r. 1.

1835

ANON.
Diary, 1835. 94 leaves.
Contents: journal of a tour in the Balkans.
Oxford, St. John's College Library, MS. 229.

ANON., (M. T. G?).
Diary, August, 1835. 1 vol.
Contents: journal compiled in verse; from Cambridge via Yorkshire to the Lake District; return through Lancashire and Derbyshire Peak District.
Berkshire Record Office: MS. D/EE Z26.

ANDERSON, Captain.
Diary, 1835.
Contents: journal of his expedition to Manitoulin Island and Sault Ste. Marie (Ontario).

E*

Private: Papers of Sir John Colborne, 1st. Baron Seaton: J.E.C. Mackrell Esq., Beechwood, Plympton, Devon: Seaton Papers, Situation f.

BALFOUR, Arthur Lowry, Lieutenant in 52nd. Foot Regiment.
Diary, 1835–37.
Contents: journal kept during the Kaffir Wars.
National Library of Ireland: Dept. of MSS.

BALY, William (1814–1861), Physician-extraordinary to Queen Victoria.
Diaries, 1835–36. 3 vols.
Contents: (i) Sept–Oct., 1835 journal of a walking tour from Heidelberg to Berlin; Rhineland, Hartz Mountains, Berlin; scenery, people, etc; (ii) another record of his travels in France, Switzerland, and Germany.
Cambridge University Library: Add. MS. 6651.
London, Royal College of Physicians: MSS. 92 BAL.

BARNES, Mrs. Margaret (née Stapleton).
Diaries, 1835–58, 1844–45, and 1856.
Contents: first diary has intermittent entries, principally at Whitchurch, Gloucestershire; the second was kept at Rome; and the third at Umballah, India.
Private: Col. A. C. Barnes, D.S.O., O.B.E., Foxholme, Redhill Road, Cobham, Surrey. Hammond MSS.

BELDAM, [——], of Royston.
Diary, July, 1835–rest not dated. 1 vol.
Contents: journal of a stay in Paris by a male member of the Beldam family.
Cambridgeshire Record Office: MS. R58/8/14/16.

COBDEN, Richard (1804–1865), of Dunford House, Heyshott.
Diaries, 1835–61 (with gaps). 25 vols.
Contents: journal of honeymoon tour in France and Switzerland, 1840; journal of a tour in America, 1835; journal of a tour around the Mediterranean, Oct., 1836–April, 1837; Cairo, Constantinople, Gibraltar, Cadiz, with notes on shipping and trade; other travel journals, London to Vienna, Spain, Italy, Austria, Russia, Germany, France, Algiers, at various times.
West Sussex County Record Office: Cobden MSS. 441–469, 1026, 6051.

COKE, D. E., of Debdale, Nottinghamshire.
Diaries, Aug., 1835–Jan., 1843. 13 vols.
Private: Mrs. R. Coke-Steel, Trusley Old Hall, Sutton-on-the-Hill, Derbyshire. Coke MSS. 896.

CULLUM, Anne, wife of Rev. Sir Thomas G. Cullum.
Diaries, 1835–58 (with gaps).
Contents: journals of journeys in England and Ireland; notes of trees and plants.
West Suffolk Record Office: MSS. E2/44/60.

EDWARDS, Edward (1812–1866), Manchester City Librarian, 1850–58.
Diaries, 1835–84 (extracts). 2 vols.
Manchester Public Libraries: Archives Dept., MSS. G 920. 2 E5.

FILMER, Sir Edmund, of East Sutton Place, Staplehurst, Kent.
Diaries, 1835–37, 1839–44, and 1856. 10 vols.
Contents: entries in the printed *Kentish Companion and Almanac*, probably made by Sir Edmund Filmer, related to his movements; results of the elections, 1832 and 1835; a wealth of printed (local) information; similar detail in pocket books, 1839–44; the late diary is entered for six days only by Edmund Filmer when in the Grenadier Guards, 1856.
Kent Archives Office: Filmer MSS., U 120, F27/3–12. (Acquired 1945).

GIBBON family, of Benenden, Kent.
Diaries, [?] 1835 and 1838. 1 vol.
Contents: first journal of travel in Holland and Germany, July 21–Aug., 3, probably 1835; journal of a visit to the Isle of Wight, 27-30 Aug., 1838.
Kent Archives Office: MS. U1272, F3.

HOWARD-VYSE, Major-General R. W. (1784–1853), of Stoke Poges, Bucks.
Diary, 1835–37 (with gaps). 4pp.
Contents: long entries relating to travel, excavation, etc. in the Middle East.
Buckinghamshire Record Office: MS. D/HV (uncat.).
R. W. Howard-Vyse, *Operations Carried on at the Pyramids of Gizeh in 1837* (London, 1840).

HUDSON, J. C., of Beverley, Yorkshire.
Diary, 1835–60.
East Riding of Yorkshire County Record Office: (on loan).

JAGO, Rev. Francis Vyvyan (1780–1846), (assumed surname of Arundell in 1816), rector of Landulph, 1805–46, antiquarian.
Diary, 1835–36. 1 vol.
Contents: journal of travels in the near East.
Cornwall County Record Office: MS. DD.LR.239.

LAYARD, Sir Austen Henry (1817–1894), archaeologist.
Diaries of travel, Aug., 1835–May, 1850 (with gaps).
Contents: Aug–Oct., 1835, journal in France with the painter Brockedon; April–Nov., 1841 (gaps), archaeological work and travel in Persia; Aug., 1842–March, 1843, in European Turkey and Constantinople; Aug., 1849–May, 1850, archaeological expedition from Constantinople to Khabour (Nineveh and Babylon) and Mosul; most of these diaries are kept with archaeological purpose relating to Biblical sites; they are partly used in his *Early Adventures* (London, 1887), and his *Autobiography* (London, 1903).
London, British Museum: Add. MSS. 39091–39096.

[?] LIGHT, Mrs., of London.
Diary, 8-21 Sept., 1835. 78 pp.

Contents: notes of a tour of France by road and river-boat, travelling from Brighton to Dieppe, Rouen, Havre, and Paris; amusing and witty; dangers of travel by new-fangled steamboat.

Wigan Central Public Library: Edward Hall coll.

LUTTRELL, Rev. T. F.

Diary, 1835–64.

Somerset Record Office: Dunster Castle MSS., III. E. A. 2.

MURRAY, Alexander, of Blackhouse, Peterhead.

Diaries, 1835–54.

National Library of Scotland: Dept., of MSS.

NEVILLE, Rev. Christopher.

Diary, 1835. 1 vol.

Contents: miscellaneous jottings.

Nottinghamshire Record Office: MS. DDN 233/4.

[?] NUSSEY, Rev.,——, [a member of the Nussey family.]

Diary, 1835–47. 3 vols.

Contents: the diarist was a reverend gentleman, an inhabitant of Leeds, Yorkshire.

Lincolnshire Archives Office: Nussey Deposit.

RIDLEY, Lady Cecilia (1819–1845), wife of Matthew White Ridley, 4th. Bart.

Diaries, 1835–37 and 1839–44. 6 vols.

Contents: mostly entries concerning social life, etc.

Northumberland County Record Office: Ridley of Blagdon MSS., NRO 138, ZRI 32/6. (R. M. Gard, County Archivist).

Cecilia: the Letters of Viscountess Ridley (London: Hart Davis, 1958).

SEYMOUR, Francis Hugh George (1812–1884).

Diary, 1835. 1 vol.

Contents: private matters.

Warwickshire Record Office: MS. CR114A/644.

SOUTHCOMB, Rev. John Ladevez Hamilton (1817–1886), Rector of Rose Ash, near South Molton, north Devon.

Diaries, Nov., 1835, 1845, 1846–52, and 1870–77. 7 vols.

Contents: early journal of a schoolboy at Mr. Patey's school; journals of 1845–52 kept while a curate at Dunsford, Devon, noting ordinary daily events; a fuller and more descriptive journal of his days at Rose Ash in the 70's, church duties and parish affairs.

Private: Miss Viola Southcomb, Pennington, Lymington, Hants.

SQUIRE, Sarah, a Quaker.

Diary, June–Sept., 1835.

Contents: religious visit to the Shetland Islands, the Orkneys, and north Scotland, in series of letters home; travel notes and religion; visits to Friends' meetings.

London, Friends' Society Library: Box G.

THOMAS, John, of Llanllwni, Wales.
Diary, 1835–36.
Contents: entries made in almanacs.
National Library of Wales: Add. MS. 264–B.

WEBBER, Mary and Charles.
Diary, June–July, 1835. 42 fols.
Contents: journal of a tour through England to Wales and back through Malvern where the entries end; Gloucester, Hereford, Hay, Rhayader, Aberystwyth, Barmouth, Harlech, Bala, Shrewsbury, etc., extended comments on the scenery and local people.
Oxford, Bodleian Library: MS. Top. gen. e. 59.

WINSTANLEY, James Winckworth (1816–1891), of Riverside, Chester, barrister-at-law.
Diaries, Jan., 1835–March, 1891. 9 notebooks.
Contents: social and family events relating to London, Rickmansworth, Epsom, Chester, and Worthing; details of prices of goods, wages, and hotels. (Typed manuscript in preparation).
Private: C. W. Winstanley, 68 The Main Way, Chorley Wood, Hertfordshire.

WOOD, Richard, of Diss, a solicitor.
Diary, 1835–37. 1 vol.
Contents: brief entries in day book.
Ipswich and East Suffolk Record Office: MS. 50/20/5.

1836

ANON.
Diary, 1836.
Contents: journal of an excursion to Cornwall.
Whereabouts of MS. uncertain. When the Herries MSS. were sold to B. M. this diary was retained by Lieut-Col. Spottiswood who has since died; there is no record of what happened to this MS., Herries 183.

ANON.
Diary, 1836.
Contents: brief journal of tour to Wales.
Oxford, Bodleian Library: Eng. misc. e. 392, fols. 39–40. (Acquired 1952).

ANON.
Diary, 1836–74.
Contents: a farm journal kept at Sudborne.
Ipswich and East Suffolk Record Office: MS. HA 28: 50/23/1.8 (12).

BAKER, Rev. Samuel, headmaster of Shrewsbury School.
Diary, June–Aug., 1836.

Contents: details of the ceremonies and formalities concerning his appointment as bishop of Lichfield.

Shrewsbury School Library: MS. S. v. 78.

BALFOUR, J.

Diaries, 1836–92.

Contents: journals of travels abroad, and those of spiritual matters, probably by J. Balfour.

Scottish Record Office: GD 126/Box 24.

CHRISTIE, Col. W. Harry, officer of the 38th. Foot.

Diary, June–Nov., 1836. 1 vol.

Contents: journal by the commander of the escort for the convicts consigned to Botany Bay; detailed description of the voyage, layout of the ship, information on the conditions, incidents, etc. in a lively manner; disembarkation at Port Jackson.

Private: Mrs. Hodgson.

National Army Museum: typescript only, 6401/17.

CORNER, Rev. Edmund (1807–1839), of Edinburgh, C.M.S. missionary.

Diaries, March., 1836–Jan., 1839 (with gaps). 4 vols.

Contents: detailed journal of life while stationed at St. Andrews, Grove, Jamaica; family life, people met, eclipses of the sun, northern lights, etc.

Church Missionary Society: MS. Acc. 100 F/1. (Acquired 1914).

DICKENSON, Eliza, later wife of Francis Wemyss of Westbury-on-Severn.

Diaries, 1836–46. 9 vols.

Contents: personal matters.

Gloucestershire Records Office: MSS. D 36 F 33–41.

FARNBOROUGH, Thomas Erskine May, 1st. Lord (1815–1886), Clerk of the House of Commons, 1871–86.

Diaries, Jan., 1836 and 1857–82. 2 vols.

Contents: an early personal journal, 1836, when he was Assistant Librarian at the House of Commons; personal journal entries from 1857 onwards.

House of Lords Record Office: Hist. coll. (H. S. Cobb, Senior Assistant Clerk of the Records).

GRAFTON, 5th Duke of.

Diaries, 1836–49.

Private: His Grace the Duke of Grafton, Euston Hall, Thetford, Norfolk: Grafton MSS., 44, 45.

HALLIWELL-PHILLIPPS, Mrs. Henrietta Elizabeth Molyneux, of Middle Hill, Worcestershire.

Diaries, March, 1836–July, 1875. 4 vols.

Contents: notes on her domestic, social, and family life in Worcestershire; work with her husband on literary and scholary affairs; literary and scholarly friendships; details of her husband's daily work; a full record.

Edinburgh University Library: Halliwell-Phillipps coll. 327–330.

JONES, Captain Edward, 1st. Royal Lancashire Militia.
Diary, July–Sept., 1836.
Contents: journal of a tour in Ireland; tourist's topographical and archaeological notes.
Manchester, John Rylands Library: Eng. MSS. 1029.

MANSFIELD, C. B.
Diaries, 1836–41 and 1852–53. 2 vols.
Hampshire Record Office: MSS. uncatalogued.

MAYNARD, Nathan, of Whittlesford, Cambs., village storekeeper.
Diary, Nov., 1836 and April, 1837–Jan., 1839. (Copied extracts).
Contents: local events and domestic life.
Cambridgeshire Record Office: MS. R58/5/5 184, 468–485.

MILMAN, John Borman (b. 1815), of Thorne, Yorkshire, a farmer.
Diary, Jan., 1836–Aug., 1852. 1 vol.
Contents: a fairly detailed account of his life during this period including local history, family history, and agricultural information; diarist titles it "An Universal Journal".
Sheffield University Library: MS. 630.942742 (M).

POLHILL, Mrs. Fanny M. (b. c. 1802), of Howbury Hall, Bedford, and wife of Frederick Polhill, M.P.
Diary, Jan–Dec., 1836 (with gaps). 1 vol.
Contents: brief entries concerning family, callers, dinners, etc., mainly while resident in London.
Hertford County Record Office: MS. D/P78.29/1.

POUNTNEY, Richard.
Diary, 1836–70 (with gaps).
Worcestershire Record Office: MS.

POWELL, George Eyre (Jnr.) (1820–1836), son of Commander G. E. and Catherine Powell.
Diary, and letterbook, Jan–July, 1836.
National Library of Wales: George Evans Bequest, MS. 11.

REES, William, of Llandovery, printer and bookseller.
Diaries, 1836, 1855, 1857, 1859–61, 1866–69, 1871. 13 vols.
Contents: brief notes mostly; business transactions; local events and personalities; weather; expenditures; local railway business; visits, London, Manchester, Crystal Palace; work as Town Clerk; some religious introspection; family affairs.
Cardiff Public Library: MSS. 2.647.

RUSSELL, Charles.
Diary, Sept., 1836–Feb., 1837. 138 leaves.
Contents: journal of a tour through France and Italy.
Oxford, Bodleian Library: MS. Eng. misc. e. 392 (Russell of Swallowfield Papers). (Acquired 1952).

SHEDDEN, Samuel (c. 1818–1891), of Cheltenham.

Diary, 18 April–8 May, 1836. ca. 5,500 words.

Contents: journal of a tour to Paris via London; notes on social life of Paris under the Orleans monarchy; diarist accompanied by his sister and brother-in-law; tourist's notes on Notre Dame, the steam packet, etc.

Cheltenham Public Library: Local coll. 63GT44 is a typescript of original by Henry Collett, its owner, presented in 1947. Mr. Collett has since died and the original MS. is untraced.

WAIDE, Francis (1800–1873), farmer in the Leeds district of Yorks.

Diary, 1836–Aug., 1873 (with gaps).

Contents: personal matters; terse entries on daily affairs; some introspection; deaths; mostly factual reportage.

Leeds City Archives (Sheepscar): MSS. Acc. 1152.

Jean Radford, *Annual Report and Bulletin of West Riding Libraries* 8 (1965), 47–68.

WALLING, Richard, a miller.

Diary, 1836–95. 1 vol.

Contents: emphasis on weather and local affairs.

West Sussex County Record Office: MS. MP 745.

WEMYSS, Francis, of Westbury-on-Severn, Glos.

Diaries, 1836–40. 4 vols.

Contents: details of personal matters and life in India.

Gloucestershire Records Office: MSS. D 36 F 42–45.

WILLIAMS, Esther Phillips, of Maidenhead, Buckinghamshire.

Diary, July, 1836. 92 pp.

Contents: journal of a tour in Glamorgan, South Wales; notes on places and people, Gloucester, Ross, Chepstow, Newport, Cardiff, Bridgend, Margam; visits a tin works and clothing factory; tourist's comments on towns en route for home.

Cardiff Public Library: MS. 1.521.

1837

ANON.

Diary, 1837. 74 pp.

Contents: journal of tour to Sligo and Longford; topographical and antiquarian comments in English; with notes or extracts (mainly in Irish) at end of notebook; pencil sketches of archaeological objects, caves, etc.

Dublin, Royal Irish Academy: MS. S.R. 23L.44.

ANON.

Diaries, 1837–39. 10 vols.

Contents: journals of teachers in Protestant schools converted from Roman Catholicism.

Warwickshire Record Office: MSS. CR229/Box 16/2.

ANON.

Diary, 1837.

Contents: journal describing a tour through Wales.

Private: G. Taylor Esq., of Bishops Court, Sowton, Devon: Garratt MSS.

ADDAMS-WILLIAMS, Rev. Charles (1821–1861), of Langibby, Monmouthshire.

Diaries, Jan., 1837–April, 1852.

Contents: notes of a private nature; weather, clerical duties, recreations; farm work.

Newport Public Library: MS. 3112–3113, qM 453.4.

BACON, Jane M.

Diaries, 1837–43, 1846–51, to 1870 (with gaps).

Contents: brief occasional notes of engagements; visits, social life, etc.; a journal of a purely domestic nature.

Cambridge University Library: MSS. Add. 6253.

BAINES, Hewley John, of Haxby, near York.

Diary, Aug. 1837.

Contents: journal of an excursion to Hambleton, Coxwold, Byland Abbey, Rievaulx Abbey, Duncombe Park, Ampleforth College and Helmsley; with pen and ink sketches, by schoolboy diarist.

East Riding of Yorkshire County Record Office: coll. DDBH/27/3.

BRANDLING, [?———], of Middleton Hall, Leeds.

Diary, 1837. 1 vol.

Contents: an account in diary form of disturbances during elections.

Northumberland County Record Office: MS. Brandling of Gosforth NRO 233, ZBG 24.

BROADBENT, John (1803–1842), of Liverpool, architect.

Diaries, 1837 and 1840. 2 vols.

Contents: architectural work; notes on St. Anthony's Church, the tower of Walton parish church, etc.

Liverpool Archives Office: MSS. Eq. 794.

BUNBURY, Sir Charles J. F., Sheriff of Suffolk, 1868.

Diary, 1837–38.

Bury St. Edmunds and West Suffolk Record Office: MS. 147.

CARRINGTON, Robert Smith, 1st. Baron (1752–1838).

Diaries, 1837–38. 2 vols.

Contents: uniformly brief entries re. engagements, health, etc.

Buckinghamshire Record Office: Carrington coll., D2.

CLAUGHTON, Rt. Rev. Thomas Legh (1808–1892), Bishop of Rochester, and of St Albans.

Diary, Dec., 1837–July, 1887 (with long gaps). 97 fols.

Contents: personal and family life at Oxford and as parish priest at Kidderminster; religious thoughts and his own unworthiness; his verses, partly in Latin ; social life ; only four entries after becoming Bishop of St. Albans.

Private: Francis W. Steer Esq., Patmers, Duton Hill, Great Dunmow, Essex.

CLINTON, Lord William Pelham (1815–1850), son of the 4th Duke of Newcastle, of Clumber Park, Nottinghamshire.

Diaries, July–Sept., 1837 and Aug., 1850. 3 vols.

Contents: earlier journal is of a Grand Tour made in the company of his elder brothers ; the volume at Birmingham runs 13–16 July only with a description of travels from London, through Belgium, as far as Aix-la-Chapelle. Later volume is incomplete journal of his travels in Greece, 1850.

Birmingham University Library: MS. 6/i/2. (D. W. Evans, Rare-Book Librarian).

Nottingham University Library: MSS. Ne2 F9 Ne C 5932.

De ROTHSCHILD, Lady Louisa (1821–1910), philanthropist.

Diary, July, 1837–Dec., 1907 (with gaps).

Contents: quiet details of family life in London ; her reading ; court life and society ; Victoria and Albert ; musical evenings and musicians ; visits to Italy ; Jewish life ; sport and family country life.

London, British Museum: Add. MSS. 47949–47962 (Lady Battersea Papers).

Lucy Cohen, *Lady de Rothschild and Her Daughters* (London, 1935), pp. 6–174.

DICKSON, David (b. 1821), of Minto Street, Edinburgh, wholesale stationer ; (family firm is James Dickinson).

Diaries, 1837, 1839–46, and 1856–84. 26 vols.

Contents: journal giving details of life in the city with special reference to the wholesale stationery trade ; some entries by William Dickson.

Edinburgh Central Public Library: Edinburgh Room, MSS. YDA 1820 D 55.

EDEN, Frances ("Fanny").

Diary, 1837–38.

India Office Library: MSS. Eur. c. 130.

GIROD, Amury.

Diary, Nov.–Dec., 1837.

Contents: translated from German and Italian ; not seen.

Private: J. E. C. Mackrell, Beechwood, Plympton, Devon: Seaton MSS., Sit, a.

HORNER, Joshua (1812–1881), artist.

Diaries, 1837 and 1842. 2 vols. (See also p. 234).

Contents: journals of journeys to Paris.

Halifax Central Public Library: local hist. coll. MSS. 091.

Trans. Halifax Antiquarian Soc. (1962).

JEDDERE-FISHER, Mrs. J.
Diaries, 1837 and 1844.
Contents: travel journals.
Oxford, Pitt Rivers Museum: Balfour Library MS. coll.

JOHNSTONE, Lockhart, of Worcester, a Bencher of Gray's Inn.
Diaries, 1837–42. 6 vols. in one.
Contents: chiefly consists of notes of professional engagements and fees, entered in copies of *Ree's Improved Diary and Almanack*.
Liverpool University Library: Western MSS., 86.

KNOWLES, George, of Bradford, Yorkshire, architect and land agent.
Diaries, Sept., 1837–July, 1843 and Jan.–Dec., 1885. 6 vols.
Contents: brief notes on family and professional matters.
Bradford Central Library: MSS. D.B. 37/1.

LEWIS, Miss J. E.
Diary, August, 1837.
Contents: diary of Harriet Brough's visit to Leek.
Staffordshire Record Office: Brindley Papers (typescript only).

LOVELL, Charlotte.
Diary, 1837–41.
Private: Captain A. D. C. Francis, The Grange, Malmesbury, Wiltshire.

MURRAY, Sir Charles Augustus (1806–1895), courtier and diplomat.
Diaries, 1837, 1844, 1854–59 (with gaps). 8 vols.
Contents: opens with private journal of his first three weeks as Master of the Household to Queen Victoria; later journal includes visit of the Emperor of Russia, 1844; journals of his mission to Persia, a tour of the Middle East; private journal while Ambassador to Persia, and several travel journals, to Baghdad, Poti, Tiflis, etc.
Scottish Record Office: GD 261–1, 5–10, 22.
Selections from the Writings of Sir Charles Augustus Murray, ed. Edith Murray (Edinburgh, 1900).

NEWCASTLE, Henry Pelham-Clinton, Earl of Lincoln, later 5th. Duke of Newcastle.
Diaries, June, 1837–Oct., 1838, Feb.–May, 1850, and June–Oct., 1855. 5 vols.
Contents: journal of Lord Lincoln's North European tour, June–Oct., 1837, with his former tutor, Mr. Thompson and his family, and of his European tour with his wife, Aug.–Oct., 1838; then three volumes kept on a Mediterranean cruise and tour, 1850; finally, journal kept during his tour to and in the Crimea.
Nottingham University Library: MSS. Ne C 12,980a, 12,981–12, 983, Ne2 F10 (Ne C 10,884a is typescript of the last).

ORMSBY-GORE, W. R. (See also, HARLECH, 281).
Diary, 1837.
Contents: journal of a tour of Greece and Turkey.

National Library of Wales: Harlech of Brogyntyn MSS. (Acquired 1955).

PIERREPONT, Augusta Sophia Anne (1820–1893), only child of Hon. Henry Manvers Pierrepont, m. Lord Chas. Wellesley, 1844.

Diaries, 1837, Aug., 1838–Dec., 1848, and July, 1857–May, 1860. 2 vols.

Contents: an early tour journal, 1837 ; daily journal thereafter.

Private: Duke of Wellington, Reading, Berkshire.

POWELL, Lewis, of Cardiff.

Diaries, 1837–57. 2 vols.

Contents: local affairs and social life in South Wales.

Cardiff Public Library: MSS. 1.141.

RIDDELL, Sir Walter Buchanan (1810–1892), of Whitefield.

Diary, Aug.–Sept., 1837. 1 vol.

Contents: journal kept on a tour of the Low Countries and German States. Northumberland County Record Office: MS. Riddell of Whitefield (Hepple), NRO 282, ZRW 149.

SCOTT, John, of Exeter.

Diary, 1837–38.

Contents: notes on events when the diarist was Magistrate of the Island of Trinidad, West Indies.

Exeter City Record Office: MS.

SIMCOE, Henry Walcot (1823–1848).

Diary, June–Sept., 1837.

Contents: inscribed at Penheale, Launceston, Cornwall.

Toronto Public Library (Ontario): MS.

"S.N."

Diary, 1837–38. 1 vol.

Contents: not seen ; MS. among the papers presented by Sir Charles Bunbury.

Bury St. Edmunds and West Suffolk Record Office: MS. 139.

TOTTENHAM, John L., a soldier.

Diary, 1837–42.

Contents: journal including much information on the Afghan War. India Office Library: MSS. Eur. D. 456.

TOWER, Christopher, of Weald Hall, South Weald.

Diary, 1837. 1 vol.

Essex Record Office: MS. D/DU 301.

TREACHER, John (b. 1817), of Sonning, Berks.

Diary, July, 1837–Dec., 1842 (with gaps). 1 vol.

Contents: local events, deaths, religious notes; his reading, weather, local gossip ; local Chartist meeting; some national events ; Aurora Borealis ; the building of the railway between Sonning and Reading ; his angling exploits.

Reading Public Library: MS. B/TU/TRE.

TRYE, Henry Norwood, of Hardwicke and Leckhampton, Glos.
Diary, 1837. 1 vol.
Contents: journal kept during his year of Shrievalty.
Gloucestershire Records Office: MS. D 303 F 5.
WIMBERLEY, Mary (1796–1887), wife of Rev. Charles Wimberley.
Diary, July–Dec., 1837.
India Office Library: Photo. Eur. 72.

1838

ANON.
Diaries, 1838, and 1851–62.
Nottingham City Libraries: Green MSS.
ANON.
Diary, Aug.–Sept., c. 1838.
Contents: journal of travel in north of France; antiquities and buildings.
Cambridge University Library: Add. MSS. 4215.
ANON.
Diary, Aug.–Sept., 1838
Contents: journal of travel through Belgium and Holland; scholarly and art interests.
Cambridge University Library: Add. MSS. 4216.
ANON., an army officer.
Diary, Nov., 1838–Sept., 1839. 1 vol.
Contents: journal of officer serving with Shah Shiyas' contingent in the army of the Indus during the First Afghan War.
National Army Museum: MS. 6910/16.
ADAM, Charles Brydone.
Diary, 1838–39.
Contents: a private journal by a naval man kept on board H.M.S. *Vanguard* in the Grecian archipelago.
Private: Captain C. K. Adam of Blair Adam, Blair Adam, Kelly, Fife.
BACKHOUSE, Capt. J. B., an army officer.
Diary, 1838–42.
Contents: journal kept at H.Q. Artillery Brigade under the command of Brigadier A. Graham during the First Afghan War.
Private: Brig. E. M. W. Backhouse.
National Army Museum: photocopy, 6305/115.
BENSON, Col., an army officer.
Diary, 1838–39. (extracts only).
Contents: from journal kept while diarist was (?) resident at Rangoon, India.
Scottish Record Office: GD 45/26/74.
DAVID, Noah, of Dulais Higher, near Seven Sisters, farmer.
Diaries, 1838–69. 37 vols.

Contents: early vols. of accounts ; brief entries and many gaps.
Glamorgan County Record Office: MSS. D/D Xjx 2–38.

DUCKWORTH, Susanna Catherine, of Countess Wear, near Exeter, Devon.
Diary, 1838. 1 vol.
Contents: mostly dinner engagements, etc. ; no entries for some days.
Exeter City Record Office: MS.

EMLYN, Lord.
Diaries, 1838, and 1839. 2 vols.
Contents: journals of tour in Europe.
Carmarthen County Record Office: Cawdor MSS. 1/245.

GALTON, Emma, of Claverdon, Warwick, sister of Sir Francis Galton.
Diary, 1838–98 (with gaps). (Typescript).
Contents: very brief notes of travel and events.
London, University College Library: Galton I, Item 37.

GARNETT, William James.
Diaries, 1838–73.
Lancashire County Record Office: Garnett of Quernmore MSS., DDQ.

HALL, Ellen A., of West Wickham, Kent.
Diaries, 1838–1901 (with gaps). 22 vols.
Contents: full and lively entries ; daily activities ; weather ; her health ;
reflections ; personal relationships ; frequently dialogue reproduced ;
travels, often lengthy, in England, Europe, and North Africa.
Kent Archives Office: MSS. Hall U923, F/3, 1–22. (Acquired 1962).
A. R. Mills, *The Halls of Ravenswood* (London: Muller, 1967).
O. A. Sherrard, *Two Victorian Girls* (London: Muller, 1966).

HALL, Emily Mary, of West Wickham, Kent.
Diaries, Dec., 1838–Jan., 1901 (with gaps). 23 vols.
Contents: social relationships ; weather ; thoughts and feelings ; health ;
lively dialogue recorded ; daily events ; tours in England and abroad.
Kent Archives Office: MSS. Hall U923 F/2, 1–23. (Acquired 1962).
A. R. Mills, *The Halls of Ravenswood* (London: Muller, 1967).
O. A. Sherrard, *Two Victorian Girls* (London: Muller, 1966).

HUGHES, William, of Trysglwyn, near Amlwch, Anglesey.
Diary and account book, 1838–48.
Contents: farming matters ; Baptist observance in Anglesey ; celebration
of Victoria's coronation at Amlwch ; local emigrants to the U.S.A., etc.
Bangor, University College Library: MS. 1483.

JEWITT, Arthur (1772–1852), apprentice cutler, schoolmaster, surveyor,
artist, and tutor/poet ; of Sheffield.
Diary, May, 1838–June, 1839.
Contents: a few scattered entries, no more than a dozen ; but MS. does
include an autobiography.
Wigan Central Public Library: Edward Hall coll. M 963, 964, and 967.

LAL, Gunga Narayan, evangelist.
Diaries, c. 1838. 2 vols.
Contents: entries giving an account of his intinerant preaching; he was an evangelist (Baptist) who worked with William Robinson in the Calcutta area.
London Baptist Missionary Society: IN/6.

LINCOLN, Lady Susan Harriet Catherine Pelham-Clinton, Countess of.
Diary, Nov., 1838–Feb., 1839. 1 vol.
Contents: journal kept during a visit to Italy with her husband (later 5th. Duke of Newcastle) and children.
Nottingham University Library: MS. Ne C 12,890b.

MACAULAY, Thomas Babington Macaulay, Baron (1800–1859), historian.
Diaries, Nov., 1838–Dec., 1859 (with gaps). 11 vols.
Contents: travels in Italy; his studies, reading, criticism and writings; notes on theatre and plays; political affairs.
Cambridge, Trinity College Library: MSS. coll.
George Trevelyan, *Life & Letters of Lord Macaulay*, 2 vols. (London, 1876); Richmond C. Beatty, *Lord Macaulay* (Norman, Oklahoma, 1938).

MACKENZIE, Rt. Hon. J. A. Stewart, diplomat.
Diary, 1838–39.
Contents: journal kept in Ceylon while Governor.
Scottish Record Office: GD 46/20/21.

MADDISON, R. R., Colliery apprentice, of Chester-le-Street, Durham.
Diary, Jan., 1838–Oct., 1838.
Contents: details of pit life, etc.; personal reflections and observations; diarist was apprenticed to a Mr. Easton.
Wigan Central Public Library: Edward Hall coll., Mun. Room Cases 1 & 2. (Typescript also available).

MEAN, Rev. Joseph Calrow.
Diary, and registers of baptism, 1838–77.
National Library of Wales: G. E. Evans Bequest, MS. 411.

MURRAY, James.
Diary, June–July, 1838. 1 vol.
Contents: journal of travel in Ireland; scenery, people; Dublin, Co. Wicklow.
Manchester, Chetham's Library: MS. Mun. A.2.44.

PURDUE, John, of Abbotford Place or South Portland St., Glasgow.
Diary, March, 1838–Aug., 1840. 1 vol.
Contents: journal describing trips made with his father, an inspector of stamps and taxes, to Arran, Campbelltown, Inveraray, Dunoon, etc.; notes on scenery, history, and geology.
Edinburgh Central Public Library: Scottish Dept., R.B.R. XDA 865.

RATHBONE, William (the 6th.) (1819–1902).
  Diaries, 1838–39 and 1875.
  Contents: first is a journal of a tour in Germany and Italy; the second
  is a pocket diary with few entries.
  Liverpool University Library: Rathbone Papers.
RHINELANDER, Philip.
  Diary, May, 1838–Jan., 1839.
  Contents: journal of tour of Great Britain; New York to Liverpool;
  travel through Scotland, England, Ireland, etc.; an American's notes
  on British towns, scenery, and life.
  New York Public Library: MS. 41.M.119.
ROGERS, William (1817–1890), of Mawnan rectory, Cornwall, a clerk.
  Diary, 1838 (with gaps). 1 vol.
  Contents: certain days only; spasmodic entries about journeys made
  and events.
  Cornwall County Record Office: MS. DD.X.112/129.
SALVIN, Anne Andrews, of Finchley, wife of Anthony Salvin (1799–1881)
  the architect.
  Diary, Sept., 1838. 1 vol.
  Contents: journal kept during a fortnight's excursion to Devonshire and
  the Wye Valley.
  London Borough of Barnet Public Library: MS. Acc.6787/6.
STANLEY, Maria Margaret (1797–1882), of Alderley Park, Alderley,
  Cheshire.
  Diary, Aug., 1838–May, 1839. 1 vol.
  Contents: personal journal; family events.
  Cheshire Record Office: MS. DSA 123/4.
  Nancy Mitford, ed. *The Ladies of Alderley* . . . *1841–50* (London, 1938).
STONE, John (1818–1899), Town Clerk of Bath, Somerset.
  Diaries, Nov., 1838–Nov., 1899. 5 vols.
  Contents: continued in his old age until his death by his son, John
  Harris Stone; articled to Bath solicitors, went to London, set up practice
  in Bath; Town Clerk, 1860–98; brief daily entries of personal activities;
  rough pencil index 1860–87; the same for obituary lists 1859–99.
  Bath Municipal Libraries: MSS. 991–995.
THOMAS, William (d. 1870), Baptist missionary.
  Diary and letters, 1838 (with gaps).
  Contents: journal describing his work in Calcutta, Nov.–Dec., 1838;
  letters in the form of a journal cover the period May and June, 1838.
  London, Baptist Missionary Society: MS. IN/11.
THROCKMORTON, Sir Robert, 8th. Baronet.
  Diary, Aug., 1838–June, 1862 (with gaps).
  Contents: mostly brief daily entries; some days omitted altogether.
  Warwickshire Record Office: Throckmorton MSS., 5/1–10.

TURNER, Sharon (1768–1847), the historian.
Diary, c. 1838 (extracts).
Contents: extracts from a diary found in her *Autograph*.
London, British Museum: Add. MS. 51055. (Acquired 1963).
WEBB, William, Master of Clare College, Cambridge.
Diary, June–Sept., 1838. 64 fols.
Contents: journal of tour to Scotland; from Cambridge to the High-
lands and back to Liverpool; mostly touristic notes in Highlands; notes
on the Lakes; scenery and beauties.
Cambridge University Library: Add. MS. 5871.
WHITEHEAD, Thomas (b. 1818), of London.
Diary, Jan., 1838–Aug., 1839.
Contents: journal of a Quaker; religious observances and introspection;
some later entries outside above dates.
Private: Rev. C. N. Whitehead, St. Michael's, Wigan, Lancashire. (Yale
Univ. microfilm, By3 Whitehead).
WRIGHT, Ichabod (1767–1862), banker, of Nottingham.
Diary, April, 1838–Dec., 1862, with prior autobiographical memoranda.
Contents: entries emphasize family matters rather than outside events;
some banking notes; later entries are spasmodic; after May, 1860 entries
are made by Sophia, his daughter.
Nottingham Public Libraries: MSS. M 5586–5588.

1839

ANON.
Diary, 1839.
Contents: brief notes, chiefly religious.
Surrey County Record Office: Goulburn Papers, Acc. 249.
ANON.
Diaries, 1839, 1841–45, 1847, 1849, and 1850.
Contents: brief entries of the household stewards for Baronet de
Trafford of Trafford.
Lancashire Record Office: MSS. DDTr.
ANON.
Diary, Aug.–Sept., 1839. 33 fols.
Contents: journal of a visit to the Isle of Wight; holiday notes.
London, British Museum: Add. MSS. 36532.
ANON.
Diaries, 1839, 1859, 1862, and 1863. 4 vols.
Contents: journal kept while living in S.E. Devon, perhaps Seaton or
district, 1839; another kept while in Weymouth, Dorset, and on holiday
in the Lake District, 1859; 1862 volume kept while in Weymouth and
including a visit to the Great Exhibition in London; final volume kept

while in [?] Weymouth and on holiday in Switzerland. Brief daily entries; social and personal matters.

Devon Record Office: MSS. 337 B add. /235/1–4.

BELL, Miss Henrietta, of Liverpool.

Diaries, April–May, 1839 and Jan.–April, 1840.

Contents: religious matters; introspection, musings, spiritual welfare.

Wigan Central Public Library: Edward Hall coll. M. 981, 960. (Acquired 1951).

BERESFORD-PEIRSE, Sir Henry de la Poer, of Bedale, Yorkshire.

Diary, March–April, 1839. 1 vol.

Contents: journal of a tour of France, Germany, and Italy.

North Riding of Yorkshire County Record Office: MS. ZBA 20.

BORRADAILE, John (b. 1815), of London and Calcutta, merchant.

Diary, 1839–Feb., 1852 (with gaps).

Contents: first two years summarized in retrospect: irregularly maintained; considerable amount of excision, apparently by the diarist; business fluctuations; business relations and his moods; family affairs; illustrates the growth of industrialism in England, and also Victorian business philosophy; journey to Devonshire, 1842.

Wigan Central Public Library: Edward Hall coll. M. 789.

Exeter City Record Office; MS. (has tour journal for 1842).

CASTOR, George, a soldier in the Indian Army.

Diary, 1839–61. (Copied & revised in 1890).

Contents: description of his service as a sergeant-major in the Indian Army.

India Office Library: MSS. Eur. E.262.

CATHCART, William, 1st Earl of.

Diaries, 1839–43. 5 vols.

Private: Lord Cathcart. D.S.O., M.C., Eaton Mews, London, S.W.1.: Cathcart Papers, A/101–105.

DENNISTOUN, James.

Diary, 1839.

Contents: journal of a visit to the baths of La Battaglia, near Padua, Italy.

Edinburgh University Library: MSS. (Acquired 1963).

GARNETT, William.

Diary, 1839–59.

Lancashire Record Office: Garnett of Quernmore MSS., DDQ.

JOHANNES, John (d. 1864), Baptist missionary.

Diary, June–July, [?]1839.

Contents: journal of a Baptist missionary who was appointed in 1820 and who went out to Chittagong to help Peacock at the Benevolent Institution.

London, Baptist Missionary Society: MS. IN/5.

JONES, Ernest Charles (1819–1868), of London, Chartist politician, poet and novelist.

Diaries, July, 1839–May, 1847. 2 vols.

Contents: life of a man of means; social calls, dances, opera; comment of his own writings, publishers, etc.; domestic events; post–1846 and the beginning of his political career the entries become irregular; notes on remarks at lectures and meetings of Chartists; diarist, Secretary to Chartist Co-operative Society.

Manchester Public Libraries: Archives Dept., 923.2 J 18.

Frederick Leary, *The Life of Ernest Jones* (London, 1887).

Ernest Jones, Chartist: Selections from the Writings and Speeches, with Introduction by John Saville (London, 1952).

KERMODE, Rev. William (1814–1890), of Ramsey, Isle of Man.

Diary, March, 1839–Feb., 1844.

Contents: diary forms an almost continuous record from March, 1839 until Aug., 1839, and then becomes increasingly fragmentary; of some general interest, although confined to local and personal incidents; William Kermode was a man of upright character, reflective, and benevolent; his ordination as deacon took place in 1839; he then held two curacies before his appointment as chaplain of St. Paul's.

Douglas, Isle of Man, The Manx Museum: MS. 1584.

LLOYD, D., of Carmarthen, South Wales.

Diary, 1839.

Contents: journal of a trip to Europe.

Carmarthen County Record Office: Museum MS. 308.

LYON, Thomas Henry (1825–1913).

Diaries, 1839–52. 3 vols.

Contents: personal logs of voyages on the following ships: H.M.S. *Ganges,* H.M.S. *St. Vincent,* H.M.S. *Impregnable.*

Warrington Municipal Library: MS.

MARSDEN, Col.

Diaries, 1839, 1848–53, and 1857. 4 vols.

India Office Library: MSS. Eur. 139.

[?]PARKER, George.

Diary, Sept., 1839.

Contents: journal of a voyage to the Hebrides.

Liverpool Record Office: Arch. 920 PAR III. (Acquired 1955).

POWNALL, Henry.

Diary, 1839–40.

London, British Museum: Add. MS. 52501.

SHIFFNER, Rev. Sir George Croxton, 4th. Bart. (1819–1906).

Diaries, 1839–96. 58 vols. Diaries and memoranda, 1840–1900 (with gaps). 18 vols.

Contents: entries are not very detailed; memoranda jottings.

East Sussex Record Office: Shiffner arch. 3414–3489.

Francis W. Steer, ed. *A Catalogue of the Shiffner Archives* (Lewes, 1959).

STANLEY, Arthur Penrhyn (1815–1881), Fellow of University College, Oxford ; later Dean of Westminster.

Diary, c. 1839–41. (copied by his sister, Mary). 1 vol.

Contents: interesting accounts of religious affairs in England and on the Continent ; court and social life, mostly undated.

Cheshire Record Office: MS. DSA 86.

STANLEY, Lady Gertrude Sloane, of Paultons House, Hants.

Diaries, 1839–69. 10 vols.

Hampshire Record Office: MSS. 10M55/104/113.

WILKINSON, Charles Nelson, R.N., surgeon.

Diary, 1839–42. 1 vol.

Contents: private journal kept while diarist was assistant surgeon of H.M.S. *Benbow*.

National Maritime Museum: JOD 51, MS57/015.

WINTOUR, Rev. Fitzgerald, rector of Barton-in-Fabis.

Diary, 1839–43. 1 vol.

Contents: daily happenings, expenditures, etc.

Nottinghamshire Records Office: MS. DD 257/1.

WOOD, Thomas Peploe (1817–1845), of Great Haywood, Staffs., artist.

Diary, Jan., 1839–Nov., 1844. 5 almanacks.

Contents: tours through Staffordshire on painting expeditions ; visits to London ; painting local people ; sketches inserted ; interesting personal details.

Stafford Public Library: MS.

WORSLEY, Harriet, daughter of Marcus Worsley of Terrington, Yorkshire.

Diary, 1839.

Contents: journal of a Continental tour.

Private: MS. at Hovingham Hall, Yorkshire. (Information: County Archivist, North Riding of Yorkshire).

1840

ANON.

Diary, 1840. 2 vols.

Contents: journal of a visit to Swanage, Dorset.

Berkshire Record Office: MSS. D/EMt F18/2,3.

ANON.

Diary, 1840–41.

Contents: farming matters ; almost daily entries, record of sales, plantings, lambings, etc. ; some personal entries.

Leicester Museum: Swinford House Records, MS. 12.

ANON., [?]Bassett.
Diary, 1840–98.
Private: The Earl of Scarborough, Sandbeck Park, Rotherham, York-shire: Lumley MSS.

ANON., a home missionary of Wakefield, Yorkshire.
Diary, 1840–44.
Contents: record of visits to families and the holding of evening meet-ings.
Wakefield Public Library: MS. 83.

BAYLIS, Joseph Robert.
Diary, 1840.
Contents: journal of his travels.
London, British Museum: Add. MS. 52502. (Acquired 1964).

BELL, Sir Charles.
Diaries, 1840. 3 vols.
Contents: journals of a three-month tour in Italy; notes and some watercolour sketches.
London University Library: MSS. 386.

BLIGH, J. D.
Diary, June, 1840.
Contents: tour from Hanover to Prague and Dresden; notes on towns, buildings, antiquities.
London, British Museum: Add. MS. 41287.

CRANBROOK, Gathorne Gathorne-Hardy, 1st. Earl of (1814–1906).
Diaries, 1840–1906. 20 vols.
Contents. his legal and parliamentary career; Home Secretary, Secretary for Ireland; India Office; President of Council; his own ambitions and fears, with some social and family notes.
Ipswich and East Suffolk Record Office: MSS. HA 43: T501/286–306.
A Memoir, ed. A. E. Gathorne-Hardy, 2 vols. (London, 1910).

DANIEL, Rev. Alfred (1810–1875), of Frome, Somerset.
Diaries, 1840–75. 36 vols.
Contents: parish calls noted; church meetings, organizations, and services; brief entries in the main; references and some specimens of the Toy and Albion presses, later to become the Daniel Press.
Bath Municipal Libraries: MSS. 1114–1149.

DAVIS, Thomas Osborne (1814–1845), poet and Irish patriot.
Diary, 1840–45. 97 pp.
Contents: political and historical reflections, commentary on scenes and travels in the south of Ireland, ideas for essays, rough maps, and drawings.
Sir Charles Gavan Duffy, *Thomas Davis, the Memoirs of an Irish Patriot 1840–46* (London, 1890).
Dublin, Royal Irish Academy: MS. SR.12.P.19.

DURHAM, Louise Grey, Countess of.
Diary, Jan.–July, 1840.
Contents: private notes dealing with the last months of the Earl of Durham's life.
Private: Viscount Lambton, Lambton Park, Chester-le-Street, Co. Durham.

FREMANTLE, Admiral Sir C. H. (1800–1869), of London.
Diaries, 1840–68 (except 1863 and 1865). 27 vols.
Contents: mainly brief memoranda of naval and other activities; occasional longer entries; was in charge of naval transport at Balaclava, 1855–56.
Buckinghamshire Record Office: Fremantle coll. D/FR.

GOULBURN, Mrs. Jane, wife of Harry Goulburn.
Diaries, 1840, and 1843–44. 3 vols.
Surrey Record Office: Goulburn Papers.

HICKEY, Edward.
Diary, 1840–44.
Carmarthen County Record Office: Museum MS. 307.

HOWLDEN, Richard, of Sheffield, steel merchant.
Diary, 1840–43. 263 pp.
Contents: began as a scrapbook but gradually became a written narrative of his life as an apprentice to a firm of steel, saw, and file manufacturers; matters of local interest; a picture of adolescent life.
Sheffield City Libraries: Special coll., Misc. Documents 1761.

LOEWE, Dr. Louis (1809–1888), of London.
Diary, July–Nov., 1840.
Contents: written on his travels with Sir Moses Montefiore in the relief of the Jews of Damascus; public affairs in this connection at Alexandria and Constantinople.
Private: Raphael Loewe, 85 Milton Road, Cambridge.
The Damascus Affair, ed. Paul Goodman (Ramsgate, 1940).

MARTIN, Miss Sarah (1791–1843), of Great Yarmouth, dressmaker.
Diaries, April–Aug., 1840, and other records, 1823–42. 3 vols.
Contents: her daily activities in connection with prisons in Yarmouth; other of her social work among prisoners there.
Great Yarmouth Public Library: MSS.

MENCE, Miss Sarah, a schoolgirl.
Diary, 18 Feb., 1840.
Contents: one entry for one day; an inconsequential trifle cherished by its collector, Mr. Edward Hall, as possibly the shortest diary on record.
Wigan Central Public Library: Edward Hall coll. M 812.

MEWBURN, Francis (1786–1867), of Larchfield, Darlington, solicitor.
Diaries, Aug., 1840–June, 1863 (with gaps). 5 vols.
Contents: local records, occurrences and remarks; the diarist was

solicitor for the Stockton and Darlington Railway. (Five other volumes were in existence formerly.)
Darlington Public Library: MSS. U 418 y MEW.
The Larchfield Diary (Darlington: Bailey, 1876).
MOUNT, T. E., of Reading, Berks.
Diaries, 1840. 3 vols.
Contents: one proper journal of a visit to Swanage; other two books are made up of accounts and cricket scores.
Berkshire Record Office: MSS. D/EMt F18/1–3.
NAPIER, Captain Charles Elers, step-son of Admiral Sir Charles.
Diary, 1840. 1 vol.
Contents: journal of a walking and fishing tour in Wales, Scotland, and Ireland; some engravings.
National Maritime Museum: JOD 80, MS. 810.
NICOL, James, geologist.
Diary, 1840–41.
Contents: journal kept while studying at Berlin University.
Edinburgh University Library: MS. Gen.713D.
NORTHWICK, George Bowles, 3rd Baron (1811–1888), M.P.
Diary, 1840–41. 1 vol.
Worcestershire Record Office: MS. E. 153 (Acquired 1953).
ORMEROD, George (1785–1873), of Sedbury Park, Gloucestershire.
Diaries, 1840 and July, 1845.
Contents: notes, 1845, of a tour along the former Marches of Wales; along Offa's Dyke from Ledbury to Chirk Castle; thence around North Wales, ending at Chester; the first diary contains notes made on a tour of the Low Countries and in Normandy.
National Library of Wales: MSS. 5844B.
PALFREYMAN, Mrs. M. servant of Haddo House, Co. Aberdeen.
Diaries, Jan., 1840–May, 1861. 10 vols.
Contents: among Stanmore papers.
London, British Museum: Add. MSS. 49276–49285.
QUEKETT, John Thomas (1815–1861), Conservator of Hunterian Museum, Royal College of Surgeons of England, histologist.
Diaries and notebook, 1840–48. 7 vols.
Contents: memoranda concerning work of the Museum and of experiments carried out.
London, Royal College of Surgeons Library: MSS. 42.c.49–55.
RAMSDEN, Charlotte Louisa (1815–1895), of Buckden, Yorkshire.
Diary, April–Nov., 1840. 1 vol.
Contents: journal of a Continental tour with her mother and young brother, John William (later 5th. Bart. Ramsden); tourist's notes on places and people; art galleries visited; Paris, Geneva, Chamonix, Zurich, Constance, Berne, Milan, Venice, Padua, and Bologna.

Leeds City Archives Office (Sheepscar): MS. Acc. 1270.

Catherine Murdoch, "Some Yorkshire Innocents Abroad", *Annual Report and Bulletin of the West Riding* (Northern Section) 10, 1967, 35–49.

RASHLEIGH, William (1817–1871), of Menabilly, Fowey, landowner.
Diary, June, 1840. 1 vol.
Contents: journal from Cairo to Cataracts on the Nile.
Cornwall County Record Office: MS. DD.R(S)/51.

REVELEY, Hugh John, of Brynygwin, Merioneth, landowner.
Diaries, 1840–77. 5 vols. (Transcript).
Contents: journal and reminiscences of Merionethshire life.
Merioneth County Record Office: M/781/6 and 84.

ROLLS, Martha, wife of E. N. Macready, sister of John Etherington Welch Rolls.
Diary, Sept.–Dec., 1840. 1 vol.
Contents: journal covers the first months after her marriage; activities notes; feelings and reflections.
Monmouthshire Record Office: MS. D361 F/P6.

SMITH (Smythe), F.
Diary, July–Nov., 1840.
Contents: journal of a voyage from Gravesend, Kent, to Sydney, New South Wales.
Lancashire Record Office: Blundell of Crosby MSS.

TARLETON, Vice-Admiral Sir John Walter, K.C.B.
Diaries, 1840, 1855–58, and 1862.
Contents: an autobiographical narrative in journal form covering the years 1824–75; private journal of a voyage to the West Indies, 1840; then a journal, 1855–58, while in command of H.M.S. *Eurydice* and H.M.S. *Euryalus*; an office diary for 1862 with brief notes.
Liverpool Record Office: Archives, Tarleton Family Papers, 123, 117–122, 140, 141.

WILLIAMSON, R. A.
Diary, 1840–53. 1 vol.
Contents: brief entries; some accounts.
Bedfordshire Record Office: MS. D 3/5.

WOOLLCOMBE, Henry, sometime Mayor and Recorder of Plymouth.
Diaries, 1840–47. 5 vols.
Contents: contains valuable information on Plymouth activities during this period.
Plymouth City Public Libraries: Archives Dept., Woollcombe Documents.

1841

ANON.
Diary, 1841. 1 vol.
Contents: journal of a Continental tour.
Scottish Record Office: GD 152/93.
ANON., (a tea agent probably for George Dent, London tea merchant).
Diary, April, 1841–April, 1842. 1 vol.
Contents: general experiences at Macao at the time of the Opium Wars;
voyage from Macao to Sydney, Australia, via Manilla and Hobart, on
the ship *Lord Amherst.*
London, Guildhall Library: MS. 11,891.
ANON.
Diary, 1841.
Contents: journal of a tour of Wales.
Gloucestershire Record Office: Guise MSS. D 326.
ANON.
Diary, 1841.
Contents: an account of a tour from Birmingham to Wales.
National Library of Wales: MS. 748B.
BARRINGTON, R. M.
Diary, c. 1841.
Contents: one journal and papers connected with him found loose in
the diary.
Sheffield Central Public Library: Ballitore MSS., Bundle J2 (on loan).
BEMBRIDGE, James, a home missionary.
Diaries, May, 1841–June, 1853. 13 vols.
Contents: missionary activities in Manchester.
Manchester Public Libraries: Archives Dept., BR MS. 259.B1.
BLUNDELL, John.
Diary, Aug., 1841–Dec., 1842.
Contents: journal of a stay at Thirsk, Yorkshire.
Lancashire Record Office: Blundell MSS.
CONOLLY, Arthur (d.1842), a Capt. in the Indian Army.
Diary, 1841–42. (Typescript).
Contents: journal kept while imprisoned at Bokhara; diarist was Envoy
to Khiva and was executed June, 1842.
India Office Library: MSS. Eur. B. 29 ff.3–43.
John Grover, *The Bokhara Victorians* (London, 1845).
J. W. Kaye, *Lives of Indian Officers* (London, 1895).
GUISE, Sir William Vernon (?d. 1887).
Diaries, 1841–80 (with gaps). 18 vols.
Contents: journals of tours made in Great Britain and the Continent;

F

central and north Wales, the Lake District, Scotland, Ireland, Northumberland, south-west counties; Switzerland, Italy, France on several occasions; notes on matters of geology, fishing, tourists' comment.
Gloucestershire Record Office: Guise MSS., D 326 F 46–57.

HUMPHREYS, Roderick.
Diary, 1841.
Contents: some entries made in Welsh also by the coachman who served John Jones, rector of Llanaber, Merionethshire.
National Library of Wales: MS. 2707A.

Le VESCONTE, Lieutenant Henry Thomas Dundas, R.N.
Diary, Jan., 1841–Oct., 1844. 1 vol.
Contents: personal diary written in retrospect of his time on the China coast on board H.M. ships *Calliope, Cornwallis,* and *Clio.*
National Maritime Museum: JOD 89, MS69–045.

NEWDIGATE, Colonel Francis William.
Diaries, 1841, 1857–58, 1862, 1867–69, and 1876–78.
Contents: journal of a tour to Italy, 1841, and some personal diaries.
Warwickshire Record Office: MSS. CR136/A5, A9, A10.

NEWLAND, John (b. 1805), an emigrant to New Zealand.
Diary, Mar., 1841–Jan., 1873. (Copy).
Contents: journal begins with voyage to N.Z. in the barque *Amelia Thompson*; v. brief notes: deaths of fellow passengers; St. Salvador; Cape of Good Hope; Taranaki; encounters with Maoris; earthquake tremors; people met; gossip; events including Maori attacks and killing.
Oxford, Rhodes House Library: 850.12.s.3. (Original in New Plymouth Public Library, New Zealand.)

NORTON, Capt. Robert Bruce (1821–1852), officer in the 35th. Bengal Native Infantry.
Diary, Oct., 1841–April, 1842. 1 vol. (Typescript).
Contents: journal, with some letters, kept during the First Afghan War while on duty with the Bengal Native Light Infantry at Jellabad.
National Army Museum: MS. 6807/224.

OATES, Edward, of Meanwoodside, Leeds, Yorkshire.
Diaries, 1841–64 (with gaps). 10 vols.
Contents: mostly terse entries; pious reflections; notes on the weather; and on plants, flowers, shrubs, and gardens; the activities of local people; church visits and notes on sermons; some letters.
Leeds Archives (Sheepscar): MSS. Acc. 1164 and 1258. (Acquired 1942).

PEASE, Edward (1767–1858), of Darlington, Co. Durham, a Quaker industrialist.
Diary, 1841–57. 1 bundle of loose sheets.
Contents: extracts in the C.R.O. were made by his son, John Pease (1798–1868).

Durham County Record Office: MS. D/Ho/F 93.
Darlington Public Library: MSS. (originals).

PINE, Chilley, an Army surgeon.
Diaries, 1841–May, 1848, and April and October, 1854.
Contents: private journals kept while serving with the 58th. Foot and
with the 4th Dragoon Guards at Balaclava, Crimea.
National Army Museum: MSS. 6807/262/1–3.

ROBERTS, William ("Nefydd") (1813–1872), of Blaenau, Monmouthshire,
author and non-conformist minister.
Diaries, 1841, 1854, 1857, 1865–66, and 1868–71.
Contents: some entries in Welsh; personal matters and notes relating
to British and Foreign School Society of which diarist was an agent; he
was also a Baptist minister.
National Library of Wales: Nefydd MSS. 7073–7076 and 7096.

SALE, Lady Florentia.
Diary, Nov.–Dec., 1841.
Contents: journal kept at Kabul during nine months of captivity in
Afghan hands.
London, Public Record Office: 30/12 32(Pt. 1)3 (Ellenborough Papers).
The First Afghan War: Lady Sale, ed. Patrick McCrory (London, 1969).

TALFOURD, Sir Thomas Noon (1795–1854), M.P. and playwright.
Diaries, 1841–42, 1847–49, and Sept., 1852–March, 1854. 7 vols.
Contents: private and personal memoranda; some relating to his work
as a judge and as M.P. for Reading; friendships with Mary Russell
Mitford, Charles Lamb, and other literary figures.
Reading Public Library: MSS R/TU/TAL.

TERRY family.
Diaries, 1841–62.
Hampshire Record Office: uncatalogued.

THOMSON, G. E., of Plymouth, naval officer.
Diary, 1841–65.
Contents: journals with notes on routes of voyages; some watercolours.
Private: A. H. Lemar, Esq.
Plymouth Central Library: (on loan).

THORNLEY, Caroline (1822–1888), of Liverpool.
Diaries, 1841–58. 6 vols.
Manchester, John Rylands Library: Eng. MSS. 1173–78.

VERE, Hannah C. Hope.
Diary, 1841–43.
Contents: detailed journal.
Scottish Record Office: GD 46/15/137.

VYVYAN, Sir Richard Rawlinson, Bt. (1800–1879), of Trelowarren, near
Helston, Cornwall, M.P. and landowner.
Diaries, 1841–46 (with gaps). 30 vols.

Contents: night journals (written in Italian) with analyses of dreams; philosophical matter; diarist was M.P. for Helston 1841–57.
Cornwall County Record Office: MSS. DD.V.22M/FC/41/13–43.
WELLS, Dr. Edward.
Diaries, 1841–47. 8 vols.
Contents: mostly tour journals; Prussia, Switzerland, and Austria as Travelling Fellow in the University of Oxford; visits to various watering places; medicinal properties of springs detailed; also a tour of Italy.
West Sussex County Record Office: Misc. MSS.
WHITTENBURY, John Llewellyn.
Diary, Oct., 1841–April, 1842. 1 vol.
Contents: journal kept during journey to and residence at Rome.
Birmingham University Library: MS. 5/vi/10.

1842

ANON.
Diary, Jan., 1842–Dec., 1844. 1 vol.
Contents: journal kept by a schoolboy.
Nottinghamshire Records Office: MS. DD7/2.
ANON.
Diary, 1842–84 (with account book).
Contents: farm journal at Swakeleys-Herries Farm, Hillingdon.
Greater London Record Office (Middlesex Records): MS. Acc. 443.
ANON.
Diary, July, 1842.
Contents: account of a continental tour including Belgium, the Rhine Valley and Paris.
National Library of Wales: Baker Gabb MS. 1206.
ANON.
Diaries, 1842 and 1852.
Contents: journals made in the company of one Thomas Hunt to Chester and North Wales in the first instance and in 1852 to South Wales.
National Library of Wales: MSS. 4946C.
BARLOW, Henry Clark (1806–1876), medical doctor and author.
Diaries, 1842–56 (with gaps). 12 vols.
Contents: journals of travel, mainly in Italy, but also to Athens, Constantinople, Austria, Germany, France, Sweden, and Denmark; notes on topography, history, and especially the art of places visited.
London University College Library: Barlow Papers.
CHAPMAN, Elizabeth (née Fry), of Great Warley.
Diaries, 1842–45. 3 vols.
Essex Record Office: MSS. D/DU 353/1–3.

CHICHESTER, Charles Raleigh (b. 1830), eldest son of Sir Charles Chichester, soldier.

Diary, 1842–68 (with gaps).

Contents: early journal kept at boarding school, Stonyhurst; later in Paris; soldiering in Barbados and Crimea; later diaries kept in Ireland.

East Riding of Yorkshire County Record Office: DDCH/93–103.

COLERIDGE, Henry James, D.D.

Diary, Dec., 1842–Feb., 1845. 1 vol.

Contents: journal of a clergyman, together with various theological notes.

Birmingham University Library: MS. 6/i/9.

COLLIER, Dr. Howard E. (d. 1849).

Diary, 1842–46.

Contents: records of medical practice, especially in obstetrics.

Worcester Friends' Meeting House: MS. Bulk Acc. 22–8/898/2.

Worcestershire Record Office: Typescript.

FITZHERBERT, Lady Agnes (d. 1863), wife of Sir Henry Fitzherbert (1783–1858), of Tissington.

Diaries, 1842–63.

Contents: mostly short notes on family and social happenings entered in various printed diaries and almanacks.

Derbyshire Record Office: Fitzherbert coll.

FORBES, James David (1809–1869), geologist.

Diary, winter 1842–43. 549 pp.

Contents: travels in the Alps of Savoy, etc.

St. Andrews University Library: MS. DQ823.F7.

HOPKINS, Eliza Ann (1806–1866), of Brandy Carr, Lincs.

Diary, Nov. 1842–Feb., 1866 (copy).

Contents: Quaker religious life and observances; health and spiritual life; visits to neighbouring meetings; God's mercies.

Lincolnshire Archives Office: MS.

LAWLEY, Bielby Richard.

Diaries, 1842–44 and 1860.

Contents: journal of his tours of Europe, and of a stay in 1843 at Escrick, Nun Appleton and York.

East Riding of Yorkshire County Record Office: MSS. DDFA/40–27.

LAWRENCE, Captain with Captain Beresford, Lieut. Dundas, and Lieut. R. Lloyd.

Diary, May–Aug., 1842.

Contents: journal of a tour of the United States.

National Library of Wales: Aston Hall MSS. 8011.

MILNE, Lieut.-General Henry, Army officer.

Diary, Jan., 1842–Feb., 1843.

Contents: journal kept at Kelat-Ghilai during the First Afghan War.

National Army Museum: MS. 6807/207.

MONSON, 6th Lord.
Diaries, 1842–61 (with gaps). 22 vols.
Contents: most describe travel and residence abroad in Italy, France, etc.; one undated describes a tour in Lincolnshire, with some church notes.
Private: Lord Monson, The Manor House, South Carlton, Lincs.

PHILIPS, Ellen Laetitia (d. 1913).
Diaries, 1842, 1850–79, and 1881–1913. 48 vols.
Contents: details of family affairs; tour journals in the Lake District, 1842, and Wales, 1856.
Gloucestershire Records Office: Dyrham Park MSS.

POWELL, Eleanor (1817–1842).
Diary c. 1842. 1 vol.
Contents: journal assumed to be by Eleanor Powell copied into a diary for 1836.
Kent Archives Office: MS. U934 Powell, FO/1, 2.

RAMSDEN, Sir John William Bart., M.P.
Diary, Aug., 1842–Dec., 1846.
Contents: irregular entries; introspective comment and self-examination; journal of a tour of the continent in Autumn, 1846, with most entries made in Italy.
Leeds City Archives (Sheepscar): MSS. Acc. 1270.
Catherine Murdoch, "Some Yorkshire Innocents Abroad", *Annual Report & Bulletin of the West-Riding (Northern Section)*, 10, 1967, 35–49.

REEVE, John, son of General John Reeve.
Diary, c. 1842.
Contents: journal of a stay in Canada.
Private: Leadenham House, Lincoln.

REEVE, Miss.
Diaries, 1842–50. 9 vols.
Private: Leadenham House, Lincoln.

SMITH, James, of Padham, Lancashire, farmer and cabinet-maker.
Diary, 1842–44.
Contents: references to the state of markets; Accrington's civil disturbances.
Private: Miss Smith, formerly of Burnley, Lancs.; present location unknown.

SMYTHE, Agnes M. A.
Diaries, 1842, 1855, 1872, and 1886.
Contents: mostly journals of tours on the continent; Germany, the Tyrol, northern Italy, and Switzerland.
Lancashire Record Office: Blundell MSS., 53, 57–59. (Acquired 1947).

TAYLOR, Helen (1818–1885), author.
Diary, Jan., 1842–Jan., 1847, 185 fols.
Contents: economics interest; associated with John Stuart Mill.
London School of Economics Library: R (S.R.) 1033.

THURSBY, Rev. M. W. Frederic, rector of Abington.
Diaries, 1842–49, 1852–58, 1862–67, and 1869.
Northamptonshire Record Office: MSS. coll.

TREFFREY, J. T. (Austen) (1782–1850), of Place, Fowey, industrialist and landowner.
Diaries, 1842–50. 3 unbound gatherings.
Contents: memoranda about rebuilding Place.
Cornwall County Record Office: MSS. DD.TF.996.

TROWER, Lieut. F. C., officer of the 33rd. Bengal Native Infantry.
Diary, April–Dec., 1842. 218pp.
Contents: journal kept during the First Afghan War.
National Army Museum: MS. 6807/128.

VANSITTART, Mary Amelia, wife of Henry Vansittart (b. 1817).
Diaries, c. 1842–58.
Contents: fragments mostly.
India Office Library: MSS. Eur. B. 167.

WILLIAMS, William Morris, of Bron-y-Fuches, Dinorwig, Llanddeiniolen, a quarry official.
Diaries, 1842 and 1844. 2 vols.
Contents: little mention of his work at Dinorwig Quarries; general matters.
Caernarvon County Record Office: M/1256/1.

WIRE, William (1804–1857), of Colchester, clockmaker.
Diary, April, 1842–March, 1857. 1 vol.
Contents: largely archaeological interest; discoveries of Roman remains; building of railway; new bridge; notes on town grammar school; the Devil's footprints in the Colchester snow; details of small town life.
Colchester, Colchester & Essex Museum: MSS.

YERBURY, Capt. John William, officer of the Light Dragoons.
Diary, Feb.–Oct., 1842.
Contents: journal kept by an officer of the 3rd. Light Dragoons during the First Afghan War.
National Army Museum: MS. 6807/319.

1843

ANON., probably a member of the Rashleigh family, Fowey, Cornwall.
Diaries, July–Sept., 1843, 1846, and Aug.–Oct., 1850. 3 vols.
Contents: travel journals in France, in Netherlands, Germany, Switzer-

land and Italy, and finally in Belgium, Switzerland, Austria, and Scotland.
Cornwall County Record Office: MSS. DD.R(S) 52/1–3.

ANON., [Lapidge family of Portsmouth].
Diary, March–Dec., 1843. 1 vol.
Contents: scrappy and irregularly maintained; jottings of visits made, illnesses, and deaths.
Wigan Central Public Library: Edward Hall coll.

ANON.
Diary, 1843–44.
Contents: pocket diaries, with brief notes of money matters.
Private: Sir Robert Throckmorton, Coughton Court, Near Alcester, Warwickshire.

ABBOT, Keith Edward, sometime Consul at Tehran, Persia.
Diary, 1843–44. (Copy only)
Contents: journal of a journey from Tabriz to Tehran.
London, British Museum: Add. MS. 46409.

BARTLETT, Lavinia F.
Diaries, May–June, 1843 and July, 1850–April, 1851. 2 vols.
Contents: journal of a trip to Paris with her husband, 1843; journal of a trip to the Pyrenees and Riviera with her husband, daughters and a niece, 1850–51.
Birmingham University Library: MSS. 6/iii/30.

[?]BELDAM family, of Royston, Hertfordshire.
Diary, c. 1843. 1 vol.
Contents: journal of a journey from Boulogne to Paris and Rouen; the diarist may have been a travelling companion to Mr. & Mrs. Beldam, and the journal may have been as late as 1848.
Cambridge Record Office: MS. R58/8/14/17.

BRIGHTWELL, Cecilia L. (1811–1875), author and etcher.
Diary, 1843–67.
Contents: her work and social life.
Norwich Public Library: MS.

BRODIE, Alexander Oswald.
Diary, Oct., 1843–Sept., 1844. 1 vol.
Contents: journal kept at Tobermory.
St. Andrews University Library: TA.140B8E43.

FORBES, Rev. Robert, of Leith.
Diary, 1843. 182 pp.
Contents: journal of a journey to Ayr to organize a chapel.
Edinburgh University Library: MSS.

FORTESCUE, John William (1819–1859), of Castle Hill, Filleigh, Lieu-tenant-Colonel of the East Devon Militia, and M.P.
Diaries, 1843–51. 5 vols.
Contents: detailed daily entries of travels in Austria, Palestine, Egypt,

Greece, Italy, Ceylon, India, Denmark, Sweden, Norway and Portugal.
Devon Record Office: MSS. 1262 M/FD 23–27.

FRY, Rachel, granddaughter of Elizabeth Fry the philanthropist.
Diary, 1843–44. 1 vol.
Essex Record Office: MS. D/DQ 14/39.

GALTON, Sir Francis (1822–1911), of Westminster, London, scientist.
Diaries, 1843, 1853, and 1854. 3 vols.
Contents: mostly appointments; there is also a precise diary entitled "Childhood to 1883", includes particularly notes of journeys, though probably written all at one time.
London, University College Library: Galton Desk 1.
D. W. Forrest, *Francis Galton* (London: Elek, 1974).

GILSON, John.
Diary and notebooks, 1843–46.
Contents: journals kept in Germany and Russia.
London, British Museum: Add. MSS. 50245–50248 (Hodgson papers).

HUGHES, Thomas (1822–1896), novelist.
Diary, Aug., 1843–June, 1844.
Contents: journal written for Frances ("Fanny") Ford, later his wife; personal and social life in London, and travel in England.
Private: Mrs. H. V. d'Agostino, formerly of New York, present location unknown.

LLOYD, Mrs. A. M., landowner.
Diary, 1843.
Carmarthen County Record Office: Cynghordy MSS. 1145.

MAR and KELLIE, W. C. Erskine, Earl of, officer of the Bengal Native Infantry.
Diary, 1843 (Extracts only).
Contents: journal containing observations on fellow officers of the 73rd.
Bengal Native Infantry, before diarist had succeeded to the title.
National Army Museum: MS. 7106/24.

PAMPLIN, S., of Battersea, Surrey.
Diary, 1843–51.
Contents: private notes kept at Battersea; mainly sermon texts.
Private: Rev. Henry E. Ruddy, formerly of Rugby, Northamptonshire; present location unknown.

PRATTINGTON, Adam, of Birmingham.
Diary, 1843 (Transcript, 1953).
Worcestershire Record Office: MSS. coll.

PUGH, David, of Llanerchydol.
Diary, 1843–61.
Private: Captain A. D. C. Francis, The Grange, Malmesbury, Wiltshire.

ROW, Thomas Broom, of Thorverton, accountant and land agent.
Diary, 1843. 1 vol.
F*

Contents: brief daily entries; business matters, diarist was agent to West of England Fire and Life Office; social items; kept at Thorverton and one summer holiday at Bude.

Devon Record Office: MS. 1044 B/ MF 33

WEBSTER, John, of Thame, Oxfordshire, solicitor.

Diary, 1843. 1 vol.

Contents: personal matters.

Oxfordshire Record Office: MS. Misc. Har. Acc. 197.

WHITMORE-JONES family.

Diary, 1843 and some mid-century.

Private: A. Clutton Brock Esq., Chastleton House, Moreton-in-the-Marsh, Oxfordshire.

1844

ANON.

Diary, 1844–45.

Contents: journal of tours in Europe by a resident of Wicken Bonhunt, Essex.

Cambridge University Library: MSS. Add. 7631. (Acquired 1963).

ANON.

Diary, 1844.

Contents: various entries in *The Lily or Ladies Annual Pocket Book*; some tracings and maps for railways.

National Library of Wales: Bontdolgadfan MSS. 16765A.

ANON.

Diary, 1844.

Contents: journal of a tour in North Wales.

Monmouthshire Record Office: Rolls MSS.

ANON., [?]James Brown.

Diary, 1844–46. 175 pp.

Contents: log of the ship *Gossypium*, the master being James Brown; voyages between Liverpool and New Orleans.

Liverpool Record Office: MS.KF227.

BELL, G. J.

Diary, Jan–March, 1844.

Contents: journal of journeys from London to Holland, Hanover, Prussia, Saxony, Vienna; tourist's notes, with medical and scientific interests; anatomy.

National Library of Scotland: MS. No. 32.7.3.

BEST family.

Diary, 1844. 1 vol.

Contents: journal of journey to Constance, Trieste, Venice, and Germany; met Strauss.

Kent Archives Office: MS. U480 Best, F 64.

BLACK, William Henry (1808–1872), of Goodman's Fields, and later of Mill Yard Meeting House, Whitechapel, Assistant Keeper of Public Records.

Diary, Jan., 1844–April, 1846. 1 vol.

Contents: this volume is the second of a series; regular entries recording his work done at the Public Record Office; some notes on his mediaeval studies; very little about his religious activities.

Manchester, Chetham's Library: Mun. A.2.111.

F. H. Amphlett Micklewright, *N&Q* Vol. 192, 4 (Feb. 15th, 1947); and diverse entries in same journal of that year, 14 June, 29 Nov., and 13 Dec.

BROMLEY, William Davenport.

Diaries, 1844 and 1854–55. 2 vols.

Contents: a travel diary, 1844; and a diary kept in the Crimea.

Manchester, John Rylands Library: Bromley Davenport Mun. MSS. 18 and 19.

COWBURN, Rev. Allan.

Diary, 1844.

Contents: journal kept following his marriage to Rebe Mary Randall.

Kent Archives Office: U1127 Smith Masters, F 13.

DALTON, Thomas M., of Merthyr, Glamorgan.

Diaries, 1844 and 1862. 2 vols.

Contents: journal kept by a solicitor and clerk of the peace to Glamorgan; South Wales interest; entries brief and infrequent; jottings of memoranda, names and cases.

Cardiff Public Library: MS. 2.1085.

DAVIES, Lieutenant Thomas, R.N., later a Captain.

Diaries, 1844–47 and 1850–52. 2 vols.

Contents: journals kept on board H.M.S. *America* in the Pacific, and also H.M.S. *Cygnet*, off the coast of West Africa mostly.

National Maritime Museum: JOD 42, MS57/045.

FORST, Matthew.

Diary, 1844. 1 vol.

Contents: journal containing notes on travel and business in connection with the lead mining industry.

Derbyshire Record Office: MS. 504B/L242.

FRYER, Frederick (d. 1872), of Toothill Grove, York.

Diary, Oct., 1844–June, 1845.

Contents: journal of journey in Europe; France, Malta, Egypt, Italy, Germany in company of T. Pease; tourist's notes, with remarks on Quaker life abroad.

London, Friends' Society Library: MS. S.50.

HANSARD, Luke Henry (1816–1890), of Hove, printer.

Diary, 1844–51. 1 vol.

Contents: personal matters; entries concerned with printing.
Southampton University Library: MS. Acc. A9.
HARNESS, Rev. William.
Diary, 1844 (Typed copy).
Contents: journal of a visit to Stratford-Upon-Avon.
Stratford, The Shakespeare Birthplace Trust: DR 125.
Shakespeare Survey XV (1961), pp. 110–115.
HOMRIGH, Henry Davis Van (d. 1845), officer of the Bengal Native Infantry.
Diary, Jan., 1844–Dec., 1845. (Typescript of extracts).
Contents: journal kept by officer of the 48th. Bengal Native Infantry during the First Sikh War up to his death at Moodhee.
National Army Museum: MS. 6305/55.
HUNTLY, Marchioness Marie Antoinette, wife of the 10th. Marquess.
Diaries, 1844–93. 16 vols.
Huntingdonshire Record Office: Small coll. MSS. Acc. 539.
JARVIS, Hon. Caroline, [?] of Gonalston.
Diaries, 1844–71. 5 vols.
Contents: entries of miscellaneous interests.
Nottinghamshire Records Office: MSS. DDF 8/38–42.
JERMYN, Lieut. Turenne, an officer of the Bombay Native Infantry.
Diary, 1844 (Part only).
Contents: journal of an officer kept during the Sind War while serving with the 2nd. Bombay Native Infantry.
National Army Museum: MS. 6602/61.
JOHNSTON, Dr. George (1797–1855), of Berwick, naturalist.
Diary, 1844.
Contents: notes of a visit to Jardine Hall.
Proc. Berwickshire Naturalists' Club (1873–75), pp. 406–418.
LENTHALL, F. Kyffin.
Diaries, 1844–48 and 1888–89.
Contents: jottings and accounts.
Berkshire Record Office: MSS. D/EL 1.
MAX-MULLER, Rt. Hon. Friedrich, P.C., K.M., M.A., LL.D., D.C.L. (1823–1900), Corpus Professor of Comparative Philology, Oxford
Diary, 1844–49.
Contents: journal written in English, German, and French.
Oxford, Bodleian Library: MS. Dep. d. 185.
N. C. Chaudhuri, *Scholar Extraordinary* (London: Chatto and Windus, 1974).
MURDOCH, John (1819–1904), teacher and missionary.
Diary, March, 1844–Oct., 1849.
Contents: journal of his first four years as teacher and missionary in Ceylon and India, 1844–1904.

Glasgow University: MS. Gen. 41 (Special Collections Dept.).

H. B. Timothy, "He took words with him", *Other Lands* XL, No. 1, (January, 1959), 14–16.

NICHOLS, Miss M. A. I. [? daughter of John Nichols, antiquary].

Diaries, 1844–66 (gaps). 4 vols.

Contents: journeys to various places in England and on the Continent; some family matters; much antiquarian detail; cuttings on antiquarian matters, engravings, drawings, etc.

Private: Norman S. Angus, Esq., formerly of Sheffield; present location unknown.

PALGRAVE, William Gifford (1826–1888), diplomat.

Diary, 1844.

Contents: journal of a tour from London to Italy.

Yale University Library: William M. Odom coll.

PERCY, Lord Henry Hugh Manvers (1817–1877), general.

Diaries, 1844–45, 1849–57, 1859, 1863–76. 19 vols. or boxes.

Staffordshire Record Office: MSS. D260/M/F/5/69.

ROLLS, Elizabeth Mary (b. 1813), wife of John Etherington Welch Rolls, of the Hendre, Llangattock-vibon-avel, near Monmouth.

Diaries, April–May, 1844, 1849, and 1852–53. 3 vols.

Contents: generally journals of the voyages in the Rolls' yacht, *Esmeralda*. The day-by-day accounts are quite full, vividly describing the effects of bad weather and showing Mrs. Rolls' interest in her family.

Monmouthshire Record Office: MSS. D361 F/P4.

SEWELL, William (1804–1874).

Diary, 1844–45.

Oxford, Pusey House Library: MSS. coll.

SEYMOUR, Emily Charlotte, wife of 2nd. Baron Harlech.

Diaries, 1844–45 and 1847.

Contents: journal giving account of voyages with her father, Admiral Sir George Seymour, on H.M.S. *Collingwood*, to Chile and Peru, and around Cape Horne, and later to Callae.

National Library of Wales: Harlech of Brogyntyn MSS. (Acquired 1955).

STANLEY, Joseph, of Manchester.

Diaries, Jan–June, 1844 and Oct., 1851–Jan., 1852. 2 vols.

Contents: travel journals, first to Italy, via France; later to Rome and Naples; notes of places visited; personal jottings; itinerary and some note of expenses.

Manchester Public Libraries: Archives Dept., MSS 923.9 S 126.

STEVENS, W., of Fleet St., London.

Diary, 1844–45. 1 vol.

Contents: an illustrated journal by a man of a scientific turn of mind; an engraver designer, an amateur photographer, astronomer, optician, musician and mathematician in interests.

London, University College Library: Ogden MS. 89.

TARLETON, Finetta Esther (née Dimsdale).

Diaries, 1844–45 and 1852. 2 vols.

Contents: entries relate to her social life in Hertfordshire and London.

Liverpool Record Office: Tarleton Family papers: MSS. 184–185.

WARE, T. Hibbert, of Cheshire, England and (briefly) of Orillia, Ontario, a barrister.

Diary, 1844.

Contents: voyage to Canada; early months in Canada near Toronto at Orillia; Canadian society and life; diarist is critical, and eventually books a return passage.

Toronto Public Library: MSS. coll.

1845

ANON.

Diary, 1845. 1 vol.

Contents: journal containing miscellaneous memoranda and accounts of journeys to the Low Countries, Italy, and Germany; some appear to be retrospective.

Scottish Record Office: GD 18/2123.

ANDERSON, Mrs. (d. 1845), wife of Capt. James Anderson, Hollam Hall, Titchfield, Hants.

Diary, Jan., 1845. 1 vol.

Contents: notes concerning the usual pattern of her day, her children's studies and masters, etc; diarist died on 31st. Jan.

Portsmouth City Record Office: MSS. Ref. 16A/137.

BARRETT, John B.

Diary, 1845.

Private: Mrs. E. J. Mockler, Milton House, Abingdon, Berkshire.

Berkshire Record Office: Barrett MS. F 33 (on loan).

BECHER, General Sir Arthur, K.C.B.

Diary, Dec., 1845–March, 1846. 1 vol.

Contents: journal kept during the First Sikh War.

National Army Museum: MS. 5407/1.

BEVILLE, Henry.

Diary, 1845. 1 vol.

Contents: journal relating to his journey to India, with poems and other notes.

National Army Museum: MS. 7201/47.

CAMPION, Caroline Florence.

Diary, 1845?–47.

Contents: journal of her travels.

Oxford, Bodleian Library: MS. Dep. Monk Bretton Box 36.

CASS, Brevet Major George.
Diary, 1845–50 (with gaps). 9 pp.
National Army Museum: MS. 5201/55/1–2.

CLARK, William Southern, of The Mardy, Aberdare.
Diary, 1845–58 (with gaps).
Contents: occasional brief entries by the chief mineral engineer to the Bute Trustees.
National Library of Wales: MSS. 7454–7460. (Acquired 1833).

CRAY, Lieut–General William John, of the Bengal Artillery.
Diary, 1845–58. (2 MS. transcripts).
Contents: journals kept during service with Bengal Artillery; includes the Indian Mutiny and an account of commanding the seige train from Ferozepore to Delhi, 1857.
National Army Museum: MS. 6807/201.

EWEN, George W., son of T. L. Ewen.
Diary, 1845–79 (with gaps).
Contents: mostly domestic memoranda; a very brief account of special events; includes many notes of local interest.
Berkshire Record Office: MSS. D/EE F73. (On loan).

EWEN, Charles, son of T. L. Ewen.
Diaries, 1845. 3 vols.
Contents: journal kept during his visit to New Zealand.
Berkshire Record Office: MSS. D/EE F70. (Owned and kept at The Elms, Sonning, Berkshire).

FERGUSSON, Sir William (1808–1877), Hon. L.L.D., F.R.S., surgeon.
Diaries, 1845–77. 33 vols.
Contents: a general record of his life.
London, Royal College of Surgeons Library: MSS. Add. 90/1–33.

FREER, Dr. George Robert, of Church Street, Donington-in-Holland, Lincolnshire.
Diaries, June, 1845–Dec., 1850; Jan–Oct., 1856; March–Dec., 1857. 3 vols.
Contents: brief entries almost daily summarizing events; some illustrations with pen and ink, some coloured sketches.
Lincolnshire Archives Office: Misc. Dep. 88. (Acquired 1957).

GRANT, Lady Lucy of Kilgraston, near Perth.
Diaries, 1845–55.
Contents: journals of her travels in Germany, Austria, Switzerland, and France.
Scottish Record Office: GD 6/2182.

GRIFFITH, Rev. John, of Merthyr Tydvil, Glamorgan.
Diaries, 1845, 1860–64, 1866–67, and 1870. 11 vols.
Contents: diaries of a clerical nature kept by the vicar of Merthyr Tydvil.
Cardiff Public Library: MSS. 3504.

HANFORD, C. J.

Diary, 1845–60.

Contents: personal notes and many newspaper cuttings.

Private: A. W. Whitworth, Esq., Woollas Hall, Pershore, Worcs.

Worcestershire Record Office: Whitworth MS. 1204 (on loan).

HANNAN, William, of Cornham Farm, Exmoor.

Diary, 1845–57.

Contents: a record of twelve years of living on Exmoor ; farm matters.

Oxford, Agricultural Economic Research Institute: A.E.R. 1. Cupboard.

HOLT, George (1790–1861), of Liverpool.

Diary, 1845–61 (copy and extracts only).

Contents: extracts from George Holt's diary which relate to Alfred Holt, the probable copyist.

Liverpool Record Office: Arch. Holt Papers 2/38.

PEARN, Edward J. P., Master Commander, R.N.

Diary, Sept., 1845–Sept., 1846. 1 vol.

Contents: private journal kept aboard H.M. Troopship *Atholl*.

National Maritime Museum: JOD 83, MS62/001.

PHILSON, T. M., assistant surgeon, R. N.

Diary, 1845–54.

Contents: a medical journal kept by the assistant surgeon and C. Pine, surgeon, in H.M.S. *British Sovereign* to Sydney and Aukland [Auckland?], and in H.M.S. *Castor* from Aukland [Auckland?] to Sydney.

National Maritime Museum: JOD 26, MS54/015.

WELSH, General James (1775–1861), C.O. of the Northern Division of the Madras Army at Waltair.

Diary, June, 1845–Feb., 1848.

Contents: journal records crude meteorological & astronomical observations, the texts of sermons, ailments, daily routine, births & deaths ; account of rebellion in Golconda which he subdued. "Trivial and intimate".

India Office Library: MSS. Eur. D. 168.

J. Welsh, *Military Reminiscences . . . of Nearly Forty Years' Active Service in the East Indies* (London, 1860).

WINFIELD, John Fawkener.

Diary, Aug–Oct., 1845.

Contents: notes on a tour of Belgium and Germany.

Birmingham Public Library: MS. 660 877.

WOOD, John, of Thedden Grange, a landowner.

Diaries, 1845–70. 28 vols.

Contents: life of a country squire, especially interested in hunting.

Hampshire Record Office: MSS. 28M67/1–28.

1846

ANON.
Diary, 1846–1909. 1 vol.
Contents: brief entries on local and national events kept by incumbents, Moulsford.
Berkshire Record Office: MS. D/P 88/1/1.
ANON.
Diary, 1846. 1 vol.
Carmarthenshire County Record Office: Cynghordy MSS. 1146.
ANON.
Diary, July, 1846–Sept., 1847. 1 vol.
Manchester Public Libraries: Archives Dept., MS. 923.4 D.1.
ANON. (of Edinburgh).
Diary, Jan., 1846–March, 1850. 74 fols.
Contents: notes of a man educating himself; Edinburgh life; music, studies, and lectures on practical, cultural, and intellectual matters; weather; walks.
National Library of Scotland: MS. 3107.
BAXTER, William, a Wesleyan Methodist preacher.
Diary and commonplace book, 1846–71.
Contents: notes on his work while at Manavon and Welshpool, Montgomeryshire.
National Library of Wales: MS. 6211B. (Acquired 1929).
BLUNDELL, Nicholas, 28th. Lord, of Little Crosby, Lancashire.
Diaries, 1846–89, and 1847. 61 vols.
Contents: personal jottings; includes the journal of his honeymoon with Agnes (née Smythe) on the Continent; France, Italy, Switzerland, and Germany.
Lancashire Record Office: Blundells of Crosby MSS. (Acquired 1947).
CARR, Thomas, first Bishop of Bombay.
Diaries, 1846–59 (copy). 18 vols.
Contents: journal of his work in India.
Buckinghamshire Record Office: Arch. of the Earl of Bucks., Hampden House, Great Hampden.
COLLINSON, Samuel (1812–1895), of Nottingham, stockbroker and poet.
Diaries, 1846; Oct., 1854–June, 1868; Sept., 1869–70. 2 vols.
Contents: personal life and Nottingham activities; lectures; volunteers; reading; public affairs; general observations; walks; local obituaries.
Nottingham Public Library: Arch. M 382–383. (Acquired 1922).
V. W. Walker, "Sam. Collinson's Diary", *Transactions of Thoroton Society*, LXVII (1943), 53–61.

FLOWER, Mrs. Sarah, (d. 1908), of Stratford-Upon-Avon.
Diary, 1846–92 (with gaps). 1 vol.
Contents: journal of the wife of Charles Edward Flower.
Stratford, The Shakespeare Birthplace Trust: DR 195.

GARDINER, Capt. Allen F., missionary.
Diaries, 1846–47 and 1850–51. 3 vols.
Contents: journals kept while serving at Tierra del Fuego.
London, South American Missionary Society; MS 1.

G——, Harry, of Camberwell, London.
Diary, Oct–Nov., 1846. 84pp.
Contents: journal of a Rhine tour: from London to Ostend, Koln, Koblenz, Frankfurt, Bonn, Liege, Brussels, Antwerp; local customs; paintings; churches; diarist writes in affected style but not without sense of humour.
Oxford, Bodleian Library: MS. Eng. misc. f.412. (Acquired 1971).

HORSMAN, Charlotte Louisa, wife of Edward Horsman (1807–1876).
Diaries, Oct., 1846–March., 1847 and Feb–July, 1855.
Contents: journal of a visit to Italy, Germany and Switzerland, winter of 1846; later vol. mostly concerned with her husband's political activities and parliament.
Buckinghamshire Record Office: Ramsden coll. D/RA.

HUGGINS, William Sidney (1822–1862).
Diary, 1846.
Contents: journal of an American's tour of Scotland.
Yale University: MS. misc. coll., diaries.

LANG, Major F. H., of the 34th. Foot.
Diary, Jan–Dec., 1846. 1 vol.
Contents: journal kept by officer of the 34th. Regiment; service life, etc.
National Army Museum: MS. 7203/28.

MILLS, Dr. John, surgeon, H.E.I.C.
Diaries, 1846–59. 5 vols.
Contents: journals kept in the medical services, includes the Persian War, 1856–57, and the Indian Mutiny.
National Army Museum: MSS. 6306/25.

SHIRLEY, Mrs. Maria, wife of Walter Augustus Shirley (consecrated Bishop of Sodor and Man, Jan., 1847, died April, 1847).
Diary, April, 1846–May, 1848. 1 vol.
Contents: personal diary kept at Shirley, Derbyshire, and Bishop's Court, Isle of Man.
Nottingham University Library: MS. 1264.

STANLEY, Henry Edward John, later 3rd Baron (1827–1903), of Alderbury Park, Alderbury, Cheshire, a diplomat.
Diary, July–Aug., 1846, Feb–June, 1847, and Nov–Dec., 1847.
Contents: mostly concerned with public mattters; last item is concerned

with diplomatic work and life at Foreign Office where he was Assistant Precis Writer.

Cheshire Record Office: MS. DSA 203.

STEPHEN, Rt. Hon. Sir James (1779–1859), statesman.

Diary, Jan–May, 1846.

Contents: a general personal diary, quite long entries for most days; political affairs; the Colonial Office; written at Downing Street.

Cambridge University Library: MS. Add. 7511.

Caroline E. Stephen, *The First Sir James Stephen* (pr. ptd., Gloucester, 1906).

THOMPSON, George (1804–1878), anti-slavery advocate.

Diaries, 1846–47, 1856–57, and 1861. 5 vols.

Manchester, John Rylands Library: MSS. Raymond English Dep.

VERULAM, James Walter Grimston, 2nd. Earl of (1809–1895), of Gorhambury, St. Albans, Herts.

Diaries, 1846–95. 50 vols.

Contents: printed diaries; personal, political, sporting, social and business matters.

Hertford County Record Office: MSS. Ref. AR 942.

WESTWOOD, John Obadiah [? died 1886].

Diary, 9-26 Sept., 1846.

Contents: journal of a tour in South Wales; tourist's comment; antiquarian interests; some sketches.

Oxford, Bodleian Library: MS. Eng. misc. c. 143. (Acquired 1930).

1847

ANON., clergymen of Wantage, Berks.

Diaries, 1847–1953. 11 vols.

Contents: volumes of parochialia, thought to have been begun by Rev. W. J. Butler and carried on by successive vicars; some more personal than others; journals of parish events, visits, services & offertories, school matters, etc.

Berkshire Record Office: MSS. D/P. 143/28/1–11.

ANON., clergymen of Milton, Berks.

Diaries, 1847–75. 32 vols.

Contents: printed diaries with lists of families in the parish, their occupations, an attempted directory for 1859; boys attending the Church school, etc.

Berkshire Record Office: MSS. D/P 85/28/2.

ANON.

Diary, Feb., 1847. 1 vol.

Contents: journal of an expedition to Bunnoo.

India Office Library: MSS: Eur. E. 213.

168 *British Manuscript Diaries* [1847

ANON.

Diary, 1847. 1 vol.

Contents: journal of a visit to the West Indies by a passenger in S.S. *Forth*.

National Maritime Museum: JOD 13, MS55/010.

ANON., of Halifax, Yorkshire.

Diary, 1847.

Contents: religious journal of a Halifax minister; Nonconformist life in the area.

Halifax Public Library: Archives Dept.

BLUNT, Lady Anne Noel (née King) (1837–1917).

Diaries, July, 1847–Nov., 1917. 214 vols.

Contents: kept by the grand-daughter of Lord Byron, and wife of Wilfred Scawen Blunt.

London, British Museum: Add. MSS. 53817–54030 (Wentworth Bequest).

BENTHAM, D[aniel, of Regent Square, London.]

Diaries, 1847, 1849, and 1852. 2 vols.

Contents: detailed daily entries describing three holidays spent with his family at Weymouth, 1847, at Torquay and Ilfracombe, 1849, and at Ilfracombe and Tiverton, 1852; places visited, people met, church services attended; expenses; food; monument inscriptions copied.

Ilfracombe Museum: MSS. coll.

Mervyn G. Palmer, "A Diarist in Devon", *Trans. of Devonshire Assoc.* 75, 211–243, 76, 215–247, and 77, 199–233.

CATHCART, Charles Murray, later 2nd. Earl.

Diary, April–Dec., 1847.

Contents: part of a diary kept in Montreal by the C-in-C, Canada.

Private: Lord Cathcart, 14 Eaton Mews, London, S.W.1.

CLARK, Sir James (1788–1870), Royal Physician.

Diaries, 1847–49 and 1848–58. 2 vols.

Contents: journals include notes of his journeys with the Royal Party to Scotland in 1847 and 1848, and to Ireland and Scotland in 1849; records of comments by the Queen and Prince Albert on many of the political and literary figures of the day.

London, Royal College of Physicians: MSS. 92 CLA.

COLLET, Sir Mark Wilkes, Bart. (1816–1905), businessman and merchant banker, a director of the Bank of England.

Diaries, 1847, 1851, 1860–65, 1867–68. 4 vols.

Contents: business and social appointments, travels to various towns in the U.S.A., 1847; elsewhere family and social matters; notes on sermons; a visit to Philadelphia.

Kent Archives Office: MSS. U1287, F 9–14.

DUNDAS, John Charles, M.P., of Woodhall, Wetherby, Yorkshire.

Diaries, 1847–65 and 1861–63.

Contents: the major journal is principally concerned with political events; the other volume is a journal of tours abroad.

North Riding of Yorkshire County Record Office: MSS. ZNK X 7.

ELLIOTT, Captain W. C. P., R.M.

Diary, 1847–56.

National Maritime Museum: JOD 31, MS54/014.

EXLEY, Eli, of Kirkburton, near Huddersfield, Yorkshire.

Diary, 1847–93 (with gaps). 1 vol.

Huddersfield Central Public Library: local coll.

GRAHAM, Sir Frederick Ulick, Bt. (1820–1888), of Netherby, near Carlisle.

Diaries, 1847–48. 3 vols.

Contents: volumes 2, 3, & 4 only of diaries; includes account of a hunting trip in Upper Canada; vivid, detailed, some connected narrative. MSS have been altered in such a way as to suggest preparation for publication.

Hertford County Record Office: MSS. Ref. AR 925.

GÜNTHER, Dr. Albert Charles Lewis Gotthilf, F.R.S. (1830–1914), Zoologist and president of Linn. Society.

Diaries and letters, 1847–62. 4 vols.

Contents: journals of eminent scientist, who joined the British Museum, eventually becoming Keeper of the Zoological Department; he founded the *Record of Zoological Literature* in 1864.

London, British Museum: Add. MSS. 54488–54491. (Acquired 1968).

HALL, Sir John (1795–1866), physician.

Diary, 1847–51.

Contents: army matters: Spain, West Indies, and South Africa.

London, Royal Army Medical College Library: MS. coll.

HARRIS, Katherine.

Diary, 1847–50.

Contents: journal of her travels.

London, British Museum: Add. MS. 52503.

HURST, Joseph.

Diary, Oct., 1847–Jan., 1849. 1 vol.

Contents: journal of a voyage from Liverpool to U.S.A. on board the ship *Robert Burton*; observations on the customs of New Jersey.

Manchester Public Libraries: Archives Dept., MS. 910.4 H1.

JACSON, Roger (Junior).

Diary, 1847–55.

Lancashire Record Office: MS. DX (Barlow, Preston, Estate).

JENKINS, John, of The George, Llantrisant, and The Bush, Llantwit Major, Glamorgan, maltster.

Diary and notebook, 1847–60 (with gaps). 2 vols.

Contents: journal of personal and local matters; family, footraces, people leaving for America and Australia; some medicinal and culinary

recipes ; bell-ringing changes ; some poetry in Welsh and English.
Glamorgan County Record Office: MSS. D/D Xnv 1, 2.

LEAROYD, Rev. Amos, Methodist minister.
Diary, 1847. 1 vol.
Contents: personal and social matters.
Halifax Public Library: Archives Dept., MS. BIOG.

LEVER, Charles, of Liverpool.
Diary, 1847.
Contents: a hosier's work and social life in Lancashire. Whereabouts of MS. is unknown at present. Wrongly ascribed in *British Diaries* to Manchester Central Library ; see, *Notes and Queries* (May, 1968).

LONG, R. W.
Diary, summer 1847.
Contents: notes of a ten-day tour in North Wales.
National Library of Wales: MS. 5912.

LOWE (formerly Holden), William Drury Nathaniel Drury, son of William Drury Holden/Lowe of Locko Park, Derby.
Diaries, 1847, 1853, 1856–81 (with gaps). 24 vols.
Contents: an early travel journal from Mainz to Constance ; a journal of a tour of Canada and North America, 1853 ; a military diary, when he was A.D.C. to Lord Cardigan, 1856 ; and a series of rough diaries.
Nottingham University Library: Drury-Lowe coll., MSS. Dr F 104–127, Dr2 F 1.

NORMANBY, Constantine Henry Phipps, 1st. Marquis of (1797–1863).
Diary, Dec., 1847–Dec., 1848.
Contents: journal kept in Paris ; background of revolution ; analyses and comments on situation ; much factual detail.
A Year Of Revolution, 2 vols., (London, 1857).

PEARSON, Rev. Thomas (1809–1873), of Market Lavington, Wiltshire.
Diaries, Jan., 1847–73. 33 vols.
Contents: life and work of a curate and vicar in various Wiltshire parishes ; chronical of parish visiting and social calls ; picture of the life of an earnest Tractarian priest.
Private: Rev. J. H. Adams, formerly of Saltash, Cornwall; present location unknown.

PORTMAN, Hon. the Rev. Walter Berkeley (1836–1903), fourth son of Viscount Portman, rector of Corton Denham, Somerset.
Diaries, 1847–1903. 11 vols.
Contents: hunting and game diaries only ; diaries are continued by his son until 1937.
Somerset Record Office: MSS. DD/PMN.

ROSCOE, Mrs. F. C., wife of Edward Stanley Roscoe (d. 1932).
Diaries, 1847–48 and 1876.

Contents: first volume is typescript; latter is for June only, kept while in Paris.

Buckinghamshire Record Office: Roscoe Papers 53.

SALVIN, Eliza Anne, daughter of Anthony Salvin (1799–1881), of East End Road, Finchley, London, and Hanover Terr., Regent's Park.

Diaries, 1847–59 (with gaps). 5 vols.

Contents: one volume "copied without correction from various books kept at the time, 1847, 1849–51"; travel journals, in Paris and Normandy, Aug–Sept., 1851, in Heidelberg, 1856, Scotland, 1853, Germany and Switzerland, 1856; many sketches.

London Borough of Barnet Public Library: MSS. 6787/2–6.

TOOKEY, George (d. 1849), of the 14th. Light Dragoons.

Diary, 1847–49.

Contents: journal in letter form by soldier who fell during the Second Sikh War at Chillianwalla; includes account of operations in the Punjab, 1847–49.

Manchester, Queen's Park Museum: 14th./20th. Hussars coll.

National Army Museum: typescript only (6405/61).

VANE-TEMPEST, Lord Adolphus, third son of the 3rd. Marquis of Londonderry, of Wynyard Park, Co. Durham.

Diary, 1847–48. 5 booklets.

Contents: journal of a tour from Bombay to Calcutta, Lucknow, the North-West Provinces, Lahore, and of a return by the Indus.

Durham County Record Office: MS. D/Lo/F 490.

VAWDREY, Benjamin Llewelyn (1809–1892), of Kinderton by Middlewich and Tushingham Hall, Cheshire, solicitor.

Diaries, 1847–63. 16 vols.

Contents: office diaries, containing memoranda and business appointments.

Cheshire Record Office: MSS. DMD/L/9/1–3.

WAUGH, Edwin (1817–1890), of Manchester, poet and writer.

Diary, July, 1847–Feb., 1851. 540pp.

Contents: substantial daily entries; meditations on sermons; his failings and self-discipline; poverty, illness, and melancholy; domestic unhappiness; separation from wife; his reading and conversations; several poems; publication of "Tim Bobbin"; work as assistant secretary to Lancashire Public School Association; notes on secular education.

Manchester Public Library: Archives Dept., MS. Q. 928.28 W87. (Available on microfilm).

1848

ANON., of Woodbury, Devonshire.

Diaries and accounts, 1848–54 and 1893.

Contents: farming matters.

Private: W. B. Hallett, Esq., 38 Bellvue Road, Exmouth, Devon.

ANON., [apparently a passenger on the ship].

Diary, July–Dec., 1848. 140 pp.

Contents: journal of a voyage to Australia in the ship *Artimesia*; from Granton to Deptford where, after a brief tour of London, the diarist boards the *Artimesia*; technical details of shipping; hours of the watch, etc.

Glasgow, Mitchell Library: MS. 596848a.

BABINGTON, Rev. Matthew Drake (1788–1851), of Thringston, Leicestershire.

Diary, Jan–Sept., 1848. 146 fols.

Contents: kept at Messina; interesting account of revolution against Neapolitan government; much detail; lively and amusing.

London, British Museum: Add. MS. 38067.

BIDDULPH, Sir Michael Anthony Shrapnel, G.C.B. (b. 1823).

Diary, 1848–49 (with gaps).

Contents: journal of holiday rambles among the fields and fjords of the central and western districts; remarks on political, military, ecclesiastical, and social organization.

Oxford, Bodleian Library: Ant. Sketches MSS. Dep. c 276.

Thomas Forester, *Rambles in Norway in 1848 & 1849* (London, 1850).

CLARKE, Robert Eagle, of Thetford, Suffolk.

Diary, Feb–May, 1848. 310 fols.

Contents: a visit to the peninsular of Spain and Portugal; no regular daily entries, but reflections and comments.

Oxford, Bodleian Library: MS. Eng. misc. d. 622.

COMPTON, Mrs.

Diary, 1848.

Contents: journal of her voyage from Bombay to England.

India Office Library: MSS. Eur. A. 39.

DAVIES, William of Abergele, Denbighshire, a farmer.

Diaries, 1848–76.

Contents: records of farming at Brynffanigl Farm; data on prices, wages, etc.

National Library of Wales: MSS. 10755B–10765B.

DODSON, John George (1825–1897), 1st. Baron Monk Bretton.

Diary, Feb., 1848–May., 1896.

Contents: accounts of travels; books read; accounts, etc.

Oxford, Bodleian Library: Monk Bretton Papers, Box 36. (Acquired 1960).

GRANVILLE, Richard de la Bere.

Diary, 1848–51. 1 vol.

Contents: private journal on the cruise of H.M. ship *Meander*, to Hong Kong and Canton, etc.

Exeter City Record Office: MS.

GREENOCK, Alan Cathcart, Lord (later 3rd. Earl Cathcart), (b. 1828).
Diaries, 1848–52 and June–July, 1852. 6 vols. and 1 vol.
Contents: the majority of the diaries are filled with business jottings; the short travel is of a tour in Holland, Germany and Belgium.
Private: Lord Cathcart, 14 Eaton Mews, London S.W.1.

GRIFFITHS, Evan (1795–1873), minister and author.
Diaries, 1848–69.
Contents: journal of a Welsh Congregational minister who was also a translator of Matthew Henry's *Commentary*.
National Library of Wales: MSS. 2188–2189A.

HARRISON, R. B. (b. 1833), 55 Briggate, Leeds, Yorkshire, the son of the Stationer to the Leeds Town Council.
Diary, 1848. 65pp.
Contents: notes on his father's bookselling business; weather; recording of daily doings; personal interests; accounts of various visits in and around Leeds, including a railway journey to Wakefield.
Leeds Public Library: MS. L.920.4 H247.

HUTCHINSON, Peter Orlando, of Sidmouth, Devonshire.
Diaries, 1848–72 and 1878–94. 5 vols.
Contents: notes on topography and antiquities of the Sidmouth area; comments on national events; some illustrations.
Exeter City Record Office: MS.

MacDIARMID, Mrs. Duncan.
Diary, Aug–Oct., [?] 1848.
Contents: journal of a voyage from Quebec to Liverpool aboard the ship *Tuscar* with her family in order to rejoin her husband, presumably in 1848.
Liverpool Public Library: local hist. coll. 920MD289 Acc. 872.

MANN, William Thompson.
Diary, Dec., 1848–June, 1849. 1 vol.
Contents: journal of a trip to America.
Liverpool Record Office: MS. G 6590.

PALGRAVE, Francis Turner (1828–1897), anthologist.
Diary, April, 1848. 177 pp.
Contents: diary of his visit to Paris with Benjamin Jowett, A. P. Stanley, and R. B. Morier; literary interest.
Oxford, Bodleian Library: MS. Eng. misc. e 249.

PEARSE, General George Godfrey.
Diary, 1848–49.
Contents: journal kept during the seige of Moottan, the Punjab War, and also on the Afghan frontier.
India Office Library: MSS. Eur. B. 115.

RUSSELL, Robert (d. July, 1849) and George, brothers; of Ferniegair Cottage, Ferniegair, near Hamilton, Scotland.

Diaries, Jan., 1848–Feb., 1852. 2 vols.
Contents: weather; domestic and farming observations; journal continued by George after his brother's death.
Glasgow, Mitchell Library: MS. 202396 SR.171.

SIMPSON, William, R.M.
Diary, 1848–50. 1 vol.
Contents: journal kept in H.M. Discovery ship, *Plover*, on an Arctic voyage in search of Sir John Franklin.
National Maritime Museum ; JOD 76, MS59/0.

STANMORE, Sir Arthur Hamilton Gordon, 1st. Baron (cr. 1893) (1829–1912), diplomat and colonial governor.
Diaries, Nov., 1848–Aug., 1904 (with gaps). 15 vols.
Contents: journal describing his tours and residences in many parts of the world: India, Mauritius, Ceylon, Fiji, New Zealand, Canada, etc.
London, British Museum: Add. MSS. 49253–49269, 49271. (Acquired 1953–56).

WHITE, Charlotte.
Diary, ca. 1848. 1 vol.
Contents: journal of a holiday in Bognor ; visit to Chichester Cathedral, etc.
West Sussex County Record Office: MS. MP 700.

1849

ANON., [?]GARDINER, John Webber (c. 1813–1849).
Diary, July–Dec., 1849. 1 vol.
Contents: journal of a sea voyage taken for health reasons, written very probably by Gardiner, of Wellesford House, Langford Budville, a solicitor.
Somerset Record Office: MS. DD/TBR 18.

ANON.
Diary, 1849–65. 1 vol.
Contents: a personal journal consisting mainly of religious reflections.
East Sussex Record Office: Add. MS. 4507.

ANON., (a lady of Bovingdon, Hertfordshire).
Diary, June–Aug., 1849. 1 vol.
Contents: journal of a visit to Oxford, Cheltenham, and Malvern by the diarist and her daughters.
Oxford, Bodleian Library: MS. Top. Oxon. e 383. (Acquired 1962).

ANON., a soldier.
Diary, July, 1849–April, 1850. 1 vol.
Contents: journal includes a voyage from England to Calcutta in the troopship *Monarch*, July to November.
National Army Museum: MS. 6907/351.

AYRE, John, R.N., M.R.C.S., surgeon.

Diaries, June, 1849–Jan., 1850 and Feb.–Dec., 1850. 2 vols.

Contents: medical and sea journal, 1849–50 kept as Surgeon Superintendent on board the emigrant ship *Cheapside* bound for Australia; includes prescriptions. Similar journal on board emigrant barque *Duchess of Northumberland.*

Cheshire Record Office: MSS. DDX 106.

BLATHWAYT, Rev. W. T., rector of Dyrham, 1875–1909.

Diaries, 1849, 1853–55, 1858–71, and 1873–75. 21 vols.

Contents: family affairs; includes a diary of his honeymoon, 1849, with his first wife Frances Elizabeth; irregular entries.

Gloucestershire Records Office: Dyrham Park MSS., D 1779 F 227–248.

BLATHWAYT, Frances Elizabeth (née Philips), wife of Rev. W. T. Blathwayt.

Diaries, 1849–62 and 1864–68. 11 vols.

Contents: family affairs, chiefly at Langridge, Somerset, and Pau, France; 1855 journal includes an extract from a letter of Capt. Edward Hibbert describing conditions in the Crimea.

Gloucestershire Records Office: Dyrham Park MSS., D 1799 F 249–259.

BOWEN, Gwynne Vaughan, farmer of Ffynnow y Derwyddon, Pembrokeshire.

Diary, 1849–57.

Contents: entries of the commonplace-book kind in English and Welsh.

National Library of Wales: MS. 6641B.

BRABOURNE, Rt. Hon. Sir Edward Knatchbull-Hugessen, 1st. Baron, politician.

Diaries, 1849–93, 1851, 1857–98, 1887–88. 59 vols.

Contents: various journals, personal and political; a tour to Italy, 1851; a journey around the world, 1887–88; political journals kept 1857–80 while diarist was M.P. for Sandwich and later in the Upper House; 45 volumes personal in character from 1849, excluding 1890.

Kent Archives Office: MSS. U951 Knatchbull, F25/1–45, F26, F27/1–12, F28.

BROOKS, John Hatfield (1824–1907), of Flitwick Manor House, Bedfordshire, a major in the 19th. Hussars.

Diaries, Oct., 1849–Jan., 1851, Aug., 1859–Dec., 1863 and Jan.–Dec., 1871. 3 vols.

Contents: earliest journal was kept in India; the second contains family and local items, India; the third mostly family and local.

Bedfordshire County Record Office: MSS. LL 17/ 288, 286, 289.

BURTON, David (b. 1787), Deputy Lieutenant of the East Riding of Yorkshire.

Diary, 1849–53.

Contents: journal and commonplace book kept during his year as Deputy Lieutenant.

East Riding of Yorkshire County Record Office: MS. DDCB/25/38, (acquired 1958).

CARRINGTON, Lady Charlotte Augusta.

Diaries, 1849–56, 1858–64, 1869, and 1871–77. 24 vols.

Contents: brief memoranda re: London society engagements; travel journals to Europe, 1862, and 1871–76 of visits to German spas.

Buckinghamshire Record Office: Carrington coll. D3.

EDWARDE, Major, an army officer.

Diary, 1849 (excerpts only).

Contents: service in India, including Mooltan after capture.

Scottish Record Office: GD 45/6/355.

FIELD, Robert, of Longhope, Glos., farmer and contractor.

Diaries, 1849–84. 7 vols.

Contents: mostly detail of farming and work on many farms and private homes in the parish.

Private: F. W. Baty, Longhope, Glos.

HALE, Rev. Richard, vicar of Harewood, Yorkshire.

Diaries, 1849–53 and one volume without date.

Contents: entries initially are autobiographical, only the later part becoming a day-to-day journal; the undated MS. is a journal of a journey to the Lakes with Chalenor; diarist is the son of General Hale.

North Riding of Yorkshire County Records Office: MSS. ZFM, Bundle 316.

KENNEY, John, of Stow Hill, Litchfield, Staffordshire, a gardener.

Diary, 1849–54. 1 vol.

Contents: contains brief notes covering his daily work; of little value.

Litchfield Public Library: MS. (Information: H. Appleyard).

LEES, Edwin, F.L.S.

Diary, summer, 1849. 1 vol.

Contents: notes of a tour among the scenery of North Wales in company with two ladies; some original sketches.

National Library of Wales: MS. 1250D.

LLOYD, Emmeline M.

Diaries, 1849, 1851, and 1852. 3 vols.

Carmarthen County Record Office: Cynghordy MSS. 1147–1149.

MARSH, John (1788–1872), of Dorking, Surrey.

Diary, 1849.

Contents: journal kept on a trip with William Forster to Denmark and Sweden, via France and Germany, to present petition against slavery; travel notes; visits to hospitals; Christian conversations recorded by the Quaker diarist.

London, Friends' Society Library: MS. Box Q.

MEYNELL, Henry, of Brasenose College, Oxford.
Diary, 1849–51.
Private: Godfrey Meynell, Esq., Meynell Langley, Derbyshire.

NORMAN, Lieut.–General Sir Francis Booth (1830–1901).
Diary, 1849–89 (copied extracts).
Contents: concerning his service in Bhutan campaign, 1864–66; also the
Black Mountain expedition, 1868; the Second Afghan War, 1879–80; his
time in Burma, 1885–86.
India Office Library: MSS. Eur. D. 659/15.

PONSONBY, Col. Arthur (1827–1868), soldier.
Diaries, 1849–68. 14 vols.
Contents: weather, sport, social notes; military life; games, racing,
theatricals, dinner parties; plays, operas in London; love affair in Greece;
regular daily entries; service abroad.
Private: General J. Ponsonby.
Arthur Ponsonby, *English Diaries* (London, 1923), pp. 397–399.

POWELL, Ophelia Catherine (1823–1866).
Diaries, July, 1849–July, 1864. 3 vols.
Contents: personal matters; work done and books read; diarist was the
wife of Rev. Prof. David Lewis Evans.
National Library of Wales: G. E. Evans Bequest, MSS. No. 13–15.

PUSEY, Sidney Edward Bouverie (d.1911), son of Philip Pusey, M.P., of
Pusey, Berkshire, a noted agriculturalist.
Diary, 1849–50. 1 vol.
Berkshire Record Office: MS. D/EBp F17.

SHERIDAN, Richard Brinsley (d. 1888), of Frampton Court, Dorset.
Diaries, 1849–50, 1854–55, 1857–58, 1864–65, 1872–73, and 1875. 11 vols.
Contents: local and estate affairs at Frampton, with some references to
farming and labour; life in London including parliamentary business,
visits to Millais and other artists; electioneering at Dorchester; family
affairs and visits to Europe.
Dorset County Record Office: MSS. D51/15/1–11.

THROCKMORTON, Courtney.
Diary, 1849. 1 vol.
Contents: contains a few entries relating to a journey to Malta, thence
to Corfu, Albania, and return via France.
Warwickshire Record Office: Throckmorton MSS. Drawer 5/15 (on loan).

WHITEHEAD, David (1790–1865), of Rawtenstall, Lancashire, a cotton-mill
owner.
Diaries, 1849 and n.d. 2 vols.
Contents: a journal of the Brussels Peace Congress of 1849, and one
other.
Rawtenstall Central Library: MSS.

1850

ANON.

Diary, 1850. 1 vol.

Contents: journal of a tour through North Wales; Aberystwyth, Oswestry, Llangollen, Bangor, Caernarvon, Tremadoc, and Dolgelly.

National Library of Wales: MS. 7999C.

ANON.

Diary, 1850–87.

Contents: journal of gardening and farm matters, with memoranda on cows, how to remove the taste of turnips from milk, mixture for destroying vermin in lambs and sheep, and weather prognostics; kept at Farley.

Staffordshire Record Office: Bill MSS. D554/140.

AIREY, Lieut-Col. Sir Richard, C.O. of 34th Regiment.

Diary, 1850–51.

Contents: journal kept while in Port Talbot with his family; dispute with his uncle, Co. Thos. Talbot about former's lands in Canada; details of weather conditions, animals bought and sold, employment of servants, buying of provisions and his uncle's health and temper.

Herefordshire Record Office: MS. G/1V/A/E47/70.

BAINES, W. M. of Auckland, New Zealand.

Diary, Aug.–Dec., 1850.

Contents: journal of a voyage to New Zealand on the ship, *Sir Edward Paget*; fellow passengers; first impressions of New Zealand.

Private: present location unknown.

BARNES, Alfred, of Farnworth.

Diary, 1850. 1 vol.

Contents: journal of a tour in Ireland.

Lancashire Records Office: MS. DDX/75.

BAYLEY, Sir John.

Diaries, 1850–55 and 1857–69. 19 vols.

Private: Major-General Sir John Laurie, Bart., C.B.E., D.S.O., Maxwelton, Moniaive, Co. Dumfries.

BRAY, Louisa, daughter of Edward Bray and Mary Ann Malthus.

Diary, c. 1850.

Contents: her memoirs were written around the mid-century; MS. is now lost and only imperfect transcripts exist.

Guildford Muniment Room, Surrey: MS. (transcript only).

DARNLEY, [?]6th. Earl of.

Diary, 1850. 1 vol.

Contents: journal of a visit to France with Lady Darnley.

Kent Archives Office: U565 F31.

DURHAM, 2nd. Earl of.

Diaries, c. 1850–76.

Private: Viscount Lambton, M.P., Lambton Estate Office, Lambton Park, Chester-le-Street, Co. Durham.

ELTON, Rev. Edward, vicar of Wheatley, Oxon.

Diaries, May, 1850–Dec., 1884. 10 vols.

Contents: record of his delight in the world of nature, flowers, birdsong, walks, rare butterflies; notes on his periodic visits to parishioners; parish work (he was an appointee of Wilberforce.)

Private: Lord Elton, Adderbury, Oxfordshire.

W. O. Hassall, ed. "Wheatley Records: 956–1956" *Oxon Record Society* (1956), pp.96–106.

Diana McClatchey, *Oxfordshire Clergy* (Oxford, 1960).

GULSTON, Miss Josepha, ("Talbot Gwynne"), of Carmarthen, a landowner's daughter.

Diary, 1850–59 (with gaps).

Carmarthen County Record Office: Derwydd MSS. H41.

HERVEY, Isabella Mary, daughter of Lionel Charles Hervey, later wife of Walter Drummond, of Sevenoaks and London.

Diaries, Jan., 1850–Dec., 1857. 2 vols.

Contents: descriptions of daily activities, dinners, visits, her friends, etc.

Birmingham University Library: MSS. 7/iii/6.

HORSMAN, Edward (1807–1876), politician.

Diary, 1850–66 (with gaps). 40pp.

Contents: occasional entries, mainly personal in nature.

Buckinghamshire Record Office: Ramsden coll. D/RA.

HUTTON, Capt. Robert, an officer of the 61st. Foot.

Diary, June, 1850–April, 1855. (Photostat).

Contents: journal kept in India while serving with the 61st. Regiment.

National Army Museum: MS. 6309/109.

LIDDON, Rev. Henry Parry (1829–1890), canon of St. Paul's and biographer of Pusey.

Diary, 1850. 1 vol.

Oxford, Bodleian Library: St. Edmund Hall MS. 69–1.

MacGEORGE, Andrew (1810–1891), lawyer and antiquary.

Diary, Sept., 1850–Oct., 1866 (with gaps). 1 vol.

Contents: notes made in cruises in the ships *Raven* and *Wave* with James Smith of Jordanhill, a keen yachtsman and geologist; cruises in the Clyde and around the Western Isles; natural history; geology.

Glasgow University Library: MS. Murray 167.

MIERS, Mrs. S. M., of Rio de Janeiro, wife of Francis Charles Miers, shipbuilder.

Diary, July, 1850–June, 1860. 478 pp.

Contents: preparations for bridal voyage; intimate record of domestic and social life in South America; devoted wife and mother; visit to

England, 1853; record of voyages between England and Brazil; well documented picture of upper middle-class life.
Wigan Central Public Library: Edward Hall coll., M 795.

MILLAN, Thomas (1819–1861), of Tilston Fearnall, Cheshire, a farmer.
Diary, Mar., 1850–Mar., 1860. 1 vol.
Contents: personal diary; records local events, sensational events, deaths of local people, price of bread, etc.
Cheshire Record Office: MS. Acc. 1276A.
B. Tunstall, "Thomas Millan's Diary", *Cheshire Life* (April, 1953), p. 16.

NIGHTINGALE, Florence (1820–1910), organizer of nursing in the Crimean War.
Diaries, 1850, 1877, and July, 1888–Feb., 1889.
Contents: commonplace book; accounts, etc.
London, British Museum: Add. MSS. 45846–45849.
Mrs. C. Woodham-Smith, *Florence Nightingale* (London, 1950).

RAVEN, Rev. John James, D.D. (1836–1906), of Fressingfield, Suffolk, antiquary.
Diaries, 1850–1906. ca. 54 books.
Contents: personal, parochial, and antiquarian, with many entries concerning Suffolk campanology.
Ipswich and East Suffolk Record Office: MSS. S2/4/1.1-1-54.

TAYLOR, Francis C., an emigrant.
Diary, Feb.–June, 1850.
Contents: journal kept aboard the ship, *Stag*, on its voyage from Deptford taking emigrants to Adelaide, South Australia.
National Maritime Museum: JOD 75 MS59/0.

THOMSON, M. A.
Diary, 1850.
Private: Col. Thomson, Woodperry House, Oxford.

VIVIAN, Richard Glynn, of Sketty Hall, Glamorganshire.
Diary, with memoranda books and accounts, 1850–1903 (with gaps).
Contents: mainly journals of voyages in various parts of the world.
Cardiff Public Library: MS. 1.597.

WALKER, Frances Elizabeth, of Norton-juxta-Kempsey, Worcs.
Diaries, and household account books, 1850–74. 25 vols.
Worcestershire Record Office: Ogier MSS., Dep. H.924.

WILLIAMS, Eleanor, of Blaenllynant, Gwynfe, Carmarthenshire.
Diaries, 1850, 1854, 1856–60, 1863, 1867–74, and 1876–78.
Contents: entries in English by the mother of Sir John Williams, 1st Bart., M.D., F.R.C.P.
National Library of Wales: MSS.

WYNDAM-QUIN, Augusta Emily (1839–1877), first wife of A. Pendarves Vivian (m. 1867).

Diaries, 1850–52 and 1856–59. 2 vols.
Contents: personal matters.
Cornwall County Record Office: MSS. DD.PV. 12M/FD/65–66.

1851

ANON.
Diary, 1851–52.
Contents: voyage accounts and sundry disbursement vouchers for the barque, *Ellen*.
Liverpool Records Office: MS. KF 255.
AUSTIN, William Banks, of Birmingham, lay preacher.
Diary, 1851–52. 1 vol.
Contents: mostly religious matters.; jottings by diarist who was a member of Heneage Street Chapel.
Birmingham Public Library: MS. Ref. Branch, L 78.1 710101.
BAGNALL, George.
Diaries, 1851–56, 1857–62, 1863–68, 1868–71, and 1875–76.
Carmarthen County Record Office: Museum MSS. 309–314.
BELLEW, Henry Walter, a soldier.
Diary, 1851–61.
Contents: kept during the Crimean War; includes a description of Scutari; later entries from the Afghan War.
National Army Museum: MS. 5112/21.
BICHARD, Rev. John Gallienne (1817–1894), of Guernsey and Norfolk.
Diary, Nov., 1851–May. 1894 (with gaps). 1 vol.
Contents: contain items of his work when Port Chaplain at Mauritius and the Seychelles, interspersed with periods in England and Guernsey, preaching, etc. while on sick leave; personal and religious matters; texts of his sermons; his sea voyages; his last years as a vicar in Norfolk.
Lancaster Public Library: Local History Records, MS. 7503.
BLATHWAYT, Capt. George William (1824–1899).
Diaries, 1851–56. 5 vols.
Contents: chiefly entries concerning sporting matters at Dyrham, Gloucestershire.
Gloucestershire Records Office: Dyrham Park MSS., F 222–226.
BROWN, George Alexander.
Diaries, c. 1851–63.
Liverpool Records Office: MSS. 58–61, 63, 66.
BUCCLEUCH, Louisa, Duchess of.
Diaries and correspondence, 1851–1911.
Scottish Record Office: GD 224/11–13.
CAWDOR, 2nd. Lord.
Diaries, 1851–59, 1863, 1878, and undated. 4 vols.
G

Contents: pocket diaries and one journal, 1878.
Carmarthen County Record Office: Cawdor MSS. 1/245.

CHADWELL, Miss M. A. (d. March, 1909).
Diary, 1851–1908.
National Library of Wales: Baker Gabb MSS., Deeds and Documents.

CHAPMAN, John (1822–1894), critic and editor.
Diaries, Jan–Oct., 1851, and Jan.–Aug., 1860.
Contents: work on *Westminster Review* while George Eliot was living at his house in the Strand ; his editorial work, reading, and business ; social life and health.
Yale University Library: MSS. Vault. Section 14, Drawer 3.
Gordon S. Haight, *George Eliot and John Chapman* (New Haven, 1940), pp. 123–251.

DALY, Charles Patrick (1816-1899), of New York City, judge.
Diaries. March–April, 1851, and May–June, 1874.
Contents: first MS. is an American's tour and social life in London ; meetings with Wellington, Herschel, etc. ; the second is a journal of a tour in Ireland.
New York Public Library: MS.

DUNNE, R. E., of Limerick, Ireland.
Diary, May–June, 1851.
Contents: religious visits to the poor ; parish work and charity ; scenes from Irish life ; writing classes ; writer was apparently a puritan clergyman.
London. Dr. Williams's Library: MS.

ELMHIRST, Rev. William (1827–1899), of Elmhirst, near Barnsley, clergyman and landowner.
Diaries, 1851–74, and 1898. 25 vols.
Contents: pocket diaries ; brief notes of sermons and where preached ; clerical business.
Sheffield City Libraries: Dept. of Local History and Archives, Elmhirst MSS. 1185.

FANE, Lady Rose, daughter of Lord Westmorland.
Diary, 1851–55. 1 vol.
Contents: journal kept while she was living in Vienna when her father was British Ambassador there.
Kent Archives Office: MS. U1371 Weigall, F 17.

GRAY, William (Junior) (1815–1883), of York, the Secretary to the York & North Midland Railway Co.
Diary, July–Aug., 1851. 1 vol.
Contents: journal of a tour of Scandinavia ; some rough sketches included.
York City Library: Archives Dept., MS. Acc. 5 & 6. T/9.

GURNEY, Isabel, of Earlham, Norfolk.
Diary with Letters and autobiography, 1851–1929. 3 vols.
Private: Samuel Gurney, Esq., Compton Beauchamp, Shrivenham, Swindon, Wiltshire.

INGILBY, Sir Henry, 1st. Bt. (1790–1870).
Diaries, 1851, 1855, 1861, 1862, and 1864–70.
Contents: pocket books mostly containing cash entries; very brief recording of domestic events.
Leeds City Libraries: Archives Dept., Ingilby Records No. 3598.

JUPP, George, agricultural labourer and pioneer.
Diary, April, 1851–60. (Copy).
Contents: journal of a pioneer at Taranaki, New Zealand; his first years as a colonist, from leaving London via Great Exhibition to voyage in the *Simlah* from Gravesend; notes on progress, weather, an albatross; life at New Plymouth: people met, events, weather, daily tasks, etc.
Oxford, Rhodes House Library: 850.12.S.4. (Original with the Jupp family in New Zealand).

LLOYD, Sir Horatio (1829–1920), of Chester, barrister.
Diaries, 1851–52. 2 vols.
Contents: legal and private journals by diarist when he was Chairman of Cheshire Quarter Sessions; business engagements and social activities.
Cheshire Record Office: MSS. DDX 24/59, 60.

MARLAY, Charles Brinsley (1829–1912), son of Lt. Col. George Marlay.
Diaries, 1851–52, and 1852–64. 2 vols.
Contents: first is a journal of a tour with his mother and Lady Beaujolais Bury down the Rhine to Italy and back to Paris; second volume is of a commonplace nature.
Nottingham University Library: Marlay coll. MSS. My 4057–4058.

MORAN, Benjamin (1820–1886), American diplomat.
Diaries, May, 1851–Jan., 1875. 42 vols.
Contents: kept while secretary to the American Legation in London; private secretary to Buchanan, Dallas, Adams, Johnson, Schenck, and Motley.
Washington, Library of Congress: MSS.

PAMPLIN, William (1806–1899), of London and Llandderfel. Merionethshire.
Diaries and notebooks, 1851–94.
Contents: a botanical record and natural history journal; notes on his garden, his fruit-trees, and his bees; some personal and family affairs and public events; Christian reflections.
MS National Library of Wales 7492B–7508B

RANDALL, Richard William (1824–1906).
Diary, 1851–61.
Oxford, Pusey House Library: MSS. coll.

RICHARDS, Dr. Owen, of Bala, Merionethshire, surgeon.
Diary and memoranda, 1851–81 (with gaps).
Contents: brief, often impersonal, entries made by diarist while at Bala and Llandderfel.
National Library of Wales: Bronwylfa, Llandderfel MS. 7519B.

SOMERSET, Arthur Edward (d. 1853), of Woolhampton, Berks., barrister.
Diary, April, 1851–April, 1853. (With gaps). 1 vol.
Contents: refers to his work, personal and family affairs, politics and public events, including political events in France; visits to the Great Exhibition; failing health.
Berkshire Record Office: MS. D/EX 396. (Acquired 1971).

SUTHERLAND, George Granville William, 3rd Duke of (1828–1892).
Diaries, 1851–90 (with gaps). 33 vols.
Staffordshire Record Office: MSS. D593/P/24/4.

TARLETON, Frances (née Egerton), wife of Thomas Tarleton (d. 1862).
Diaries, 1851 and 1853.
Contents: day-to-day entries, mostly domestic.
Liverpool Records Office: Arch. Tarleton Family Papers.

TWISDEN, Mary.
Diary, 1851–52. 1 vol.
Contents: illustrated journal; visits.
Kent Archives Office: MS. Twisden U49, F 21.

VIVIAN, Sir Arthur Pendarves (1834–1926), of Taibach, S. Wales and St. Columb Minor and Bosahan, Cornwall, industrialist.
Diaries, 1851–1923 (with gaps). 64 vols.
Contents: personal and travel journals; some give precis of letters written, references to family smelting business; travel in Hartz Mountains, 1851; Algeria, 1861; Albania, 1861; Spain, 1861; Baltic and Russia, 1864; Egypt, 1871; Albania, 1866 and 1876; and America, 1877. Journal of his yacht, *Ina*, 1888–1903.
Cornwall County Record Office: MSS. DD.PV. 12M/FD/1–64.

WATSON, Henry (1834–1907), of Glasgow, a shipbroker.
Diary, June, 1851. 1 vol.
Contents: journal kept of a visit to London for the Great Exhibition.
Glasgow City Archives: MS. TD 120/1.

WHARNCLIFFE, Edward Montagu Stuart Granville Montagu-Stuart-Wortley-MacKenzie, 1st Earl (1827–1899), of Wortley Hall, Sheffield, Yorkshire.
Diary, 1851. 1 vol.
Contents: journal describing his tour in New Zealand.
Sheffield City Libraries: Department of Local History and Archives, Wharncliffe Muniments 458.

1852

ANON.
Diary, Jan–Dec., 1852. 1 vol.
Contents: entries by the wife of a farmer living near Uxbridge, Middlesex.
Wigan Central Public Library: Edward Hall coll., M 923.
ANON.
Diaries, 1852–53. 2 vols.
Contents: journal of a tour in Italy.
East Riding of Yorkshire County Record Office: DDSY/102/58/59.
ANON.
Diary, July–Nov., 1852. 1 vol.
Contents: journal kept by a passenger on board the ship, *Abel Gower*,
on a voyage from Gravesend to Port Philip, Victoria, Australia.
National Maritime Museum: JOD 90, MS70/097.
ARBER, Edward.
Diaries, 1852–53, 1859, 1860, 1865, and 1859–62. 2 vols.
Contents: volume kept at school at the Institution Bellagret, Paris; March,
1852–Feb., 1853; travel journals to Lake District, June–July, 1859, to
West Wales, Aug., 1860, and the Lakes again July, 1865; notes for King's
College, Aug., 1859–May, 1862.
Birmingham University Library: MSS. E.A. 270, 274.
ARNOLD, Matthew (1822–1888), poet and critic.
Diaries, 1852–88. 44 vols.
Contents: notes on his reading; literary interests, etc.
William Bell Guthrie, *M. Arnold's Diaries, the Unpublished Items: a
Transcript and Commentary.* Doctoral Diss. 1957, University of Virginia,
(University of Michigan Microfilms, 1959).
BARRINGTON, Selina.
Diaries, 1852–59. 10 vols.
Private: Mrs. M. R. Backhouse: Ballitore MSS. Bundle J.
CHAMBERLAIN, Richard.
Diary, May–Aug., 1852. 1 vol.
Contents: journal of a tour to Lisbon, Cadiz, Seville, Gibraltar, Malaga,
Grenada, Malta, Constantinople, Smyrna.
Birmingham University Library: MS. AC 1/1/6.
CLOUGH, Arthur Hugh (1819–1861), poet.
Diary, 1852.
Contents: very brief entries in diary among a register of letters exchanged
with Blanche, Oct., 1852–June, 1853.
Oxford, Bodleian Library: MS. Eng. misc. c 359. (Acquired 1959).
CURZON, Hon. Sophia.
Diary, 1852–89.

Private: Rt. Hon Viscount Scarsdale, Kedleston, Derbyshire, Muniment Room, Serial 1–30.

DARBISHIRE, Charles James, of Bolton, Lancashire.
Diary, 1852. 22 fols.
Contents: journal recording the activities of a Bolton Unitarian, magistrate, and landowner.
Liverpool University Library: Western MSS.
H. McLachlan, "Diary of a Bolton layman, 1852", *Trans. of the Unitarian Historical Society* IX, No. 4 (1950), 225–231.

DOMVILLE, W. T., ship's surgeon.
Diary, 1852–53. 1 vol.
Contents: journal and observations on Board H.M.S. *Resolute*.
National Maritime Museum: JOD 67, MS58/1.

DUBERLY, Frances Isabella, wife of Henry Duberly, Paymaster of the 8th. Hussars.
Diary, 1852–64 (with gaps).
Contents: relating to the Crimean War and the Indian Mutiny.
London, British Museum: Add. MS. 47218. (Acquired 1950).

FIELD, Mary.
Diaries, Aug–Sept., 1852. 2 vols.
Contents: experiences of journeys in the Isle of Wight and abroad.
Isle of Wight Record Office: MSS. coll.

FITZHERBERT, Sir William (1808–1896), of Tissington.
Diaries, 1852–53, 1857–58, and 1861–96.
Contents: mostly short notes on family and social happenings kept in printed copies of Pawsey's pocket Diary; he also continued a diary begun by his father in 1806 with notes on farming, crops, cows, and weather, 1859–95.
Derbyshire Record Office: Fitzherbert coll. 3.4.

HALL, Col. Montague (d. 1904), army officer.
Diaries, 1852–53. 4 vols.
Contents: memoranda of his service with the 101st. Foot Reg. Bengal Fusiliers and the Royal Munster Fusiliers.
National Army Museum: MSS. 5705–11.

HEFFER, Edward Arthur, of London, apprentice student in architecture.
Diary, March–Dec., 1852. 71 pp. (and typescript).
Contents: journal of a young man about to take an extension course in the Arts; exemplifies Victorian "self-help"; his love affair; Victorian domesticities and morality.
Wigan Central Public Library: Edward Hall coll., M 831.

HOTHAM, Lady Frances.
Diaries, 1852–54, and 1856–57.
Contents: domestic matters; family and friends; visits, etc., with a pocketbook for 1834 and very brief journal items 1837–48.

East Riding of Yorkshire County Record Office: DDHO/18/6, 7–11, 12.

HUNT, Ebenezer.
Diary, July–Dec., 1852.
Contents: journal of a voyage from Plymouth to Australia.
Oxford, Rhodes House Library: Australia MS. r 2.

JONES, Daniel.
Diaries, 1852–66.
Contents: travel journals in Germany and elsewhere.
Shropshire Archives Office: MSS. coll.

LITHGOW, Stewart, of Edinburgh.
Diaries, Jan., 1852–Nov., 1853.
Contents: an Edinburgh University medical student's brief notes of daily life, medical studies, social life; miscellaneous lectures and musical notes.
National Library of Scotland: MSS. 2550–2551.

MEDLYCOTT, Sir Mervyn Bradford, bart. (1837–1908), of Von House, Milborne Port, Somerset, naval officer (ultimately Rear-Admiral).
Diaries, 1852–55, 1857–59, 1864–66, 1868–72, July–Oct., 1874, Feb–Sept., 1875, 1880–81. 8 vols.
Contents: journals kept while serving in all parts of the world; includes his service in the Crimea.
Somerset Record Office: MSS. DD/MDL.

MELLISH, Richard, a soldier.
Diary, 1852. 1 vol.
Contents: account in diary fashion of four days in the Water Kloof with the Rifle Brigade under Colonel Eyre against the Kaffirs; diarist was a private.
Nottingham University Library: MS. Me 185–124.10.

MOORSOM, William Robert (d. 1858), A.D.C. and Q.M.G. to Sir Henry Havelock.
Diaries, 1852–58. 4 vols.
Contents: journals begin in Dublin; leave in Kashmir and period spent surveying there; journal kept at Lucknow and Ceylon; another begun in Colombo and ending at Lucknow where he was killed.
India Office Library: MSS. Eur. E. 299 (on loan).

TARLETON, Commander.
Diary and official papers, 1852–53.
Contents: concerned with the Burmese War.
Liverpool Records Office: Arch. Tarleton Family Papers.

[?]THOROLD, Sir John Charles.
Diaries, 1853–55 and 1861–66. 3 vols.
Lincolnshire Archives Office: Thorold Deposits, 12/2/5–7.

WOOD, Mrs. Eliza, of Market Overton, near Oakham, Rutland.
Diaries, 1852 and 1856.
Private: F. C. Norman, Esq., Whitcot, Branscombe, near Seaton, Rutland.

1853

ANON., an Army officer.
Diary, Aug., 1853–March, 1854.
Contents: journal of an officer describing voyage down the Ganges from Chunar to Calcutta, and other tours.
India Office Library: MSS. Eur. B. 242.

ANON.
Diary, 1853. 1 vol.
Contents: account of a journey to Scotland; mostly expenses.
Berkshire Record Office: MS. D/EBp A4/11.

ANON.
Diary, 1853–83.
Contents: journals of farming interest kept in the West of England and Trewman's Pocket Journal and Besley's West of England and Exeter Pocket Book.
Devon Record Office: Partridge Deposit, MS. 181/M/E 8–28.

BRADLEY, Mrs. Marian Jane, wife of Rev. G. G. Bradley, Headmaster of Marlborough and later Dean of Winchester.
Diaries and a notebook, 1853–70 (with gaps). 3 vols.
Contents: contain allusions to her husband's friendship with the Tennyson family.
London, British Museum: Add. MSS. 3766A–C (Acquired 1961).

FRAZER, James, of Wrexham, Denbighshire.
Diary, 1853–58.
Liverpool University Library: MSS. coll.

GEE, Jonathan, Royal Navy.
Diary, 1853–71.
Contents: a complete record of eighteen years spent at sea.
Keele University Library: Archives Dept. (on loan).

GRAHAM, Sir Lumley, Bt., an officer of the 41st. Foot.
Diaries, Jan–Sept., 1853 and April, 1854–April, 1855.
Contents: journal kept as an infantry officer during the Kaffir War in the Cape, 1853; later vols. kept while a major in the Crimean War and A.D.C. to Major-Gen. Eyre.
Oxford, Rhodes House Library: MSS. Afr. r. 8.
National Army Museum: MSS. 6807/231. (Typescript).

HARWOOD, John Thomas (b. Aug., 1838), of Sneinton, Nottingham.
Diary, 1853. 1 vol., 6 pp.
Contents: manuscript of little value begins on May 1st, and gives a retrospective account of his life and upbringing. Then follows a gap with three brief entries in April and June, 1855.
Nottingham City Public Library: MS. 23, 821.

HINDS, Rev. Robert.
Diary, 1853–56. 1 vol.
Contents: journal kept mostly aboard H.M.S. *Rodney*; Crimea and Black Sea.
National Maritime Museum: JOD 65, MS58/095.

JONES, Arthur F. (c. 1836–c. 1915), of Brixton, Peckham, then Petersfield, Hants., and finally Cranleigh, Surrey, an accountant or clerk.
Diaries, 1853–59 and 1868–1910. 8 vols.
Contents: social life, personal, domestic and family affairs; some detailed travel accounts; work in "the City".
London Borough of Lambeth: Local Hist. coll. 8/25 (S 1654).

KEMP, Caleb Rickman, of Dorking, a Quaker.
Diaries, May, 1853–Sept., 1908.
Contents: attendance at Quaker meetings in Dorking and Bedford Lodge; visits to meetings in southern counties, etc; religious emotions and reflections; Quaker social life; his health and family affairs.
London, Friends' Society Library: MSS. S3–S8.

KIRK, Sir John, explorer.
Diary, 1853–63.
Contents: an account of the Zambesi Expedition; Kirk, Livingston's lieutenant on the expedition, was one of the first explorers to carry a camera.
Kirk on the Zambesi: a Chapter of African History, ed. Sir Reginald Coupland (orig. 1929, Oxford, 1969).

LEGGE, Lt. Colonel Edward H., soldier.
Diaries, 1853–77 (with gaps). 24 vols.
Contents: travel diaries kept in Switzerland, Crimea, West Indies, North America, Italy, Holland, Middle East, Germany, France, Switzerland; army diaries kept at Aldershot, 1855, and elsewhere in service with the Coldstream Guards.
Greater London Record Office (S.E.I.): MSS. F/LEG 894–915, 935.

[?] LOVELL, J.
Diary, Jan–May., 1853. 1 vol.
Contents: journal kept in the barque *Elizabeth,* taking emigrants from Bristol to Melbourne; authorship uncertain.
National Maritime Museum: JOD 79, MS60/0.

MacGILLIVRAY, Mrs. Margaret Colquhoun.
Diary, 1853.
Contents: journal of the voyage of the clipper, *Torrens,* from London to Adelaide, kept by a passenger.
National Maritime Museum: JOD 78, MS60/0.

MAX-MÜLLER, Georgina Adelaide, wife of Professor Max-Müller, of Oxford.
Diaries, May, 1853; Dec., 1853–April, 1854; Jan., 1856–Sept., 1867;
G*

Feb–May, 1875 ; and a children's diary, July–Aug., 1869.
Contents: sporadic journal-keeping ; first two are mainly concerned with
the Crimean War ; 1863 is written in Germany and Italy ; the 1875 MS. is
also written in Italy.
Oxford, Bodleian Library: MS. Dep. 198–200.
RICHARD, Rev. Ebenezer (and his son, Henry Richard, M.P.), Dissenter.
Diary, Jan., 1853–Dec., 1863 (with gaps).
Contents: public events ; reflections on politics ; meetings attended ;
observations on society ; talks with Cobden and Bright ; religious matters ;
Peace Society affairs.
National Library of Wales: MS. 10100B. (Acquired 1935).
SCROPE family.
Diaries, Jan., 1853–June, 1854, and one undated.
Contents: journals of a tour in France and of an undated tour of Egypt,
seemingly from the same period.
North Riding of Yorkshire County Record Office: ZPT/V/2.
SHORTHOUSE, John William.
Diary, 1853. 1 vol.
Birmingham Public Library: MS. 612 498.
SYLVESTER, John Henry, army surgeon.
Diary, 1853–67 (with gaps).
Contents: journal kept in India while serving as Deputy Surgeon General
in the Bombay Army.
India Office Library: MSS. Eur. C. 241.

1854

ANON.
Diary, 1854. (Fragment).
Contents: journal made on voyage of discovery for the North-West
Passage.
Edinburgh University Library: Dc. 4. 102, f. 80.
ANON., an army officer.
Diary, May–June, 1854. 1 vol.
Contents: part of the journal of a British officer serving with the Turkish
Army during the Crimean War.
National Army Museum: MS. 6807/232.
ANON.
Diaries, 1854–82. 8 vols.
Scottish Record Office: GD 38/1/1259.
ANON.
Diaries, 1854–58.
Warwickshire Record Office: MSS. CR136/A5.
ANON.
Diary, May, 1854–Feb., 1857. (Typescript copy).

Contents: journal kept during the Crimean War by a naval lieutenant.
Greater London Record Office (S.E.I): MS. F/LEG 954–957.

ANON.
Diary, April–Nov., 1854. (Photostat copy).
Contents: logbook of the screw steamship *Andes*; voyage on government service from Liverpool to the Black Sea; call at Plymouth; carrying the 1st. Royal Regiment to the Crimea; ship under the command of John Muir.
Liverpool Records Office: Arch. 387 MD4 Acc. 525. (The original is in the possession of the Cunard Steamship Company).

AMBERLEY, John Russell, Viscount (1792–1878), statesman.
Diaries, Feb., 1854–75.
Contents: a detailed account of his private and social affairs up to his courtship and marriage to Kate Stanley; then notes of outstanding events; Harrow, Edinburgh, Cambridge; and travel notes.
The Amberley Papers, ed. Bertrand and Patricia Russell, 2 vols., (London, 1937).

AMPHLETT, John (1845–1918), of Clent, Worcestershire.
Diaries, 1854–1918 (with gaps). 42 vols.
Contents: extremely full accounts, mostly of personal matters, by a prominent Worcs. figure.
Oxford, Worcester College Library: MS. coll. CCLXXVI. (Restricted access; MSS. formerly on loan to the Bodleian Library, MS. Top. Oxon. d. 464).

BURGOYNE, Sir John Montague (1832–1921), 10th. Bart., Lieut–Col. Grenadier Guards, of Sutton Park, Bedfordshire.
Diaries, Feb–Nov., 1854 and 1872. 2 vols.
Contents: his experiences in the early part of the Crimean War; battle of Alma; wounded and sent home; the later journal is of a cruise on the yacht, *Iolanthe*.
Bedfordshire Record Office: MSS. X. 143/20 and 23.
Bedfordshire Hist. Records Soc. XL with introduction.

BUT(T)LER, Capt. James Armar (d. 1854), of Ceylon Rifle Regiment.
Diary, 1854. 18pp.
Contents: brief journal kept during the Crimean War by man who was killed while serving with the Turkish Army at the seige of Silistria, June 1854.
National Army Museum: MS. 6803/45.
Scottish Record Office: GD 45/26/91 (Copy).

CARMICHAEL, Lieut–Col. G. L., of 95th. Foot.
Diaries and letters, 1854 and 1857–58.
Contents: journals kept during the Crimean War and the Indian Mutiny.
National Army Museum: MSS. 6807/264.

CHAPMAN, Capt. W., of the 20th. Regiment.
Diary, 1854–56.

Contents: his service during the Crimean War.
Plymouth City Library: Archives Dept.

CHESSON, F. W., son-in-law of George Thompson, the anti-slavery advocate.
Diaries, 1854–70. 16 vols.
Manchester, John Rylands Library: Raymond English Deposit.

COLCHESTER, Lady Elizabeth.
Diary, Aug–Sept., 1854. 1 vol.
Contents: part of a diary kept during her tour of Wales and the Midlands.
London, Public Record Office: MS. 30/9 3 Part 1 No. 6 (Colchester Papers).

COLVILLE, Hon. Sir William James, K.C.V.O., C.B., (b. 1827).
Diary, 1854–55.
Contents: kept during the Crimean War; diarist was serving with the 2nd. Batt. Rifle Brigade, and was on the staff of General Simpson, commander of the army at the fall of Sebastopol.
Private: Viscount Colville of Culross, Fawsyde, Kinneff, by Montrose, Angus. [Enquiries to National Register of Archives (Scotland)].

EYRE, Major-Gen. Sir William, K.C.B., C-in-C in British North America, 1856–59.
Diaries, Feb., 1854–Sept., 1856. 4 vols.
Contents: journal kept in the Crimea and in British North America; commander of 2nd Brigade, 3rd Division in Crimea.
London, Public Record Office: MS. 30/46 Box 9 Nos. 2–5.
(Eyre Papers, presented mostly in 1939, having been given originally to the War Office.)

FANSHAW, Ellen, wife of the Rector of Adwell and South Weston, Oxfordshire, 1862–1900.
Diaries, 1854, 1860–64, and 1866–90.
Private: Miss Fanshaw, Adwell with South Weston, Oxfordshire.

GARRETT, Major-General Sir Robert (d. 1869), of Ramsgate.
Diary, 1854. 1 vol.
Contents: diary of a journey to the Crimea; daily position noted; weather.
Kent Archives Office: MS. U888 F9.

GILHAM, Sara Jane, of Walworth, London.
Diary, Aug–Sept., [?] 1854. 1 vol.
Contents: effusions of a young lady, with many quotations, while holidaying on the Isle of Wight; date uncertain, probably 1854.
Southampton University Library: MS. Acc. A179.

GOLDSMID, Sir Frederick John (1818–1908).
Diary, 1854.
India Office Library: MSS. Eur. C. 168. (Acquired 1963).

GRAVES, Lieutenant Thomas Molyneux, R. E. (d. 1855).
Diary, 27 Sept–15 Oct., 1854.
Contents: journal of the seige of Sebastopol; diarist died in the attack upon Redan, 1855.
London, British Museum: Add. MS. 54483 (formerly Philips MS. 15676) (Acquired 1968).

GREIG, (——), an army medical officer.
Diary, 1854. 1 vol.
Contents: journal kept during the Crimean War.
R.A.M.C. Historical Museum: MS. 226.

GRUNDY, Sir Cuthbert.
Diary, 1854–57 and [?] 1863.
Contents: journal with autobiographical notes; the later volume, attributed to him, contains notes of a tour made in the Netherlands.
Lancashire Record Office: DDX/207.

HOWARD, Samuel Lloyd (1827–1901), grandson of Luke Howard, the industrialist, of Chigwell, Essex.
Diary, 1854. 1 vol.
Contents: journal of journey to America, including visits to New York, Philadelphia, and Baltimore.
Greater London Record Office (Middlesex Records): MS. Acc. 1017/1618.

JAMES, Henry Ridley, a soldier.
Diary, Sept., 1854–May, 1855.
Contents: journal kept during the Crimean War.
National Army Museum: MS. 6901/46.

KENRICK, Caroline Mary.
Diaries, April–Dec., [?] 1854, Aug., 1858–Oct., 1859, and Nov–Dec., 1859. 3 vols.
Contents: journals of tours, on the Continent with her parents, probably 1854.
Birmingham University Library: MSS. AC 1/1/1–3.

KINGSCOTE, Colonel Sir Robert Nigel FitzHardinge, K.C.B. (b. 1830).
Diary, 1854–55 (with gaps). 27 pp.
Contents: journal kept during the Crimean War; diarist was with the 4th. Batt. Gloucestershire Regiment.
Private: Kingscote, Wotton-under-Edge., Gloucestershire.

LAUGHTON, J. K., a naval instructor.
Diary, 1854–56.
Contents: journal kept aboard the ship, *Algiers*.
National Maritime Museum: MS. (Acquired 1963).

LEITH-HAY, Alex, army officer.
Diary, 1854.
Contents: journal kept while serving in the Crimea as commander of the 93rd Highlanders.

Private: Leith-Hay MS. (Present location unknown).

McKELLAR, R. W.

Diary, July–Nov., 1854. 133 pp.

Contents: journal of a voyage from Greenock, Scotland, to Sydney, New South Wales ; many interests.

Glasgow, Mitchell Library: MS. 706419 S.R. 161.

MAULE, Lauderdale, a soldier.

Diary, 1854.

Contents: journal describing journey from Southampton via Algiers and Malta to Turkey, then Gallipoli, Istanbul, Scutari, and Varna.

Scottish Record Office: GD 45/26/91.

MURRAY, John Ivor, F.R.C.S.

Diary, 1854–55. 1 vol.

Contents: journal of travels in Asia, Egypt, Palestine.

National Library of Scotland: Dept. of MSS. (Acquired 1963).

NAPIER, Sir Charles, Admiral.

Diaries, Feb–Dec., 1854. 2 vols.

London, Public Record Office: 30/16/15–16 (Napier Papers).

(Other Napier Papers were presented to the British Museum in 1921, Add. MSS. 40018–40058.)

OWEN, Lieut. Charles Henry (1830–1921), later Major-General.

Diary, July, 1854–Nov., 1855. 1 vol.

Contents: journal of the Crimean War ; diarist served with 1st. Company, 12th. Batt., Royal Artillery ; additional notes on the voyage out, June–July, 1854.

Oxford, Bodleian Library: MS. Eng. hist. e. 219. (Acquired 1960).

Jocelyn, *The History of the Royal Artillery: Crimea Period* (London, 1911).

PRICE, George, of Birmingham.

Diaries, 1854–July, 1864. 3 vols.

Contents: journal kept on various excursions in this country and abroad.

Birmingham University Library: MSS. 6/i/4–6.

RADCLIFFE, Lady (née Doughty).

Diaries, Oct., 1854 ; March–May, 1866 ; Feb–May, 1888. 3 vols.

Contents: first journal is started on her wedding day and has few entries ; the last is a travel journal describing a pilgrimage to Rome.

Private: Capt. Radcliffe, Harrogate, Yorks.

RUSSELL, Miss Helen J. M., of Ashiesteel.

Diary, Nov., 1854–March, 1855. 31 fols.

Contents: her studies and lessons ; daily activities of a well-bred young girl ; music, reading, country life in Scotland ; prim formal picture of Victorian domestic life.

National Library of Scotland: MS. No. 3233.

SAUNDERS, Katherine, wife of James Renault Saunders, a pioneer in Tongaat, Natal, South Africa.

Diaries, 1854–74. 2 vols. (Microfilm).

Oxford, Rhodes House Library: Micr. Afri. 430.

Originals in private possession: Mrs. M. M. K. Robinson, 31 Golf Road, Pietermaritzburg, S. A.

SHARPE, John Henry, an officer with the 55th. Regiment.

Diaries, Jan., 1854–July, 1855. 2 vols.

Contents: deal with his last year at Sandhurst and the first few months of service with the 55th. Regt. in Ireland.

National Army Museum: MSS. 6905/31.

SHIFFNER, Lady Elizabeth (d. 1897).

Diaries, 1854–97. 45 vols.

Contents: one volume is a listing of principal events, 1854–96; the remainder contain daily brief notes of engagements and activities.

East Sussex Record Office: Shiffner arch., MSS. 835–879.

Francis W. Steer, ed. *A Catalogue of the Shiffner Archives* (Lewes, 1959).

STEPNEY, Lieut.-Col. Stepney Cowell, of the Guards.

Diary, 1854 (fragments).

Contents: leaves from the journal of an officer of the Guards.

Carmarthen County Record Office: Derwydd MS. CA 50.

THOMAS, John, of Nant y ty, Llanllechid, Caernarvon.

Diary, 1854. 1 vol.

Contents: accounts of farm life.

Caernarvon County Record Office: M/1222/1.

TIPPET, (——), army surgeon.

Diary, (?) 1854.

Contents: journal of the early part of the Crimean War by a surgeon of the 7th. Fusiliers.

R.A.M.C. Historical Museum: MS. 703.

TOWER, Harvey.

Diaries, April, 1854–Nov., 1870 (with gaps). 7 vols.

Contents: a journal kept in the Crimea campaign, April, 1854–July, 1856; a volume of tours in Mexico, California, 1858, and Spain, 1859; another volume describing tours in India and Ceylon, 1861–62; another volume of a cruise in the Mediterranean, 1862–63; and a further two describing journeys to Copenhagen, Dublin, the Crimea, and even Africa.

Private: Col. E. H. Goulburn, D.S.O., Betchworth House, Betchworth, Surrey.

WALKER, Mark, V.C., officer of the 3rd. Foot.

Diary, April, 1854–July, 1860. 1 vol.

Contents: journal includes brief notes on his service in the Crimean War as Adjutant of 30th. Foot, till June, 1855; his days commanding a

Company of the Buffs, until he lost an arm—indicated by an abrupt change of writing.

National Army Museum: MS. 6807/85.

WELLESLEY, Major Edward (d. 1854), officer of the 73rd. Foot.
Diary, April–Sept., 1854.
Contents: journal kept while serving in the Crimean War.
National Army Museum: MS. 7006/8.

1855

ANON.
Diary, 1855–56. 1 vol.
Contents: the log of H.M.S. *Hannibal* in the Crimea.
Cambridge University Library: Add. MS. 6659.

ANON.
Diaries, 1855–59. 5 vols.
Carmarthen County Record Office: Cynghordy MSS. 1150–1154.

ANON., a Russian officer.
Diary, Jan–April, 1855. (MS translation).
Contents: private journal of a Russian artillery officer in the Crimea; the original found in Sebastopol after the capture of the city.
National Army Museum: MS. 6709/36.

ANON.
Diary, 1855. 1 vol.
Contents: a detailed account of a visit to Paris.
Berkshire Record Office: MS. D/EMt F17.

BEAMONT, William John (1828–1868).
Diary, 1855.
Contents: an account of a visit to the Seven Churches of Asia.
Warrington County Public Library: MS. coll.

BORROW, George Henry (1803–1881), author.
Diaries, 1855, 1857, and 1858.
Contents: a travel journal of a visit to the Isle of Man, Aug–Sept., 1855; a brief record of a tour in Wales, Aug–Sept., 1857; and brief topographical notes of a tour in Scotland and the Highlands, 1858; antiquities, folklore; rough drawings.
New York Public Library: Berg coll. has 1858 volume.
Y Cymmrodor, XII (1910), 159–170 (quotes 1857 journal).
R. A. J. Walling, *George Borrow* (London, 1909), pp. 197–228, 263, 267.

BURGESS, Ann, of Leicester, a Quaker.
Diary, Jan., 1855–June, 1865 (occasional entries).
Contents: attendances at Quaker meetings; visits from Friends; brief notes of travels as a ministering Quaker, and of activities of her husband, Joseph Burgess.
London, Friends' Society Library: MS. Box D.

CALDER, (——), an army officer.
Diary, July, 1855–May, 1856. 1 vol.
Contents: full and vivid journal of Scutari and Sebastopol during the Crimean War.
R.A.M.C. Historical Museum: MS. 701.

CAMPBELL-BANNERMAN, Sir Henry (1836–1908), Prime Minister.
Diaries, 1855; 1860; 1862–64; and 1886–1908.
Contents: the early volumes are travel diaries; as an undergraduate in France and Switzerland, 1855; on his honeymoon tour in France, Switzerland, and Italy, 1860; other tours in France and Spain; tourist's notes on scenery, towns, antiquities, art, etc; finally, the volumes 1886–1908 contain brief and cryptic notes of social and political engagements and business; biographical interest only.
London, British Museum: Add. MSS. 41248 A–D, 41249 A–W.

ELIOT, George (1819–1880), novelist. (Mary Ann Cross, née Evans).
Diaries, 1855–77 and Jan–Dec., 1879.
Contents: brief notes on her writing, reading, music, travels, health; reception of her novels; her intellectual pursuits and despondencies; her love for George Henry Lewes (1817–1878) and her life with him. The later diary contains verses, reading, business notes; reflections on Lewes' death; work and health; brief notes.
New York Public Library: Berg coll. (Yale Microfilm 1874) has the diary MS. for 1879. Extracts from the diary, 1855–77 are in G. W. Cross, *Life of George Eliot*, 2 vols., (London, 1884).

ELWES, Valentine Dudley Cary, soldier.
Diary, 1855.
Contents: journal of a voyage made, as a soldier, to Egypt and the Far East.
Lincolnshire Archives Office: Elwes of Elsham Hall MSS.

GABB, Thomas Stead.
Diary, 1855. 1 vol.
Contents: journal of the sailing ship *Canning* on a voyage from the Port of London to Madras and Calcutta; ship, commanded by Capt. Lewis Brown, sailed March 16.
National Library of Wales: Baker-Gabb MSS., Deeds & Don. No. 1185.

GRIFFITH, W. Tyndal, of Bangor, North Wales, a medical student.
Diaries, 1855–61. 3 vols.
Contents: personal diary kept by a Welsh medical student and apothecary in London; work in Bloomsbury Dispensary, Royal London Orthopaedic Hospital, and St. Luke's Hospital for Lunatics; religious life and introspection; public events; peace celebrations; some shorthand.
National Library of Wales: MSS. 10209A, 10210B, 10211B.

HOBHOUSE, Charlotte Mary.
Diary, 1855.

Contents: journal of a holiday in Wales.
Wiltshire Record Office: MS. 112/41.

HUNT, William Holman (1827–1910), pre-Raphaelite painter.
Diaries, 1855 and 1872. 2 vols.
Contents: journals of visits to Egypt and the Holy Land.
Manchester, John Rylands Library: MSS. Ryl. Eng. 1211–1212.

MAXSE, Frederick Augustus (1833–1900), admiral.
Diary, Jan–June, 1855. 1 vol. (copy).
Contents: notes on the Crimean campaign; copied by Lady Caroline Maxse.
West Sussex County Record Office: Maxse Ms. 179.
Francis W. Steer, ed. *The Maxse Papers* (Chichester, 1964).

POWELL, Laura Hirtzel (1828–1901), daughter of Cmdr. G. E. Powell.
Diaries, 1855, 1860–62, and 1863–1901. 38 vols.
Contents: family matters; some holiday journals.
National Library of Wales: G. E. Evans Bequest, MSS. 19–62.

RANSOM, Edwin (1842–1927), of Kempston, owner of "Bedfordshire Times", and proprietor of Kempston Mill and Gas Works.
Diaries, 1855, Feb., 1857–July, 1871, and undated. 3 vols.
Contents: journals of travel in France, 1855, and France and Germany, undated; other journals begin when the diarist was a schoolboy and continue to marriage; religious reflections and travel in Europe.
Bedfordshire Record Office: MSS. X 67/926–928.

REID, David, of Peasehill Farm, Fife.
Diaries, 1855–56 and 1878–83. (Copy only).
Edinburgh University Library: Gen. 1719. (Original is in private hands).

ROLLS, John Allan (b. 1837), later Lord Llangattock, son of J. E. W. Rolls.
Diaries, 1855–1912 (with gaps). 57 vols.
Contents: short, precise and not very informative entries; good on weather.
Monmouthshire Record Office: MSS. Rolls, D361. F/P3.

SCROPE, Emily Jane, wife of Simon Thomas Scrope, of Danby, Yorkshire.
Diary, Nov., 1855–April, 1856. 1 vol.
Contents: journal of a tour in Spain on her honeymoon.
North Riding of Yorkshire County Record Office: ZPT/V/2.

SCROPE, Simon Thomas (1882–1896), of Danby, Yorkshire.
Diary, Nov., 1855–April, 1856. 1 vol.
Contents: journal of a tour in Spain on his honeymoon.
North Riding of Yorkshire County Record Office: ZPT/V/2.

TRYE, Henry Norwood (the younger) (1835–1902).
Diaries, 1855–56. 2 vols.
Contents: journal kept while at Oxford University.
Gloucestershire Record Office: MSS. D303 F6.

1856

ANON.
Diary, 1856–57.
Contents: journal of work on some farms in Heysham; lists of owners, acreage and number of tithe plan of lands and premises in Heysham.
Lancaster Public Library: Local Record Room.

ANON.
Diary, 1856. (Microfilm).
Scottish Record Office: RH 4/35/390/64.

BALFOUR-MELVILLE, James, of Strathkiness, Scotland.
Diary, 1856–62. 1 vol.
Edinburgh University Library: MS. coll.

BARNETT, Canon Samuel Augustus.
Diaries, [?] 1856, April–June, 1867, and 1890–91. 3 vols.
Contents: journal of a trip to Ireland with his parents, probably 1856; part of a journal kept on a trip to the United States, 1867; finally, in diary form, an account of his trip around the world.
Greater London Record Office (S.E.I.): MSS. F/BAR–557–559. (Head Archivist).

BROUGHTON, Delves [?] 9th. Bt. (b. 1846), of Broughton Hall, Staffordshire.
Diary, 1856–58.
Contents: journal of a young boy, started on his 10th birthday, 17 May, 1856.
Private: Sir Evelyn Delves-Broughton, Bt., Doddington Park, near Nantwich, Cheshire. Delves-Broughton MSS. on loan to Cheshire Record Office: MS. Box A, Bundle U.

CAMBELL, Robert, a Methodist minister.
Diary, 1856–58. 1 vol.
Contents: journal of the Methodist Town Missioner at Leeds.
Leeds City Libraries (Sheepscar): Archives Dept., MS. Acc. 999 GA/Z/53.

CLIFFORD, Richard Henry, Bengal Civil Servant, 1853–78.
Diaries, Nov., 1856–Jan., 1860. 2 vols.
Contents: journals include account of the Sepoy Mutiny.
India Office Library: MSS. Eur. D. 568 & 720.

CODRINGTON, General Sir William John (1804–1884), C-in-C in the Crimea.
Diary, April–July, 1856.
Contents: journal of embarkation kept at Balaclava during the Crimean War.
National Army Museum: MS. 6807/381.

COLCHESTER, Reginald Charles Edward Abbot, 3rd. Baron, F.S.A., F.R.G.S. (b. 1842), barrister.
Diaries, July, 1856–Feb., 1919 (with gaps). 54 vols.
Contents: many of these are travel diaries, especially of tours of the Continent, like the first one kept as a young man accompanying his father and mother; political matters dominate for the rest.
London, Public Record Office: MSS. 30/9/53–104 (Colchester Papers).

DIXON, Edward Livesey, Assistant-Surgeon, Bengal Establishment.
Diary, April, 1856–Nov., 1859.
Contents: journal kept during the Indian Mutiny and in Central India by diarist who served with the 24th. Regt. S. Wales Borderers and the 21st. Punjab Infantry.
National Army Museum: MS. 6012/247.

FISHER, Charles (d. 1883), of Distington Hall.
Diaries, 1856–83.
Contents: personal, sporting, and business affairs; entries in the fifties and early sixties on the coastal shipping trade (Liverpool area).
Cumberland and Westmorland Record Office: MSS. DX/199.

GOULBURN, Frederick (1818–1878).
Diary, 1856. 1 vol.
Contents: journal mostly describing the last illness of Henry Goulburn.
Surrey Record Office: MS. Goulburn Acc. 426/16/6c.

HICKS-BEACH, Caroline Julia.
Diary, 1856–59 (copy extracted).
Contents: extracts made by Gwendoline Llewelyn, her daughter, and sent to Lady Victoria Hicks-Beach, Aug., 1927.
Gloucestershire Record Office: Hicks-Beach MSS., PPD/8. (On loan from the Earl St. Aldwyn).

MILLER, Mrs. Harriet, wife of W. H. Miller, geologist.
Diaries, 1856, etc. (with gaps).
Contents: journals of tours in the Alps and Germany.
Cambridge University Press: MSS. Add. 6230.

MORLAND family.
Diaries, 1856–1948.
Contents: journals of various members of the family which are not available for public inspection until forty years after the writer's death.
Kent County Archives Office: Morland MSS. U 200.

NEWBOLT, Rev. George Digby (1829–1907), incumbent of Knotting-cum-Souldrop, Bedfordshire.
Diaries, 1856–95. 2 vols.
Contents: church events.
Bedfordshire Record Office: Souldrop Parish Records, MSS. P 108/28/1.
Bedfordshire Hist. Record Soc. XL.

OWEN, John (1815–1902), of Manchester, antiquarian.
Diary, May, 1856–May, 1857.
Contents: antiquarian interests.
Manchester Public Libraries: Archives Dept., Owen MSS. v.12, pp. 85–114.

PEASE, Henry Fell (1838–1895), of Darlington, Quaker industrialist.
Diaries, 1856–96 (with gaps). 20 vols.
Contents: tour journals, to America, 1856 and 1876, to the Continent, 1858, and to Palestine, 1861 ; personal diaries are very abbreviated, except for 1860–61.
Durham County Record Office: MSS. D/Pe (not listed).

POWELL, Delia (1832–1923), daughter of Cmdr. George Eyre Powell.
Diary, Nov., 1856–June, 1894.
Contents: personal matters ; a record of conduct in the face of the diarist's rules of life, especially to help the formation of the writer's Christian character.
National Library of Wales: G. E. Evans Bequest MSS. 65–68.

RODD, F(rancis) R(ashleigh), of Trebursye House, South Petherwin, and Trebartha Hall, Northill, Cornwall.
Diary, July, 1856–Jan., 1858 (with gaps). 1 vol.
Contents: a shooting diary ; game etc.
Cornwall County Record Office: MS. AD. 156.

SYMONDS, Henry Eld, of Kirkdale, merchant.
Diary, Nov., 1856–Dec., 1860.
Liverpool Record Office: Archives 380 MD No. 2 Acc. 027.

TERNAN, Captain Augustine Henry, soldier (later General).
Diary, 1856. 1 vol.
Contents: letters in journal form, by diarist serving in the East India Co.'s 3rd. Bengal Native Infantry to his wife.
London, British Museum: Add. MS. 49521. (Acquired 1956).

WRENCH, Edward Mason (1833–1912), of Baslow Lodge, near Bakewell, Derbyshire, army surgeon.
Diaries, 1856–1912. 57 vols.
Contents: activities as surgeon in the Crimea ; daily record of life in India at the time of the Indian Mutiny ; mess gossip and comment ; life on troopship coming home ; marriage and army life in England until 1862 ; details thereafter of travel at home and abroad ; parish and family matters ; comment on scientific progress ; descriptions of functions at Chatsworth and people met there ; newspaper cuttings, photos., etc.
Nottingham University Library: MSS. Wrench coll. (uncatalogued).

WYNDHAM, Constance (née Primrose, later Lady Leconfield). (1846–1939), of Petworth House, Sussex.
Diaries, 1856–1907 (with gaps). 11 vols.

Contents: journals of travel in France and Italy; personal matters, the illness of her son, Reginald.

West Sussex County Record Office: Petworth House arch. MSS. 1680–1690.

1857

ANON., (R. M.).

Diary, May–Sept., 1857.

Contents: journal of events during the Indian Mutiny.

India Office Library: MSS. Eur. C. 148.

ANON.

Diary, 1857. 1 vol.

Contents: journal of a tour in Italy, possibly by a member of the Hale family.

Bristol Archives Office: MS. HB/J/10.

ARMSTRONG, Ensign A. M.

Diary, 1857.

Contents: journal of a journey from Quebec westwards to the Red River Settlement.

London, Public Record Office: MS. 30/46 Box 14 Fos. 52–77.

BAILLIE, Lieutenant-Colonel Charles Deymer.

Diaries, Dec., 1857–Jan., 1874. 2 vols.

Contents: journal of his service in the Far East, including the Chinese War of 1860.

London, British Museum: Add. MSS. 50954–50955. (Acquired 1962).

BARTRUM, Mrs. Katherine, wife of Surgeon Robert Henry Bartrum (1831–1857).

Diary, June, 1857–Feb., 1858.

Contents: journal gives an account of Lucknow during and after seige; life in the Lucknow residency; her journey to Calcutta after her husband's death during the relief of Lucknow.

India Office Library: MSS. Eur. A. 69.

BINGHAM, General G. W., C.B.

Diary, 1857. (Typescript).

Contents: journal kept during and after the Indian Mutiny.

National Army Museum: MS. 5903/105.

BLAKE, Col. Pilkington, of the 84th.

Diary, 1857. 1 vol.

Contents: brief journal describing events during the Indian Mutiny.

National Army Museum: MS. 6405/98.

BROWN, William Tod, soldier in Horse Artillery, formerly with the Bengal Artillery.

Diary, Nov., 1857 and Jan–June, 1858. 1 vol.

Contents: journal of events while diarist was Officer Commanding Seige Train in the Cawnpore-Lucknow area during the Indian Mutiny.
Cambridgeshire Record Office: MS. R57/24/21/3.

CADELL, Lieut. Thomas, of 104th.
Diary, Sept–Nov., 1857. (Photostat).
Contents: extracts from his journal during the Indian Mutiny when serving with the 2nd. European Bengal Fusiliers.
National Army Museum: 6702/90. (Original belongs to Mrs. Chitty).

CAMPBELL, Mrs. Catherine (née Cole).
Diary, 1857. 1 vol.
Manchester, John Rylands Library: Bromley Davenport Mun. MS. 20.

CHANCELLOR, Henry Alexander Robertson (1841–1915), of Newton.
Diaries, July, 1857–1915. 41 vols.
Contents: rather dull brief notes of engagements and activities of a society man in Scotland, from schooldays on; undeveloped and uncommunicative record; where he went and what he did; brief mnemonic notes and no more.
National Library of Scotland: MSS. 17.2. 5–45.

COLE, Col. Arthur Lowry, of the 43rd. Foot.
Diary, 1857–58. 1 vol.
Contents: journal kept while serving in Canada with his regiment.
National Army Museum: MS. 6807/399.

CONNOLLY, Capt. W. P. (1829–1864), officer of the Jodhpore Legion.
Diary, 1857. (Photostat).
Contents: journal kept during the Indian Mutiny; includes an account of the mutiny at Erinpoorah where diarist was the Adjutant of the Jodhpore Legion.
National Army Museum: MS. 6702/71.

COWPER, Lady Adine (1842–1868), of Panshanger, Hertford.
Diary, Aug., 1857–Aug., 1861 (with gaps). 1 vol.
Contents: a young girl's account of family, social, and religious events, etc; she was later the mother of Lord Desborough's wife, Ethel Fane.
Hertford County Record Office: MS. Ref. AR 1287.

CUMBERLAND, Capt. C. E., of the Royal Engineers.
Diary, Nov., 1857–April, 1859.
Contents: journal kept when in command of the 11th. Coy. of the R.E. during the Indian Mutiny.
National Army Museum: MS. 6407/47.

CURWEN, Mrs. Frances, married (1833) Edward Stanley Curwen, of Workington Hall.
Diary, Jan., 1857–April, 1862. 1 vol.
Contents: family affairs, daily life; comments upon her surroundings, in France, Isle of Wight, Brighton, etc.
Cumberland and Westmorland Record Office: MS. D/Cu.

FitzWILLIAM, Charles Wentworth, 3rd. Earl, (1786–1857), of Wentworth Woodhouse, Yorkshire and Milton, Northamptonshire.
Diary, Feb–Sept., 1857. 1 vol.
Contents: daily activities, weather, etc.
Sheffield City Libraries: Department of Local History and Archives, Wentworth Woodhouse Muniments, G.90.

FORWOOD, Sir William Bower (b. 1840), of Bromborough Hall, Cheshire, merchant and shipowner.
Diaries, Nov., 1857–Jan., 1858. 2 vols.
Contents: journal of a voyage from Liverpool to Melbourne in the ship, *The Red Jacket*; the second volume also contains the brief notes of a voyage from Sydney to Valparaiso in the barque, *Queen of the Avon*, some mercantile letters, etc.
Liverpool Record Office: Archives Dept., MSS. EQ 491.

GERMAN, Mrs. R. C.
Diary, May, 1857–Jan., 1858.
Contents: journal of the seige of Lucknow.
India Office Library: MSS. Eur. B. 134.

HALE, Lieut-Col.
Diary, 1857. 1 vol.
Contents: journal of a voyage to India and a return in 1860.
Gloucestershire Record Office: Hale (Adderley) MSS. (Deposited on permanent loan 1954).

HALE, Rev. S. A., of Claverton, near Bath.
Diary, 1857.
Bristol Archives Office: MS. HB/J/3.

HECTOR, Sir James, explorer.
Diaries, 1857–62 (with gaps).
Contents: journals kept while exploring the Rockies in Western Canada; another of a trip with Palliser to Marseilles en route to New Zealand.
New Zealand, University of Otago, Hocken Library: MS. coll.
Irene Spry, *Palliser Papers* (Toronto, 1964).

HORNE, (——), V.C., army surgeon.
Diary, 1857.
Contents: journal kept during the seige of Lucknow by a surgeon who was awarded the Victoria Cross.
R.A.M.C. Historical Museum: MS. 268.

INGILBY, Sir William (1829–1918), of Ripley Castle, Yorkshire.
Diaries, 1857–1914 (with gaps). 41 vols.
Contents: early diaries contain many references to hunting and include brief accounts of trips abroad to France, Switzerland, Italy, Austria, Germany, Poland, Scandinavia, and later Teneriffe. Following his marriage 1874, entries are of a domestic nature concerning family at Farnham; daily life in London after his move in 1893; weather, etc.

Leeds City Libraries (Sheepscar): Archives Dept., Ingilby Records MSS.
3600.

Murdoch, Catherine, "The Ingilby Records", *Annual Report & Bulletin
of the W. Riding (Northern Section)* No. 8, 1965, 27–46.

LIND, James, an officer of 5th. Punjab Infantry.
Diary, 1857.
Contents: journal of the activities of the Infantry during the Indian
Mutiny.
National Army Museum: MS. 5105/89.

MAITLAND, Rev. John Whitaker, of Loughton, Essex.
Diary, 1857–1907.
Private: Maitland MS. (Enquiries to National Register of Archives,
Scotland).

MOORE, Richard (d. 1870), of Kirkham, Lancashire, solicitor.
Diaries, 1857–69. 12 vols.
Contents: miscellaneous notes of local interest, kept by a Lancashire
solicitor and clerk to the magistrates.
Lancashire Record Office: MSS. DDD/217–227, 230.

NEILL, General James.
Diary, June–Sept., 1857.
Contents: journal kept during the Indian Mutiny.
India Office Library: MSS. Home misc. 726–23.

OMMANEY, Col. E. L.
Diaries, 1857–58. 6 vols.
Contents: journals covering the Indian Mutiny; escorting the King of
Delhi; the Black Mountain Expedition etc.
National Army Museum: MSS. 6301/143.

PICKERING, Mathew (sic), of Winlaton, Co. Durham, a Primitive
Methodist local preacher.
Diary, 1857–67. 1 vol.
Contents: concerned mainly with church affairs and including details of
congregations and comments on sermons.
Durham County Record Office: MS. M/SS 385.

POWLETT, Col. P.W., C.S.I.
Diary, Sept., 1857–Jan., 1858. 1 vol.
Contents: journal relating to the Indian Mutiny, when he was a junior
officer (Lieutenant).
National Army Museum: MS. 6702/66/1.

PRUEN, Rev. H., vicar of Huddlecote.
Diary, Sept., 1857–May, 1860. 1 vol.
Gloucester City Library: Glos. coll., MS. C.18.

RANSOM, Edward.
Diary, 1857–71.
Norwich Central Library: MS. 926.

ROBERTS, Sir Henry Gee (1800–1860).
Diary, 1857–58. (part only).
India Office Library: MSS. Eur. E. 265.

SARGENT, John Young.
Diary, summer 1857. 88 fols.
Contents: journal of a tour in Norway; notes on language; some verses by the diarist and his companion H.P. ("Pot"); some pen and ink drawings.
Oxford, Bodleian Library: MS. Eng. misc. d. 246. (Acquired 1935).

SHERER, Col. G. M., C.O. at Jalpaiguri, India.
Diary, June–Sept., 1857.
Contents: journal in the form of letters to Col. Corbett, C.O. at Lahore (presumed) by commander of Native Infantry at Jalpaiguri, at the time of the Mutiny.
India Office Library: MSS. Home misc. 7271.

SNEYD, Mary Emma.
Diary, 1857. 1 vol.
Contents: travel journal of travel in Scotland.
Greater London Record Office (S.E.I.): MS. misc. 960.

SPURGIN, Sir John (1821–1903).
Diary, 1857. (Copied extracts).
Contents: matters relating to the Indian Mutiny.
India Office Library: MSS. Eur. D. 747.

SULLIVAN, (——), explorer.
Diary, 1857–60.
Contents: journal kept while a member of the Palliser Expedition in Western Canada.
New Zealand, University of Otago, Hocken Library: MS. B784.
Irene Spry, *The Palliser Papers* (Toronto, 1964).

THORNTON, Richard.
Diaries and notebooks, Aug., 1857–March, 1863. 7 vols.
Contents: entries partly in diary form; African matters; native vocabulary; copies of articles from scientific journals; sketchbook.
Oxford, Rhodes House Library: MSS. Africa S. 27–53.

WEST, Walter, of St. Pancras, Islington, and India.
Diaries, 1857 and 1860. 2 vols.
Contents: incomplete diary for former year; later year has accounts and journal of journey in France, Switzerland, and Italy.
Greater London Record Office (S.E.I.): MSS. F/WST/19–20.

WHITLOCK, Maj-General George Cornish.
Diary, July, 1857–April, 1858. 1 vol.
Contents: journal kept during the Indian Mutiny; an expedition under his command from Bangalore to Bandeh.
National Army Museum: MSS. 6802/5.

WILSON, Capt. T. F., D.A.A.G. Oudh Field Force.

Diary, 1857.

Contents: journal of the seige of Lucknow; lists of casualties.

National Army Museum: MS 5702/23.

WOOD, J. A., soldier in the Indian Army.

Diary, March, 1857–July, 1859 (with gaps).

Contents: irregular memoranda of the writer's personal finances; occasional entries of intimate nature; in Bombay; personal reflections on army personnel; an expedition to Karachi; family news from home.

India Office Library: MSS. Eur. B. 34.

YEO, W. Arundell, an Oxford undergraduate.

Diary, 1857–62.

Contents: details of life as a student at Oxford; visits to Devonshire, etc.

Exeter City Record Office: MS.

1858

ANON.

Diary, 1858.

Contents: diary of a farmer living near Ilminister and Chard, Somerset; farming and weather notes.

Reading University Library: Archives MSS. (On long-term loan from Rothamsted Experimental Station, Harpenden, Herts).

ASHURST, Mrs.

Diary, 1858.

Contents: journal of a stay in Rome.

Oxford, Bodleian Library: MS. D.D. Ashurst e.l. (Acquired 1954).

BAMFORD, Samuel (1788–1872), of Moston, Lancs., reformer and poet.

Diaries, Feb., 1858–Dec., 1861. 4 vols.

Contents: his last weeks of employment at Somerset House; retirement at Moston; poverty contrasted with public recognition of his services to the cause of Reform; livelihood from readings and recitings to mechanics' and literary institutes; support to local Reform associations, and attendances and speeches at banquets and meetings; local affairs; some information on the "Lancashire poets".

Manchester Central Library: Archives Dept., MSS. 923. 2 B99.

The Autobiography of Samuel Bamford, ed. and intro. W. H. Chaloner, 2 vols. (London, 1967).

BASTARD family, of Kitley, Yealmpton, Devonshire.

Diaries, 1858–75.

Contents: brief notes in pocket diaries.

Plymouth Public Library: Archives Dept., MSS. Acc. 74/416–420.

BRIDSON, Paul (1809–1876), of Virginia, Braddan, Isle of Man.

Diary, March–Dec., 1858. 1 vol.

Contents: his work as secretary to the newly-founded Manx Society; memoranda, correspondence, interviews, etc.
Douglas, I. o. M., Manx Museum: MS. 1794.
BULL, Rev. Charles (d. 1883), curate of St. Anne's Church, Soho, 1857–59, later priest in the Falkland Islands, Yorkshire, and Lambeth.
Diary, Jan–Dec., 1858. 1 vol.
Contents: mostly engagements, church services; includes an account of a holiday spent in Switzerland.
Westminister City Library: Archives Dept., MS. A2374.
CADOGAN, Cadogan Hodgson (1821–1888), of Brinkburn.
Diary, 1858–82 (with gaps). 1 vol.
Contents: mostly describing the restoration of Brinkburn Priory Church initially, then continued as a personal diary; family events; political matters.
Northumberland County Record Office: Fenwick (Brinkburn), NRO 234, MS. ZFE 21.
CHESSON, Amelia (née Thompson), daughter of the anti-slavery advocate, George Thompson.
Diary, 1858.
Manchester, John Rylands Library: Raymond English Deposit.
DAVENPORT, Augusta Bromley.
Diaries, 1858–60. 3 vols.
Manchester John Rylands Library: Bromley Davenport Mun., 21.
DAVIS, Rev. Samuel (d. Aug., 1883), vicar of Burrington, Chulmleigh, Devon.
Diary, 1858–80. 2 vols.
Contents: notes on sermons preached; some personal details of this thrice-married clergyman of the old Evangelical school.
Exeter City Record Office: MSS.
DEVERY, Sgt. M., of the 53rd. Foot.
Diary, Oct., 1858–May, 1859. 1 vol. (Typescript).
Contents: journal kept during the campaign in Oudh, India.
National Army Museum: MS. 6012/266/6.
GARNETT, James of Clitheroe, Lancashire, mill owner.
Diaries, 1858–1900.
Manchester Public Libraries: Archives Dept. (Microfilms 872–879).
HARLEY, John Pritt, actor.
Diary, Jan–Aug., 1858. 1 vol.
Greater London Record Office (S.E.I.): MS. 0/54/1.
HEYWOOD, Mrs. Robert (née Elizabeth Shawcross), wife of a manufacturer in Bolton, Lancashire.
Diary, June–July, 1858. 1 vol.
Contents: journal of a journey to Russia.
London, Dr. Williams's Library: MS. 28.162.
JONES, Owen (1833–1899), non-conformist minister, of Liverpool and Llansantffraid, Montgomeryshire.

Diaries, 1858–62 ; 1864 ; 1871 ; and 1875–98. 9 vols.

Contents: religious life of a Calvinistic Methodist minister who was also an author ; his reading and literary pursuits ; some entries in Welsh.

National Library of Wales : MSS. 2650–2659.

LAING, Rev. F. H.

Diary, 1858.

Private : Mrs. George Labouchere, c/o Foreign Office, Whitehall, London, S.W.1 ; in custody of Capt. G. C. Wolryche-Whitmore, Dudmaston, Bridgenorth, Salop.

ONION, Ensign.

Diary, 1858.

Contents : journal account of his journey with a detachment of soldiers from York Factory to Fort Garry (modern Winnipeg, Manitoba).

London, Public Record Office : MS. 30/46 Box 20 fos. 15–19 (Eyre Papers).

PALLISER, Capt. John (1817–1887), explorer of W. Canada.

Diary, 1859.

Contents : journal of journey from Edmonton to Fort Colville.

New Zealand, University of Otago, Hocken Library : MS. B519.

Saskatchewan Public Archives : microfilm.

Irene Spry, *The Palliser Papers* (Toronto, 1964).

PERSE, Ensign.

Diary, 1858.

Contents : journal account of his journey with a detachment of soldiers from Quebec to Fort Garry (modern Winnipeg, Manitoba).

London, Public Record Office : MS. 30/46 Box 20 fos. 8–14 (Eyre Papers).

REYNOLDS, Lady Russell (Mrs. Frances Crepigny), of London.

Diary, April, 1859–March, 1863. 1 vol.

Contents : sporadic entries ; social engagements, concerts, opera, theatre, Royal Academy, National Gallery, etc ; some visits to France, Switzerland, Cheltenham, Gosport, Isle of Wight, etc. (Diarist was Mrs. Crepigny at time of writing).

Hertford County Record Office : MS. Ref. 86135.

RUDDY, T. (b. 1842), geologist.

Diary, 1858–1912. 8 vols.

Contents : private journals kept at Llandderfel, Llangollen ; geology, natural history.

Private : Rev. Henry E. Ruddy, formerly of Rugby, Northants ; present location unknown.

SHERRARD, Louisa (née Hall), of West Wickham, Kent.

Diaries, 1858–97 (with gaps). 19 vols.

Contents : in small printed diaries entries concerned with her children and other family matters; her own activities; she spent a considerable amount of time in Switzerland and in Germany.

Kent Archives Office: Hall of Ravenswood MSS., U923 F1/1–19.

O. A. Sherrard, *Two Victorian Girls* (London: Muller, 1966).

A. R. Mills, *The Halls of Ravenswood* (London: Muller, 1969).

SORBY, Henry Clifton, F.R.S. (1826–1908), of Sheffield, geologist and natural scientist.

Diaries, 1859–70, 1883–94, 1896–1902, and 1905–08. 11 vols.

Contents: journals recording his day-to-day activities; some mention of the scientific work he was engaged on; interest in the founding of Firth College (afterwards Sheffield University).

Sheffield University Library: MSS. 550.92 (S).

N. Higham, *A Very Scientific Gentleman: the Major Achievements* (London, 1962).

TRAHERNE, Mrs. J. M., of South Wales.

Diaries, Aug., 1858–Feb., 1860. 2 vols.

Contents: kept by the wife of the Rev. J. Montgomery Traherne; entries end with her husband's death.

National Library of Wales: Mansel Franklen coll. supp. MSS. 19–20.

1859

ANON.

Diaries, 1859–70. 12 vols.

Kent Archives Office: MSS. Norman, U310. (Acquired 1952).

ALLNUTT, W. B., sailor.

Diary, 1859–60. 1 vol.

Contents: journal kept aboard H.M.S. *Hero* by the Captain's clerk.

National Maritime Museum: JOD 28, MS54/063.

AMBERLEY, Kate Stanley Russell, Lady (d. 1874).

Diary, 1859–Jan., 1872.

Contents: scattered entries up to her marriage in 1865; then detailed; notes on political affairs and society life; her family, domestic and social life; rich in detail.

The Amberley Papers, ed. Bernard and Patricia Russell, 2 vols. (London, 1937).

BAKER-GABB, John, author.

Diaries, 1859–63; 1870; 1872; 1878; and 1892–93.

Contents: journals kept in Rome by the author of the One-Act farce, *A Husband to Order or Matched but not Mated.*

National Library of Wales: Baker-Gabb MSS., Deeds & Docu. Nos. 1170–1179.

BENSON, Mary.

Diaries, 1859 following. 10 vols.

Oxford, Bodleian Library: Benson coll. MSS. Dep. 1/71–80.

FORTESCUE, Lady Georgina Augusta Charlotte Caroline (d. 1866), wife of Hugh, 3rd. Earl Fortescue.
Diary, 1859. 1 vol.
Contents: brief daily entries of family and social activities whilst staying in Madeira.
Devon Record Office: MS. 1262 M/FD 28.

GREEN, John Richard (1837–1883), historian.
Diary, Aug–Nov., 1859.
Contents: fragmentary notes of his life at Oxford.
J. R. Green and G. Robeson, *Studies in Oxford History*, XLI (Oxford Hist. Soc., 1901), vii–xv.

HICKS-BEACH, Rt. Hon. Sir Michael Edward, 9th. Bt. (b. 1837).
Diaries, 1859; 1859–60; 1860; 1862; 1863; 1864; 1869–70; 1890; 1900–01; and some without date. 13 vols.
Contents: a series of travel journals, mostly to Europe; a trip on the Rhine and to Switzerland, May–June, 1859; to Egypt, 1859–60; to Syria and the Continent, 1860; to Germany, 1860 and 1862; to Spain, March–June, 1863; to Italy, Feb–March, 1864; one undated volume of a tour of Turkey and Syria; Vienna, 1864; Canada and the U.S.A., 1869–70; a cruise on the yacht *Irene*, 1890; St. Helena; and a trip to India and Ceylon via Egypt and Sudan without date.
Private: Rt. Hon. Earl St. Aldwyn, Williamstrip Park, Coln St. Aldwyn, Fairford, Gloucestershire; at present deposited with Gloucestershire Record Office: MSS. PPD/11–20.

HORROCKS, John (b. Aug., 1820), of Lambeth and Wandsworth, a schoolmaster.
Diary, Aug., 1859–March, 1866. 176 pp.
Contents: irregularly maintained journal; mostly memoranda of a forceful and keen young man; the maladministration of a Wesleyan School; a visit to Lancashire; family items; the diary ends when he breaks with the Methodist school and becomes a shop keeper.
Wigan Central Public Library: Edward Hall coll. M825.

IMAGE, J. M., later Fellow and Tutor at Trinity College, Cambridge.
Diary, 1859–63.
Contents: journal kept while an undergraduate.
Cambridge, Trinity College Library: Add. MS. d. 12. (Acquired 1849).

JOHNSON, Rev. E., a missionary.
Diaries, 1859–67 and 1863–66.
Contents: partly written in an Oriental script.
Cumberland Record Office: Curwen MSS., D/Cu/1/26, 27.

LYNCH, E. W.
Diary and memoirs, 1859–1913.
Plymouth City Public Library: Arch. Acc. 228/2.

MOORE, Mrs. Mary.
Diary, 1859–72 (with gaps).
Contents: journals of her holidays.
Lancashire Record Office: Garnett of Quernmore MSS., DDQ misc.
PRICE, John J., of Birkenhead, Cheshire.
Diaries, 1859 and 1861 (with gaps).
Contents: calls, letters, engagements briefly noted; weather; short and rather trivial entries.
Cardiff Public Library: MSS. 4.342.
RATHBONE, Frances S. (1821–1907), the second wife of Richard Reynolds Rathbone.
Diary, 1859. 1 vol.
Contents: journal, with some sketches, of her wedding tour in France.
Liverpool University Library: Rathbone Papers.
RATHBONE, Lucretia (d. 1859), the first wife of William Rathbone (1819–1902).
Diary, [?] 1859.
Contents: journal of a tour in Scotland.
Liverpool University Library: Rathbone Papers.
WHELER, E., of Bertie Terr., Leamington, Warwickshire.
Diaries, 1859, 1862, and 1877. 3 vols.
Contents: mostly one-line entries of appointments.
London, University College Library: Galton Papers II.
WILLIAMS, Rowland, of Abererch, Caernarvon, a tailor.
Diary, 1859. 1 vol.
Contents: journal deals with writer's business.
Caernarvon County Record Office: M/1331/2.

1860

ANON., (? C.H.S. Blair).
Diary, c. 1860.
Contents: kept by the brother-in-law of General Blair.
National Army Museum: MS. 5604/34.
ANON.
Diary, May and July–Aug., 1860. 1 vol.
Contents: journal of a visit to Cambridge in May, and a tour through parts of Wales in the summer.
National Library of Wales: MS. 6266B.
BAKER-GABB, Captain David, soldier.
Diaries, 1860–64.
Contents: journals kept during service with H.M. 11th. Regiment of Foot at home and in West Africa where the diarist died of fever during the Ashanti campaign.

National Library of Wales: Baker-Gabb MSS., Deeds and Documents, 1095–1100.

BATTISCOMBE, Lieut. Albert, of Pelorus naval brigade at Camp Waitara, New Zealand.

Diary, June, 1860–March, 1861. 1 vol.

Contents: describes engagements with enemy, Maori defences and battle tactics, settlements and way of life; some drawings.

Dorset Record Office: MS. D239/F14.

BATTY, Mrs. Beatrice Braithwaite (1833–1933), of Oxford and Reading.

Diaries, 1860–61, 1863, 1890, and 1909–10.

Contents: travel to India with her husband who quickly dies of a local disease; her return to England, Oct., 1860–Dec., 1861; (this section includes her husband's notes on the voyage out); journal kept in Brittany, Sept., 1863; Easter and Trinity terms at Oxford, 1890; visit to Royal Holloway College, July, 1890; travel journal at Oberammergau, July–Oct., 1890; in Canada, 1909–10.

Oxford, Bodleian Library: MSS., Eng. misc. e. 103–104, f. 41–47; Top. Surrey, f. 1; Top, Oxon., e. 182–183.

BENNETT, R. D.

Diary, July–Aug., 1860, and summer 1861. 1 vol.

Contents: journal of travel through the Tyrol via the Rhine, returning through Switzerland and France, 1860; tour through Scotland, Edinburgh to the Western Highlands and back, 1861.

Oxford, Bodleian Library: MS. Eng. misc. f.24.

CAMERON, Rev. Samuel (d. 1872), minister in Perthshire.

Diary, c. 1860–1872.

Contents: religious life and resolutions; his clerical work; notes on his reading on public events; sermons; introspection.

Private: formerly owned by Miss Amy Cameron of Edinburgh.

Arthur Ponsonby, *Scottish and Irish Diaries* (London, 1927), pp. 103–105.

COLLINS, John Churton (1848–1908), Professor of English Literature at the University of Birmingham, 1904–08.

Diaries, c. 1860–80. 4 vols.

Contents: intermittent diary entries among commonplace book jottings.

Birmingham University Library: MSS. 4/V.

DAVIDSON, J. Henry.

Diary, Oct., [?] 1860–Jan., [?] 1861. 1 vol.

Contents: journal of a trip with some companions through Sicily.

Birmingham University Library: MS. 6/iii/31.

DENMAN, Emma (née Jones) (d. 1904), mother-in-law of Reginald Garton Wilberforce.

Diary, 1860. 1 vol.

West Sussex County Record Office: Wilberforce MS. 38.

Steer, Francis W., *The Wilberforce Archives* (Chichester, 1966).

H

HARWOOD, George Hopkinson (d. 1869), of Nottingham, preacher.
Diary, Jan., 1860–Dec., 1867. 1 vol.
Contents: religious matters; church business, (he was the son of a Methodist preacher); sermons and traits of fellow nonconformist preachers; comment on the lace trade; letters received and sent.
Nottingham City Public Library: MS. M23, 788.

HICKMOTT, James, of Lashenden, Biddenden.
Diary and memorandum book, 1860–62. 2 vols.
Contents: containing the text of sermons preached by members of the Particular Baptists, but also containing details of the Churches' activities, of Hickmott's own affairs, especially his farming, notes on the weather and extracts from his religious reading.
Kent Archives Office: MSS. Bennett, U1334 F3.

LANGLEY, S., secretary to the novelist, W. M. Thackeray.
Diary, Jan–Dec., 1860.
Contents: notes on Thackeray's friendships, literary opinions, business affairs; his secretarial work; notes of books and commissions; and apparently notes for a future study of Thackeray.
New York Public Library: Berg coll.

LEMPRIERE, General Arthur Reid (1835–1927), Royal Engineers.
Diary, c. 1860.
Contents: journal dealing mainly with his experiences with the R.E. in Canada.
National Army Museum: MS. 6709/70.

LLOYD, Mrs.
Diaries, 1860, 1864, 1882, 1886–88. 6 vols.
Carmarthen County Record Office: Cynghordy MSS. 1155–56, 1171–4.

MANCHESTER, William Drogo, 7th. Duke of.
Diaries, 1860–89. 27 vols.
Contents: very few entries, mostly of a personal nature.
Huntingdonshire County Record Office: MSS.

McKAY, Rev. James.
Diary, 1860–65 and 1869–70. 1 vol.
Contents: journal of the life and ministration of a missionary first in Penang and later in Meerut, 1869–70.
Oxford, Rhodes House Library: MS. Ind. Ocean, S.40. (Acquired 1966).

NEWDIGATE, Charlotte.
Diaries, 1860–63, 1866.
Warwickshire Record Office: MSS. CR136/A10.

PARRY, Richard "Gwalchmai" (1803–1897), Congregational minister, poet and eisteddfodwr.
Diaries, 1860, 1867, 1873, and 1888.

Contents: personal items made in printed Welsh diaries; some entries made in English and some in Welsh.

National Library of Wales: MSS. 5668–5671.

PEACOCK, Edward (1831–1915), of Bottesford, Lincolnshire, a local magistrate and antiquary.

Diaries, Jan., 1860–82 (with gaps). 2 vols.

Contents: scholarly interests; literary jottings; antiquarian and archaeological notes; private life and business in Lincs., and south Yorkshire; local news; reminiscences of local families and events; gardening; farming; verses of his own.

Manchester, John Rylands Library: English MSS. 125.

[?] ROWLAND, E.

Diary, Jan–May, 1860. 1 vol.

Contents: journal kept by a "scripture reader" who visited homes in Merthyr Tydvil on behalf of John Griffith, rector of the parish; observations on the social life and conditions of the town.

National Library of Wales: MS. 4943B.

SYMONDS, John Addington (1840–1893), literary critic and translator.

Diaries, 1860–88 (extracts), and 1890.

Contents: his studies, social life, and friendships at Balliol College, Oxford; his melancholy and illnesses; self-analysis; travel notes in Switzerland and Italy; literary and artistic studies. Commonplace book 1890, gives an account of a journey in Germany.

Oxford, Bodleian Library: MS. Don. d. 121.

Horatio Browne, *John Addington Symonds*, 2 vols., (London, 1895).

Phyllis Grosskurth, *John Addington Symonds* (London, 1964).

TARLETON, Mary (1806–1888), of Liverpool.

Diaries, 1860–78.

Contents: her family and social life; notes on Cheshire families; there is also a retrospective journal from Jan., 1841 onwards which begins with her recollections from birth day-to-day entries in the diary.

Liverpool Record Office: Tarleton Family Papers 78–96. (Acquired 1959).

WARD, John, of [?] Clitheroe, Lancashire, a cotton weaver.

Diary, 1860–64.

Lancashire Record Office: MS. DDX/28.

Historical Society of Lancashire & Cheshire, Vol. 105.

1861

ANON., a farmer of Ysgoldy, Fourcrosses, Caernarvon.

Diary, 1861. 1 vol.

Contents: journal with reflections on life in general, and farming in particular.

Caernarvon County Record Office: M/1228/1.

ANON., [?] possibly the 3rd. Lord Colchester.
Diary, 1861.
Contents: journal of travels in France.
London, Public Record Office: MS. 30/9 3 Part 3. 15.

ANON.
Diaries, 1861 and 1878.
Contents: journals of foreign travel.
Oxford, Bodleian Library: MSS. DD Marshall and Eldridge c 7.
(Acquired 1952).

ANON.
Diary, 1861. 1 vol.
Contents: notes of the carrier from Trefiw, Caernarvon.
National Library of Wales: Add. MS. 268B.

ANNESLEY, Capt. John Tisdall, of the Bombay Native Infantry.
Diary, Jan., 1861–Dec., 1864.
Contents: journal kept while serving with the 26th. Bombay Native
Infantry in India.
India Office Library: MSS. Eur. A. 62.

BAKER, Samuel Henry (1824–1909), of Birmingham, artist.
Diaries, Sept., 1861–Dec., 1889, Jan–Dec., 1891, Jan., 1894–Feb., 1898.
33 vols.
Stratford, The Shakespeare Birthplace Trust: DR 142/1–33.

BATTY, John (1837–1905), of Rothwell, near Leeds, an antiquary and local
historian.
Diary, Jan., 1861–Feb., 1872. 1 vol.
Contents: accounts of lectures and other activities at the mechanics'
institutes; notes on local history; much moralizing (diarist was a
Wesleyan); reports of sermons heard; letters received and sent.
Leeds Central Library: MS. L 928.28 B322.

BOUGHTON, G. R. (b. 1841), of Woburn, Bedfordshire.
Diary, Aug., 1861–May, 1881.
Contents: mostly religious matters (non-conformist).
Luton Museum: MSS. Dept.
Bedfordshire Record Office: MS. CRT 110/32 (transcript).

COBDEN, Ellen Millicent (1848–1914), daughter of Richard Cobden.
Diaries, 1861–62, 1864–65, April–May, 1874. 6 vols.
Contents: brief entries; journal of a tour of Algeria, 1874.
West Sussex County Record Office: MSS. Cobden 443, 1048–52.
Francis W. Steer, ed., *The Cobden Papers* (Chichester, 1964).

CUNNINGHAM, Rev. Francis Macaulay (1815–1898), rector of East
Tisted, Hampshire, and later at Brightwell, near Wallingford.
Diaries, Aug., 1861–Nov., 1864, and 1865.
Contents: private journal kept at East Tisted and Witney; parish and
family matters; national events; holidays at Seaview and in the New

Forest. Later diary is an account of a holiday in North Wales.
Private: R. M. Fynes-Clinton, Esq., 25 Eldon Square, Reading.

DUFF, Sir Robert William, of Fetteresso, Scotland.
Diary, c. 1861.
Contents: journal containing views of political subjects, notes for speeches and quotations, etc.
Scottish Record Office: GD 105/402.

EDMUNDS, John, a gunner aboard H.M.S. *Pearl.*
Diaries, June, 1861–June, 1864. 3 vols.
Contents: entitled "A Glimpse of the Past", an account of diarist's personal experience in China against the Tai Ping rebels in 1862, against Japan in 1862–63 ; his voyage home Feb–June, 1864.
Private: J. J. Edmunds, Esq., Upper Farm, Sharnbrook, Bedfordshire.

HALE, William, of Bristol.
Diaries, 1861, 1892, 1896, 1898, 1899–1900, 1900, 1905–12.
Contents: travel journals (in order) to Germany ; France and Italy ; the south of France ; France, Italy, and Scandinavia ; Italy ; Gibraltar and Spain.
Bristol Archives Office: Hale Bequest HB/J/11–17.

HOLT, Miss Anne, of Liverpool.
Diary, c. 1861–71 (extracts).
Contents: extracts from her diary which relate to Alfred Holt.
Liverpool Record Office: Arch. Holt Papers, 2/40.

KER, Edward S., of the 52nd. Light Infantry.
Diary, 1861. 1 vol.
Contents: journal kept while stationed at Jhansi, India ; describes life and routine in the army.
National Army Museum: MS. 7209/28.

LONG, Robert (d. [?] 1868), of Manor Farm, Upper Stondon, Beds., farmer.
Diary, 1861–68. 1 vol.
Contents: weekly diary of weather and farm work.
Bedfordshire Record Office: MS. X 159/3.

MILLER, Thomas (1807–1874), poet and novelist.
Diary, Jan–Sept., 1861. 1 vol.
Contents: domestic affairs ; finances (he was very short of money) ; gardening ; business memoranda ; some literary criticism of Dickens and Thackeray ; his own works, the country books for boys.
Wigan Central Public Library: Edward Hall coll. M 853.

MORLEY, Albert Edmund Parker, 3rd. Earl of (b. 1843).
Diaries, Aug., 1861–Jan., 1863, 1879–84, 1885–1904 (with gaps).
Contents: mostly relating to political affairs, the diarist being Lord-in-Waiting to the Queen and later Under Secretary of State for War ; some

personal affairs; the tour journals pertain to visits to Europe, with one to Egypt.

London, British Museum: Add. MSS. 48218–48301.

NORMAN, George Wade.
Diary, 1861.
Contents: portion only of a diary found among his miscellaneous papers.
Kent Archives Office: MS. Norman U310, F61.

OSWELL, William Basnett (b. 1835), of Eardiston, Shropshire.
Diary, 1861–63.
Contents: farming matters.
Salop County Record Office: Eardiston Estate Papers, MS. 370/1–4.

SANDERSON, Sir John Burdon (1829–1905), Regius Professor of Medicine at Oxford, 1889–1904.
Diaries, 1861–1905. 43 vols.
Contents: social and personal items; includes his time as Joderell Professor of Human Physiology at U.C.L., 1874–83.
London, University College Library: MS. ADD. 179 17–60.
Lady Burdon Sanderson, *Sir John B. Sanderson: A Memoir* (Oxford, 1911).

SATOW, Sir Ernest Mason (1843–1929), diplomat and historian.
Diaries, Nov., 1861–Dec., 1926 (with considerable gaps). 39 vols.
Contents: some personal affairs; many travel diaries, including his residence in Japan, Siam, Uruguay, and China.
London, Public Record Office: 30/33 15, 1–17; 16, 1–12; and 20, 1.
"A Journey in Siam", *Journal of Soc. of Arts* XL 182–197.
B. M. Allen, *The Rt. Hon. Sir Ernest Satow: A Memoir* (London, 1933).

SEYMOUR family.
Diary, 1861. 1 vol.
Contents: journal of an attack upon a fortress, by a member of the Seymour family.
Warwickshire Record Office: MS. CR114A/717/2.

THOMSON, James (1834–1882), poet.
Diaries, 1861–81. 13 vols.
Contents: daily memoranda, accounts, etc; includes journal of a visit to Spain and account of his work for Champion Gold & Silver Co. in Colorado, U.S.A.
Oxford, Bodleian Library: MSS. Don. e 46–47, f 16, 18–24, g 5–7. (Acquired, 1952).

VINCENT, John Amyatt Chaundy (1826–1905), of London, an architect and genealogist.
Diaries, Jan., 1861–Dec., 1863, and Jan., 1867–Jan., 1871. 2 vols.
Contents: personal, often intimate, entries among a mass of regional

genealogical and heraldic data; vexations of lodging in London; anti-quarian matters.

Wigan Central Public Library: Edward Hall coll., M 888–889.

WHARNCLIFFE, Lady Susan, Countess of (d. 1927), of Wortley Hall, Sheffield.

Diaries, 1861–98. 3 vols.

Contents: appointments, daily activities, travels, etc., of the wife of the 1st. Earl Wharncliffe.

Sheffield City Libraries: Dept. of Local History and Archives, Wharncliffe Muniments 485–487.

WOOD, (——), an army surgeon.

Diary, 1861–67.

Contents: journal kept while serving in India.

R.A.M.C. Historical Museum: MS. 351.

1862

ANON., [?] FitzWilliams.

Diaries, Sept., 1862–March, 1865, and 1874–82. 10 vols.

National Library of Wales: FitzWilliams MSS., 62–71. (Acquired 1965).

ANON.

Diary, 1862–74.

Contents: journal of a farmer, titled "Rate book", in the Broadhembury district, near Honiton; brief entries, rates and taxes.

Devon Record Office: Dunning and Bicknell coll., 104/76.

BAKER, F. J. (with R. L. Freer), of Liverpool.

Diary, Aug–Sept., 1862. 1 vol.

Contents: an account of a voyage in *The Great Eastern* to New York, the stay in New York, a journey to Queenstown in the Cunard Line *Persia*, and return home.

Liverpool Record Office: MS. G 5120.

BONTINE, William Cunninghame, of Renfrewshire, Scotland.

Diaries, 1862–63.

Contents: mostly containing local weather reports.

Scottish Record Office: GD 22/Section 1/571.

BROUGH, W. S., of Stafford.

Diaries, 1862–1916 (with gaps). 19 vols.

Contents: entries are few and rather brief; mostly personal affairs noted.

Staffordshire Record Office: Brindley Papers, Bundles 12–14.

CAMPBELL-BANNERMAN, Lady Sarah Charlotte, wife of Sir Henry Campbell-Bannerman, G.C.B. (m. 1860).

Diaries, 1862–64 and 1881–87.

Contents: earlier group are travel diaries of tours made with her husband in France and Spain; latter contain brief private entries made occasion-

ally; weather, social engagements, visitors, travels, personal notes.
London, British Museum: Add. MSS. 41250 A–C, 41251 A–B.
FINNIE, John, a painter.
Diary, 1862–91. 1 vol.
Contents: lists of pictures painted, 1862–90, and pictures exhibited from
1869–91; with rough original sketches in pen and ink.
Liverpool Record Office: MS. DQ 3538.
FOSTER, James, of Preston, a manufacturer.
Diaries, 1862 and 1866.
Contents: mostly jottings concerning business records of the firm, W. & J.
Foster Ltd., knitting machine manufacturers.
Lancashire Record Office: MSS. DDX/438.
GORHAM, Jane.
Diary, 1862. 12 pp.
Oxford, Bodleian Library: MS. Eng. lett. d 142 fol. 160. (Acquired 1953).
GRIFFITH, Mrs. John, minister's wife.
Diaries, 1862, 1866, and 1885.
Contents: personal affairs and some accounts; diarist was the second wife
of Rev. John Griffiths, rector of Merthyr Tydfil, Glamorgan.
Cardiff Public Library: MS. 3.504.
HEWKIN, Edward, of Saddleworth, Yorkshire.
Diary, 1862. 1 vol.
Contents: mainly about the weather; slight entries in a printed *Wesleyan
Methodist Kalendar.*
Saddleworth Central Library: Irad Hewkin coll. 54a.
HOOPER, Rev. Richard (d. 1894), vicar of Upton, Berks.
Diaries, 1862–94. 13 vols.
Contents: journals of parish life; records of services and communicants;
personal events; includes parish of Aston Upthorpe after 1866.
Berkshire Record Office: MSS. D/P 20C/28/2–14.
LEGATT, Miss Frederica Constance (1843–?1920), of London.
Diaries, Oct., 1862, March, 1863–July, 1864, Oct., 1867. 3 vols.
Contents: a valuable cross-section of mid-Victorian domesticities and
socialities; London life.
Wigan Central Public Library: Edward Hall coll. M 968.
LITTLEHALES, R. H.
Diary, 1862–66.
Contents: include a record of plays performed and gossip at the pit
entrance of the Theatre Royal, Birmingham.
Birmingham Public Library: MS. 378 723.
LOW, Lieutenant John, R.N.
Diaries, 1862, 1863 and 1864. 3 vols.
Contents: journals of several voyages; on the ship *Alabama*, July–Oct.,
1862 and Nov., 1862–May, 1863; on the ship *Tuscaloosa*, June–July, 1863

and Dec., 1863–Jan., 1864 ; on the barque *Virginia* from New Bedford, U.S.A. towards the Fayal Islands, Aug–Sept., 1962 (the last possibly by a different hand).

Liverpool Record Office: photostat only.

Private: Miss Kathleen Crippen, Kenilworth Road, Blundellsands, Lancashire.

POOLE, Rev. William, son of Edward Poole, Rector of Hentland.

Diary, 1862. 1 vol.

Contents: journal of a tour in France.

Herefordshire Record Office: MS. C 95.

REES, Rev. Thomas, vicar of Verwick, Cardiganshire.

Diary, 1862–76 (with gaps).

Contents: a few notes of minor interest ; entries in both English and Welsh.

National Library of Wales: Add. MSS. 390–A.

ROBINSON, Sir William le Fleming (1829–1895), Bengal Civil Servant.

Diaries, May–Dec., 1862 and Jan., 1866.

Contents: journals kept while serving in India (1851–78).

India Office Library: MSS. Eur. A. 91.

ROSCOE, Mrs. Katherine E. (née Gawne), wife of Edward Stanley Roscoe (d. 1932).

Diaries, 1862, 1872–89, 1897–93, 1895–1900 and 1911.

Buckinghamshire Record Office: Roscoe Papers AR1/70G.

SALKELD, Joseph (d. 1875), of Penrith, Temple Sowerby, and of Ranbeck, Cumberland.

Diaries, 1862, and 1865–75. 12 vols.

Contents: comments on the weather, and briefly on events of the day ; accounts of his stays at Penrith, Temple Sowerby, Dublin and with his sister at Ranbeck, Kirkland.

Cumberland and Westmorland Record Office: MSS. D/BS.

SIM, George (1835–1908), of Aberdeen, a naturalist.

Diaries, 1862–1900. 12 vols.

Contents: private diaries which embody many of his scientific journeys and investigations through Aberdeenshire and along the Kincardineshire coast.

Aberdeen Public Library: MSS. Lo. 508 Si4.

SLINGSBY, E. H.

Diary, 1862–90.

Contents: domestic and general, relating to Yorkshire and North Lancashire.

Private: present location unknown.

SPERLING, Lieutenant Rowland M., sailor.

Diary, 1862. 1 vol.

Contents: mostly rough notes on his daily observation of birds.

National Maritime Museum: JOD 25, MS9326.

H*

1863

ANON.
Diary, Aug., 1863–Dec., 1864. 1 vol.
Contents: detailed account of day-to-day activities by a clergyman.
Birmingham University Library: MS. 6/i/21.
ANON.
Diary, 1863. 1 vol.
Contents: journal of a tour in Scotland.
National Library of Scotland: Dept. of MSS. (Acquired 1963).
ANON., [?M. H. Hicks-Beach].
Diary, 1863. 1 vol.
Contents: journal of a trip to the Continent.
Gloucestershire Records Office: Hicks-Beach MS. PPD/19.
ANON.
Diary, 1863. 1 vol.
Contents: journal of a tour in Pembrokeshire, with visits to Swansea,
Cardiff, etc.
Cardiff Public Library: MSS.
ANON., [an attorney].
Diary, May, 1863–April, 1870 (Jan–Dec., 1864 missing).
Contents: descriptions of business done for clients; may have been a
member of legal firm of Kaye, Weld, & Lawrence of Liverpool.
Liverpool Public Library: 920 MD 305.
ANDREWS, Captain, sailor.
Diary, 1863. 1 vol.
Contents: journal of a voyage from London to Shanghai aboard the ship
Osprey.
National Maritime Museum: JOD 18, MS53/48.
BAGE, William, formerly of Shrewsbury and Chester, of Cardiff and
Penarth.
Diaries, 1863, 1865, 1871, and 1874–85. 15 vols.
Contents: brief diaries, including his work in Sweden.
Glamorgan County Record Office: MSS. D/D Xje 4/1–15.
BOISSIER, Richard Arthur.
Diary, 1863. 1 vol.
Contents: a schoolboy's journal kept in France and Germany.
Kent Archives Office: MS. Woodgate U1050.
COBDEN, Emma Jane Catherine (1851–1949), daughter of Richard Cobden,
married T. Fisher Unwin.
Diary, 1863–98. 1 vol.

Contents: a volume of extracts from [?her] diaries.
West Sussex County Record Office: MS. Cobden 1071.
Francis W. Steer, ed., *The Cobden Papers* (Chichester, 1964).

CUNNINGHAM, Alison ("Cummy") (1822–1913), nurse to Robert Louis Stevenson, residing with the Stevenson family in Edinburgh.
Diary, Jan–June, 1863 and part of 1866.
Contents: journal of a tour of the Continent while accompanying R.L.S. to Mentone and returning by Naples, Florence and Bavaria ; later entries record a holiday at Torquay.
Edinburgh, Huntley House Museum: MS. R.L.S.C. 327.

FITZPATRICK, Rev. Richard William (1819–1871), first vicar of Holy Trinity Church, Bedford.
Diary, March, 1863–Dec., 1870.
Contents: mostly an account of his work.
Bedfordshire Record Office: photocopy of pub. vol. 130 Bedford.
N. R. Fitzpatrick, ed., *Memoir of Rev. R. W. Fitzpatrick* (Bedford, 1878).

HARRISON, Frederic (1831–1923), writer.
Diary, 1863.
Contents: journal of a cotton famine in Lancashire.
London School of Economics Library: MS. 8109.

HERRIES, Marmaduke Francis Constable Maxwell, 11th. Lord.
Diaries, 1863, 1877, and one undated. 3 vols.
Contents: journal of a tour of Egypt, Rome and Russia, 1863 ; the undated one is of a tour of Italy, Austria, Germany, and Switzerland ; the 1877 volume contains personal matters, hunting, family births ; estates and farm matters.
East Riding of Yorkshire County Record Office: DDEV/61/33–35.

MANSFIELD, George John, a merchant in Singapore.
Diary, June, 1963–Dec., 1866. 1 vol.
Contents: journal of a voyage to Singapore and his time as a merchant there.
Oxford, Rhodes House Library: MSS. Ind. Ocn. r. 11. (Acquired 1968).

MORRIS, Sir Lewis (1833–1907), of Carmarthen, lawyer, poet and educationalist.
Diary, 1863. 1 vol.
Contents: journal of a tour through Belgium, Holland, and Rhine district.
National Library of Wales: MS. 6938A.

RUSHTON, Edward, of Bolton, Lancashire.
Diary, 1863.
Contents: journal of a voyage from Liverpool to Lagos (extracts).
Liverpool Records Office: Archives, MD 266.

SHACKLETON, Robert, a steward.
Diaries, 1863–87. 25 vols.

Contents: simple account of his daily work as steward to the Stourhead estate of the Hoare family.

Wiltshire Record Office: MSS. 383/127.

STRACHEY, Mrs. Jane Maria, wife of General Sir Richard Strachey.

Diaries, June, 1863, Oct., 1868, and Oct., 1869. (photostat).

Contents: mostly social notes.

India Office Library: Photo. Eur. 38.

THOMAS, Rev. T., rector of Disserth, Radnorshire.

Diary, Sept., 1863.

Contents: journey from Disserth to Tenby, Pembrokeshire, begun 22 Sept; it is not clear how or when he reached Tenby.

Trans. Rad. Soc. VIII (Dec., 1938), 29.

TWISDEN, Charlotte.

Diaries, 1863–74 and 1876–78. 6 vols.

Contents: entries are very full; personal matters mostly.

Kent Archives Office: MSS. Twisden U49 F22/1–6. (Acquired 1954).

WHITE, James Espie (1846–1865), Laverockbank, Trinity, Edinburgh, a student.

Diary, 1863. 1 vol.

Contents: journal in narrative style of the principal events which occurred on board the ship, *Henry Fernie*, on her voyage to Australia.

Edinburgh Central Public Library: Edinburgh Room, MS. YDA 8120 W58.

WYVILL, Marmaduke D'Arcy, M.P., of Constable Burton, Yorkshire.

Diary, 1863–65.

Contents: journal kept while at Eton College.

North Riding of Yorkshire County Record Office: MS.

1864

ANON.

Diary, 1864. 1 vol.

Contents: mostly personal matters; diarist lived in the Sparkhill area of Birmingham.

Birmingham Public Library: MS. 660 360.

AMHERST, Rev. the Hon. Percy.

Diaries, 1864 and 1868.

Contents: illustrated journals of visits to Egypt and Palestine.

Kent Archives Office: MSS. Amherst U1350.

BARROW, Lieutenant-Colonel John (1808–1898), of Kingham, Oxon.

Diary, Aug., 1864–Nov., 1894.

Contents: extensive record of personal affairs; social and family life near Chipping Norton, walking, sketching; travel in England and on the

Continent; London life; notes and cuttings relating to military affairs, sport, and public events.

Oxford, Bodleian Library: Eng. Hist. d 18–81.

BERRY, Henry, of Shelley, Yorkshire.

Diary, 1864–88. 1 vol.

Huddersfield Central Library: local coll.

BRAND, Thomas Seymour (1847–1916), later Admiral.

Diaries, 1864–66, 1866, 1866–67. 3 vols.

East Sussex Record Office: Glynde arch. 763.

Richard F. Dell, ed., *The Glynde Place Archives* (Lewes, 1964).

BRETT, Albert (b. 1843), of Andover, Hants., and Puddletown, Dorset, assistant schoolmaster.

Diary, Sept., 1864–May, 1865. 1 vol.

Contents: activities while teaching at the British School, Andover, with holidays at home in Puddletown.

Dorset Record Office: MS. D255/1.

BROOKS, Charles William Shirley (1816–1874), of London, editor of *Punch*.

Diaries, 1864, 1865–Dec., 1873.

Contents: daily entries; much family history; notes on Thackeray, Dickens, Leech, and other *Punch* contributors; a witty record of a man about town, 1864; his work on *Punch*; contributions and notes on eminent contributors; literary life and friendships in London; his social and family life.

Harvard University, Houghton Library: Eng. MSS. 601.20. (1864).

London, The London Library: Safe 4 (1869, 1871, 1873).

George Somes Layard, *A Great "Punch" Editor* (London, 1907), pp. 229–577.

COULMAN, J.

Diary, 1864. 1 vol.

Contents: journal of a tour in Switzerland.

Cambridge, Trinity College Library: Add. MSS. c.108. (Acquired 1964).

FITZGIBBON, Sarah Ann, 3rd. wife of Lt. Richmond Allen FitzGibbon (c. 1805–1871).

Diary, 1864–76.

India Office Library: MSS. Eur. B. 205.

HATHERTON, Edward George Percy Littleton, C.M.G., 3rd. Lord (b. 1842), of Teddesley Park, Penkridge, Staffordshire.

Diaries, 1864–1930 (with gaps). 3 vols.

Contents: brief entries pertaining to his military career, including service in Canada as Military Secretary to the Governor-General, 1874–79.

Staffordshire Record Office: Hatherton MSS., D 260.

PARRY, Sir Charles Hubert Hastings (1848–1918), musician and composer.

Diary, 1864–1918 (extracts).

Contents: include entries made at Eton College, where he had been a pupil since 1861.

Gwilym Beechey, *Musical Times* (Oct., 1968), 956–958.

C. L. Graves, *Hubert Parry* (London, 1926).

SALKELD, Mary, of Ranbeck, parish of Kirkland, Cumberland.
Diaries, 1864–65, 1869, 1872–76. 9 vols.
Contents: pocket diaries with very brief entries; daily events, etc.
Cumberland and Westmorland Record Office: MSS. D/BS.

SNELLING, Rev. Oscar T. (1845–1916), of Swansea, missionary.
Diaries, Aug., 1864–May, 1867 and Oct., 1871–Aug., 1875. 3 vols.
Contents: diaries of the founder of the Swansea Gospel Mission, with notes concerning his activities in Swansea; these three volumes are only a part of a collection of records relating to the G.M. Soc; and other diaries of his appear to be missing.
Swansea Public Libraries: MSS. coll. 435–537.

WADE, Rev. Thomas Russell (1839–1914), missionary.
Diary, 1864–65.
Contents: kept in Kashmir while in charge of local medical mission.
Church Missionary Society: MS. Acc. 110.

WEBSTER, Wentworth (1829–1907).
Diary, Nov., 1864–May, 1865. 1 vol.
Contents: titled "Nile Diary", with personal affairs and accounts.
Oxford, Bodleian Library: MS. Eng. misc. d.104 (fols. 16–43, 203–205). (Acquired 1921).

WOODHOUSE, Rev. Thomas.
Diaries, 1864–84.
Hampshire Record Office: MSS. 8M65/5–6.

1865

ADAM, R. A., of Lindsay, Ontario, Canada.
Diary, 1865–71 (with gaps).
Contents: journal of tours to Scotland.
Edinburgh University Library: Dc. 8. 170–172.

ANON.
Diaries, 1865 and 1874. 2 vols.
Contents: short diary of a journey round the coast of Asia Minor, 1865, and of a trip through Switzerland, 1874.
Berkshire Record Office: MSS. D/EFu F10–F11.

AWDRY, Miss S. V. ("Susie"), of Seagry, near Chippenham, Wilts.
Diary, July–Aug., 1865. 1 vol.
Contents: somewhat guidebookish account of a trip to Ireland and the

Isle of Man with her mother in the yacht of a Mr. Dendy, *Star of the Sea*; social comments; numerous illustrations.
Wigan Central Public Library: Edward Hall coll.

BEVERIDGE, Annette Susannah (née Ackroyd) (1842–1929), wife of Henry Beveridge (1837–1929), mother of 1st. Baron Beveridge (1879–1963).
Diaries, 1865–1928. 62 vols.
Contents: mostly recording her life in India; the founding of a school for girls in Calcutta; her work on translation of the *Humayun-Nama* and the *Babur-nama*.
India Office Library: MSS. Eur. C. 176, B. 41–103. (Acquired 1963).
Lord Beveridge, *India Called Them* (London, 1947).

COXE, Henry Octavius, a Bodleian librarian.
Diary, March, 1865 (copied extracts).
Contents: copied parts of Coxe's diary which relate to the Bodleian Library: the rest is believed to have been destroyed.
Oxford, Bodleian Library: MS. Don. d. 145 (fol. 215). (Acquired 1935).

CRADDOCK, M. William, of Birmingham.
Diary, 1865–91 (with gaps). 1 vol.
Contents: personal entries concerning the diarist's life in Birmingham when he lived at 69 Camp Hill.
Birmingham Public Library: MS. L78.1.

DUNDONALD, Thomas Barnes, 11th. Earl.
Diaries and notebooks, 1865–1881.
Contents: few and brief entries.
Scottish Record Office: GD 233/17.

[?] FOLEY, Henry, of Canterbury.
Diary, Aug–Sept., 1865.
Contents: journey via Paris to Switzerland; travel conditions; hotels; guidebook details; some drawings.
Wigan Central Public Library: Edward Hall coll. 45.

HAWKER, Rev. Dr. Robert Stephen (1803–1875), vicar of Morwenstow, Cornwall, and poet.
Diary, Nov.–Dec., 1865.
Contents: very brief entries among miscellanea; contributions to journals (copied by his great nephew).
Oxford, Bodleian Library: MSS. Eng. misc. b. 93 (fols. 45–64). Acquired 1968).
D. M. Hopkinson, "Parson Hawker of Morwenstow", *History Today* XVIII, No. 1 (January, 1968), 38–44.
S. Baring-Gould, *The Vicar of Morwenstow* (London, 1876).

INGILBY, Lady Elizabeth, wife of Sir Henry Ingilby (1790–1870).
Diary, 1865.
Contents: consist of daily family doings.

Leeds Public Libraries (Sheepscar): Archives Dept., Ingilby Records, 3601.

Catherine Murdoch, "The Ingilby Records", *Annual Report & Bulletin of the West Riding Nat. Reg. of Arch.*, (No. 8, 1965), 27–46.

JENNINGS, Miss Hermione, of Gellideg, Carmarthenshire.
Diaries, 1865–71. 4 vols.
Contents: journals of social life of a landowner's daughter.
Carmarthen County Record Office: MSS. Acc. 2033–2036.

JONES, Edward, of Llanfyllin, Montgomery, Wales.
Diaries, 1865–71.
Contents: the official journals of a police constable and member of the Montgomeryshire Police Force.
National Library of Wales: MSS. 6227–6229D.

[?]KIRKE, Mrs. Ann.
Diary, with account book, 1865. 1 vol.
Nottingham University Library: Dept. of MSS., Kirke of East Markham Papers. (On loan).

PAYNE, Joseph Frank (1840–1910), of Wimpole St., London, a physician.
Diaries, 1865(?) and 1879. 2 vols.
Contents: early MS kept during a travelling scholarship; the later records his visit to Russia to report on the plague for the Government. (There are also 21 small diaries, 1876–1910 briefly noting engagements, social and professional).
London, Royal College of Physicians: MSS. 92 PAY.

PRITCHARD, Dr. Edward William (1825–1865), of Glasgow, poisoner.
Diary, 1865.
Contents: twin diaries, the one kept purposely to mislead those who might suspect him of the murder of his wife and mother-in-law; brief entries in the one, some sanctimonious entries in the other. (The ruse failed and he was hanged!)
Arthur Ponsonby, *Scottish and Irish Diaries* (London, 1927), pp. 16–17.

SIDWICK, Arthur (1840–1914), Fellow & Tutor of Corpus Christi College, Oxford, and brother of Henry Sidgwick.
Diaries, Dec., 1865–March, 1914 (with gaps). 5 vols.
Contents: brief notes on his life and work; some autobiographical notes; personal affairs; holidays; weather.
Oxford, Bodleian Library: MSS. Eng. misc. e. 655–659.

WILSON, James Moncrieff (d. 1886), of Claughton, Birkenhead, an actuary.
Diary, Dec., 1865–March, 1866. 1 vol.
Contents: journal of a visit to the United States and Canada on business; voyage via the *Scotia* from Liverpool to New York; his travel in Canada, Montreal, Quebec, Ottawa, Toronto; private interests recorded as well as official matters.
Liverpool Record Office: Arch. MS. 920 MD 154 Acc. 645.

WOODS, Rev. H. G., afterwards President of Trinity College, Oxford.
Diary, 1865. 1 vol.
Contents: journal of a tour in Switzerland.
West Sussex County Record Office: Add. MS. 2728.

1866

ANON.
Diaries, 1866 and 1873.
Contents: in the same hand a "photographic diary" kept while at Torquay, 1866, and a journal of a journey in Kent, 1873.
Private: Mrs. R. Coke-Steel, Trusley Old Hall, Sutton-on-the-Hill, Derbyshire.

BIDDULPH, John.
Diaries, 1866–1903 (with gaps). 10 vols.
Contents: journals of travels in the Himalayas, Pamirs, Gilgit, Japan, Canada, West Indies.
Herefordshire Record Office: MSS. A 87/1–10.

BROWNE, Commander Hon. E. M. D., R.N.
Diary, 1866–70.
Contents: not seen.
Private: Lord Kilmaine, The Mount House, Brasted, Kent.

COKE, S. Talbot.
Diary, Jan.–Dec., 1866.
Contents: journal of an English military man during his tour of duty at Montreal.
Private: Mrs. Coke-Steel, Trusley Old Hall, Sutton-on-the-Hill, Derbyshire.

DANIEL, Rev. Wilson Eustace (b. 1842), vicar of Frome and of East Pennard, Somerset.
Diaries and business notebooks. 1866–1923 (with gaps).
Contents: clerical work, parish life; his literary and printing interests (Daniel Press) with some samples; earlier entries deal with east end of London, when diarist was assistant curate of St. Mark's, Whitechapel; outbreak of cholera. Sketchy entries.
Bath Central Reference Library: MSS. 1150–1201.

DAVIES, Rev. John, of Pandy, Monmouthshire.
Diaries, 1866, 1875–76, and 1886–1916 (with gaps).
Contents: relates to the Abergavenny district; his preaching and travels among Welsh Calvinistic Methodists; Sunday meetings, engagements, etc.; some entries in Welsh.
National Library of Wales: MSS. 11385A (Welsh), 11386A–11400A (English).

DUNDAS, Mary L.
Diary, 1866–69. 1 vol.
Edinburgh University Library: MS. Gen. 822.

FULLER, Juliana, wife of John Stratton Fuller (m. 1866), of Chesham, Buckinghamshire.
Diaries, Oct.–Nov., 1866, June–Aug., 1867, and July–Sept., 1868.
Contents: a honeymoon tour of Bath and Devon, 1866; journal of a foreign tour, Switzerland, 1867; a Welsh tour, 1868.
Wigan Central Public Library: Edward Hall coll. MS. 993.

GLADSTONE, Mary (1847–1927), daughter of W. E. Gladstone, and later wife of Canon Henry Drew.
Diaries, 1886–1920. 14 vols.
Contents: personal entries mostly; includes a journal of a cruise to Norway, Aug.–Sept., 1885 with her parents.
London, British Museum: Add. MSS. 46254–46267. (Acquired 1946).
Lucy Masterman, ed., *Mary Gladstone* (London, 1930).

HEALD, Walter.
Diaries, 1866–70. 4 vols.
Contents: journal of a voyage and residence in Buenos Aires.
Manchester, John Rylands Library: Eng. MSS. 1217.

HEWETT, Mrs. Agnes Frances (neé Anderson), of Posbrooke, Tichfield, Hants.
Diaries, 1866, 1869, 1870, 1872, 1874, 1876–77, 1894, 1899, 1900, and 1905. 11 vols.
Contents: brief jottings in pocket diaries.
Portsmouth City Record Office: MSS. Ref. 16A/139/1–11.

JENKINSON, F. J. H. (d. 1923), Cambridge University Librarian.
Diaries, 1866, 1880–81, and 1886–1923.
Contents: a record of personal and official affairs; work in the University Library; information on natural history.
Cambridge University Library: MSS. Add. 7406–7447.

LASH, Rev. Augustus Henry, missionary.
Diary, Oct., 1866–Jan., 1867. 1 vol.
Contents: journal of a voyage round the Cape to Madras; sailors' customs noted; life on board ship.
Church Missionary Society: MS. Acc. 42 (Acquired 1942).

LLOYD, Howard, of Carmarthen.
Diaries, 1866 and 1868. 2 vols.
Carmarthen County Record Office: Cynghordy MSS. 1157, 1159.

MORTON, Clara D'Orville, wife of Rev. H. S. Gorham.
Diaries, 1866–1907.
Oxford, Bodleian Library: MSS. DD Gorham/D'Orville d. 1. (Acquired 1953).

ROBERTS, Captain J. S.
Diary, 1866–95. 1 vol.
Contents: an abstract journal of the East India ships *Malabar* and

Highflyer, and the cable ships, S.S. *Britannia, Bucaneer*, and *Silverstone*, kept while the diarist was a midshipman and fourth officer.

National Maritime Museum: JOD 54, MS57/027.

SEWALL, Mary, of Hitchen, Hertfordshire, a Quaker.

Diary, Jan–Dec., 1866. 135 pp.

Contents: Quaker religious, social and family life in Hitchen.

Hitchen Public Library: MS. (R. F. Ashby, Librarian).

SEYMOUR, Lady Emily Charlotte.

Diaries, 1866, 1869, and one without date.

National Library of Wales: Harlech of Brogyntyn MSS. (Acquired 1955).

SMITH, Charles Edward, of Hull, Yorkshire, ship's surgeon.

Diary, March, 1866–April, 1867.

Contents: journal kept aboard the whaler *Diana* of Hull, on a voyage under Capt. Gravill to Baffin Bay, where the ship was trapped and spent the winter in the ice; deaths among the crew; drifting on the ice to Frobisher Bay; subsequent freedom and journey home.

Hull Maritime Museum: MS.

C. E. Smith Harris, ed., *From the Deep of the Sea* (London, 1922).

The Listener (17th April, 1969), 525–526.

STENTON, John (c. 1842–1870), of Attercliffe, Sheffield, a silversmith designer.

Diary, July–Dec., 1866. 1 vol.

Contents: journal with account of daily life, his outings, and his interest in natural history.

Sheffield University Library: MS. 942.741 (S).

H. Armitage, *Sorrelsykes* (London, 1913).

THORNTON, Miss M. S., of Kingsthorpe.

Diaries, 1866–99.

Northamptonshire Record Office: MSS. 1936/34.

1867

ADNUTT, Rev. R. T., Rector of Croft and Cadeby, Leicestershire.

Diary, 1867–70.

Leicester Museum: MSS. coll. (on loan from Freer & Co.).

ANON.

Diary, 1867.

Contents: diary for the year with entries by unknown lady.

Gloucester City Library: Glos. coll. MS. N30.15.

ANON.

Diary, Oct., 1867–March, 1868. 1 vol.

Contents: journal of a continental tour in the South of France and in Italy.

Glasgow University Library: MS. Gen. 13.

ANON.

Diary, 1867. 46 leaves.

Contents: a journal of a tour through part of Switzerland via Belgium, returning by Paris.

Oxford, Bodleian Library: MS. Eng. misc. e 364. (Acquired 1953).

ANON., [?Kynaston] of Liverpool.

Diaries, 1867 ; 1886–87 ; 1901.

Contents: journals of travels on holiday on the Continent ; interests in chemicals ; fullish narratives which include sketches of items of interest.

Liverpool Record Office: Arch. MS. 920 MD 146 Acc. 608.

ANON.

Diary, c. 1867. 20 fols.

Contents: journal of a tour of the Rhine, through Switzerland and back by Paris.

Oxford, Bodleian Library: MS. Eng. misc. e 365. (Acquired 1953).

ANON.

Diary, 1867.

Contents: journal of a six-week visit to Palestine.

Ipswich and East Suffolk Record Office: MS. 63/1.

ANON.

Diary, 1867.

Contents: journal of a voyage to South America and Africa.

Warwickshire Record Office: MS. CR136/A5.

ARDAGH, Major-General Sir John Charles, K.C.I.E. (1840–1907).

Diaries, 1867–1900.

Contents: pocket diaries and memoranda of soldier who was a member of various commissions of enquiry, delegate to international conferences, and private secretary to successive Governors-General of India.

London, Public Record Office: Ardagh Papers 30/40, 22 Boxes.

Susan Hamilton, *J. C. Ardagh, a biography* (London, 1909).

AWDRY, Miss Cecile, of Seagry, near Chippenham, Wiltshire.

Diary, Sept–Oct., 1867. 1 vol.

Contents: journal of a trip to Paris with her sister and parents, primarily to see the Great Exhibition ; Victorian sentiment ; guidebook details.

Wigan Central Public Library: Edward Hall coll.

BELDAM, E. A., Josephine, of Royston, Herts., gentlewoman.

Diary, Oct., 1867–Feb., 1868. 1 vol.

Contents: journal kept on voyage to Madeira ; social life in Madeira.

Cambridgeshire Record Office: MS. R58/8/14/18.

BRADLEY, Katherine Harris (1846–1914), pseudonym with Miss Edith Emma Cooper, "Michael Field".

Diaries, 1867–68, 1868–69, 1889–1914.

Contents: journal of literary interest ; record of thought and events ;

drafts of their poetry; much of it about the literature and literary celebrities of the time.

Oxford, Bodleian Library: Eng. misc. e 336 [1867–68]. (Acquired 1942).

London, British Museum: Add. MSS. 46776–46804 [1866–1914]. (Acquired 1948).

BRET, Isabella.

Diaries, 1867 and 1872–73.

Ipswich and East Suffolk Record Office: MSS. HA 71/B/1–3.

CODRINGTON, Rev. Robert Henry, Fellow of Wadham College, Oxford, and later missionary in the Far East.

Diaries, 1867–1922. 32 vols.

Contents: journal with letters and lectures relating to his missionary work in Melanesia up to 1887; then entries during his years as Prebendary of Chichester.

Oxford, Rhodes House Library: Pacific Ocean MSS. s. 2–33.

DAVIS, Rev. Francis Neville (b. 1867), of Rowner, Hampshire, an antiquarian.

Diary and autobiography from 1867.

Contents: his work with the Oxfordshire Record Society, and church and Hampshire scholarly societies; detailed diary of everyday life in his parish and neighbourhood.

Southampton University Library: Strong Room, cupboard 3.

Not available for consultation until 1996.

DICKENS, Charles John Huffam (1812–1870), novelist.

Diary, Jan–Dec., 1867.

Contents: very brief notes, some in shorthand, in a pocket diary; his engagements; his readings; his second trip to America and his readings there; bald memoranda, of biographical interest only. (This MS. has figured prominently in the search for information on the Dickens-Ternan story).

New York Public Library: Berg coll.

HAMILTON, Sir Edward Walter, G.C.B. (b. 1847), civil servant.

Diaries, 1867, 1880–1906, 1890–1906. 71 vols.

Contents: early journal of a stay in Brittany, 1867; sixteen volumes of engagement diaries, 1890–1906; the remainder are personal diaries, April, 1880–May, 1906, when he was private secretary to Gladstone, 1880–85, and later Assistant Financial Secretary.

London, British Museum: Add. MSS. 48629–48699.

HILL, [——].

Diary, 1867. 187 pp.

Contents: journal of a tour on the Continent; Edinburgh, London, Paris, Geneva, Venice, Florence, Rome, Naples, Genoa.

Oxford, Bodleian Library: MS. Top. gen. e. 77. (Acquired 1955).

HILLS, George, of Hepworth, Suffolk.
Diary 1867–1922 (extracts).
Contents: notebook with extracts from journals and letters; brief items mostly, more detailed for 1914–22.
West Suffolk Record Office: MS. E5/2/6.2a.

HORNER, Josua (1812–1881), of Halifax, Yorkshire, a portrait painter.
Diary, Jan., 1867–Dec., 1868. 1 vol. (See also p. 134).
Contents: a working diary entered in *Mr. Punch's Pocket Book: 1867–68.*
Wigan Central Public Library: Edward Hall coll. M858.

LEIGHTON, Stanley.
Diaries, 1867–68.
Contents: travel journals of journeys in India and Ceylon.
India Office Library: MSS. Eur. B. 132.

LLOYD, Mrs. Howard, of Carmarthen.
Diaries, 1867, 1869–70, and 1876–77.
Carmarthen County Record Office: Cynghordy MSS. 1158, 1160–61, 1164–65.

MELVILLE, Lady Susan (1828–1910), daughter of eighth Earl of Leven and seventh Earl of Melville, Lady of the Bedchamber to Princess Christian, 1868–83.
Diaries, 1867–1910. 32 vols.
Contents: weather; social engagements; foreign travel; mostly very brief entries.
Glasgow City Archives: MSS. T/PM CXXIII/1–31.

MORRIS (Clark), Josie.
Diary, 1867.
Contents: touristic notes made during a tour of England.
Yale University Library: Diaries, Misc. coll.

PEASE, Elizabeth Mary (d. 1903), of Darlington, wife of Henry Fell Pease.
Diary, 1867. 1 vol.
Contents: very abbreviated entries.
Durham County Record Office: MS. D/Pe (not listed).

PHIPPS, Charles N.P. (1845–1913), of Westbury, Wiltshire, a country gentleman.
Diary, Oct., 1867–Feb., 1868. 1 vol.
Contents: full journal of a voyage from Rio de Janiero round South America to Panama, and then to Jamaica, calling at various places.
Wiltshire Record Office: MS. 540.

SCOTT, G. R., a schoolboy at Winchester School, from Stowey.
Diary, May, 1867–Sept., 1869. 191 pp.
Contents: cricket games at school; social life and sport at Winchester; schoolboy's affairs; school gossip; slangy; account of holiday rambles,

Devon in 1869 ; camping ; weather ; books read ; cuttings from the *Times* ;
copies of school songs.
Oxford, Bodleian Library: MS. Top. Hants. e. 9. (Acquired 1929).
SMITH, Sidney, an apprentice aboard the ship *Whampoa.*
Diary, Sept., 1867–Oct., 1868. 1 vol.
Contents: journal of voyage to Calcutta and New York, and passage from
New York to Liverpool in S.S. *Helvetia.*
National Maritime Museum: JOD 87, MS69/061.
STANTON, David, of Church End Farm, Keysoe, Beds., farmer.
Diaries, Jan., 1867–Dec., 1905. 7 vols.
Contents: farming matters.
Bedfordshire Record Office: CRT 160/54 (photocopy).
STOTT, Walter Barton, of Manchester, surgeon.
Diary, Jan–Dec., 1867. 1 vol.
Manchester Public Libraries: Archives Dept., MS. 926.1 S105 V2.
TRYE, Rev. C. B., Rector of Leckhampton, near Cheltenham.
Diaries, 1867–84. 4 vols.
Gloucestershire Records Office: MSS. D 303 F 15. (Acquired 1961).
YOUNG, Major-General Ralph.
Diary, 1867.
Contents: journal of a trip to Kashmir.
India Office Library: MSS. Eur. B. 133.

1868

ANON.
Diary, 1868–69.
Contents: journal of a voyage to Australia.
Cornwall Record Office: MSS. (Acquired 1963).
ARBUTHNOT, Herbert R. (1851–?1919), schoolboy at Eton, son of George
Arbuthnot, Elderslie, near Ockley, Surrey.
Diary, Dec., 1868–Dec., 1869. 1 vol.
Contents: entries made while in the VIth. form at Eton ; schoolboy
interests. (Latterly diarist became a director of the London and West-
minster Bank).
Wigan Central Public Library: Edward Hall coll. M 925/140.
BALDWIN, Lord Alfred of Bewdley (b. 1841), industrialist and politician.
Diaries, 1868–1908. 7 vols.
Private: Earl Baldwin of Bewdley, Showborough House, Twyning, near
Tewkesbury, Gloucestershire. (Formerly in Dudley Public Library,
Worcestershire).
BROWNE, William D., Town missionary. (c. 1857–77).
Diary, Aug., 1868–Jan., 1870.
Plymouth Public Library: Local History and Archives 920BRO.

CARTWRIGHT, Julia, later wife of Rev. W. Henry Ady (m. 1880), of Edgcote, Northants, and Charing, Kent, a biographer and fiction writer.
Diaries, 1868–1919. 52 vols.
Contents: personal notes by the author of *The Pilgrims' Way* (1892), *Life and Work of Sir Edward Burne-Jones* (1894), etc.
Northamptonshire Record Office: MSS. Acc. 1961/81.

DICKSON, William Joseph, of Preston, Lancs., a solicitor.
Diaries, 1868–1900. 32 vols.
Contents: miscellaneous notes of local interest; clerk to the justices of the peace.
Lancashire Record Office, Preston: MSS. DDD/193–216, 228–229, 231–237.

GORHAM, C. A.
Diary, April–June, 1868. 90 leaves.
Contents: journal of an excursion to Syria and Palestine.
Oxford, Bodleian Library: MS. Eng. misc. e. 366. (Acquired 1953).

HALLAM, William Henry (1868–1956), of East Lockinge, Berkshire, and Swindon, railway engineer.
Diaries, 1868–1952. 63 vols.
Contents: autobiographical memoranda growing into a record of daily life, work, and expenditure; his efforts to educate himself through lectures and reading at the Swindon Mechanics Institute; archaeological interests; local customs and folklore.
Reading Public Libraries: Local Hist. coll., MSS. B/TU/HAL.

HART, Eliza Julia F. (d. 1886), of Durban, South Africa.
Diary, 1868–70.
Contents: journal and fragmentary letters home, describing life in South Africa, including hunting expedition with husband into the interior.
Oxford, Rhodes House Library: MSS. Afr. s. 1004.

HASLAM, W. H. (b. 1857), of Crosspool, Sheffield, a Sunday School teacher and probably manual worker.
Diaries, July, 1868–July, 1869. 4 vols.
Contents: daily activities, local events.
Sheffield City Libraries: Dept. of Local History & Archives, Misc. Doc. 1115–1118.

JEFFERY, Edward, of Northampton.
Diary, 1868.
Contents: journal of a lay assistant at Saint Katherine's Church, Northampton.
Northamptonshire Record Office: MS.

JONES, David, of Aberystwyth, an apprentice seaman.
Diaries, 1868–69.
Contents: log books kept by Jones, an apprentice on board the ship

Alexandria on two voyages from Liverpool to Calcutta and the two return voyages.
National Library of Wales: MSS. 1469–1470.
KENDRICK, James (1809–1882).
Diary, 1868–69.
Contents: journal of his researches at Wilderspool.
Warrington Municipal Library: MS.
NEWDIGATE, Rev. C. J.
Diary, 1868. 1 vol.
Warwickshire Record Office: MS. CR136/A5.
PAGET, Catherine.
Diary, 1868.
Contents: a visit to Osborne, Isle of Wight; very brief.
Oxford, Bodleian Library: MS. Eng. misc. d. 244, (fol. 184). (Acquired 1960).
PRYSE, Marianne.
Diary, 1868.
Carmarthen County Record Office: Aberglasney MSS. 35.
REYNOLDS, W., of Welbeck Street, Nottingham.
Diary, Feb., and June, 1868, June, 1869, and Feb., 1873.
Contents: occasional entries, 1–6 Feb., 17–26 June, and one entry for 6 Feb., 1873; the first is occasioned by a visit to London; then a visit to Hamburg, N. Germany in June; entries made on a visit to Manchester and Liverpool, June, 1869.
Nottingham City Public Library: MS. M 12, 297.
ROBERTS, Lady, wife of Field-Marshal Lord Roberts.
Diary, 1868.
Contents: journal with brief memoranda.
National Army Museum: MS. 7101/23/94.
STANDEN, William (1804–1889).
Diary, 1868–82. 1 vol.
Contents: a journal of wind and weather; monthly graphs showing barometer and thermometer recordings for each day; comments on direction and force of wind and state of weather; notes on gardening progress and temperatures at certain hours of the day.
East Sussex Record Office: Add MS. 3253.
STONE, Eleanor, of Banbury, Oxfordshire.
Diaries, 1868–94. 3 vols.
Contents: very few entries; includes some reminiscences of childhood and family history (especially an account of the Paris Exhibition).
Private: Brigadier J. S. W. Stone, 22 Rutland Gate, London, S.W.1.
TABOR, H. S., of Bocking.
Diaries, 1868–1910. 18 vols.
Essex Record Office: MSS. D/DTa F6–23.

1869

ANDERSON, Capt. James, R.N., of Westbury House, Fareham, Hants.
Diary, 1869. 1 vol.
Portsmouth City Record Office: Hewett coll., 16A/138.
BOUGHTON, Elizabeth, of Hushborne Crawley, Bedfordshire.
Diaries, Jan–Feb., 1869 and Jan., 1870.
Contents: daily life of an invalid; her health, visits from neighbours, etc.
Luton Museum: MSS. coll.
Bedfordshire Record Office: CRT 110/32 (transcript).
CHICHESTER, Rev. William, of Drewsteignston, near Crockernwell, Devon.
Diaries, 1869–95. 6 vols.
Contents: regular daily entries by the incumbent.
Private: Rev. A. R. W. Peak, The Rectory, Drewsteignton, Devon.
COWHAM, Henry, soldier of the 39th. Foot.
Diary, 1869. 59pp.
Contents: journal of an overland route taken by the 39th. Foot from Cork to Ferozepore, India.
Private: F. R. Cowham, Great Rissington, Cheltenham, Glos.
National Army Museum: 7212–4 (Photostat).
DIXEY, Frederick Augustus, D.M., F.R.S. (1855–1935), Fellow of Wadham College, Oxford.
Diaries, 1869–1935. 20 vols.
Private: H. G. Dixey, 102 Kingston Road, Oxford. (Papers destined for the Bodleian Library, Oxford).
FORBES, Lieut-Col. Henry Erskine.
Diaries, 1869–70 and 1891.
India Office Library: MSS. Eur. B. 222.
HOTHAM, Henry Edward.
Diaries and memorandum, 1869 and 1878–79. 2 vols. (See also p. 299).
Contents: latter is a pocket notebook with military notes, and a fragmentary journal relating to service in South Africa.
East Riding of Yorkshire County Record Office: MSS. DDHO/11/16–17.
KRABBÉ, Emily Isabel, of Buenos Aires, later married Walter Heald.
Diaries, 1869–71. 2 vols.
Manchester, John Rylands Library: MSS. Eng. 1218.
RAMSAY, Robert W. (1861–1951), of Yarm-on-Tees, Darlington, and after 1882 of London.
Diaries, April, 1869–Jan., 1951. 44 vols.
Contents: juvenile notes; concerts; plays; national events; antiquarian interests.
Greater London Record Office (S.E.I.): MSS. F/RMY/1–44.

SCOTT-GATTY, Sir Alfred Scott (b. 1847), York Herald of the College of
Arms and composer.
Diary, 1869–92. 270 leaves.
Contents: few entries ; some transcripts of letters Boosey & Co.
Oxford, Bodleian Library: MS. Eng. misc. b. 81. (Acquired 1966).
SOWDEN, John, of Bradford, Yorkshire, an artist.
Diaries, 1869–1923 (with gaps). 32 vols.
Bradford Central Library: MSS. DB. 39/14.
WATTS, James, of Abney Hall, Cheshire.
Diaries, 17-28 Aug., 1869 and May–June, 1872. 2 vols.
Contents: journals of holidays in Holland and Germany.
Manchester Public Libraries, Archives Dept., MS. C1/1/3–4.

                                      1870

ANON.
Diary, 1870. 1 vol.
Contents: a brief journal of a tour to Calais, Lille, Brussels, etc ; tourist's
interests.
National Library of Wales: MS. 3015C (Haverfordwest MSS., 95).
ANON.
Diary, 1870. 1 vol.
Contents: travel journal of a tour in the Hebrides and central Highlands ;
notes on scenery and beauties
National Library of Scotland: MS. 2562.
ANON., (a member of the Freemantle family).
Diary, 1870. 1 vol.
Contents: journal of a journey in Spain and France.
Buckinghamshire Record Office: Freemantle coll., Box 234.
BAKER, Charles Edward, of Sherwod, Nottinghamshire.
Diaries and personal history, c. 1870–1929. 2 vols.
Contents: opens with autobiographical notes before becoming a diary
proper.
Birmingham Public Library: Baker coll. (Acquired 1940).
DOUGHTY, Frederick Proby, R.N.
Diary, 1870–74.
Ipswich and East Suffolk Record Office: MS. HA 75/A1/1.
DUNDAS, Captain James, military officer.
Diary, 1870.
Contents: journal of the Red River (Canada) Expedition, kept by an
officer in the 60th. Rifles.
Private: Miss Dundas, of Arniston, Arniston House, Gorebridge, Mid-
lothian. (Enquiries to N.R.A., Scotland). Microfilm at S.R.O.: RH4/15/1.

FRATER, James (1833–1875), clerk of works at Chester Cathedral.
Diaries, 1870–73. 5 vols.
Contents: professional diaries kept during the restoration of Chester Cathedral (1868–75).
Chester Cathedral Muniments: MSS. coll.
G.W.O. Addleshaw, " Architects, sculptors, . . . Chester Cathedral", *Architectural History* XIV (1971), pp. 82–96.

GRIMSTON, (Hon.) William (1855–1900), naval officer.
Diary, 1870–71. 1 vol.
Contents: journal and "remark book" during service as a midshipman on H.M.S. *Trafalgar*.
Hertford County Record Office: MSS. Ref. AR 942.

HALL, Colonel Charles Thomas, of Osmington Lodge, Dorset.
Diary, Jan–Dec., 1870. 1 vol.
Contents: brief notes of social and sporting activities.
Dorset County Record Office: MS. D83/26.

HERRIES, Lady Angela Fitzallan Howard, wife of 12th. Baron Herries, of Everingham Park, York.
Diaries, 1870, 1872–73, 1877, and 1883. 5 vols.
Contents: mostly notes on social and family affairs.
East Riding of Yorkshire County Record Office: MSS. DDEV/61/36/40.

HEWETT, James, of Posbrook, Titchfield, Hants.
Diaries, 1870, 1872–77, and 1894. 8 vols.
Portsmouth City Record Office: MSS. Ref. 16A/140/1–8.
K.C.M.G. (1848–1923), subsequently C-in-C of the Dominion Militia.

HUTTON, Lieutenant-General Sir Edward Thomas Henry, K.C.B.
Diary, Oct–Nov., 1870. 60 pp.
Contents: journal kept during a visit to the battlefields of the Franco-Prussian War by a then young officer.
London, British Museum: Add. MS. 50107 (Vol. 30 of Hutton Papers). (Acquired 1926 and 1948).

MARTIN, Robert Frewen, of Woodhouse Eaves, Leics., civil engineer.
Diaries, 1870–76. 5 vols.
Contents: brief notes of expenses and journeys.
Leicestershire Record Office: MSS. DG6/C/41.

NICHOLL, Rev. J. B., of Llanegwad, Carmarthenshire.
Diaries, 1870–77 (with gaps).
Contents: brief memoranda in pocket diaries.
Carmarthen County Record Office: Museum MSS. 318–324.

ROLLS, Georgiana Marcia (later, Lady Llangattock), of the Hendre, Llangattock-vibon-avel, near Monmouth.
Diaries, 1870, 1889, 1892–93, and 1907. 5 vols.
Contents: domestic concerns ; full entries.
Monmouthshire Record Office: MSS. D361 F/P8.

STRATHERN, Alexander.
Diary, 1870–72.
Contents: journal of trip to Sedan, visit to Cluny Hill Hydropathic and voyage from Glasgow to Melbourne and back to Liverpool.
Scottish Record Office: GD 1/471/1.

WHYLEY, Rev. G. E., of Eaton Bray, Bedfordshire, incumbent.
Diary, Jan–Dec., 1870. 1 vol.
Contents: brief entries; accounts; church matters.
Bedfordshire Record Office: MS. A.D. 3808.

WOOD, A. H.
Diary, Sept., 1870–Feb., 1871.
Contents: journal kept in Paris during the seige which occurred in the Franco-Prussian War.
Oxford, Bodleian Library: MS. Fr. d. 20–23.

1871

ANON.
Diaries, 1871–91. 11 vols.
Scottish Record Office: GD 18/2124.

ANON., [?Henry Francis Brown (1840–1920), of London, bachelor].
Diary, Aug., 1871–Sept., 1875. 132 pp.
Contents: occasional record of home interests, but mostly devoted to annual Continental trips; treatment at various spas, Salzburg, Ischl, etc; visits to Paris, including one after the German occupation contrasting with memories of Paris in its heyday; stays in Rome, Venice, Cologne; the Oberammergau Passion play; Christmas in a Brighton hotel; journal of some individuality, a military bore at home and abroad. [Edward Hall].
Wigan Central Public Library: Edward Hall coll. Muniment Room, cases 1 & 2.

CLIFFORD, Edward John (1849–1931), of Stow-on-the-Wold, Gloucester-shire, a stonemason.
Diaries, 1871–1919.
Contents: originally kept in shorthand, but converted into longhand at the suggestion of Rev. J. T. Evans, rector of Stow-on-the-Wold.
National Library of Wales: MSS. 1454–1459C.

DANIEL, David Robert.
Diaries, 1871–1930.
National Library of Wales: D. R. Daniel coll. MSS. 509–552.

DENSHAM, Thomas Row, of Luke Street, Bampton, a solicitor.
Diaries, 1871–87. 11 vols.
Contents: brief daily entries; mostly business matters; he was clerk to the Tiverton Highways District Board, to Bampton School Board, and Agent for the West of England Insurance Co.
Devon Record Office: MSS. 1044 B add. 2/1–11.

EDWARDS, E. E. M., of Caerynwch, Brithdir, Merioneth.
Diaries, 1871–83 (with gaps). 3 vols.
Contents: sporting journals, game, etc.
Merioneth County Record Office: M/73.

GARNETT, William.
Diary, 1871–72.
Lancashire Record Office: Garnett of Quernmore MSS., DDQ.

GAUNTLETT, J. L.
Diary, 1871.
Contents: journal of a tour in Scotland.
Edinburgh University Library: Dc.3.102.

[?]HOLT, Alfred, son of George Holt, senior, of Liverpool.
Diary, July–Aug., 1871. 1 vol.
Contents: journal of a holiday in France and south-west England, with Frances, his wife.
Liverpool Record Office: Archives Dept., Holt Papers, 2/9.

JAMES, David.
Diary, 1871. 1 vol.
Contents: entries relating to Tabernacle Chapel, Aberystwyth, made in *The Gentleman's Illustrated Pocket Diary & Almanack*; some English and some Welsh used.
National Library of Wales: Evan Evans coll., MS. 7484A. (Presented 1923).

LAYARD, Lady.
Diary, Aug–Nov., 1871.
London, British Museum: Add. MS. 50182. (Acquired 1960).

MAXWELL, Marmaduke Constable.
Diaries, 1871–72. 2 vols.
Contents: family affairs; chapel at Dumfries; farm and estate matters; social events; etc.
East Riding of Yorkshire County Record Office: MSS. DDEV/61/41–42.

ROBERTS, of Waterford and Kandahar, Frederick Sleigh, 1st. Earl (1832–1914), Field Marshal.
Diaries, 1871–72 and Dec., 1899–March, 1900. 2 vols.
Contents: journal of the Lushai Expedition, 1871–2; and a Staff journal kept at Ladysmith, South Africa.
National Army Museum: MSS. 7101/23/93, 185.

SANDERSON, Jane Charlotte Burdon (c. 1836–1889), of Oxford.
Diaries, April, 1871–March, 1872. 3 vols.
Contents: travel journals of a Cook's Tour; France, Italy, and Palestine. (MSS. may be copies; attributed to the above).
London, University College Library: MSS. ADD. 179/83 a–c.

SMITH, B. L.
Diary, May–Oct., 1871. (Typescript).

Contents: journal of his voyage to Norway and the Arctic regions in the schooner *Sampson* ; explorations in the Spitzbergen seas.
Edinburgh University Library: Gen. 76.

STANSFIELD, T. W., a major in the Indian army.
Diary, July, 1871–Dec., 1878. 1 vol.
Contents: journal of life in Madras, London, and Rangoon.
Birmingham University Library: MS. 6/vi/14.

SUFFIELD, Sir Charles Harbord, K.C.B., 5th. Baron (d. 1830), A.D.C. to the Queen.
Diaries, 1871, 1879, 1881, and 1883.
Contents: book diaries, none of which is complete.
Private: Mrs. J. M. Cuthbert, c/o Midland Bank, High Street, Winchester.

WARD, Thomas Humphry (1845–1926), of Stocks, Aldbury, Herts., Oxford undergraduate and later journalist with (London) *Times*.
Diaries, 1871 and 1887. 2 vols.
Contents: record of studies, dinner and other engagements.
London, University College Library: MSS. ADD. 202.

WHITMORE, F. H.
Diaries, 1871, 1884, 1890–91. 14 vols.
Private: Mrs. George Labouchere, owner ; custodian ; Capt. G. C. Wolryche-Whitmore, Dudmaston, Bridgnorth, Salop.

WILLIAMS, Nathaniel.
Diaries, 1871, 1874, 1876, 1877, and 1880.
Contents: sparse entries in both English and Welsh made by the brother of Sir John Williams, the first president of the National Library of Wales.
National Library of Wales: MSS. 2178A.

1872

BOLTON, Charles Henry.
Diary, Feb–May, 1872. 1 vol.
Contents: journal of a voyage from Tilbury to Melbourne, Australia, kept by a passenger on board the ship *Lincolnshire*.
National Maritime Museum: JOD 91, MS68/103.

BOSANQUET, Charles B. P., of Rock, Northumberland, son of Charles Bosanquet, 1769–1850.
Diary notebook, 1872–1903.
Contents: farming, weather, crops, stock, prices ; relating to three farms at Rock ; in summary form ; interesting for farm methods and economics.
Private: C. C. Bosanquet, Esq., Christ Church College, Oxford.

BROWN, Thomas Lloyd, of South Parade, Leeds, a wine and spirit merchant.
Diaries, 1872–85. 9 vols.
Contents: brief but regular entries ; local events, deaths, disasters, murders ; local history jottings ; observations on birds and their habits ;

the weather ; a mixture of local and public happenings mostly culled from newspapers.

Leeds Public Libraries (Sheepscar): Archives Dept., MSS. GA/C39–47.

BUND, Mrs. Harriette Penelope Willis, of London and Worcestershire.
Diaries, 1872–73. 2 vols.
Contents: pocket diaries with occasional notes.
Worcestershire Record Office: MSS. Ref. 705:36. (Acquired 1949).

CHENNELLS, F. St. T., of Church Farm Great Gaddesden, Herts.
Diary, 1872.
Contents: personal items ; farm matters.
Hemel Hempstead Town Hall: local records coll., MS. LC/GG/1X.

CROSWELL, Henry.
Diaries, Nov., 1872–Sept., 1886. 2 vols. (Transcript only).
Contents: records of his weekly visits to 500 various London churches ; notes on architecture, style of service, quality of music, sermons, seating and size of congregation, parson, hymns, organ, length of service, etc.
Oxford, Bodleian Library: MSS. Eng. misc. c. 402/1–2 (typescript).
M. Donovan, *Church Quarterly Review* (April–June, 1965), 178.

HAMPDEN, Sir Henry Bouverie William Brand, 1st. Viscount (1814–1892), Speaker of the House of Commons, 1874–84.
Diaries, 1872–84. 13 vols.
Contents: his diaries appear to relate almost exclusively to his official duties ; he was Speaker 1874–84.
House of Lords Record Office: Historical collections.

HOLT, Alfred. (1829–1911), of Liverpool.
Diary, April–July, 1872. 1 vol. (See also pp. 242, 257).
Contents: journal of a voyage to North America with his wife Fanny, her sister Harriet, and Isobel Green ; boat left Southampton for New Orleans via Havana ; visits to Denver, San Francisco, Utah, Chicago, Niagara, New York, Boston, and Montreal ; returned to Liverpool from Quebec.
Liverpool Record Office: Archives Dept., Holt Papers 2/5.

LLOYD, Mrs. Aimée (née Peel), of Carmarthen.
Diaries, 1872 and 1890–92. 4 vols.
Carmarthen County Record Office: Cynghordy MSS. 1162, 1176–1178.

SMEATON, John, of Glasgow, wright and builder.
Diary, Jan–March, 1872. 1 vol.
Contents: church-going ; his work ; social activities, entries very brief.
Glasgow City Archives: MS. TD 109/1.

WALKER, Alfred Osten.
Diaries, 1872–1924. 53 vols.
Contents: notes of business and social activities ; observations in natural history and meteorology, in North Wales and (from 1899 onwards) in Kent.
Liverpool University Library: Western MSS., 100. (Acquired 1950).

WILLCOX, D. (b. 1845), of the Glasgow area.

Diary, 1872–86. 145 pp. (Transcript only).

Contents: haphazard entries, with great gaps in the later years; includes a retrospective survey of family history; family tragedy of young son lost in house outbreak of fire.

Glasgow, Mitchell Library: MS. B.645163 (Acquired 1951).

1873

ANON.

Diary, 1873–74.

Contents: journal for the Inspector of Nuisances for Wallingford district, Berks.`

Berkshire Record Office: MS. D/Ex 288 02.

ANON.

Diaries, Jan., 1873–March, 1874. 2 vols.

Contents: apparently kept by a bailiff or similar officer; brief notes on farming activities, weather, etc., at Frampton; some mention of the Sheridan family, whose bailiff at Frampton in 1874 was Frederick Luscombe.

Dorset Record Office: MSS. 3900.

ANON.

Diary, 1873.

Contents: journal of a tour in Kent.

Private: Mrs. R. Coke-Steel, Trusley Old Hall, Sutton-on-the-Hill, Derbyshire.

ANON.

Diary, 1873.

Royal Commonwealth Society: MSS. coll. (on loan from Mrs. Fairfax).

ANON.

Diary, 1873–74.

Contents: journal kept during the Ashanti War.

Private: Glover MSS. (Present location unknown).

CHILSTON, Aretas Akers-Douglas, 1st. Viscount (1851–1926), of Chilston Park, Maidstone, Kent, a parliamentarian.

Diaries, 1873–1925. 52 vols.

Contents: entries in printed Lett's diaries, usually recording appointments and movements; he led a distinguished, though not spectacular, career in the House of Commons.

Kent County Archives Office: MSS. U564 Chilston/F1–53.

COCHRANE, Lord Douglas, army officer.

Diaries, 1873, and 1878–85.

Contents: journals include a journey to South America, 1873, and one kept during the Sudan campaign, 1884–85.

Scottish Record Office: GD 233/167–8, Bundle 3 and 170.

I

CRAIG, James Whitelaw (1849–1880), of Paisley, engineer.
Diary, Sept., 1873–March, 1877. 283 pp.
Contents: travel in south of France and in Australia; collecting natural history specimens; detailed account of natural history; climate, life of countries; sketches, general interest.
Paisley Public Library: MS. P.C.137.

EDWARDS, R. J.
Diary, 1873–74.
Contents: journal notebook of a trip to Britain.
Rhodes University, South Africa: Cory Library, MS. Acc. 22.

EVANS, George Eyre (1857–1939).
Diaries, 1873, 1874, 1877, 1890–1901 (with gaps). 56 vols.
Contents: mostly small pocket diaries with sparse entries; two travel diaries of 1899 are kept in Ireland in early July and 13–30 an incomplete journal of a tour of U.S.A.
National Library of Wales: G. E. Evans Bequest, MSS. 100–156.

GORHAM, G. D'O.
Diary, 1873. 1 vol.
Contents: domestic journal, with household accounts.
Private: Rev. H. M. Gorham, formerly of Croft, Leicestershire.

KNATCHBULL-HUGESSON, Eva, daughter of the 1st. Baron Brabourne.
Diaries, 1873–93. 9 vols.
Contents: entirely personal; series of diaries is incomplete.
Kent Archives Office: MS. Knatchbull, U951 F30/1–9. (Acquired 1962).

LISTER, John (1847–1933), of Shibden Hall, Southowram.
Diaries, 1873–1922. 9 vols.
Contents: personal and social matters.
Halifax Public Library: Archives Dept., MSS. SH:7:JN 8–16.

LYTTON, Lady Edith, later Countess of (1841–1936), of Knebworth, Herts.
Diary, April–May, 1873. 8pp.
Contents: journey to, settling in Paris, friends, entertainment, etc; her husband had been appointed First Secretary at the Embassy.
Hertford County Record Office: MS. Ref. 57462.

McLAREN, William Forbes.
Diary, 1873–74. 386 pp.
Contents: journal kept by a Gold Coast trader, who entitled the volume, "From Glasgow to the River Volta, West Coast of Africa".
Oxford, Rhodes House Library: MS. Afr. S. 710. (On permanent loan from Dr. L. Goodman since 1966.)

MACQUEEN, Archibald, soldier of the 98th. Foot.
Diary, 1873. (Typescript).
Contents: journal of journey to Jamaica by a member of the 98th. Foot.
National Army Museum: MS. 6603/68.

NARES, Sir George Strong.
Diary, 1873–74. 1 vol.
Contents: journal kept aboard H.M.S. *Challenger.*
National Maritime Museum: JOD 15, MS. 9981.

RAMSAY, Charles Maule, schoolboy and later cadet.
Diaries, 1873–77.
Contents: journals kept at Wimbledon School and Royal Military
Academy, Woolwich.
Scottish Record Office: GD 45/26/93.

RASHDALL, Hastings (b. 1858), schoolboy and later an Oxford Fellow.
Diary, 1873. 56 fols.
Contents: journal kept by young scholar at Harrow School.
Oxford, Bodleian Library: MS. Eng. misc. e 361. (Acquired 1953).

RIDLEY, Sir Edward (1843–1928), 2nd. son of Sir M. W. Ridley, 4th.
Bart.
Diaries, 1873–74, 1876, 1889, and 1899. 4 vols.
Contents: journals of travels on the Continent.
Northumberland Record Office: MSS Ridley of Blagdon, NRO 138,
ZRI 31/1.

SHUVALOV, Lieutenant Count Paul.
Diary, March–April, 1873.
Contents: journal of the Khiva Campaign.
London, British Museum: Add. MS. 47841/Q.

1874

BARROW, Percy H. S., of the 19th. Hussars.
Diaries, 1874–85. 2 vols.
Contents: journals kept while serving in the U.K.
National Army Museum: MSS. 6009/14.

BIRCH, James Wheeler Woodford (1826–1875), Colonial Civil Servant.
Diary, March, 1874–Sept., 1875 (with gaps).
Contents: journal kept while British Resident of Perak, Malaya; includes an expedition through the States of Salangor and Perak; his work
there. (Diarist was assassinated there in Nov., 1875. MS currently not
available to readers).
Oxford, Rhodes House Library: MSS. Ind. Ocn. s.242 Box 1.

BODLEY, John Edward Courtney (1853–1925), historian and politician.
Diaries, Jan., 1874–Dec., 1875, Oct., 1884–Jan., 1885 and Aug.–Oct., 1888.
4 vols; 1887–8 (TS), 2 vols.
Contents: people met; dinner parties; political talk and society gossip;
visits made; theatre-going; life in Oxford and London; encounters with
prominent personages. 1888 volume is journal of a tour in Canada and
the U.S.A. MSS. have been cut in several places; visit to S. Africa, 1887–8.

Oxford, Bodleian Library: MSS. Eng. misc. e 459–461, d 498. (Acquired 1956). Balliol College Library: MSS. No. 443.

BROWN, Robert, sailor.
Diary, 1874–75.
Contents: an account of a voyage to China and New York in the ship *Tamesa* by the third mate.
National Maritime Museum: JOD 64 MS58–080.

BRUNE, E. S. Prideaux.
Diary, 1874.
Contents: journal of a Continental tour.
Hampshire Record Office: MS. 19M59/12.

FANSHAWE, Herbert Charles, an Assistant Commissioner.
Diary, 1874–75.
Contents: journal with title, "What I saw of the '74 famine in Bengal"; also entries relating to his leave.
India Office Library: MSS. Eur. E. 217.

FORTESCUE, John William (b. 1859), of Castle Hill, Filleigh, Major Royal in North Devon Cavalry.
Diary, 1874. 1 vol.
Contents: detailed daily entries of travels in the U.S.A.; observations on the differences between life in America and in England; at home his sporting and social activities.
Devon Record Office: MS. 1262 M/FD 23–27.

GOODSALL, Walter (1849–1913), a master mariner.
Diaries, May–July, 1874 and 1876–1900.
Contents: after a volume of intermittent entries the major span has daily entries without a break; the record covers many voyages between London and Bombay, and cable work in the ship, *Kangaroo*, off or between Lisbon, Malta, Alexandria, Aden, Suez, Zanzibar, etc.; includes an account of the bombardment of Alexandria, 1882, while he was in command of the Eastern Telegraph Co. ship, *Chilton*, between voyages and after his 1888 retirement there is a detailed account of family life in south London.
Private: Robert Goodsall, Esq., Stede Court, Harrietsham, Nr. Maidstone, Kent.
E. W. Polson Newman, *Great Britain in Egypt* (London: Cassell, 1928).

HADDOW, Sir William Henry (1859–1937), Fellow of Worcester College, Oxford.
Diaries and correspondence, 1874–1900.
Oxford, Worcester College Library: MS. coll.

LLOYD, H. M., of Carmarthen.
Diaries, 1874 and 1893. 2 vols.
Contents: journal of a tour on the Continent, 1874.
Carmarthen County Record Office: Cynghordy MSS. 1163, 1179.

MORGAN, John D., of Genesse Shrub, Utica, New York. U.S.A.
Diary, March, 1874–March, 1875. 1 vol.
Contents: journal containing general notes on everyday life.
Caernarvon County Record Office: M/1236/3.

MOSS, William Flint, of Mansfield, Notts., a cooper.
Diary, Jan., 1874–Nov., 1879. 400 pp.
Contents: local events at Mansfield; public events recorded rather than personal interests: local deaths, crimes, weather, accidents; his journeys.
Nottingham Public Library: Arch. Dept., MS. M 379. (Appears in Matthews, *British Diaries* under Anon, 1874.)

NORRIS, William Harris, of Loxbeare Barton, of Gunstone in Crediton, and finally of Searle Street, Crediton, a farmer.
Diaries, 1874–90. 2 vols.
Contents: brief entries; sometimes daily but more often every two or three days; farming matters, farmwork and stock; some details of personal and social activities.
Devon Record Office: MSS. 500 M/F 1–2.

PICKERING, William Alexander.
Diary, Oct.–Nov., 1874. (Typescript)
Contents: journal of a journey from Singapore to Sungie Ujong and of his stay there.
Oxford, Rhodes House Library: MSS. Ind. Ocn. s. 74. (Originals among the Government Papers of Perak Library).

RIDLEY, Matthew White (1842–1904), 1st. Viscount.
Diary, Jan.–March, 1874. 1 vol.
Contents: journal of a French tour.
Northumberland Record Office: MS. Ridley of Blagdon, ZR1.

WELD, Constance Elizabeth, daughter of Edward Joseph Weld, of Lulworth Castle.
Diaries, Jan.–Oct., 1874 and Jan.–Dec., 1876. 2 vols.
Contents: daily activities of a young lady in Lulworth, London, Cannes, and Italy.
Dorset Record Office: MSS. D10/F109.

WREY, George.
Diaries, 1874, 1876, and 1877. 3 vols.
Contents: journals of a visit to Venice and travels round Italian lakes, 1874, of a hunting trip in the Rocky Mountains, 1876, and of travels in Spain, 1877.
Scottish Record Office: GD 21/480 and 21/482/2–3.

1875

ANON., of Oldham, Lancashire, an architect.
Diary, Jan.–Dec., 1875. 1 vol.

Contents: entries mostly refer to building mills; diarist is possibly A. H. Scott.
Manchester Public Libraries: Archives Dept., MS. MISC/117.

ABEL, William Jenkinson (b. 1838), of Boston, Lincolnshire, and east London, schoolmaster.
Diary, 1875. 1 vol.
Contents: rather terse entries, and some gaps; affairs of the New Street school; his engagement to A.S.P.; attends a public lecture by Huxley.
Nottingham Public Library: Arch. Dept., MS. ABL/1. (Acquired 1966).

COLQUHOUN, A. S. D.
Diary, June, 1875. 46 pp.
Contents: journal of a summer tour to St. Petersburg and Moscow; rather overdramatic in style.
Glasgow, Mitchell Library: MS. 392 688 S.R. 175.

COURTNEY, Catherine, 1st Baroness Courtney of Penwith.
Diaries, Oct., 1875–July, 1919. 17 vols.
Contents: social and political affairs; meetings with political and literary figures; domestic rounds; accounts of tours home and abroad (Egypt, 1879; Norway, 1885, etc.).
London School of Economics: Courtney coll. R (S.R.) 1003/21–38.

ELLIS, Thomas Edward (d. 1899).
Diaries, 1875–76 and 1878 (with copied notes from his diaries for 1889–90).
Contents: notes by a student at New College, Oxford, and later a member of Parliament.
National Library of Wales: D. R. Daniel coll. 6 & 7.

FORTESCUE, John Seymour (b. 1856), of Castle Hill, Filleigh, a naval Captain and equerry-in-waiting to the King, and naval A.D.C. to Lord Roberts.
Diaries, 1875–1900. 10 vols.
Contents: detailed daily entries of his activities at home and abroad, including his travels in India, Australia, New Zealand, China, U.S.A., South Africa, and Germany.
Devon Record Office: MSS. 1262 M/FD 29–53.

GALTON, Mrs. Louisa (d. 1897), wife of Sir Francis Galton, of Claverdon, Warwick.
Diary, 1875–96. 1 vol.
Contents: personal matters briefly noted; yearly summaries.
London, University College Library: MSS Galton I item 2.

HAMPTON, Sir John Somerset Pakington, Baron (b. 1800).
Diaries, 1875–80. 5 vols.
Worcestershire Record Office: Pakington MSS., 4732:1i.

SEEBOHM, Henry.
Diaries, 1875, 1876, 1877, and 1881. 3 vols.
Contents: travel journals; to Great River Petchora in land of Samoyeds, 1875; ornithological trip to Holland, 1876; journey to the Yenisei, 1877; in Norfolk, 1881.
Cambridge University Library: Add. MSS., 4471, 4472, 4474.
SHIRLEY, Evelyn Philip.
Diaries, 1875–82.
Warwickshire Record Office: MSS. CR229–175–176.
SMITH, James Parker (1854–1929), of Jordanhill, barrister, M.P., and P.P.S. to Joseph Chamberlain.
Diaries, 1875, 1877, and Nov., 1880–Feb., 1882. 4 vols.
Contents: brief and scattered entries; life at Trinity College, Cambridge; late volumes mainly about his state of mind and feelings for the woman he wants to marry.
Glasgow City Archives: MSS. TD 1.

1876

ANDERSON, M. W., of Carmarthen, South Wales.
Diary, 1876–78.
Carmarthen County Record Office: Derwydd MSS. CA30.
CALVERTT, J. S., of Tothill, Lincs., and Shipton-under-Wychwood, Oxfordshire, farmer.
Diaries, 1876–1900. 3 vols.
Contents: personal and farming matters.
Gloucestershire Records Office: MSS. D 2550.
CHAMBERLAIN, Joseph.
Diaries, Aug., 1876–Oct., 1905 (with gaps). 4 vols.
Contents: undated journal of a visit to Paris; diaries of Continental tours; diaries of a trip to New York, 1887 and 1888.
Birmingham University Library: MSS. AC 1/5/1, 2/2/17, JC 8/1/2–3, 5.
CLARK, Frederick and Elmira.
Diary, 17–25 May, 1876. 25 pp.
Gloucester City Library: Gloucestershire coll., MS. 6957. SA 4.27.
COLLIER, C. D.
Diary and commonplace book, 1876–81.
National Library of Wales: G. E. Evans Bequest, MS. 412.
CUNINGHAME of THORNTON, Lord.
Diary, 1876. 1 vol.
Contents: journal of a hunting trip in the Rocky Mountains.
Scottish Record Office: GD 21/482/2.

D'ABERNON, Sir Edgar Vincent, 1st. Viscount (1857–1941), diplomat.
Diaries, 1876–98 and 1920–23 (with gaps). 19 vols.
Contents: initially soldier's affairs, the Coldstream Guards from which
diarist resigned in 1882; diplomatic career, mostly in Europe. [Some of
the 1920's diaries have been published.]
London, British Museum: Add MSS. 48941–48959. (Acquired 1955).
MILLS, Dr. John, of Yateley, Hants., Army Medical Corps.
Diaries, 1876–80.
Contents: journals kept while serving as Indian Army Doctor.
Hampshire Record Office: MSS. 99.M.71.
SIMCOX, Edith.
Diary, May, 1876–Jan., 1900 (with gaps). 189 leaves.
Contents: brief entries; contains many references to George Eliot;
bears the title, "Autobiography of a Shirtmaker".
Oxford, Bodleian Library: MS. Eng. misc. d 494. (Acquired 1958).
THOMPSON, Dr. Herbert (1876–1945), of Malton, Yorkshire, a musician.
Diary, and autobiography, 1876–1945. 71 vols.
Contents: details of purely personal interest, accounts of domestic events
and social activities, as well as travels abroad and music criticism; they
also describe his meeting with famous men, notably Brahms.
Leeds University Library: MSS. No. 80.
WYNNE, Dr. W. A. S.
Diaries, 1876–1920.
Norfolk and Norwich Record Office: MSS. (Acquired 1963).

1877

ANON.
Diary, Jan.–Dec., 1877. 1 vol.
Contents: an account of day-to-day events in the life of a young woman
living near Bath; visits to friends, to London, etc.
Birmingham University Library: MS. 6/i/35.
BILLSON, Theodora, Mabel, and Edgar.
Diary, 1877–98 (with gaps).
Contents: a journal of tours in Yorkshire, Westmorland, and North
Wales.
National Library of Wales: Harry Williams MSS. 5644B.
COGHILL, Lieut. Nevill Josiah Aylmer (1852–1879), V.C., officer of the
24th. Foot.
Diaries, 1877 and June, 1879, 2 vols.
Contents: journals kept while serving; the latter belongs to the period
of the Zulu War and was found on the battlefield of Isandhlwana.
National Army Museum: MSS. 7112–38.
COLBORNE, Ellen.
Diary, 1877.

Private: Seaton MSS; formerly owned by J. E. C. Mackrell, Beech-wood, Sparkwell, Devon.

COLBORNE, H. L.

Diary, 1877–78.

Private: Seaton MSS; formerly owned by J. E. C. Mackrell, Beech-wood, Sparkwell, Devon.

COOK, A. M., of Brighton and London.

Diaries, March, 1877–July, 1886, and Dec., 1912–July, 1921. 12 vols.

Contents: chiefly notes of political events and public affairs; comments on literary matters and the theatre, social meetings and calls; occasional weather notes.

Oxford, Bodleian Library: MSS. Eng misc. e. 166–177. (Acquired 1927).

HOLWORTHY, Joseph Matthew (b. 1822), of Bromley and London, merchant.

Diary, Dec., 1877–Jan., 1878. 1 vol.

Contents: journal of a voyage aboard S.S. *Lusitania* from Saint Vincent via Adelaide to Melbourne, Australia.

Cambridgeshire Record Office: MS. 279/F2.

KINCHINGTON, John., soldier of the 2nd. Bn. of the Buffs.

Diary, 1887.

Contents: journal of shipwreck of the troopship S.S. *St. Lawrence.*

National Army Museum: MSS. 6603–66.

LAGDEN, Sir Godfrey Yeatman, K.C.M.G. (1851–1934), Resident Commissioner, Basutoland.

Diaries, 1877–1934. 67 vols.

Contents: diaries, along with his correspondence relating to Basutoland, Swaziland, etc., 1833–1934, are only to be consulted with permission of Miss Diana Wilbraham, owner.

Oxford, Rhodes House Library: MS. Afr. s. 142–215 (on loan).

LUTTRELL, Alexander Fownes (1855–1945), of Dunster Castle, Somerset, soldier.

Diaries, Oct., 1877–April, 1878 and Nov., 1879–Aug., 1884. 2 vols.

Contents: former is a hunting diary; latter is kept while serving at home as an officer in the Grenadier Guards.

Somerset Record Office: MSS. DD/L.

MORLEY, Countess, wife of the 2nd. Earl.

Diaries. 1877–78. 2 vols.

London, British Museum: Add. MSS. 48263–48264.

RORKE, John.

Diary, 1877. 1 vol.

Contents: journal kept while 2nd. cabin passenger on the clipper ship *Loch Vennachar.*

National Maritime Museum: JOD 44, 37. MS. 1693.

I*

SCHLUTER, Augusta, a lady's maid.
Diaries, 1877–90. 6 vols.
Contents: mostly domestic items by the Hanoverian servant of the Gladstone family.
London; British Museum: Add. MSS. 46271. (Acquired 1946).
M. Duncan, *A Lady's Maid in Downing Street* (London, 1927).

TAGGART, Thomas, of Kerrowkeeill, Malew, Isle of Man, tailor and crofter.
Diary, 1877.
Contents: business diary, with jottings, memoranda, prices, and measurements in connection with his tailoring work; occasional references to church music and practices, weather, his neighbours and the croft.
Douglas, I.o.M., Manx Museum: MS. No. 1498.

VANE-TEMPEST, Lord Henry John (1854–1905), 2nd. son of 5th. Marquis of Londonderry, of Machynlleth, Merioneth.
Diaries, 1877–85 and 1892–1900. 6 vols.
Contents: detailed accounts of social activities, regimental duties, etc.; horse-racing, cricket; visits to Wynard Park, Co. Durham.
Durham County Record Office: MSS. D/Lo/F 511–516.

YEOMAN, James Brown, of South Shields, merchant seaman.
Diary, 1877–80. 1 vol.
Contents: journal of voyages to the Mediterranean, Bombay, Boston (U.S.A.), etc., in the ships, *Cervin*, *Albula*, and *James Barrass*.
Durham County Record Office: MSS. D/X 108–2.

YONGE, Rev. D. (1836–1920), vicar of Broxted (1869–85) and Boreham (1885–1918).
Diaries, 1877 and 1890–1919. 31 vols.
Essex Record Office: D/Du 358/1–31.

1878

ANON.
Diary, 1878–80.
Contents: journal kept aboard the ship, S.S. *Sorthella*.
Lincolnshire Archives Office: MSS. (Acquired 1963).
ANON.
Diary, April, 1878–Feb., 1904. 1 vol.
Manchester Public Libraries: Archives Dept., MS. 920.9 Sc 1.
ANON.
Diary, 1878. 1 vol.
Contents: journal of a trip to France.
Northumberland Record Office: Soc. of Antiquaries MSS., NRO 93, ZAN M17/12.

BANDINEL, Julia Maria.
Diary, June, 1878–Jan., 1898. 1 vol.

Contents: in two parts, 4–15 June, 1878 on a journey through Switzerland and Germany; the remainder is an intermittent journal of life at home.

Birmingham University Library: MSS. 7/iii/11.

BENSON, Rt. Rev. Edward White (1829–1896), Archbishop of Canterbury.

Diary, Feb. 1878–Sept., 1896 (extracts).

Contents: notes of his clerical work and administration in his various episcopates; travels on the Continent; public and church affairs in the House of Lords; private affairs; social and family life, reading and studies.

Cambridge, Trinity College Library: Benson Papers.

Oxford, Bodleian Library: Benson coll. MSS. 2/77–79.

Arthur C. Benson, *The Life of Rt. Rev. Edward White Benson* (London, 1901), pp. 174–547.

CAMPBELL, Ronald, a soldier.

Diaries, 1878–79. 2 vols.

Contents: journals kept of his service in South Africa.

Carmarthen County Record Office: Cawdor MSS. 1/245.

CHAMBERLAIN, Sir Austen.

Diaries, Aug., 1878–Nov., 1901 (with gaps). 7 vols.

Contents: almost all journals kept on tours; Switzerland and Canada, 1884, Constantinople, Greece, Italy, 1886; Germany and Austria, 1891–92; Spain and the Pyrenees, 1895; central Europe, 1897 and 1898; and Turkey and Greece, 1901.

Birmingham University Library: MSS. AC 2/2/2–8.

GEDGE, Ernest (1862–1935), explorer and prospector.

Diaries, Oct., 1878–Nov., 1919 (with gaps). 53 files.

Contents: journals of expeditions in various parts of the world: in Uganda with Sir Frederick Jackson, 1889–93, and Rhodesia; work as "Times" correspondent; prospecting trips to Kenya etc. Later work in Yukon, Mackenzie Delta, in Malaya, Borneo and Java, and Iraq.

Oxford, Rhodes House Library: MSS. Brit. Emp. s.290, Box 6.

GILBERT, William Schwenk (1836–1911), of Harrowweald, Middlesex, dramatist and lyric writer.

Diaries, 1878, 1889, and 1905–11.

Contents: his autograph diaries are irregularly entered; the 1878 volume contains a telegraphic code, presumably for use on his tour of the U.S.; many are written in French.

London. British Museum: Add. MSS. 49322–49329. (Acquired 1965).

GORDON, Major Alexander.

Diary, Nov., 1878–Sept., 1879. 1 vol.

Contents: journal kept during the 2nd. Afghan War (1878–80) by the Brigade Major to General Sale.

National Army Museum: MSS. 7103–26.

HUGHES, Isaac, a Welsh author.

Diaries, 1878, 1886, and 1894. 3 vols.

Contents: very brief entries; first two volumes are in Welsh.

Cardiff Public Library: MSS. 4.592.

LLOYD, male member of the family, of Carmarthen, South Wales.

Diaries, 1878, 1881, and 1882. 3 vols.

Carmarthen County Record Office: Cynghordy MSS. 1166, 1168, and 1170.

LUCKHAM, Alexander Minty, of Studland, Dorset, a farmer.

Diaries, 1878–1906. 29 vols.

Contents: mainly family events; frequent weather records and some farming references.

Dorset Record Office: MSS. D97/3–31. (Acquired 1960).

SIMPSON, Mrs. L. M. (b. 1839), widow.

Diary, July, 1878–July, 1880. 274 pp.

Contents: the unpleasant lot of a soured middle-aged widow living with and upon a round of relatives in England and Ireland; mid-Victorian domesticities and family life.

Wigan Central Public Library: Edward Hall coll. M 822.

STEVENSON, Robert Louis (1850–1894), man of letters.

Diaries, 1878–90 (with gaps). 5 vols.

Contents: journal kept during the cruise of the *Janet Nicholl* in the South Seas, 1890 (fragment); visits to the South Seas, July, 1888–Dec., 1889; volume kept on a walking tour in the Cevennes, Sept.–Oct., 1878; and some undated journals kept in the South Seas travels.

San Marino, California, Henry Huntingdon Library: MSS.

Sister Martha Mary McGaw, *Stevenson in Hawaii* (University of Hawaii Press, 1950).

STILL, Mrs., of Burgar & Smoogrow, Orkney.

Diary, 1878–82.

Scottish Record Office: GD 1/585/8.

WILSON, John T., of Birmingham, a missionary.

Diary, 1878–80.

Contents: diary and reports of the missionary to the Birmingham Police Mission.

Birmingham Public Library: MS. 426 677.

1879

ANON.

Diary, 1879–80.

Private: Major C. J. Vernon Wentworth, formerly of Stanborough, Hertfordshire.

ANON.

Diary, 1879.

Contents: an army journal kept in South Africa ; the Boers.

Private: Viscount Colville of Culrose, Fawsyde, Kineff, By Montrose, Angus. (Enquiries to N.R.A., Scotland.)

BLATHWAYT, Mrs. W. T. (née Oates).

Diary, 1879–80. 1 vol.

Contents: mostly family affairs, diarist was the second wife, born Mary Sarah Oates.

Gloucestershire Record Office: Dyrham Park MSS., D 1799 F 260.

COUCHMAN, Susan, of Temple Balsall, Warwicks.

Diary, c. 1879.

Contents: additions of a devotional kind, presumably by Susan Couchman, in the diary of Henry Couchman (d. 1838).

Warwickshire Record Office: MS. CR347/6.

COWPER, Matthew, a mariner.

Diary, July–Sept., 1879. 1 vol.

Contents: journal of a cruise to the Norwegian fiords kept by the second officer of the yacht *Argo* ; Alfred and Philip Holt of Liverpool were among the passengers.

Liverpool Record Office: Arch. Dept., Holt Papers 2/3 (with 4 a copy of the same by Agnes Cowper, the diarist's daughter.) (Acquired 1942).

FAIRLIE, W. G., a soldier.

Diary, 1879. 1 vol.

Contents: journal kept while serving during the Zulu War ; some sketches of Natal, etc.

National Army Museum: MSS. 6302–48. (Acquired 1963).

HOLT, Alfred (1829–1911), of Liverpool, the Founder of the Blue Funnel Line.

Diary, 1879–95. (See also pp. 242, 244).

Contents: notes for a journal, mainly of holidays on the yacht *Argo II*. There is also an autobiographical narrative and recollection of his first 50 years. Diary includes description of the inception of the Far Eastern Service.

Liverpool Record Office: Arch. Dept., Holt Papers 2/20 (on loan).

JAMES, H., a soldier of the Connaught Rangers.

Diary, 1879. 1 vol.

Contents: journal of a private kept while serving in the Zulu War.

Private: J. H. Whittaker, Esq., Fleetwood, Lancashire.

National Army Museum has photocopy, 7205–73.

JONES, David (b. 1843), of Wallington, Surrey.

Diaries, 1879–83, and 1887. 6 vols.

Contents: antiquarian and general interest ; weather ; local personalities ; jottings of national news interests ; transcripts of church tablets ; description of Father Ignatius ; visits in S. Wales ; some sketches.

Cardiff Public Library: MSS. 1.640.

MERCER, Col. C. A. (1847–1923).

Diary, 1879. 1 vol.

Contents: journal kept during the Afghan War; begins at Jellabad; descriptions of daily life in camp and the foray marches; returned to depot at Bakloh in September before joining his battalion in Afghanistan.

National Army Museum: MSS. 6903/5/33.

OWEN, David Edmundes (1866–1922), later vicar of Llandovery, Carmarthenshire.

Diary, 1879. 1 vol.

Contents: youthful jottings.

National Library of Wales: MS. 2864B.

ROW, Thomas, of Fore Street, Bampton, solicitor.

Diaries, 1879–1905. 16 vols.

Contents: daily entries, mostly pertaining to his business; clerk of Bampton U.D.C. and the School Board, Commercial Union Insurance agent, and agent to the Devon and Exeter Savings Bank.

Devon Record Office: MSS. 1044 B add. 2/12–17.

SMITH, Joseph.

Diaries, 1879–80. 3 vols.

Contents: written on a voyage to New Zealand and other places.

National Maritime Museum: MSS.

STEPHENSON, Henry (b. 1842), of Haslingden, Lancashire, a schoolmaster.

Diary, Jan., 1879–Dec., 1881. 652 pp.

Contents: school records and family affairs; local genealogy, local families; gravestones and local data, indexed; travels in the neighbourhood; church and Sunday-school work.

Rawtenstall Central Public Library: MSS. coll.

THOMAS, (?H)., of St. Andrew's Major, Glamorgan.

Diaries, 1879, 1881, 1886, and 1889–93. 8 vols.

Glamorgan County Record Office: MSS. D/D Xen.

TUCK, M. M., soldier of the 58th. Foot.

Diary, Feb., 1879–April, 1882. 1 vol.

Contents: journal of a private serving in the Zulu and Transvaal Wars; accounts of the battles of Ulundi and Laing's Nek, where diarist was wounded.

National Army Museum: MSS. 7005/21.

1880

ANON.

Diary, 1880–84. 5 vols.

Contents: personal items and affairs of a member of the Goulburn family.

Surrey Record Office: Goulburn MSS., Acc. 147.

BAKER, Oliver (b. 1856), of Birmingham and Stratford-upon-Avon.
Diaries, Sept., 1880–Dec., 1884, Feb–Nov., 1892, and Jan., 1897–Dec., 1898. 4 vols.
Stratford, The Shakespeare Birthplace Trust: DR 142/51–54.

BLATHWAYT, Rev. Wynter Edward (1859–1929), rector of Dyrham, Gloucestershire, 1909–29.
Diaries, 1880 and 1889–1929. 21 vols.
Contents: the first diary was kept during the Michaelmas Term at Trinity College, Cambridge; later ones have brief entries only; family affairs; European holidays.
Gloucestershire Record Office: Dyrham Park MSS. D1799 F 261–281.

BROOKS, Marianne Sophie Eugenie (later Jenkins) (d. 1885), of Flitwick Manor House, Beds.
Diary, Sept., 1880–May, 1881. 1 vol.
Contents: journal of holiday in France, illustrated by sketches and post-cards.
Bedfordshire Records Office: MS. LL 17/291.

DILKE, Sir Charles Wentworth, 2nd. Bt. (b. 1843), M.P.
Diaries, April, 1880–Feb., 1892. 5 vols.
Contents: entries, which relate mostly to political matters, are irregular; they become less frequent after 1886, when he retired from public life; the last volume is mostly in the hand of his secretary; these diaries were intentionally compiled for eventual publication. Tour journals in Ireland, 1880, Egypt, 1881–82, and Ireland, 1883.
London, British Museum: Add. MSS. 43924–43928 (Dilke Papers, Vols. 51–55).
Birmingham University Library: JC 8/2/1 (copies of tour journals).

ELIOT, Emily M. (b. 1857), later married John H. Morison.
Diary, June, 1880. 33 pp.
Contents: a young lady's visit to Oxford, having journeyed from New York with her father; her stay at New College; walks around Oxford; college services, Convocation; Mark Pattison.
Oxford, Bodleian Library: MS. Top. Oxon. d. 314, fols. 112–128.

HALL, Francis George, a District Officer.
Diaries, 1880–1901. 9 vols.
Contents: journals with some letters and papers; brief entries, calendar of correspondence, etc. concerning his African service.
Oxford, Rhodes House Library: MSS. Afr. s. 54–62.

HOLDEN, Captain Henry (1823–1900), of Bramcote Hills, Nottinghamshire.
Diary, 1880–96.
Contents: contains many interesting references to Notts. and Derbyshire personalities, country gentry, magistrates; sport, weather, family matters.
Private: Wilfred H. Holden, 32 Southwick St., London, W.2.

KENNEDY, J. H., an officer of the 97th. Regiment, who was later Deputy-Lieutenant of Norfolk (1925).
Diary, 1880. 1 vol.
Contents: journal kept while serving with the 97th. Foot at Halifax, Nova Scotia.
National Army Museum: MSS. 6406/58/4.

LECKIE, Col. F. W. V.
Diary, 1880. 1 vol.
Contents: journal of a march with the 2nd. Brigade, 1st. Bombay Division, from Jandalar to Maiwand under the command of Brig-General A. P. Danbury, during the 2nd. Afghan War.
National Army Museum: MSS. 5911/399.

MANNERS, Capt. C. G. E. J., officer of the Grenadier Guards.
Diary, 1880–81. (Typed copy).
Contents: journal kept on service during the Boer War; the Transvaal campaign.
National Army Museum: MSS. 6807/157.

PEARSON, George Robert (1858–1908), of Bristol, an accountant.
Diary, 1880. 425 pp.
Contents: journal of a voyage from Greenhythe to New Zealand aboard the ship, *Lady Jocelyn*, for the sake of health; daily happenings on ship-board; people, sights, communal life; descriptions of London, Sydney, Melbourne. The return voyage of the S.S. *Chimborazo*, from Sydney to London.
Private: Nelson V. Pearson, Esq., 24 Lightwoods Hill, Warley Woods, Smethwick, Birmingham.

PETRIE, Sir W. M. Flinders (1853–1942).
Diaries and letters, 1880–1933.
Oxford, Ashmolean Museum: Griffith Institute MSS. coll.

TATHAM family, of Abingdon, Berks.
Diaries, 1880–1950.
Private: Misses S. A. and E. Tatham, Abingdon.

THOMAS, John, of Port Madoc, Wales.
Diaries, Jan–Dec., 1880, and Jan–Dec., 1885. 2 vols.
Contents: daily jottings of people met, things seen; weather; his literary habits; local excursions and walks; local obituaries; some newspaper cuttings; cash accounts.
Cardiff Public Library: MS. 2.1044.

TUCKER, Henry St. George, an army officer.
Diary, (?) 1880. 1 vol.
Contents: journal kept in Upper Burma.
India Office Library: MSS. Eur. E. 200.

1881

ANON.
   Diary, 1881. 1 vol.
   Carmarthen County Record Office: Cynghordy MSS. 1167.
DE CHAIR, Admiral Sir Dudley, K.C.B., K.C.M.G., M.V.O. (1864–1958),
   of Campden Hill Gate, London W.8, Royal Naval Officer.
   Diaries, Dec., 1881–Dec., 1882 and Jan–Dec., 1894. 2 vols.
   Contents: service as a Midshipman on the ironclad ship *Alexandra*,
   mostly in the Mediterranean; active duty in Egyptian nationalist rising;
   conditions while imprisoned by rebels, 1882. Later volume concerned with
   his service as Lieutenant on the battleship *Royal Sovereign*; life at H.M.S.
   Vernon, the Torpedo School at Portsmouth.
   Imperial War Museum: MSS. De C 20, 21.
HERRIES, R. S.
   Diary, 1881–98.
   Private: Herries MSS. (Present location unknown; diary formerly in the
   possession of the late Lieut-Col. Spottiswood).
HOLWORTHY, F. W.
   Diary, April–July, 1881. 1 vol.
   Contents: journal with very detailed entries of a voyage from London to
   Christ Church, New Zealand.
   Kent Archives Office: MS. Holworthy U929, F17.
LLOYD, J. Howard F., of Carmarthen, South Wales.
   Diary, 1881.
   Carmarthen County Record Office: Cynghordy MSS. 1169.
[?] MAGNIAC, Charles, (or bailiff, possibly John Burr), of Church Farm,
   Souldrop, Beds.
   Diary, 1881–89. 1 vol.
   Contents: farm journal; annual account of treatment of fields, crops,
   grazing, etc.
   Bedfordshire Record Office: MS. X 167.
MILNER, Sir Alfred (1863–1925), later Viscount Milner, sometime Governor
   of the Cape Colony and High Commissioner of South Africa post-1897.
   Diaries, 1881–1925 (some gaps). 46 vols.
   Contents: mostly annual diaries with brief entries: relate to his career,
   journalist, prospective M.P., civil servant. Special diaries relate to Egypt,
   Palestine, Rio Tinto, and South Africa.
   Oxford, Bodleian Library: Milner Papers, MSS. 250–295.
MORRIS, Hugh, of Bwlchysarnau, Radnorshire, schoolmaster.
   Diary, c.1881–July, 1891.
   Contents: notes on school attendances; weather; discipline and punish-
   ments; school inspectors; deaths in the neighbourhood; local person-
   alities; illnesses; school routines.

H. L. V. Fletcher, *Portrait of the Wye Valley* (London: Hale, 1968), pp. 49–57.

NATHAN, Sir Matthew (1862–1939), K.C.M.G., soldier and civil servant.
Diaries, Sept., 1881–1939. 75 vols.
Contents: mostly brief items, which include his expedition to Sudan, 1884–85, to Lushai, 1889–94, his career as Governor in Sierra Leone, 1899, the Gold Coast, 1900, then Hong Kong, 1903, Natal, 1907, and Queensland, 1920; also deals with his subsequent work on various commissions.
Oxford, Rhodes House Library: Nathan Papers, MSS. 1–75. (Acquired 1961).

ORMSBY-GORE, George Ralph Charles (heir to 2nd. Baron Harlech).
Diary, 1881.
National Library of Wales: Harlech MSS.

PLUNKETT, Sir Horace Curzon (1854–1923), politician, promotor of agricultural co-operatives.
Diaries, Jan., 1881–March, 1932. 52 vols.
Contents: early life in Ireland; ten years' ranching in Wyoming; Irish Agricultural Cooperative movement; parliamentary affairs; Home Rule; 1916 Rebellion; agriculture in Ireland; U.S.A. cooperation; association with Theodore Roosevelt; negotiations with U.S.A. about war; personal and political observations.
Oxford, The Plunkett Foundation: MSS. coll.

PORTAL, Sir Gerald H.
Diaries and Correspondence, 1881–95. 12 vols.
Contents: relating to his services in Cairo, Zanzibar, and Uganda.
Oxford, Rhodes House Library: MSS. Afr. s 103–114.

RUDDY, F. H.
Diary, 1881–12.
Contents: kept at Llandderfel, Llangollen, Denbighshire.
Private: Rev. D. H. Ruddy (present address unknown).

WHITE, E. S.
Diary, 1881–89 (with gaps).
Contents: journals kept during visits to Lynmouth, Keswick, Oxford, Derbyshire, and Axminster.
Private: Sir Richard White. Bt., The Vine, Presteigne, Radnorshire, Wales.

1882

ANON.
Diaries, 1882–94.
Contents: [?] official diaries of police constables of the Lincolnshire constabulary at Lindsey.
Lincolnshire Archives Office: MSS. 1/5.

ANON.
Diaries, 1882, 1884, and 1889–91.
Contents: diary of public engagements in the Bicester area; in printed Hewlett's *Almanack Diary & Bicester Directory.*
Oxford, Bodleian Library: MS. Alm. G. A. Oxon. 40709. (Acquired 1953).

ANSTEY, F. (pseud. of Thomas Anstey Guthrie) (1856–1934), of Grosvenor Square, London, a novelist.
Diaries, 1882–92 and 1894–95. (Copy).
Contents: a collection of notes drawn from his diaries.
London, British Museum: Add. MSS., Millar Bequest. (Acquired 1968).

EVANS, Dr. John Gwenogvryn, of Tremvan, Llanbedrog, Caernarvonshire.
Diaries, 1882 and 1884 (with a further undated volume). 3 vols.
Contents: Feb–April, 1882, a notebook containing daily entries describing a voyage from Melbourne; the undated MS. is also a journal of a voyage.
National Library of Wales: J. G. Evans MSS., 131–133. (Acquired 1930).

GREENSTREET, Emily.
Diary, Aug., 1882. 1 vol.
Contents: journal of her visit to France and Switzerland, illustrated by postcards.
Greater London Record Office (S.E.1.): MS. P 82/ALB/139.

HAMILTON-GORDON, Rachel, daughter of Lord Stanmore.
Diary, 1882. (Transcript).
Contents: journal of a child kept on a voyage from Wellington, New Zealand to London. Some illustrations.
London, British Museum: Add. MS. 49271 (Stanmore Papers).

MAXSE, General Frederick Ivor (1862–1958), of Dorking.
Diaries, 1882, 1884, 1886, and a 1897–98. 6 vols.
Contents: journals, including a journey to America, 1882, and the Soudan Campaign, 1898.
West Sussex County Record Office: MSS. Maxse 347–352.

McCRACKEN, General, late of 49th. Regiment.
Diary, [?]1882–1937.
Berkshire Record Office: MSS. (on loan from Mrs. B. M. N. Powell and Miss G. C. S. McCracken).

McCRACKEN, Mrs., wife of General McCracken.
Diary, [?]1882–1934.
Berkshire Record Office: MSS. (on loan from Mrs. B. M. N. Powell and Miss G. C. S. McCracken).

MacDONALD, George (1824–1905).
Diary, [?]1882. (Typescript with author's corrections).
Contents: entitled "The Diary of an Old Soul" and intended for private printing; there is an edition dated 1882 of this diary in the College Library.
Oxford, Balliol College Library: MS. 418. (Acquired 1945).

SOUTHAM, George Armitage, of Manchester.
Diary, Nov., 1882–June, 1895. 1 vol.
Manchester Public Libraries: Archives Dept., MS. 942.73081 S29.

STADDON, James Rawlinson, a soldier of 7th. Royal Fusiliers.
Diary, 1882–86. (photocopy).
Contents: journal describing his journey to India and his service there with his regiment.
National Army Museum: MSS. 7207–14.

THORNTON, Mrs. Frances (née Macadam) (b. 1854), wife of Dr. James Parsons Thornton, medical superintendent of the ship and formerly on the staff of Newcastle-upon-Tyne Infirmary.
Diary, 1882. 1 vol.
Contents: journal in narrative style, kept during the voyage of the emigrant ship *Selkirkshire* from Glasgow to Rockhampton, Queensland, Australia.
Devon Record Office: MS. 877 M/F 1.

TROUP, Lieut-Col., an army surgeon.
Diary, 1882.
Contents: journal kept while in charge of convalescents in Egypt.
R.A.M.C. Historical Museum: MS. 332.

WILSON, F., a soldier of the 60th. Rifles.
Diary, July–Oct., 1882. 1 vol.
Contents: journal kept during the Egyptian War by a private soldier; description of the campaign.
National Army Museum: MSS. 6806/18.

1883

BAGGETT, John, a sailor.
Diary, 1883–85. 1 vol.
Contents: journal kept by the signalman on the cruises of the ship, H.M.S. *Alexandra*, flagship of Admiral Lord John Hay.
National Maritime Museum: JOD 71, MS59/0.

BLATHWAYT, Robert Wynter (1850–1936), of Dyrham Park, Gloucestershire.
Diaries, personal and hunting; 1883, 1885, 1892–99, and 1888–94. 9 vols.
Contents: Personal ones contain few entries; some petty cash accounts; the hunting volumes are detailed, concerned chiefly with New Forest Hounds, Deer Hounds; also includes The Exmoor Fox Hounds, otter hunting in Hampshire, and excursions with the Duke of Beaufort's Hounds.
Gloucestershire Record Office: Dyrham Park MSS., D1799.

BRENNAND, Stephen.
Diary, Aug–Nov., 1883. 40 pp. (Transcript).
Contents: journal of a voyage to Adelaide, South Australia.
Rawtenstall Central Public Library (Lancs.): MSS. coll.

COLLIER, Rev. Carus Vale (1864–1929), of Sheffield, Yorks.

Diaries, 1883 and 1900. 32 and 70 fols. respectively.

Contents: first is a young man's diary showing antiquarian leanings as he attends Durham University; notes on historical events and genealogy; matters of local history; entries seldom personal. Journal of a summer chaplaincy at Brunenn, Lake Lucerne, Sept., [?]1896; another of a holiday in Kent, 1899, and some notes on excursions in Yorkshire, June–Aug., 1900.

Leeds University Library: Brotherton coll., case 74.

CORNISH, Rev. James (1860–1938), of Sidmouth, Devon.

Diaries, April, 1883–June, 1938. 8 vols.

Contents: a country journal; chiefly relates to shooting over dogs in Suffolk, Berkshire, and Devon; hawking; fishing in Devon, Dorset, Scotland; birds, weather, natural history; visits to Belgium, Switzerland, France, Scotland, and Wales.

Private: Mrs. Miriam Page, formerly of Street, Somerset.

DICKEN, Admiral C. G. (d. 1937).

Diary, 1883–84.

Contents: journal kept on H.M.S. *Alexandra*; some memoirs.

Cambridge University Library: Add. MS. 7351.

FISHER, Charles (junior) (d. c. 1842), of Distington Hall.

Diaries, 1883–1900.

Contents: diaries continued after his father's death; brief items concern personal, sporting and business affairs.

Cumberland and Westmorland Record Office: MSS. DX/199.

FitzWILLIAMS, Charles H. Llewelyn (d. 1925).

Diaries, 1883–98, 1900, 1902–04, 1906–09, and 1911–26.

Contents: diaries kept by the above and afterwards by one of his sons.

National Library of Wales: FitzWilliams MSS., 72–111.

FRANCKLIN, J. L., of Gonalston.

Diaries, 1883–1912. 14 vols.

Nottinghamshire Record Office: MSS., DD.F.

FRAZER, James George (1854–1941), sometime Fellow of Trinity College, Cambridge, a social anthropologist.

Diaries, 1883, 1890, 1895, and 1900.

Contents: diary of a tour in Spain, 1883; some 8 volumes of notes made while in Greece, 1890 and 1895; diary of a stay in Rome, 1900.

Cambridge, Trinity College Library: MS. R.8.43–45.

GLADSTONE, Mrs. Catherine, wife of Rt. Hon. W. E. Gladstone.

Diary, Jan–March, 1883. 1 vol.

Contents: journal kept during a visit to Cannes, South of France.

London, British Museum: Add. MS. 46269.

McCULLAGH, James B.

Diary, 1883–1905. 71 pp.

Contents: journal relating to experiences with Indians of Naas River; Aiyansh reservation.

Oxford, Rhodes House Library: MS. Canada r. 3.

ROWE, A. H.

Diary, 1883–94.

Private: The Chepstow Society (Monmouthshire).

WILLIAMS, Richard, of Eilionwy, Caernarvon, a master painter.

Diary, 1883. 1 vol.

Contents: brief accounts of day-to-day business.

Caernarvon County Council Record Office: M/1133/1.

1884

ANON.

Diary, Sept–Oct., 1884. 1 vol.

Contents: mostly an account of a return journey through Biskra, Kantara, Constantine, Metliz, and Algiers.

Church Missionary Society: MS. Acc. 82 F 1/3.

ANON.

Diaries, 1884–85. 2 vols.

Contents: soldier's journals of the brigade under the command of Sir Herbert Stewart.

Scottish Record Office: GD 16/52/57/10.

ALEXANDER, George James (1842–1922), of Portsmouth, carpenter in Royal Navy and Naval Dockyards.

Diaries, 1884–1900 and 1901–20. 2 vols.

Contents: brief record of daily and family events; references to local and world news; written mainly in Portsmouth.

Portsmouth City Record Office: MSS. coll.

CRAUFORD, Capt. H. J., officer in the Grenadier Guards.

Diary, 1884–85. (Copies only, made 1907).

Contents: journal written during the Gordon Relief Expedition.

National Army Museum: MSS. 6710/48.

DANBY, William, soldier of the 10th. Hussars.

Diary, Feb–March, 1884. 1 vol.

Contents: diary-form letters (to a cousin) concerning service in the eastern Sudan; account of the battle at El Teb in which General Graham defeated the Mahdist forces in 1st. Sudan campaign.

National Army Museum: MSS. 7003/2.

DESBOROUGH, William Henry Grenfell, 1st. Baron (1855–1945), of Taplow Court, Bucks.

Diaries, 1884–1938 (with gaps). 11 vols.

Contents: journals of a trip to America and Canada, 1884, as journalist on 2nd. Suakim campaign, 1885, later trips to Canada, 1888, 1911, 1920, for hunting; journals devoted to items concerning his harriers, 1888–94 ; a visit to Egypt and Sudan, 1913, to the armies at the Front in France, 1915 ; brief journal of journey to India, 1891–92 ; later diaries are kept in Norfolk.

Buckinghamshire Record Office: MSS. D86/1–11.

EVANS, Thomas, of Monkton, Monknash, and of Downcross, Llantwit Major, a farmer.

Diary, 1884. 1 vol.

Contents: an agricultural journal ; farm matters.

Glamorgan County Record Office: MS. D/D Xnm 2.

GORDON, General Charles George (1833–1885).

Diary, 21–24 April and 30 July, 1884. (Facsimile).

Contents: journal kept at Khartoum during the 1st. Sudan campaign.

National Army Museum: MSS. 5702/27.

HAY, Capt. Henry, officer of 1st. Bombay Lancers.

Diaries, 1884–87 (with gaps). 3 vols.

Contents: journals include accounts of his operations with Upper Burma Field Force during the 3rd. Burmese War ; memoranda on horses, rations, marches, etc ; expedition against Kanle, sketches of landscape and people.

National War Museum: MSS. 6610/45/3, 6909/43, & 7306/15.

ILBERT, Sir Courtney Peregrine (1841–1924).

Diaries, 1884–86. 3 vols.

Contents: journals relating to his period as legal member of the Council of the Governor-General of India.

India Office Library: MSS. Eur. D. 594/3–5. (Acquired 1959).

LAWRENCE, W. R., I.C. Service.

Diaries, 1884–1902. 11 vols.

India Office Library: MSS. Eur. F. 143.

PRICE, John, of Birkenhead.

Diary, 1884. 15 pp.

Contents: journal of a visit to North Wales.

Cardiff Public Library: MS.

RASTRICK, Henry, son of John Urpeth Rastrick, the engineer.

Diary, 1884. 1 vol.

Contents: entries usually brief ; daily events, accounts, and addresses.

University of London Library: Rastrick Papers, MS. 243/11.

T. D. Rogers, *The Rastrick Papers: a Handlist* (London, 1968).

SCOTT, Sir James George.

Diaries, 1884–97.

Contents: journals kept in Burma, includes the period of the 3rd. Burmese War.

India Office Library: MSS. Eur. C. 102–114.

WALKER, George (1821–1910), of Aberdeen.

Diaries, 1884–1910. 12 vols.

Contents: earlier volumes concerned with personal life and relationships, with public affairs and personages in Aberdeen; in later volumes, more generally with public men and public affairs.
Aberdeen Public Library: MSS. Lo.920.4.W15.

1885

ANON., an Army officer.
Diary, May–Aug., 1885. 1 vol.
Contents: part of a journal kept by an officer, probably in Q.M.G. Department in Egypt.
National Army Museum: MSS. 7108/35/1.
ANON.
Diary, July–August, 1885. 1 vol.
Contents: holiday journal with pen & ink illustrations of places, buildings, crosses, animals, people, etc.
Cornwall County Record Office: MSS. AD. 72/5.
I. D. Spreedbury, ed. *Impressions of the Old Duchy, Book II: 1885; Through Cornwall by Train and Bus* (Mevagissey, Cornwall, 1971).
ANON.
Diary, July–Aug., 1885. 1 vol.
Contents: notes of a holiday kept in Cornwall and Devon; some sketches.
Cornwall Record Office: MS. AD/72/5. (Acquired 1960).
ASHWIN, Henry.
Diary, 1885–86.
Contents: journal and remark book kept on board H.M.S. *Avon*.
Worcestershire Record Office: MSS. coll. (on loan).
ATHERTON, Frederick, of Gainsborough, Lincolnshire.
Diary, 1885–88.
Contents: journal kept while foreman in charge of sinking an artesian well in Gainsborough district; really no more than a working-diary or log-book, giving details of the progress of construction at the Gainsborough waterworks; no other general material incorporated into it.
Gainsborough Public Library: local coll.
CARPENTER, Rt. Rev. William Boyd (1841–1917), Bishop of Ripon.
Diaries, 1885–92, 1894–97, 1899, 1901–02, 1904–06, 1908–17.
Contents: [autobiographical memoranda on teaching theology at Oxford] journal begun when he had been elected to bishopric; church matters, appointments.
London, British Museum: Add. MSS. 46726–46758. (Acquired 1948).
CUBBON, Henry, of Ballayelse, Arbory, Isle of Man.
Diary, June, 1885–Nov., 1887.
Contents: journal of a Manx evangelist, who belonged to an old Isle of Man family.
Douglas, I.o.M., Manx Museum: MS. 249.

CURREY, Admiral Bernard.
   Diaries, 1885–1914. 3 vols.
   Contents: personal matters as well as professional life.
   National Maritime Museum: JOD 62, MS58/052.

HANNINGTON, Rt. Rev. James (1848–1885), missionary.
   Diaries, Jan–May, 1885. 5 vols.
   Contents: notes pertaining to the Bishop's work.
   Church Missionary Society: MSS. Acc. 258. (Acquired 1971).

LASCELLES, Hon. Frederica Maria (1848–91), of London.
   Diary, Jan–Dec., 1885.
   Contents: daily domestic events recorded, but rarely with detail; visits, teas, and dinners; trouble with the maids. Diarist was the wife of Hon. Fred. Canning Lascelles, brother to the 5th. Earl of Harewood, and an uncle to the future Princess Royal, Princess Mary.
   Wigan Central Public Library: MS. M.999 EHC 199. (Acquired 1954).

PORTEUS, George, of Saffron Walden, Essex, bank employee.
   Diaries, 1885–1914. 28 vols.
   Essex Record Office: MSS. D/DU 635.

ROLLS, Henry Allen (d. 1911), of Llangattock-vibon-avel, near Monmouth, gentleman.
   Diaries, 1885, and 1891–94. 5 vols.
   Contents: detailed account of the weather.
   Monmouthshire Record Office: MSS. D361 F/P11.

ROLLS, John Maclean (1870–1916), 2nd. Lord Llangattock, of the Hendre, Llangattock-vibon-avel, near Monmouth.
   Diaries, 1885–1914. 30 vols.
   Contents: generally short and vague.
   Monmouthshire Record Office: MSS. D361 F/P10.

SECCOMBE, Thomas (b. 1866), of King's Lynn, Norfolk.
   Diary, Aug., 1885–June, 1887. 79 leaves.
   Contents: chiefly a record of books read by him, with comments on them (often extensive). Little of the daily jottings. Author is a young man, writing soon after he has left school, and is studying at Balliol College, Oxford.
   Oxford, Bodleian Library: MS. Eng. misc. d. 523. (Acquired 1961).

SLADE, Cicely Maud (d. 1960).
   Diary, 1885. 1 vol.
   Contents: journal reflecting young lady's interests.
   West Sussex County Record Office: MS. 1260.

WARD, Mary Augusta (1851–1920), of London, and "Stocks", Aldbury, Herts.
   Diaries, 1885–87 and 1892–98. 10 vols.
   Contents: family journals, almost entirely made up of advance appoint-

ments, dinner guests, etc. written apparently in conjunction with Thomas Humphrey Ward.

London, University College Library: MS. Add. 202.

WHITE, Major-General Sir George Stewart (b. 1835), of White Hall, Ballymena, Co. Antrim, Ireland.

Diaries, 1885–87. 3 vols.

Contents: private journal kept while A.A.Q.G. in Egypt with the Nile Expeditionary Force, 1885 ; two volumes pertaining to the Third Burmese War, in which he commanded a Brigade.

India Office Library: MSS. Eur. F. 108/118–120.

1886

ANON., a ship's officer.

Diary, 1886. 1 vol. (Typescript).

Contents: journal dealing with ship life, also aspects of life ashore.

Caernarvon County Record Office: M/565.

ANON.

Diary, 1886–87.

Contents: journal of the Expedition up the River Gambia in the ship, H.M.S. *Racer.*

Plymouth Public Libraries: Archives Dept., MS. Acc. 335.

ANON.

Diary, March, 1886–Nov., 1888. 1 vol.

Contents: a solicitor's journal giving brief indications of his daily work ; the majority of entries deal with property transactions, mainly in Glasgow.

Glasgow, Mitchell Library: MS. 831451.

ANON.

Diary, 1886.

Contents: journal of a journey to Menton.

Kent Archives Office: MS. Smith-Masters U1127, F15.

ANON.

Diary, 1886–89.

Contents: journal of a cruise on the ship. H.M.S. *Himalaya.*

Plymouth Public Libraries: Archives Dept., MS. Acc. 140.

AULDJO, John (1805–1886).

Diary, Jan–May, 1886. 1 vol.

Contents: brief notes kept by the former mountaineer and traveller.

London, British Museum: Add. MS. 48351. (Acquired 1952).

COCKERELL, Sydney, late director of the Fitzwilliam Museum, Cambridge. Cambridge.

Diaries, Jan., 1886–c. 1951.

Contents: early contacts with Morris, Ruskin, etc ; sometime Morris's secretary ; later in same position with Wilfred Scawen Blunt ; literary executor of Morris, Blunt, and Thomas Hardy; literary and scholarly friendships.

London, British Museum: Add. MSS. 52623–52663. (Acquired 1965).

CONNOR, W. Frederick, a missionary with C.M.S.
Diary, July, 1886–Sept., 1887 (with gaps). 27 fols.
Contents: journal of a missionary recounting daily experiences in Palestine; his work and travel for the Church Missionary Society; Arab customs; religious effusions; only three entries for 1887. Moslem hostility to the mission house.
Manchester, John Rylands Library: English MS. 705.

DUNDONALD, Douglas Cochrane, 12th. Earl.
Diaries, 1886–1930.
Scottish Record Office: GD 233/139.

IWAN, Llwyd Ap.
Diaries, 1886–87.
Contents: journal of an emigrant; the voyage to Patagonia; daily record of movements; personal activities, and events among the Welsh colony there; letters; in English and Welsh.
National Library of Wales: MSS. 9652A, 9653A.

JAMES, Montague Rhodes (1862–1936), mediaevalist, author, and Provost of Eton College (from 1918).
Diaries, with bibliographical notes, 1886–1935.
Contents: not so much a day-by-day record of events as a record entered retrospectively and at intervals of several months. Much information on his publications, bibliographical and palaeographical works.
Cambridge University Library: MSS. Add. 7517.

MACKAY, Rev. Alexander, missionary in Africa.
Diary, May–July, 1886. 1 vol.
Contents: journal of his work in Uganda; lists candidates for baptism.
Church Missionary Society: MSS. Acc. 72 F3. (Acquired 1949).

MAUNDRELL, Rev. H. (1837–1896), missionary in Africa and Far East.
Diaries, 1886–93.
Contents: journals kept while serving in Japan.
Church Missionary Society: MSS. Acc. 139.

PRING, Samuel William, passenger.
Diaries, March–June, 1886 and 1903. 2 vols.
Contents: journal kept on board the ship, *Ben Cruachan*, on a voyage from London to Sydney, Australia, 1886; details of the crew and passengers. Brief diary of the return voyage.
National Maritime Museum: JOD 81, 82, MSS. 60/05, 61/04.

TEMPLE, Sir Richard (1826–1902), an Anglo-Indian official.
Diaries, 1886–95.
Contents: a Parliamentary journal, with a vivid description of Gladstone's

two Home Rule Parliaments, from the Conservative point of view.
London, British Museum: Add. MSS. 38916–38928.

WOLSELEY family.
Diary, 1886–1916.
Contents: diary narrative rather than daily entries, with notes on Wolseley memoirs and scrapbooks.
Hove Central Public Library: Wolseley Papers, MS. 126.

ZIEGELE, Otto, a company book-keeper.
Diary, May, 1886–April, 1890 (with gaps).
Contents: journal recording journey from Dover, via Paris, to Singapore to work for Brinkman & Co.; financial troubles; holiday outings; recreations, racing and riding; intimate insight into social and recreational pattern of young man in Victorian colonial days; his voyage home via Benares, Lucknow, Port Said.
Oxford, Rhodes House Library: MSS. Ind. Ocn. s. 95.

1887

ANON., a missionary in Africa.
Diary, July, 1887–Jan., 1888. 1 vol.
Contents: journal of a missionary's journey in the Congo.
Church Missionary Society: MSS. Acc. 82 F3/1.

BROOKE, Henry, curator of Manchester Art Museum, Ancoats Hall, Manchester.
Diary, Jan., 1887–Dec., 1889. 1 vol. (Copy).
Contents: the work of the Art Museum.
Manchester Public Libraries: Archives Dept., MS. 708.273 Ma 1.

BURN, Lieutenant-Colonel A. G. (1856–1929), Regular Officer in the Indian Army (14th. Madras Infantry).
Diary, Feb–May, 1887.
Contents: journal of journey with his regiment from Bangalore to Rangoon; transport by train and river to Mandalay; descriptions of the Burmese people; a good picture of the problems which the Burma Expeditionary Force had to overcome.
Imperial War Museum: MS. AGB 1.

DORMER, J. T.
Contents: journal started on board the ship, H.M.S. *Surprise*.
Warwickshire Record Office: MSS. coll. (on loan from Lord Dormer).

FLOYD, William (?1810–1898), an antiquarian.
Diary, 1887.
National Library of Wales: MS. 385A (Floyd MS 211). (Acquired 1899).

GARDNER, Ernest Arthur (1862–1939), of Maidenhead, Yates Professor of Archaeology at University College, London (1896–1929).
Diaries, Jan.–Apr., 1887, June, 1895, and Jan., 1916–Aug., 1917. 4 vols.

Contents: journals of travel to Athens, 1887, to Russia in 1895, and of war service as a Naval Officer in the Mediterranean during the First World War.

London, University College Library: MSS. Add. 82.

MATHESON, Percy Ewing (1859–1946).

Diary, 1887–88. 1 vol.

Contents: journal of his travels.

Oxford, New College Library: MSS. coll.

MORTON, Alfred (1854–1943), of Birmingham, bricklayer.

Diaries, Jan., 1887–Jan., 1942. 48 vols.

Contents: very detailed day-to-day account of a working-man's life in England and the United States, especially New York; his work, personal and household expenses; family life and social; adventures in Victorian England and nineteenth-century industrial America.

Glasgow, Mitchell Library: MSS. B 596848–596895.

OWENS, Owen, of Garnons St., Caernarvon, North Wales, a joiner.

Diary, Apr.–June, 1887. 1 vol. (Xerox copy).

Contents: journal describing sea journey to Australia.

Caernarvon County Record Office: M/857.

RAWLINSON of Trent, Henry Seymour, Lord (1864–1925), general.

Diaries, 1887–1924. (with gaps). 34 vols.

Contents: journals include his service in the Burmese War of 1887–8, the 2nd. Sudan campaign, 1898, in which he was D.A.A.G. to Kitchener, and the Boer War; later volumes deal with India, 1902–3, a trip to N. America, 1909, and various journeyings to Europe, China, and S-E Asia; journals of 1st World War, and when C-in-C in India; visits to England, 1920–24.

National Army Museum: MSS 5201/33.

RUDD, Charles Dunell.

Diary, 1887 (typescript).

Contents: journal of a trip, with F. Thompson and R. Maguire, to Lobengula (S. Rhodesia) to obtain the "Rudd concession".

Oxford, Rhodes House Library: MSS. Afr. s. 794.

WHITEMORE, Thomas (1839 or 1840–1902).

Diary, Sept., 1887–April, 1891. 1 vol. (Copy).

Contents: hunting with the Oakley Hunt.

Bedfordshire Record Office: CRT 130/3 (photocopy).

Bedfordshire Hist. Rec. Soc., XLIV

WILSON, Thomas Needham (1863–1945), of Sandbach, Cheshire and Lymington, Hants., barrister and landowner.

Diary, June–July, 1887.

Contents: journal of a cruise in the 27-ton yacht *Nova*.

Cheshire Record Office: MS. DWS 3/11.

1888

ANON.

Diary, 1888–96.

Carmarthen County Record Office: Aberglasney MSS. 17/457.

ANON.

Diary, 1888.

Carmarthen County Record Office: Cynghordy MSS. 1175.

BURNS, Rt. Hon. John (1858–1943), M.P., P.C., later President of the
Board of Trade, of Lavender Hill, Battersea, S.W.

Diaries, 1888, 1891–94, 1897–99, 1900–09, and 1906–20. 33 vols.

Contents: mostly small appointments diaries; some notes on his career
with the Labour Party.

London, British Museum: MSS. Add. 46310–46342. (Acquired 1946).

W. Kent, *John Burns: Labour's Lost Leader* (London, 1950).

CLEMENTS, Carey, of Halstead, Essex, a mill manager.

Diary, 1888. 1 vol.

Essex Record Office: MS. D/F 3/3/26.

[?]CORNWALLIS family.

Diaries, 1888–1932. 7 vols.

Contents: diaries of the Linton Beagles, with details of every run, name
of the packs, photographs, cuttings, etc. from its formation in 1888 by
Lord Cornwallis (Linton Park, Maidstone) to its final season.

Kent Archives Office: MSS. U24 Cornwallis Zi/1–7.

GWYNNE, Rt. Rev., missionary in Africa.

Diaries and papers, 1888–1953.

Contents: include his work in the Sudan; sermons, etc.

Church Missionary Society: MSS. Acc. 18. (Acquired 1963).

HEWITT, Mrs. M.

Diary and housekeeping accounts, 1888–1924.

Stafford, William Salt Library: MS.

HOLT, Robert Durning (1833–1908), of Liverpool.

Diaries, 1888 and 1894 (extracts in typescript).

Contents: notes of a Lord Mayor of Liverpool (1893).

Liverpool Record Office: Archives Dept., Holt Papers, 4/5.

HUNTER, James (b. 1866), of Didsbury, Manchester.

Diaries, June, 1888–May, 1930.

Manchester Public Libraries: Archives Dept., MSS. 926.77 H1.

LANCHESTER, Charles Compton (b. 1877), of Hannington Rectory, Hants.

Diary, Aug.–Sept., 1888. 1 vol.

Contents: journal kept on a visit to London by an 11-year old.

Hampshire Record Office: MS. 149M.71.

MILDMAY, Meriel Hariet Caroline St. John, of Dogmersfield House.

Diary, 1888. 1 vol.

Contents: journal of a tour in Northern Italy.

Hampshire Record Office: MS. 15M50/1333.

PICKARD-CAMBRIDGE, Sir Arthur William (1873–1952), classical scholar.

Diaries, 1888–1910.

Contents: mostly entomological matters.

Oxford, Hope Dept. of Entomology: MSS. coll.

POPE, Mr. ———[?], father of Elizabeth Pope, of Copplestone House, Bow, a farmer.

Diaries, 1888–95, 1897. 8 vols.

Contents: brief daily entries of farming and personal matters.

Devon Record Office: MSS. 1791 M/F 5–13.

PRESTON, Arthur Edwin (1852–1942), of Abingdon, Berks., local historian and alderman.

Diaries, 1888–1927.

Contents: giving accounts and photographs of travels on the Continent, in North Africa, on their world tour, and on cruises; some parts relate to journeys in England.

Berkshire Record Office: MSS. D/EP8 F1–13.

WALKER, Ernest (1870–1949), D. Mus., composer.

Diaries, 1888–94. 7 vols.

Contents: journal begins after diarist became a commoner at Balliol College, Oxford (1887); contents are of musical interest.

Oxford, Balliol College Library: MSS. 445.

M. Deneke, *Ernest Walker: A Memoir* (Oxford, 1951), pp. 16–39, and pp. 50–54.

WHITWELL, Charles (1871–1955), of Nottingham and London, a lace designer and latterly a librarian.

Diaries, Jan., 1888–July, 1955. 70 vols.

Contents: detailed comments on daily events, personal and public; travels; family matters, etc.

Nottingham Public Library: MSS. Acc. M10416–10486.

1889

ANON.

Diary, 1889. 1 vol.

Contents: clerical interests.

Merioneth County Record Office: MS. coll. (Acquired 1963).

ARNOTT, H. J., Plymouth Brethren missionary.

Diary, 1889–94. (Microfilm).

Contents: journal of his missionary activity in western and central Africa; details of his correspondence.

Oxford, Rhodes House Library: micr. Afr. 410. (Original is in the National Archives of Rhodesia.)

BARCLAY, Miss Evelyn.
Diary, Oct.–Dec., 1889.
Contents: private diary kept at Venice in the household of Robert Browning during his last illness; health chart; friends; funeral arrangements; funeral.
Texas, Baylor University Library: Browning Library MSS.

CADDICK, Helen (1843–1927), of Birmingham, traveller and Governor of Birmingham University.
Diaries, 1889–1914 (with gaps). 12 vols.
Contents: travel diaries kept in many parts of the world; Palestine, Egypt, South Africa, India, Japan, New Zealand, Canada, China, Australia, Java, United States, West Indies, Argentina, Peru, Philippines, Burma, etc.
Birmingham Public Library: Ref. Library, MSS. 336851.

CHAMBERLAIN, Neville.
Diaries, June, 1889, Nov., 1889–Feb., 1890, Sept.–Oct., 1895, and Sept.–Oct., 1899. 4 vols.
Contents: journal of a family trip to Paris, 1889; to Pyrenees, Blois and Paris, 1895; to Egypt, via Italy, 1889–90; and a tour to Northern Italy, with notes on Italian history.
Birmingham University Library: MSS. NC.

DIXEY, Mrs. Frederick Augustus, of Oxford.
Diaries, 1889–1916. 28 vols.
Private: H. G. Dixey, 102 Kingston Road, Oxford. (Papers are intended for the Bodleian Library.)

FISHER, Walter, a Plymouth Brethren missionary.
Diary, 1889–1903. (Microfilm).
Contents: missionary activities in western and central Africa.
Oxford, Rhodes House Library: micr. Afr. 408. (Original is in National Archives of Rhodesia.)

GARDYNE, Lieut.–Colonel A. D. Greenhill, of the Gordon Highlanders Regt.
Diaries, 1889–1919. 8 vols. (Microfilm).
Scottish Record Office: RH 4/59/1–8.

GORHAM, Mrs. C. D'O., of Southampton.
Diaries, 1889–91, 1894–1905, and 1907. 15 vols.
Contents: domestic matters.
Private: Rev. H. M. Gorham, formerly of Croft, Leicestershire.

JONES, Miss Emily A. (c.1832–post 1910), of Brixton, Peckham, Petersfield, Hants., and finally Cranleigh, Surrey.
Diary, May, 1889–Dec., 1900. 1 vol.
Contents: brief notes on social life, personal, domestic, and family affairs; some excursions.
London Borough of Lambeth, Minet Library: MS. 8/25 (S 1655).

LEWIS, Cecil Champain (1864–1948).
Diary, 1889.
India Office Library: MSS. Eur. A. 63.
ROBINSON, Rev. J. A. (1859–1891), missionary in Africa.
Diary, March, 1889–June, 1891. 1 vol.
Contents: journal of journeys in Sudan and Africa, the Upper Niger Mission; notes on his illness.
Church Missionary Society: MSS. Acc. F4/7.
SINGER, P. E., of Kensington Court, London.
Diary, 1–28 Nov., 1889. 58 pp.
Contents: travel journal of a young American, born in Paris, seeing Europe via Brussels, Vienna, Constantinople, and Athens.
Wigan Central Public Library: Edward Hall coll. (Acquired 1950).
SMITH, Capt. E. A., soldier.
Diary, 6–22 Feb., 1889. 1 vol.
Contents: journal kept during a punitive expedition which penetrated the jungle to the south of Bhamo to quell the Mohlaing Rebellion; records firings, woundings and killings; some papers found, sketch maps; triumphant entry into Bhamo.
India Office Library: MSS. Eur. B. 65. (Acquired 1920).
WARD, Dorothy M. (c.1874–1960), of Grosvenor Place, London, and "Stocks", Aldbury, Herts.
Diaries, 1889 and 1898. 2 vols.
Contents: pocket journals giving details of her work for the Passmore Edwards Settlement with which her mother was much involved; some family news.
London, University College Library: MSS. Add. 202.
VEREY, Miss L. E., of Childe Court, Streatley, near Reading.
Diary, 3–20 Sept., 1889.
Contents: journal of a boating tour down the Rivers Severn and Thames; Shrewsbury to Gloucester, Oxford, Abingdon, Streatley, following the line of travel afforded by canals and rivers.
Wigan Central Public Library: Edward Hall coll. (EHC 24).

1890

BAKER, S. H.
Diaries, 1890, 1892, and 1894.
Birmingham Public Library: Ref. Library, MSS. Acc. 662358.
CARRINGTON, Rt. Hon. Sir William (1845–1914).
Diaries, 1890–92 and 1894. 4 vols.
Contents: brief entries concerning social engagements, notes on his periods of "waiting", as equerry to Queen Victoria; attendance at court dinners and names of guests.
Buckinghamshire Record Office: Carrington coll. MSS. D4.

K

CAVELL, E., of Sheffield, an evangelist.
Diary, Jan., 1890–Jan., 1892. 265 pp.
Contents: religious diary, recording his visits for the Sheffield Town Mission to private houses; the mission was a nonconformist, but not a sectarian, evangelizing enterprise, especially concerned with promoting abstinence and education ; general interest.
Sheffield City Libraries: Dept. of Local History and Archives, MS. B.C316S.

CHAMBERLAIN, Mary Endicott.
Diaries, Jan., 1890–Dec., 1899. 10 vols.
Contents: engagements and tour journals ; to Egypt, America, Germany and Austria, 1890–91 ; to Holland, Paris, Italy, 1892 ; Paris and New York, 1893 ; Paris and the Riviera, the Pyrenees and Spain, 1895 ; further trips to central Europe, 1897 and to America, 1898.
Birmingham University Library: MSS. C5/1.

CONRAD, Joseph (1857–1924), novelist.
Diary, June–Aug., 1890
Contents: journal of travel up the valley of the Congo; details of countryside, flora, fauna ; very little personal ; navigation directions ; illustrated.
Harvard University Library: Houghton Library, Eng. MS. 46.

EVANS, Catherine Powell, sister of George Eyre Evans, 1857–1939, of Birkenhead, later of Aberystwyth and Carmarthen.
Diary, 1890.
Contents: journal kept during an expedition by members of the Liverpool Teachers' Guild to the Continent: Venice, Rotterdam, Cologne, etc.
National Library of Wales: MS. 4299B (Eyre Evans Papers 20).

ILCHESTER, Lady, wife of 6th. Earl, of Holland House, Kensington.
Diary, 1890. 1 vol.
London, British Museum: Add. MS. 51273 (Vol. 55 of Holland House Papers). (Acquired 1963).

LANGFORD, John Alfred.
Diary, Sept., 1890–June, 1895. 1 vol.
Birmingham Public Library: Ref. Library, MS. Acc. 660980.

LUGARD, Lady, wife of Lord Frederick Lugard.
Diaries, 1890 and 1907. 2 vols.
Contents: journal of a caravan journey in East Africa, describing their movements from the coast to Uganda ; later volume kept at Hong Kong, July–Dec., 1907.
Oxford, Rhodes House Library: Lugard coll. s. 39.

McLACHAN, Angus, ship's officer.
Diary, May–July, 1890. 1 vol.
Contents: journal kept while on board the windjammer, *Eurydice*, on

a voyage from Barry, Glamorgan, to Capetown; some notes by a different hand (possibly his wife's) follow and are of a domestic nature.

Glasgow, Baillie's Library: MS. 60650, Safe 387. 22 McL.

MOOR, Mrs. F. D., wife of Rev. Frewen Moor, vicar of Ampfield, Sussex.

Diary, April–June, 1890. 194 pp.

Contents: journal of an expedition to Germany to meet an occulist of Wiesbaden; some comment on London, and the journey via Harwick, Rotterdam, Cologne; a deal of self-revelatory comment.

Wigan Central Public Library: Edward Hall coll. M 924. (Acquired 1948).

STRATHERN, Mrs.

Diary, 1890–91. 1 vol.

Contents: description of a voyage from Southampton to South Africa; impressions of that country, often humorously expressed.

Scottish Record Office: GD 1/471/2.

WILLIAMS, Mrs. Eleanor.

Diary, 1890. 1 vol.

Contents: brief comments; callers; special meals; chapel-going; unflagging reports of the weather; her interests suggest that she was the wife of a farmer in South Wales.

National Library of Wales: Add. MS. 268B.

WILLIAMS, Miss Sarah, of Bontdolgadfan, Llanbrynmair, Wales.

Diary, 1890–97 with account and memorandum book, 1884.

Contents: record of daily and weekly receipts and payments; short jottings, with references to the weather; her work with bees; some entries in Welsh.

National Library of Wales: Add. MS. 16760C.

WORSFOLD family, of Birchington, near Margate, Kent.

Diary, 1890–97. 1 vol.

Kent Archives Office: Worsfield MSS., U475.

1891

ANON.

Diary, 1891–93. 1 vol.

Carmarthen County Record Office: Derwydd MSS. CA51.

ALLENBY, M., a midshipman.

Diary, 1891–93.

Contents: journal kept aboard H.M.S. *Anson*; Plymouth; notes on Spain and Ireland.

Plymouth Public Libraries: Arch. Dept., MS. Acc. 216/5.

BOWES, Frederick.

Diary included in autobiographical journal, 1891–1923. 2 vols.

Contents: the diary includes a record of his career as an administrator in Ceylon, and is itself part of the autobiography *Bows and Arrows*.

Oxford, Rhodes House Library: MSS. Indian Ocean s. 8 and 9. (Acquired 1962).

BULL, Robert Taylor, of Burnham, Essex, saddler and harness maker.
Diaries, 1891–1937. (Microfilm).
Essex Record Office: T/B 245.

COKE, J. G., a midshipman.
Diary, July, 1891–May, 1892. 1 vol.
Contents: journal kept at sea aboard H.M.S. *Rodney*.
Private: Mrs. R. Coke-Steel, Trusley Old Hall, Sutton-on-the-Hill, Derbyshire.

DRANE, Robert (1833–1914), of Cardiff, naturalist and antiquarian.
Diaries, 1891, 1893, 1898–99, and 1902–13. 16 vols.
Glamorgan County Record Office: MSS. D/D Xib 1–27.

ELGER, Thomas Gwyn Empey, of Bedford.
Diaries, 1891–96. 2 vols.
Contents: personal and public affairs in Bedford pertaining to his employment as director of a laundry, his post as trustee of the library, and his private interest in astronomy.
Cambridge University Library: MSS. Add. 7498–7499.

FISHER, Anne, a Plymouth Brethren missionary.
Diary, 1891–93. (Microfilm).
Contents: her missionary activities in western and central Africa.
Oxford, Rhodes House Library: micr. Afr. 409. (Originals in the Rhodesian National Archives.)

FOSTER, Sir William (1863–1901), superintendent of India Office Records.
Diary, March–April, 1891. 1 vol.
Contents: journal of an expedition to Florence.
India Office Library: MSS. Eur. E. 242/323.

HEWETT, Agnes Elizabeth, of Titchfield, Hants.
Diaries, 1891–1950 (with gaps). 25 vols.
Portsmouth City Record Office: MSS. Ref. 16A/141/1–25.

HOUSMAN, Alfred Edward (1859–1936), classical scholar and poet.
Diary, 1891 with jottings for subsequent years.
Contents: little used, indeed mainly blank; some pages have been cut.
London, British Museum: Add. MS. 54349. (Acquired 1968).

MACDONALD, Sir J. R. L.
Diaries, 1891 and 1892.
Contents: notebooks associated with surveying the Uganda railway for the Imperial British East Africa Company, Kenya.
Oxford, Rhodes House Library: MSS. Afr. s. 529.

MORRIS, William, of Tonyrefail, Glamorgan.
Diary, 1891. 1 vol.
Contents: mostly philosophical quotations.
Caernarvon County Record Office: M/1236/2.

PRINGLE, Sir J. W.
  Diary-cum-notebooks, 1891–92. 2 vols.
  Contents: notes made on the Imperial British East Africa Company's survey of the Kenya-Uganda Railway, with Sir J. R. L. MacDonald.
  Oxford, Rhodes House Library: MSS. Afr. s.528–530. (Acquired 1965).
SMITH-MASTERS, Mary, the wife of Allan Smith-Masters.
  Diaries, 1891 and 1898 [?]. 2 vols.
  Contents: first volume is a journal kept on a voyage to India; the second, 1898, is possibly written by her.
  Kent Archives Office: Mss. U1127 Smith-Masters, F 16–17.
WALLACE, J. W. (1853–1926), of Bolton, Lancashire.
  Diary, 1891. 1 vol.
  Contents: his visits to Walt Whitman.
  Manchester, John Rylands Library: Eng. MS. 1186.

1892

COKE, J. D., a midshipman.
  Diary, June, 1892–Nov., 1893. 1 vol.
  Contents: journal kept at sea with H.M.S. *Monarch*, H.M.S. *Camperdown*, and H.M.S. *Temeraire*.
  Private: Mrs. R. Coke-Steel, Trusley Old Hall, Sutton-on-the-Hill, Derbyshire.
CRABTREE, Rev. W. A., missionary in Africa.
  Diary, 1892. (Typescript).
  Contents: kept as a member of missionary journey of Bishop Tucker from Mombassa to Kampala.
  Oxford, Rhodes House Library: MSS. Afr. s. 1417.
[?]EVANS, Eyre (1857–1939).
  Diary, summer, 1892.
  Contents: a journal of holiday travels with the Liverpool Teachers' Guild in Switzerland; Lucerne, etc.
  National Library of Wales: MS. 7976B. (Eyre Evans MSS.).
FISHER, Rev. Arthur Bryan (1868–1955), missionary in Africa.
  Diary, 1892–1914.
  Contents: journal kept while serving in Uganda.
  Church Missionary Society: MSS. Acc. 84.
HARLECH, William Richard Ormsby-Gore, 2nd. Baron (cr. 1876), (b. 1819), Lord-Lieutenant of Co. Leitrim, formerly a Member of Parliament.
  Diary, 1892–93. (See also p. 135).
  National Library of Wales: Harlech MSS. (Acquired 1955).
JONES, R. B., a coroner in Plymouth.
  Diaries, 1892–97.
  Plymouth Public Libraries: Archives Dept., MSS. Acc. 95.

McGREGOR, Rev. James (1832–1910), of Edinburgh, moderator of the Church of Scotland.

Diaries, Sept., 1892–1898 (mostly his wife), and Jan., 1894–Dec., 1903 (copied by his wife from an original).

Contents: religious life and parish work of the minister of St. Cuthbert's Church, Edinburgh; public life, preaching, visiting, social engagements; Edinburgh life; brief notes.

National Library of Scotland: MSS. 557–566.

MONRO, Capt. Charles, policeman.

Diaries, 1892–1904.

Contents: journals concerning his service in British South African Company Police.

Scottish Record Office: GD 71/491/2.

NICKISSON, Rev. John Percy (1875–1927), missionary in Africa.

Diaries, May, 1892–Jan., 1893. 2 vols.

Contents: journal of voyage out to East Africa; journey of 750 miles through central Africa made by the missionary party under Bishop Tucker, from Mombassa to Mengo.

Church Missionary Society: MSS. Acc. 109 F1. (Acquired 1960).

RUDDY, Rev. Henry E., of Rugby, Northamptonshire.

Diary, 1892–1902.

Contents: diaries of a personal nature, kept at Manchester, Grimsby, Rugby, etc.

Private: present location unknown. (Formerly owned by Rev. D. H. Ruddy).

WILSON, Henry Joseph (1833–1914), M.P. for Holmfirth (Yorks.), a director of the Sheffield Smelting Co.

Diaries, 1892, 1900, 1909, and 1914. 4 vols.

Contents: pocket diaries with brief entries of appointments; notes of a lifelong radical and nonconformist.

Sheffield City Libraries: Local History & Archives Dept., misc. documents, 2460.

WRIGHT, Dr. Gaskoin Richard Morden (c. 1859–1923), missionary in Africa.

Diary, July, 1892–Jan., 1893. 1 vol.

Contents: journal of a journey from his station at Mengo, Uganda, to the coast, in company of Fred. C. Smith.

Church Missionary Society: MSS. Acc. 134 F1. (Permanent loan).

WYNDHAM, William Reginald (1876–1914).

Diary, 1892. 1 vol.

Contents: mainly sporting activities.

West Sussex County Record Office: Petworth House Archives, 1962. Francis Steer and Noel Osborne, eds., *Petworth House Archives*, vol. 1. (Chichester, 1968).

1893

ANON., a London gentleman.

Diary, 1893. 1 vol.

Contents: scattered groups of entries recording shooting in Scotland, visits to race meetings, theatres, etc.; diarist appears to have had private means.

Edinburgh University Library: MS. Dk.5.31.

ANON.

Diary, 1893–95.

Contents: a log-book kept on board H.M.S. *Tourmaline*, H.M.S. *Blake*, and H.M.S. *Endymion*.

National Library of Wales: FitzWilliams MS. 112.

ANON.

Diary, 1893. 2 pp.

Contents: fragment of a journal of a journey from France to England.

Berkshire Record Office: MS. D/EBy A 154.

ALLAN, Dr. James Watson (d. 1925), surgeon.

Diary, 1893. 227 pp.

Contents: journal on board the *Aurora*; the record of a sealing and whaling voyage kept by the surgeon of the ship; founded on brief journal notes; illustrated with photographs and sketches.

Glasgow University Library: MS. Gen. 154.

BLATHWAYT, Mrs. W. E.

Diary, 1893. 1 vol.

Contents: a few brief entries; domestic.

Gloucestershire Records Office: Dyrham Park MSS., D 1799 F282.

DENNIS, Rev. Thomas John, archdeacon and missionary in Africa.

Diaries, 1893–1917.

Contents: letter–journals kept while in Africa; Sierra Leone, Fourah Bay College, Onitsha; sundry visits recorded.

Church Missionary Society: MSS. Acc. 89 F1.

HEWLETT, Maurice (1861–1949), novelist.

Diaries, Jan., 1893–May, 1923, and travel diary, April, 1914.

Contents: a literary diary with brief notes of his yearly progress; reading, writing, work of magazines, lecturing; a yearly self-appraisal as a writer; family and general affairs. The travel diary was kept in a tour of Greece and Italy with his daughter; hospitality of monasteries; full account of Easter service.

London, British Museum: Add. MSS. 51075 (excluding travel diary).

L. Binyon, *The Letters of Maurice Hewlett* (London, 1914), pp. 251–290.

NEVINSON, Henry Woodd (1860–1941), LL.D., scholar.
Diaries, 1893–1941.
Contents: literary interests, etc.; notes kept consistently to within two months of his death, and continued by his wife during his last illness.
Oxford, Bodleian Library: MSS. Dep. e. 66–84.

PARRY, W. J. (1842–1927), of Coetmor, Bethesda, Caernarvon, a Welsh labour leader and representative of Welsh Patagonia Gold Field Syndicate.
Diary, 1893–94. 1 vol.
Contents: journal giving account of his journey to South America.
Caernarvon County Record Office: M/1311.

PORTAL, Captain Melville Raymond.
Diary, Jan.–May, 1893. 1 vol.
Contents: journal kept in *Letts' Colonial Rough Diary & Almanack* while he was on a mission to Uganda; at the end is a telegram announcing his death from fever, May 27.
Oxford, Balliol College Library: MS. 379. (Acquired 1927).
Sir Gerald Portal, *The British Mission to Uganda in 1893* (London, 1894), pp. 319–348.

SADLER, Dr. Michael Thomas (1834–1923), of Barnsley, Yorkshire, physician.
Diaries, Jan., 1893–June, 1923. 14 vols.
Contents: his work and studies as a doctor; travels in Switzerland, notes on travel conditions; domestic, family, and social life; his reading, and love of Gilbert & Sullivan; tastes of the Victorian era.
Oxford, Bodleian Library: MSS. Eng. misc. e. 204–217.

SWAYNE, Harold George C.
Diary, 1893. (Copy and extract).
Contents: private journal kept in Somaliland and Abyssinia.
Oxford, Rhodes House Library: MS. Afr. s.553. (Acquired 1965).

TAYLOR, Miss Ida Ashworth, daughter of Sir Henry Taylor (1800–1866).
Diary, Dec., 1893–March, 1895. 19 fols.
Contents: notes on the social and literary circles of her father: Colvin, the Meynells, the Le Galliennes, Francis Thompson, the Darwins; entertaining reports of literary opinions; visits to the theatre, some notes on Norway, its history and its legends.
Oxford, Bodleian Library: MS. Eng. misc. e. 192/1–19.

WILSON, Field Marshal Sir Henry, Bart. (1864–1922), Chief of Imperial General Staff (1918–22).
Diaries, Jan., 1893–Dec., 1899. 7 vols.
Contents: daily entries pertaining to military life; the Rifle Brigade, Staff College, 1892–4, a Captain in the Intelligence Division, a Brigade Major of the 2nd. Brigade at Aldershot from 1897–9; service in South Africa, 1899.
Imperial War Museum: MSS. HHW 1/1–7. (Acquired 1973).

C. E. Callwell, *Field Marshal Sir Henry Wilson* 2 vols. (London: Cassell, 1927).

WRAY, Rev. Joseph Alfred (1856–1948), missionary in Africa.
Diaries, 1893–1909, (with gaps). 9 vols.
Contents: journals record his work in Kilindini and Mombassa; later in Segalle; notes on temperatures etc.; a voyage home to England, 1900.
Church Missionary Society: MSS. Acc. 86 F1/1–9.

1894

BARING-GOULD, Miss, daughter of C.M.S. Home Secretary, 1888–94.
Diaries, Aug., 1894–Mar., 1939. (with gaps). 29 vols.
Contents: journals initially kept while touring with her father who was to take over Far East post with C. M. S.: New York, Toronto, Winnipeg, Vancouver, Tokyo, Osaka, Hiroshima; excursion to China and Malaya; Ceylon, Aden, Brindisi, Dover; later tours include Egypt, India, and Italy, 1899–1900; America, China and Japan, 1912, Palestine and Egypt, India and Ceylon, 1921; tour of Africa, 1927, and East Africa, 1938–39.
Church Missionary Society: MSS. Acc. 21 F1. (Acquired 1961).

Da SILVA., [?———]. A Goan clerk.
Diaries, 1894–96 and 1900–02 (typed copy).
Contents: journal of camps in Kenya, notes on chaingangs and punishments; construction work.
Oxford, Rhodes House Library: MSS. Afr. s.424/125–133.
(Acquired 1964).

GARRAWAY, George Hervey (1846–1935), painter.
Diaries, 1894–1934. 37 vols.
Contents: his life and work as an artist in Italy, chiefly at Florence where he ultimately made his home; he was a member of the Liverpool Academy of Art before moving to Italy.
Liverpool Record Office: MSS. 920GAR 1–43.

GLOVER, F., of College Road, Leeds, a schoolmaster.
Diary, June, 1894–Nov., 1895. 1 vol.
Contents: daily activities, especially at Leeds Grammar School where he coached in Latin and Greek; books read, lectures attended; walks; visits to local places of interest; whist; weather; concerts; Paderewski, etc.; family and personal matters.
Leeds Public Library: MS. L923.7 G518.

KENNAWAY, Gertrude Ella (b. 1875), daughter of Sir John Henry Kennaway of Escot, Ottery St. Mary, Devon.
Diary, Jan.–April, 1894. 1 vol.
   K*

Contents: brief daily entries, personal and social, kept in the *Church Missionary Pocket Almanack.*
Devon Record Office: MS. B961 M add./F 14.

LEVESON GOWER, William George Gresham (1883–1918), Clerk in the Parliamentary Office from 1908 onwards.
Diaries, 1894–1918. 24 vols.
Contents: relate to both official and personal matters.
London, House of Lords Record Office: H.L.R.O. Historical coll.

ORMSBY, George, colonial magistrate.
Diaries, 1894, 1898, 1901 and 1909. 4 vols.
Contents: brief pocket-diary entries, kept in North Borneo in 1898, in India, 1901, and an informal journal kept while 2nd. Class Resident in Nigeria.
Oxford, Rhodes House Library: MSS. Brit. Emp. s. 287.

OSBOURNE, Lloyd (1868–1947), of Samoa, step-son of Robert Louis Stevenson.
Diary, 1894. 1 vol.
Contents: notes in *Lett's Australasian Diary*; general household management of servants, arrangements for birthday parties etc. together with briefest mention of R. L. S's death in whose house the diarist lived.
Edinburgh, Huntley House Museum: MSS. R.L.S.C.323.

PEAKE, Edward.
Diaries, 1894–1941.
Contents: ornithological diaries and notebooks.
Oxford, Edward Grey Institute: Alexander Library MSS. coll.

POPE, Elizabeth, of Copplestone House, Bow, Devon.
Diaries, 1894–98 and 1900–07. 13 vols.
Contents: entries made in volumes of *Renshaw's Diary and Almanack.*
Devon Record Office: MSS. 1791 M/F 14–26.

SHILSTON, Richard Durant (1870–1935), of West Hartlepool, a surveyor.
Diary, 1894–1935.
Contents: family history, raising six children; national events; holidays; middle-class family.
Private: Mrs. N. M. Bayly, formerly of Burnley, Lancs.

TODD, James, of The Poplars, Hardwick, Bucks., a farmer.
Diaries, 1894–95, 1901, 1905, 1911, 1914–22, 1931, 1940, and 1951. 17 vols.
Contents: journals relating to farm matters; details of farm activities, sales and purchases.
Buckinghamshire Record Office: MSS. coll. (Acquired 1970).

Van der VLIET, Senator Basil, of the Russian Foreign Office.
Diary, 1894–1914.
London, British Museum: Add. MSS. 49068–49083 (Van der Vliet Papers, vols. 4–19). (Acquired 1956).

1895

ANON.

Diaries, 1895–97. 3 vols.

Contents: brief daily entries; work on farm in Honiton or district; some cash accounts.

Devon Record Office: MSS. 337 B add.2/ special subjects 1 c.

ANON.

Diary, and notebooks, 1895–1924.

Contents: a religious journal probably kept by the vicar; church matters.

Private: The Vicar, Long Clawson, Leicestershire.

ANON.

Diary, 1895.

Contents: very few entries, but those are of a factual nature dealing with farming matters.

Private: S. C. Good, formerly of Worcester.

ANON.

Diary, 1895–Jan., 1896.

Contents: journal of Egyptian campaigns, kept by an army man.

Private: Adrian Conan-Doyle, Esq., Windlesham, Hurtis Hall, Crowborough, Sussex.

ANON.

Diary, 1895–97. 1 vol.

Contents: a log-type journal kept on H.M.S. *Blake*, H.M.S. *Volage*, and H.M.S. *Inflexible*.

National Library of Wales: Fitzwilliams MSS., 113.

AINSWORTH, John.

Diaries, 1895–1902 and 1917. 3 vols.

Contents: journals kept in East Africa.

Oxford, Rhodes House Library: MSS. Afr. s. 377–382. (Acquired 1963).

CLITHEROW, Col. J. Stracey.

Diary, Aug., 1895–Feb., 1896. 1 vol.

Contents: journal of the Jameson Raid by one of the participants fighting against the Boers.

National Army Museum: MSS. 6603/52.

GERVERS, Brigadier F.R.S. (1873–1971), officer in the Royal Engineers, c. 1890–1930.

Diary, Mar., 1895–Dec., 1899. 1 vol.

Contents: journal covers his service as a subaltern in India; mostly stationed at Kirkee, but some action in various parts of the N-W Frontier; leave in England, June–Oct., 1898; army life at Quetta, India.

Imperial War Museum: MSS. FRG 1

JOSEPH, Horace William Brindley (1867–1943).

Diary, 1895–1902 (with gaps).

Contents: journals of his travels.

Oxford, New College Library: MSS. coll.

LONGSTAFF, George Blundell (1849–1921).

Diaries and papers, 1895–1915.

Contents: of entomological interest.

Oxford, Hope Dept. of Entomology Library: MSS. coll.

RAMSAY, Sir William (1852–1916), Professor of General & Inorganic Chemistry at University College, London (1887–1913).

Diaries, 10–20 Aug., 1895 and Aug.–Dec., 1900.

Contents: early volume is of travel in Iceland with Prof. W. P. Ker; later typescript is of travel in India, where he reported on proposed Indian University of Research.

London, University College Library: Ramsay Papers Vol. 8 & 85–88.

RUSSELL, Edward, J. H.

Diaries, 1895–97, 1899, and 1900. 5 vols.

Contents: journals kept by the Assistant Commissioner of the British East Africa Company.

Oxford, Rhodes House Library: MSS. Afr. s.118–122.

THOMPSON, Sir John Perronet (b. 1874), I.C.S.

Diaries, July, 1895–Dec., 1932. (with gaps). 30 vols.

Contents: journals begin with life at Trinity College, Cambridge, his vacations, Northern Ireland, his golf, etc.; voyage to India; full entries describing Anglo-India, social life, local customs, his reading, court-ship and marriage; jokes recorded; later journals have intermittent entries and are more domestic and routine, except those covering holidays in England.

India Office Library: MSS. Eur. F. 137.

WHITE, Robert.

Diary, March–Dec., 1895.

Contents: journal of the Jameson raid, with notes and maps relating to the raid.

Oxford, Rhodes House Library: MS. Afr. s.220–222.

H. M. Hole, *The Jameson Raid*.

WHITEHOUSE, Sir George, an engineer.

Diaries and correspondence, 1895–1903. 9 vols.

Contents: journals kept by the chief engineer of the Uganda railway construction.

Oxford, Rhodes House Library: MSS. Afr. s. 1046. (Acquired 1967).

1896

COLE, Thomas (1846–1919), Secretary of the Institution of Municipal and County Engineers.

Diary, July–Sept., 1896. 1 vol.

Contents: illustrated journal of a voyage round the world.
Somerset Record Office: MS. DD/CLE.
CONG, Col. Ulric Thynne, C.V.O., D.S.O., of the 60th. Rifles.
Diary, Feb–April, 1896. 1 vol.
Contents: journal of a sporting tour by officers of the 1st. Bn. of 60th.
Rifles in the Delhi district while on privilege leave after the Chitral
campaign.
National Army Museum: MSS. 6408/47.
FELLOWES, H. le M., a soldier.
Diaries, 1896–97. 3 vols.
Contents: daily entries kept by an officer serving in the N-W Frontier of
India.
National Army Museum: MSS. 7209/37.
HAMLYN, Nathaniel Temple, first bishop of Accra.
Diary, 1896–1910. 105 leaves.
Contents: brief, irregular entries.
Oxford, Rhodes House Library: MS. Afr. r.65. (Acquired 1966).
HEWKES, H. P.
Diaries, 1896–97. 2 vols.
Contents: journal kept in Egypt, Italy, and England.
Private: Commander Hook, 11 Woolacombe Road, Blackheath, London
S.E.3.
MAIN, Mary.
Diary, 1896–1952.
Private: Mrs. Gildersleeves, 40 Elmsleigh Drive, Leigh-on-Sea, Essex.
NORMAN, Brigadier-General Claude Lumsden, D.S.O., M.V.O. (1876–
1969), of Kingston St. Mary, Taunton, army officer.
Diaries, Jan., 1896–Dec., 1897. 2 vols.
Contents: his passage to India and his service as a Second Lieutenant on
the North-West Frontier of India ; entries are detailed in period Aug–Dec.,
1897.
Imperial War Museum: MSS. CLN 1, 2.
PASSY, Lieut. De Lacy Dayrell, officer of the 67th. Foot. in Burma.
Diary, April–May, 1896. 1 vol.
Contents: journal kept while regiment provided an escort to a mission
sent through the Kachin Hills to Mauwyne to enquire into the murder
of a British trade representative.
National Army Museum: MSS. 6909/5.
ROSE, J. C., a soldier of Rifle Coy. Mounted Infantry.
Diary, 1896–97. 1 vol.
Contents: journal kept by a private seconded from the Rifle Brigade
during his journey to South Africa, 1896, and covering his experiences in
the Matabele War.
National Army Museum: MSS. 7201/9.

WATSON, General W. M.
  Diaries, 1896 and 1902. 2 vols.
  National Army Museum: MSS. 6412/46.

1897

ANON.
  Diary, 1897–1926.
  Contents: journal of farming at Penistan.
  Ipswich and East Suffolk Record Office: MS. HA 193/A3/1.

DAVIES, Richard, of Glamorgan, farmer.
  Diaries, 1897–1902 (with gaps). 4 vols.
  Contents: journals probably kept at Ynysdawley Farm, Dulais Higher, near Seven Sisters.
  Glamorgan County Record Office: D/D Xjx 77–80.

EGERTON, Maj–General Granville G. A., officer of 72nd. Foot.
  Diaries, 1897 and Nov., 1899–April, 1900.
  Contents: typescript journal of the detachment at Canea, Crete, during the early days of the Internation occupation of the island; later journal kept while Lt-Col. of the Khartoum detachment of 1st. Bn. Seaforth Highlanders during 2nd. Sudan campaign; entries rather official and factual.
  National Army Museum: MSS. 6807/171–2.

HAMILTON, John.
  Diary, 1897. 1 vol.
  Contents: journal kept while a passenger in the S.S. *Australian* on voyage from England to Suez; the return journey overland; illustrated with sketches and photographs.
  National Maritime Museum: JOD 53 MS57/024.

MALCOLM, Sir Neill.
  Diaries, 1897–99. 2 vols. (Typescript).
  Contents: journal kept in East Africa, includes the Uganda mutiny, etc.
  Oxford, Rhodes House Library: MSS. Afr. s. 759.

TEMPLETON, Lady.
  Diaries, 1897–1906. 2 vols.
  Warwickshire Record Office: MSS. CR 426.

WARDROP, General Sir Alexander.
  Diary, 1897. 1 vol.
  Contents: journal describing shooting in various parts of India: lists of stores and shikar requirements.
  National Army Museum: MSS. 6404/81.

1898

ANON., an army officer.
Diary, 1898–99. 1 vol.
Contents: journal kept by officer in the Nigerian Army.
Hampshire Record Office: MSS. 115.M.71.

BELLISS, Mrs. M. A.
Diary, April–June. 1898. 149 pp.
Contents: journal of travels through Palestine: Jaffa, Jerusalem, Jericho, Haifa, Zahlebi; tourist's comment on sacred scenes; record of conversations, books, and personal experiences.
Private: Mrs. John Campbell, Woodcote Valley Road, Purley, Surrey CR2 3BD.

BERESFORD-PEIRSE, Sir Henry Monson de la Poer, 3rd. Bt. (b. 1850), of The Hall, Bedale, Yorkshire.
Diaries, Oct., 1898–May, 1899. 2 vols.
Contents: journal of a tour round the world.
North Riding of Yorkshire County Record Office: MSS. ZBA 20.

BROWN, Henry Francis (1840–1920), of London, a merchant.
Diary, June, 1898–Oct., 1909. 177 pp.
Contents: business and private affairs; social life in London, musical, art, and literary circles; acquaintances, especially leading politicians, of a cultured bachelor; information by Madame Novikoff, his friend, about the Dreyfus case.
Wigan Central Public Library: Edward Hall coll. M879.

FLETCHER, Charles Robert L.
Diary, 1898. 123 leaves.
Contents: journal of a "border raid in a tandem".
Oxford, Bodleian Library: MS. Eng. misc. d. 339, fol. e.

MINTO, Gilbert John Murray Kynynmond Elliot, 4th. Earl, later Governor-General of Canada.
Diaries, 1898–1904. 2 vols.
Contents: travel diary, notes on Canada.
Oxford, Rhodes House Library: MSS. Can. t. 1.

MINTO, Mary Caroline, Countess of, wife of the 4th. Earl, the Governor-General of Canada.
Diary, Nov., 1898–Nov., 1904. 1 vol.
Contents: travel diary, illustrated with photographs.
Oxford, Rhodes House Library: MS. Can. t.1,2.

NEWDIGATE, Francis William.
Diary, 1898. 1 vol.
Contents: journal of a tour of South Africa.
Warwickshire Record Office: MS. CR 136/A9.

PATTERSON, John Henry, colonial civil servant.
Diary, Feb., 1898–Jan., 1899. (Xerox copy).
Contents: journal kept by civil servant in East Africa.
Oxford, Rhodes House Library: MSS. Afr. r. 93.

WALLACE, Alexander, of Colchester, physician, bulb-importer, and experimenter in silk-worm culture.
Diaries, 1898–99. 2 vols.
Essex Record Office: MSS. D/DU 559/16–17.

WHITEHOUSE, Lady, wife of Sir George C. Whitehouse.
Diary, 1898. 21 leaves (typewritten).
Contents: journal of a trip with her husband through Kenya to the shores of Lake Victoria.
Oxford, Rhodes House Library: MS. Afr. s.1055. (Acquired 1967).

WINWOOD, William Quintyne, soldier of the Dragoon Guards.
Diaries, 1898–1923 (with gaps). 7 vols.
Contents: journals kept while serving in 5th. Dragoon Guards; details of army life in India and later South Africa (1904–7).
National Army Museum: MSS. 7105/3.

1899

BRADFIELD, General Sir Ernest, Indian Medical Services.
Diaries, 1899, 1900, 1917, 1936–39, and 1941–44.
National Army Museum: MSS. 6409/26.

CATHCART, Reginald, soldier in the King's Royal Rifles.
Diary, Nov., 1899–Feb., 1900. 1 vol. (Copy).
Contents: journal kept in South Africa during operations for the relief of Ladysmith.
Private: Lord Cathcart, 14 Eaton Mews, London, S.W.1.; Cathcart Papers A/110.

CHARLES, Sir Ronald, officer of the Royal Engineers.
Diary, Oct., 1899–May, 1900. 1 vol.
Contents: journal kept while he was serving in the Boer War with 26th. Coy. of the Royal Engineers.
National Army Museum: MSS. coll.

CLOWES, Col. P. L., commander of the 8th. Hussars.
Diary, 1899–1902. (typescript).
Contents: journal in the form of letters (to Mrs. Stanford) concerning his service in the Boer War.
National Army Museum: MSS. 5807/13.

COKE, Colonel J. Talbot, later Major-General.
Diaries, 1899–1901 and one without date. 3 vols.
Contents: first two are journals of his service with the 10th. Brigade in the South African War; the other dates from a campaign in Suakin.

Private: Mrs. R. Coke-Steel, Trusley Old Hall, Sutton-on-the-Hill, Derbyshire.

COOPER, A. S., an accountant.

Diary, 1899.

Contents: journal kept while an accountant with the Uganda railway.

Oxford, Rhodes House Library: MSS. Afr. t. 17.

DRURY, Sgt., of the Shropshire Light Infantry.

Diary, Nov., 1899–Oct., 1900. (photostat typescript).

Contents: journal kept by a sergeant of "C" Coy. of 2nd. Shropshire Light Infantry serving in the Boer War.

National Army Museum: MSS. 7005/30.

GILBERT, W. H., an army schoolmaster.

Diary, Oct–Dec., 1899.

Contents: journal in the form of letters to his mother from Ladysmith camp, Natal, including graphic account of the seige and extensive detail.

National Army Museum: MSS. 6309/114.

GROSSMAN, Col. George L., officer of the West Yorkshire Regt.

Diary, Nov., 1899–Jan., 1902. (Copy).

Contents: journal begins with disembarkation of Regt. at Durban; troop train disaster; details on artillery and regimental life; skirmishes with the Boers; Churchill's escape from Pretoria, etc.

National Army Museum: MSS. 6306/24.

HOLT, Maj–General M.P.C., army medical staff.

Diary, 1899–1900.

Contents: journal kept at Ladysmith seige during the Boer War when diarist was a Surgeon Captain.

Royal Army Medical Corps. Historical Museum: MS. 380.

IMAGE, Selwyn, later Slade Professor of Fine Arts at Oxford.

Diary, 1899–1919. 134 leaves.

Oxford, Bodleian Library: MS. Eng. misc. d. 349. (Acquired 1948).

JOURDAIN, Col. H.F.N., of 88th. Foot, Connaught Rangers.

Diaries, Nov., 1899–April, 1922 (with gaps). 31 vols.

Contents: journals begin with voyage to South Africa; details of Colenso, passage of the Tugela, and Spion Kop; operations at Rietfontein and action of Zuur Vlakle; later volumes kept in the Mediterranean (Gallipoli, Serbia, Salonika), 1915–16; service in Flanders with Royal Welch Fusiliers, 1917, Ypres etc; B.A.O.R. service in Upper Silesia, 1921–22.

National Army Museum: MSS. 5603/10–13.

KNOX, Col.

Diary, Nov., 1899–March, 1900. 1 vol.

Contents: journal kept at Ladysmith while in command of divisional troops during the Boer War.

National Army Museum: MSS. 7101–23/184.

LEWIN, Rev. Harold Brelsford (d. 1972), a missionary in Africa.
Diary, Oct., 1899.
Contents: journal of a voyage across the Victoria Nyanza.
Church Missionary Society: MSS. Acc. 276. (Acquired 1972).

LYTTLETON, Maud (1880–1953), later Lady Leconfield.
Diary, 1899–1900. 7 pp.
Contents: extracts from diary visits to Holkam Hall, Norfolk.
West Sussex County Record Office: Petworth House arch., 1965.
Francis Steer and Noel Osborne, eds., *Petworth House Archives*, vol. 1
(Chichester, 1968).

MACKINDER, Sir Halford John, Principal of Reading College.
Diary, 1899. 17 notebooks.
Contents: reporter's notebooks with journal entries relating to the first
ascent of Mount Kenya; maps and scientific readings.
Oxford, Rhodes House Library: MSS. Afr. r.11–27. (Acquired 1961).
H. J. Mackinder, *The Geographical Journal*, XV (1900), 453–486.
The Alpine Journal, XX (1900), 102–110.

MAITLAND, Captain Stuart Cairns.
Diary, 1899–1900.
Contents: journal kept by a member of the 2nd. Batt. of the Gordon
Highlanders while in action in the Boer War.
Private: Adam Maitland, Esq., Cumstoun, Kirkcudbright.
(Enquiries to N.R.A., Scotland).

MANCE, Brigadier-General Sir Osborne, K.B.E., C.B., C.M.G., D.S.O.
Diaries, Nov., 1899–Oct., 1902, and June–Aug., 1923. 4 vols.
Contents: three volumes were kept while he was a Lieutenant in the Royal
Engineers in the Boer War; interest in railway matters; the later volume
treats of a visit to Barcelona for a Conference on Freedom of Communi-
cations and Transit.
London, Public Record Office: 30/66, 1–3 and 32.

MANSEL-PLEYDELL, Mrs. [?Emily Kathleen] (née Grove), of Whatcombe
House, Winterborne Whitechurch, Dorset.
Diary, Jan–Dec., 1899. 1 vol.
Contents: brief account of daily activities.
Dorset Record Office: MS. MR45.

MEINERTZHAGEN, Richard, Military Adviser, Colonial Office.
Diaries, 1899–1965. 76 vols.
Contents: journals kept in India, Mauritius, East Africa, Palestine. (Not
yet available for examination).
Oxford, Rhodes House Library: unlisted MSS.

MELLIS, Maj-General C. J. (1862–1936), V.C.
Diaries, April–July, 1899 and Nov., 1902–May, 1903. 2 vols.
Contents: journal kept in the Ashanti War while serving with the West

African Frontier Force; later volume deals with the "Mad Mullah" Expedition with the Somaliland Field Force.
National Army Museum: MSS. 6702/91/22–24.

MIERS, Sir Henry Alexander, F.R.S., F.G.S. (b. 1858), mineralogist.
Diaries, 1899, 1901, 1905, 1913, 1918, and 1925. 5 vols.
Contents: mostly travel journals; Russia in 1899 and 1925 when he represented Oxford and the Royal Society at the Academy of Science; an account of a visit to the Klondyke, 1901, while representing the Canadian Government; 1905, to South Africa for the British Association; Toronto, 1913, for International Geological Congress; 1918 to America as Chairman of an Educational Mission.
Oxford, Bodleian Library: MSS. Don. (Formerly owned by the Misses Tatham of Abingdon).

PROCTOR, Robert George Collier (1868–1903), bibliographer in the British Museum.
Diaries, 1899–1903 and 1900–02. 5 vols.
Contents: the first three are general diaries; the last two were journals kept while on holidays.
London, British Museum: Add. MSS. 50190–50195.

RAMSDEN, Diana.
Diary, Nov., 1899–Sept., 1900. 59 pp.
Contents: irregularly maintained travel diary of an intelligent Englishwoman visiting friends in Queensland, Australia; personal affairs and observations; details of life on a station viewed through the eyes of Victorian propriety.
Wigan Central Public Library: Edward Hall coll. EHC 19.

READE, Lieut. R. E., officer of the 60th. Rifles.
Diary, Sept–Oct., 1899. 1 vol.
Contents: journal kept during the Boer War while serving with the 1st. Bn. King's Royal Rifle Corps.
National Army Museum: MSS. 6802/1.

RICHARDSON, Rev. A. E., a missionary in Africa.
Diaries, Dec., 1899–June, 1900 and April, 1903–Jan., 1904. 8 vols.
Contents: journals kept while serving in Sierra Leone and Nigeria: Lagos, Jebba, Kano; later volumes concern work in India: Poona, Calcutta, Benares, Lucknow, Agra, Delhi, Lahore, Bombay and Madras; also in Colombo (Ceylon).
Church Missionary Society: MSS. Acc. 56 F1–2. (Acquired 1954).

RICHARDSON, P. E.
Diary, 1899–1900. 33 pp.
Contents: largely a record of marches made during the South African Campaign.
Rawtenstall Borough Libraries: MSS. coll.

RUTHERFORD, (——), Army Medical Officer.
Diary, Dec., 1899. 1 vol.
Contents: journal includes an account of the battle of Magersfontein in the Boer War.
Royal Army Medical Corps. Museum: MS. 150.

THOMAS, L/Cpl. E. J., soldier of 1st. Bn. The King's Regt.
Diary, Oct., 1899–March., 1900. 1 vol.
Contents: journal includes account of the seige of Ladysmith during the Boer War.
National Army Museum: MSS. 7008/10.

VEAL, Charles Lewis, soldier of the Welch Regt.
Diary, Nov., 1899–April, 1900. 1 vol.
Contents: journal kept by member of the 41st. Foot, Welch Regiment during the Boer War.
National Army Museum: MSS. 6810/19.

WHITE, Robert Eaton.
Diaries, 1899–1913 and 1928–40. 28 vols.
Contents: not seen.
Private: Sir Richard White. Bt., The Vine, Presteigne, Radnorshire.

APPENDIX A

In the case of a number of nineteenth-century diaries in manuscript, the year in which the journal was kept has been omitted or lost. This even happens when the day's date and the month are meticulously noted. Doubtless, in some instances an explanatory fly-leaf has been lost or detached, particularly likely when the diarist was in the habit of writing upon looseleaf pages; even jottings in soft-covered booklets are often difficult to place for the same reason. At the same time these manuscripts can usually be attributed either to families or to particular writers from internal references, similar handwriting, etc.

The list which follows is in alphabetical order, and wherever the owners or archivists have been able to give some indication of the date this has been included.

ANON.
Early nineteenth-century.
Exeter City Record Office: Trehill (Brooke) MSS.
ANON.
Early nineteenth-century, possibly late eighteenth-century.
Contents: journal of travels in Germany and Switzerland.
Greater London Record Office (Middlesex): MS. Acc. 1017/1407.
ANON.
Contents: some diary entries, with cash accounts, by a Carmarthenshire man.
National Library of Wales: G. E. Evans Bequest, MS. 413.
ANON.
Early nineteenth-century.
Contents: journals of tours to the Lake District and Scotland, and through the west of England en route from London.
Lincolnshire Archives Office: MS. Ref. I ANC.
ANON.
Before 1843 (within a few years).
Contents: journal of travels in Egypt, Palestine, Asia Minor, and the Balkans. (Incomplete copy).
Nottinghamshire University Library: Mellish coll., MS. Me 2 L4/5.
ANON.
Contents: journal of a visit to Germany.
Northumberland Record Office: Middleton of Belsay MSS., NRO 79 ZMI B.33/39.
ANON.
Contents: diary of travels in Wales.
Private: R.C.C.J. Binney, Esq., Pampisford Hall, Cambridgeshire.

ANON.

Contents: journals of various journeys in England.

Private: Major H. R. M. Porter, M.B.E., The Courthouse, Birlingham, Worcs. (On loan to Worcestershire Record Office).

ASHBEE, C. R. (1863–1942).

Late nineteenth century.

Contents: some information on the Arts and Crafts Movement.

Cambridge, King's College Library: MS. coll.

CALDWELL, [——], of Hopton Wafers, Shropshire.

Late nineteenth-century.

Contents: local matters.

Salop County Record Office: MSS. coll.

CARR, Rev. Donald, of Woolstaston, Shropshire.

Diaries-cum-notebooks, (copies).

Contents: pertain to the restoration of the church and rectory.

Salop County Record Office: MSS. coll.

CODRINGTON, Lady Georgiana, wife of Sir Christopher William, of Dodington, Chipping Sodbury, Gloucestershire.

Contents: personal diaries and some commonplace books.

Private: Sir Christopher Codrington Bt., Dodington Park, Chipping Sodbury, Gloucestershire.

COWARD, Sir Henry (b. 1849), of Sheffield, choirmaster.

Late nineteenth- and early twentieth-centuries. 14 vols.

Contents: his musical life mostly; gossipy, visit to Canada.

Sheffield City Library: Department of Local History and Archives, misc. documents.

Reminiscences of Henry Coward (London, 1919), passim.

DONCASTER, Daniel (b. 1807), a steelmaster.

Contents: diary with brief entries.

Sheffield City Library: Department of Local History and Archives, misc. documents.

FitzHERBERT family, of Tissington, Derbyshire.

Diaries, both early nineteenth-century.

Contents: the first volume is a journal of an expedition from Suez to Mount Sinai made one February; notes on Mohammedan customs and Middle East geography; the other volume was made during a trip to Italy.

Derbyshire Record Office: Fitzherbert coll., D.239/2.7.

FRANCES, Mrs. [——].

Contents: 19 vols.

Private: W. J. C. Berington, Little Malvern Court, near Malvern Wells, Worcestershire. (On loan to Worcestershire Record Office).

GARLICK, Sarah, wife of the Vicar of Malmesbury.

Contents: kept while living near Painswick, Gloucestershire, when a widow.

Private: Mrs. R. F. Tuckett, Winchester, Hants. (Dr. Joan Greatrex, informant).

GRAHAME, James (1790–1842), author.
Diaries, early nineteenth-century. 3 vols.
Contents: travel journals in Britain, France, Belgium, Holland, Germany, Switzerland, and Madeira.
London, Dr. Williams's Library: MSS. 24.104–6.

GURDON, W. B.
Ipswich and East Suffolk Record Office: Cranworth coll., MS. HA 54: 970.

HADFIELD, George (b. 1789), Member of Parliament.
Sheffield City Library: Department of Local History and Archives, misc. documents.

HAYHURST, [——], of Wrockwardine Hall, Shropshire.
Mid-nineteenth-century.
Contents: mainly comments on the weather.
Salop County Record Office: MSS. coll.

HORDERN, Isaac, of Huddersfield, an Agent for Sir John Ramsden.
Late nineteenth-century. 1 mf.
Huddersfield Central Library: local coll.

[?] HOTHAM, H. E.
23–25, April. (See also p. 238).
Contents: fragment of a diary of a game-hunt in India.
East Riding of Yorkshire County Record Office: DDHO/18/13.

LEGGE, Lady Mary (or Anne Legge).
Contents: journal of a tour in Germany and Italy.
Greater London Record Office: MS. F/LEG/963.

LEGH, George Cornwall (1804–1877).
Mid-century. 38 vols.
Manchester, John Rylands Library: Cornwall-Legh mun.

LEIGHTON, Rachael.
Late nineteenth-century, even c. 1900.
Contents: journal of a tour around the world.
Salop County Record Office: MSS. coll.

MAGGS, James (1797–1890), of Southwold, Suffolk, an auctioneer and teacher.
Mid-century. 5 vols.
Private: Miss Y. Halton, Manor Lodge, Woodley's Yard, Southwold, Suffolk. (On loan to Ipswich and East Suffolk Record Office, MS. HA:56).

MARX, Admiral J. L.
Contents: diaries and correspondence.
Private: Commander G. W. C. Fowler, R.N., Broadoaks, Fronfield, Petersfield, Hampshire.

MAXWELL, Sir John (1791–1865), of Pollock, M.P.
Between 1813–15.
Contents: journal of a tour to Egypt.
Glasgow City Archives: MS. T/PM CXVI

MILNES, Mrs. Robert Pemberton, of Fryston Hall, Ferry Bridge, Yorkshire.
Early nineteenth-century.
Private: Lady Celia Milnes-Coates, J.P., Helperby Hall, Helperby, Yorkshire.

MITFORD, Margaret Emma (1836–1927), wife of William Townley Mitford.
Contents: journal of a tour of Italy.
West Sussex County Record Office: MS. Mitford 43.
Francis Steer, ed., *The Mitford Archives* (Chichester, 1961).

MONSON, Hon. Mrs. [——], mother of William John, 6th. Baron Monson.
Early nineteenth-century. 3 vols.
Private: Lord Monson, The Manor House, South Carlton, Lincoln. (On loan to Lincolnshire Archives Office).

OLIVER, William, of Chittoor, India.
West Sussex County Record Office: MS. Mitford 1426.

PARKER, Rev. John, of Llan-y-blodwel.
Contents: practically a diary account of his restoration of the church and buildings of the school; his difficulties in building the very unusual spire to a plan of his own without any expert assistance.
Salop County Record Office: MSS. coll.

PINYON, John.
Early nineteenth-century.
East Sussex Record Office: Add. MSS. D.884, 904.

PLYMLEY, Katherine (d. 1830).
Early nineteenth-century.
Salop County Record Office: Corbett of Longnor coll. (MSS. presently returned to the family).

RIGBY, Dr. E.
148 leaves.
Contents: travel journal describing his journey through France to Turin, Italy.
Oxford, Bodleian Library: MS. Dep. c. 115 e. 43. (Acquired 1952).

SCOURFIELD, Sir John Henry (1808–1876), of Williamston, near Neyland, Pembrokeshire.
Contents: journal of a Continental tour, when he went through parts of Holland, the Rhineland, Switzerland, and France.
National Library of Wales: MS. 4741B.

SELWYN, George Augustus (1809–1878), Primate of New Zealand and later Bishop of Lichfield, Staffordshire.
Cambridge, Selwyn College Library: MSS. coll.

SHEFFIELD, Julia Maria, later wife of the 1st. Lord Kesteven.
Early nineteenth-century.
Contents: one diary and some commonplace books.
Lincolnshire Archives Office: 9/66.
THISTLEWOOD family.
Presumed nineteenth century.
Lincolnshire Archives Office: Monson MSS. 31.
TWISDEN, M. M.
Contents: personal matters.
Kent Archives Office: MS. Twisden U49, F7.
WARD, William (b. 1809), Primitive Methodist minister.
Mid-century.
Sheffield City Library: Department of Local History and Archives, misc. documents.
YEATS, William Butler (1865–1939), poet and dramatist.
Late nineteenth-century.
Private: Michael Yeats, Esq. (To be deposited in the National Library of Ireland eventually).
YOUNG, Robert ("Robin Hill"), of Sturminster Newton, Devon, dialect poet.
Contents: a volume describing Sturminster Newton during his early life; a quasi-diary.
Dorset Record Office: MSS. coll.

INDEX OF DIARISTS

[303]

M*

SUBJECT-INDEX

The following subject-index concentrates upon places, people, professions, and events; it is not intended to be comprehensive but rather to suggest the range of interests to be found in nineteenth-century diaries.